CONFLICT AND CONSENSUS

CONFLICT AND CONSENSUS
The Struggle between Congress and the President over Foreign Policymaking

GERALD FELIX WARBURG

1817

Harper & Row, Publishers, New York
BALLINGER DIVISION

Grand Rapids, Philadelphia, St. Louis, San Francisco
London, Singapore, Sydney, Tokyo

International Standard Book Number: 0-88730-273-4

Library of Congress Catalog Card Number: 89-31800

Printed in the United States of America

Library of Congress Cataloging-in-Publication Data

Warburg, Gerald Felix.
    Conflict and consensus : the struggle between Congress and the
President over foreign policymaking / Gerald Felix Warburg.
        p. cm.
    Bibliography: p. 315
    Includes index.
    ISBN 0-88730-273-4
    1. United States—Foreign relations administration. 2. Legislative
power—United States. 3. Executive power—United States. I. Title
JX1706.W37 1989
328.73'0746—dc20   89-31800
                                                                  CIP

89 90 91 92 HC 9 8 7 6 5 4 3 2 1

To Joy Jacobson, who inspired, prodded, and nourished

and

to Jason Clement Warburg, who shared

CONTENTS

ACKNOWLEDGMENTS

One of the great pleasures of stepping back and analyzing a profession in which one is ordinarily immersed is the opportunity afforded to learn from friends and former adversaries. This book benefited tremendously from the thoughts and criticism of a host of professional colleagues in the executive branch, Congress, and the academic world. Their collaboration and friendship has lent me joy and encouragement.

A special word of thanks goes to two colleagues from opposite ends of the political spectrum. Jeff Bergner, former Republican chief of staff of the Senate Foreign Relations Committee, and Gordon Kerr, Administrative Assistant to Democratic Senator Carl Levin, patiently helped me to rework each chapter. They served as a constant source of motivation and a healthy "reality check," as arguments were refined and points of consensus identified. In a similar manner, Casimir Yost of the Northern California World Affairs Council, Gerald Connolly of the Foreign Relations Committee, and Ken Wollack of the National Democratic Institute reviewed key portions of the manuscript, offering helpful comments and insights. Brian Atwood also offered valuable improvements based upon his experience as Assistant Secretary of State for Congressional Relations.

This project was enriched at various stages by the counsel of Alton Frye and Peter Tarnoff at the Council on Foreign Relations, Bill Quandt of the Brookings Institution, Adele Smith Simmons of

Hampshire College, John Ritch of the Foreign Relations Committee, and Madeleine Albright of Georgetown University. I wish to express my thanks to each of them. I also wish to acknowledge the editorial assistance in Washington of Colleen Sechrest and Kara Andersen, who helped bring the manuscript to a more readable state. At Ballinger Publishing Company, Carol Franco, India Koopman, and Cindy Buck were especially loyal and diligent in moving the book to completion.

Finally, I wish to express my appreciation to three persons whose insights enriched this work immeasurably. These gentlemen made their contributions not so much as politicians but as educators, eager to examine and explain the policymaking process even as they made vigorous engagement in it their chosen careers. Jonathan Bingham, the late congressman from New York, Alan Cranston, senior senator from California, and Charles McC. Mathias, former senator from Maryland, each shared wisdom that I have endeavored to reflect in this work. For their contributions, and for much more, I am deeply grateful.

FOREWORD

The Constitutional Convention that met in Philadelphia in 1787 adopted Montesquieu's doctrine of separation of powers as a hallmark of the great charter. Having done so, it created a number of exceptions in which power was shared by the several branches of government, notably in the area of foreign policy. Treaties with foreign powers may be negotiated by the executive, but do not take effect until they are ratified by the Senate. War must be declared by the Congress, but prosecuted by the president. The secretary of state, ambassadors and ministers, and other officials with authority to execute foreign policy may be nominated by the president, but may not enter upon the duties of their offices before confirmation by the Senate.

As a result of these constitutional arrangements, the lines of authority and responsibility in the field of foreign policy are not always clear, but are always the subject of debate. For 200 years the pendulum of power has swung back and forth between the executive and legislative branches of the federal government. Each has struggled for domination over foreign policy, and from time to time, each has prevailed in one case or another. The last quarter of the twentieth century has been especially productive of such controversy.

One argument that Lyndon Johnson adopted after he moved from the Capitol to the White House was that the Congress should not attempt to lead because it did not "have the facts." Such a charge of ignorance had the effect of catnip on members of Congress, who immediately set out to get the facts. Intelligence committees were established, standing committee staffs were expanded, and the resources of the Library of Congress were augmented. The role of the legislative branch in the decisions to resort to the use of armed force, to supply military equipment to other nations, and to undertake covert action was defined and clarified by statute.

History repeated itself when the pendulum swung back in the other direction after the election of Ronald Reagan in 1980. President Reagan disputed the constitutionality of the War Powers Act and tried to evade its application to Lebanon and the Persian Gulf, with resulting compromises on both sides. He committed the United States' armed forces to combat in Grenada and Libya with more notice to and consultation with foreign governments than he accorded to the Congress.

The lesson to be learned from Vietnam and the succeeding years of controversy is that no foreign policy can succeed in the long run if it lacks the support of a majority of the American people and their representatives in the Congress.

Confirmation of this principle can be found in the success of recent American policy initiatives in Afghanistan and their lack of success in Nicaragua.

A corollary that can be derived from this principle is that foreign policy must not only be sound but it must be so perceived by the public, and that this perception will be dependent on the process by which it was formulated. I had the privilege of participating in that process for a quarter of a century, and so I had an opportunity to see what is likely to work and what is not. Failure has usually followed an attempt by one branch to blindsde or preempt the other. Early efforts to coordinate policy and to seek genuine consultation have generally been more successful.

I do not underestimate the difficulties incurred in the coordination of policy that I believe is implicitly required by the Constitution. The several branches of government may be in different political hands, which creates a climate of caution. There is great reluctance to create precedents that may impinge on the prerogatives of office. Secrecy and silence sometimes appear to be safer and easier alternatives to taking a constitutional partner into confidence.

Unfortunately, the smoke, noise, and confusion of these political battles has obscured this critical process and covered it with a veil of mystery.

This book goes a long way in parting that veil and revealing the essentials of the process. The author speaks from first-hand knowledge and personal experience on the staffs of Senator Alan Cranston and the late Congressman Jonathan Bingham, both deeply committed to foreign policy issues.

I have been the beneficiary of the excellent work done by congressional staff and have admired Gerald Warburg's achievements as an expert in foreign affairs. I have watched him at work in the Committee on Foreign Relations and with congressional delegations making official visits to foreign capitals. In each role he has been unusually successful in interacting with the principals in such sessions, as well as with his staff colleagues. He has acquired, therefore, a realistic and comprehensive view of the working of the process, both in its human aspect and in its formal evolution.

Gerald Warburg addresses fundamental problems of American democracy about which we all need greater understanding. His book is written to fulfill that need, and it does so in an important way without dictating that the reader should adopt all of his conclusions.

—Charles McC. Mathias, Jr.
former U.S. Senator

INTRODUCTION

This is a book about revolution and reaction. It chronicles the turbulent decade of congressional challenge to the president's foreign policymaking powers that unfolded in the 1970s, as well as the years of counterreformation that ensued under the administration of Ronald Reagan. This work examines two institutions in conflict, the Congress and the presidency; it assesses how these two branches of the U.S. government—granted competing and overlapping foreign policymaking authority under the Constitution—have battled for the power to set America's course in the world. Just exactly how is this fight waged today by key participants in the White House and Congress? What reforms brought about by the harrowing experiences of Vietnam and Watergate have endured? What changes have been swept away in the Reagan years, and what are the new rules of this crucial competition? These are the questions this work looks at in detail before addressing the challenge of charting a more promising course for the future of American foreign policymaking.

The struggle to shape American relations with the nations of the world is never-ending. It is a high-stakes battle that has crippled numerous presidents while intimidating many a legislator. Throughout our history, seizure of the upper hand by one branch of government has inevitably sparked reaction. In recent years, these self-correcting cycles have accelerated. The pace of change itself has become dizzying. Familiar battle lines have been drawn in Washington at a time when American leadership in the world faces extraordinary challenges. While most of our social institutions have now weathered a full generation of turbulent reform, old Washington policymaking structures have crumbled. In the 1960s, the omnipotence of the dollar and the American nuclear missile monopoly was eroded. In the 1970s, a revolution began within Congress that substantially altered America's way of doing business with the world.

The revolution in Congress was at first an internal phenomenon, striking against old patterns of dominance. The seniority system fell. Staff resources multiplied. Party identification declined—reflecting changes under way among voters at the grass roots—and crucial elements of institutional discipline eroded in the process. Then the frenetic congressional reform efforts were aimed at executive branch prerogatives, which had reached their zenith during the Nixon era. As repeated assaults were made against the accumulated powers of the modern presidency, a series of White House incumbents fell from grace. Indeed, a string of "failed" presidencies followed in the wake of the most recent congressional resurgence. Challenges to the foreign policymaking authorities of a succession of presidents have sped their downfall. In the process, the way in which American foreign policy is made has been changed. The themes of this struggle are familiar. But the legacy of the 1970s cycle of reform proved qualitatively different. The rules have been changed. Never again will they be the same.

Today, those who would shape U.S. foreign policy—the president, the members of Congress, the foreign service officers, the lobbyists, diplomats, and White House appointees—are sailing in uncharted waters. The decisionmaking process has become so strained that new procedural devices are created in the middle of even the most sensitive debates over the substance of international policy. The process has become extraordinarily confusing, and the search for a reliable road map ever more frustrating.

We are witnessing government by procedural improvisation: crucial foreign policy decisions are being shaped in Washington today by awkward parliamentary gimmicks. Controversies are resolved on the basis of last-minute presidential letters, nongermane legislative amendments, and executive orders waiving binding statutory requirements. Whether the issue is aiding the Nicaraguan rebels or arming Middle East belligerents, prosecuting a war or concluding a peace, *process* has become almost as important as *policy*. Many of the toughest issues are ducked again and again. "Bipartisan" study commissions are established and conditional appropriations are employed as means of deferring final decisions on vital questions such as modernization of strategic weapons and Central America policy. In the midst of such parliamentary confusion, it is virtually impossible to build an effective governing consensus.

The dilemma here is by no means unique to this era. The American constitutional system has always been a living experiment; the use of ad hoc procedures to solve international problems is a familiar phenomenon. But the challenge now is to weather tumultuous changes in the instruments of government in an age when American leadership in global affairs has become extraordinarily important. It is therefore long past time for policymakers to take a hard look at how the competition along Pennsylvania Avenue has evolved. We need to examine the legacy of the 1970s. We need to appreciate which of Congress's revolutionary changes have endured and recognize which have been swept aside by a Reagan administration that successfully challenged many legislative restraints.

Americans urgently require a better policymaking road map. Both the process and the participating institutions have changed dramatically. There can be no single framework that offers the key to understanding the policymaking competition because the process itself is a dynamic one, subject to change. But the shape of future disputes can be anticipated more effectively. To prepare for this challenge, we need to sort out the jumbled pieces, to reexamine the administrative flowcharts and the legislative procedures, to look at the new laws on the books and the most recent precedents for their use. We need to look at the process with less institutional partisanship and with less ideological passion. Only then can we appreciate the current state of U.S. foreign policymaking—and only then can we pursue the national interest more effectively.

The touchstone for any such inquiry must be history. We cannot fully appreciate where we are, or where we might hope to go, unless we have a clear understanding of where we have been. The scope of the congressional challenge in the 1970s was something new and different. But the flames it ignited grew from the sparks of a 200-year old dispute.

Ever since the Declaration of Independence, Americans have struggled to define their proper place in the world. The framers of the

U.S. Constitution created a new and revolutionary form of government in 1787. But this brilliant charter was neither intended nor able to resolve the fundamental ambivalence Americans have felt toward international relations. A nation of immigrants, the United States has been split since its founding by conflicting impulses of self-interested isolationism and missionary interventionism. The Constitution deliberately reflects this tension between executive and legislative predominance in foreign policymaking. This tension is inherent in our tripartite federal system; it was created by design, not accident. However, the stakes of the struggle to resolve this conflict have been raised markedly. It has become ever more important for Congress and the president to move beyond competition and to forgo a workable consensus. In a world burdened with 50,000 U.S. and Soviet nuclear warheads, a world where U.S. leadership is subject to daily challenge, the battle to shape American foreign policy has truly global stakes.

If a voter, a scholar, a commentator, or a bureaucrat wants to understand how American diplomacy is shaped today, it is essential to understand the degree to which the policymaking process itself has been irreversibly altered. Why is it that Congress and the White House seem to be in an almost constant state of confrontation over foreign policy issues? How does the United States become ensnared in prolonged procedural wrangles over initiatives as diverse as troop deployments, arms sales, and foreign aid? Whatever happened to the "bipartisam tradition" that—with the exception of the Washington debate over "who lost China"—guided U.S. foreign policy from Pearl Harbor to Vietnam? What can Americans learn from such rare periods of consensus to help avoid debilitating policy disputes in the future? These are questions that must be addressed before attempts are made to chart a better course.

Many of the differences in how the White House and Congress wage disputes over foreign policymaking power result directly from changes occurring within these two branches of government. A central truth is that there has been an extraordinary dispersion of power in both branches, making policy formulation and implementation ever more difficult. Today, the legislative branch is vastly different from what it was just twenty years ago. Indeed, more than half the current membership was not in Congress a decade ago. Legislators are younger and less experienced in the art of governance. Deals are not so readily cut between the White House and a handful of Capitol Hill powers because the ability of senior congressional leaders to deliver on the bargain is so much more open to challenge. "Go it alone" policymaking has diffused power among junior members who are skilled in the demands of the modern media campaign, who are masters of the 15-second television sound bite. This juniorization of Congress has accelerated the erosion of party discipline and created dozens of new power pockets in once obscure subcommittees. Efforts at consensus building have thus been greatly hindered.

At the same time, the modern presidency has endured a tumultuous generation of change. Five successive presidents have been weakened by foreign disasters and domestic challenges to their international priorities. Executive authority was severely weakened by the Vietnam War and the Watergate investigations. Executive power was eroded by an aggressive Congress, a vigorous adversary press, and a host of competing executive branch agencies. Unremitting sniping between key departments and a parade of national security advisers have weakened executive branch cohesion. Consequently, the ability of any president to lead has been sorely tested. After the collapse of Richard Nixon's governing authority, a likable Gerald Ford was ineffective in international affairs, and a cerebral Jimmy Carter proved politically inept. "President-bashing" was promising to become a national sport, but Ronald Reagan enjoyed a lengthy and productive honeymoon. The president's foreign policy prerogatives were resurgent during Reagan's combative first term. But the diplomatic accomplishments of the Reagan White House were modest, and with the Iran-Contra affair came a new weakening of the lame-duck president's standing. Presidential authority once again fell under sustained challenge. Despite bipartisan support for the INF treaty and improved U.S.-Soviet relations, legislators repeatedly reversed White House priorities in Reagan's waning years.

The principal constant in this recent struggle has been steadily heightened politicization of U.S. foreign policymaking. Such conflict between the White House and Congress is not inherently undesirable. The Constitution's system of checks and balances serves vital purposes: a thorough scrubbing of policy options is not only a good way to avoid disasters, it is a healthy means of building a consensus that can weather change and setback. But public debate can also be overdone, inviting disarray. The consequences—legislative gridlock and executive paralysis—provide a recipe for diplomatic failure. Thus, there is every reason for concern that this heightened struggle, which confounds our allies and adversaries alike, ill serves U.S. national interests.

"President Clashes with Congress over Arms Policy." "Legislators Hamstring White House Diplomacy." "Supreme Court Backs President in War Powers Dispute." With increasing frequency, these and similar headlines have confronted the American people in recent years. Controversies like the Iran-Contra scandal serve to revive the familiar debate. Soon, as Yogi Berra observed, "It's deja vu all over again." Congressional champions inevitably cite executive branch excesses as justification for more severe restrictions. White House partisans counter that it is precisely such "micromanagement" by Congress that underscores the need for greater presidential freedom of action on issues of war and peace. Old cliches are dusted off, old arguments unholstered. And off they go, round and round; once again the battle lines are drawn for debilitating Pennsylvania Avenue foreign policymaking struggles.

Today these conflicts are by no means an insider's game. Beyond the Washington Beltway, American voters have grown more concerned with the international issues of the day. This is a consequence not only of the omnipresent possibility of nuclear annihilation that haunts our fragile planet. Wars in Central America and economic distress in Mexico send waves of immigrants northward. Imports of cheap finished goods dislocate American workers while inexpensive raw material imports restock U.S. factories. Fighting on the West Bank or around the Persian Gulf sharpens divisions within the patchwork quilt of ethnic groups that constitute the American electorate. Economic and security issues have greater grass-roots impact in an age of growing international interdependence. Thus, the middle-class stockholder and the blue-collar worker have a greater interest in Washington policy debates. To the old adage, "All politics are local," might be added the notion that now even the town hall worries about the global village.

The worldwide reach of satellite television and gavel-to-gavel coverage of most congressional proceedings have also injected international issues into American homes with extraordinary immediacy. Innovative new stations like Cable News Network (CNN) and Cable Satellite Public Affairs Network (C-SPAN) have made Washington debates daily dinnertime fare for many—and lunchtime soap opera entertainment for more than a few. Once obscure bureaucrats have gained instant celebrity. Each new policy struggle brings us new heroes and villains—the Richard Perles, the Jim Wrights, and the Oliver Norths. Today the investigative press is far more aggressive than in years past; the rules of engagement have changed and publication of sensitive national security information is routine. In addition, new ethnic lobbies and political action committees have been formed to influence the foreign policy debate, shepherd voters to the polls, and flood enormous sums of money into campaign coffers. These new electoral pressures have introduced a host of international issues into state and local elections.

These recent developments in the political life of our nation have generated substantial press commentary. A few visionary policymakers have called for a more critical and systematic evaluation of the fruits of past reforms. But there is always a preoccupation with the crisis of the day. And the elections always just over the horizon have distracted the vast majority of those in government. On the fundamental question of how our foreign policymaking process should function, there has been a paucity of lucid analysis. Insufficient consideration has been given by legislators and diplomats alike to the question of how this process serves U.S. national interests. There is insufficient understanding at both ends of Pennsylvania Avenue about what the current foreign policymaking environment portends for the future of American diplomacy.

Lost in most recent commentary on foreign policymaking struggles have been three essential facts.

1. While the breadth of the congressional revolution in the 1970s was extraordinary, the legislative-executive contest over foreign policymaking predominance is by no means a new one. The rules of engagement *have* been fundamentally altered. But the nature of this debate is altogether familiar and is grounded in numerous precedents that are central to an understanding of our current state of affairs but, all too often, have been forgotten as institutional memory has been lost in the dizzying turnover of Washington personnel. A close examination of history can provide useful perspective here and can restrain wasteful efforts to reinvent the wheel. Those who express alarm at allegedly unprecedented congressional "unsurpation" of White House prerogatives often fail to recall the legacy of past challenges. Just as President Franklin Roosevelt's repeated conflicts with an isolationist Congress continued well into his third term, President Wilson faced insurmountable opposition to joining the League of

Nations. And for decades in the nineteenth century, no president could move forward in the negotiation of international treaties and tariffs without the express approval of key congressional powers. The fact is that there has been a constant ebb and flow, a cyclical advance and retreat by the respective branches of the federal government in asserting their foreign policymaking powers. An appreciation of this phenomenon helps us evaluate which recent policymaking changes are temporary aberrations and which are likely to have an enduring impact.

2. *The congressional revolution of the 1970s spoke more to procedure than to substance.*   Congress has rarely reversed a central policy initiative, like detente with the Soviet Union or establishing new ties with the People's Republic of China. Rather, Congress has created a formidable new gauntlet for such proposals to run. The cumulative effects of congressional reforms has been to alter substantially the way U.S. foreign policy is shaped. For example, the Nuclear Nonproliferation Act, the Arms Export Control Act, and the War Powers Resolution each created new congressional levers for redirecting or halting presidential initiatives. Because of the breakdown of the seniority system, these new parliamentary devices have empowered the most junior members. Today it is possible for even a first-term congressman in the minority party to have a significant impact on relations with China, or Panama, or Saudi Arabia. Procedural reforms have introduced complicated new hurdles into the business of setting American foreign policy, and thus have had a lasting impact on the balance of power between Congress and the White House. But they have rarely produced a fundamental redirection of America's global outlook.

3. *The counterreformation of the 1980s has curbed many legislative prerogatives that were central to the congressional revolution of the previous decade.*   The Reagan administration challenged the powers of Congress across the board. Laws governing arms sales, nuclear exports, treaty interpretation, and military deployments were confronted repeatedly. The Reagan White House ran over, around, and, occasionally, right through the legal barriers erected by Congress to assert its policymaking powers. Hill leaders prevailed in several of these confrontations. But the legislative precedents were often reshaped. For example, the 1983 Supreme Court ruling that struck down the legislative veto forced Congress to relinquish the

right of final approval, upon which a whole series of crucial foreign policy statutes had been based—a blow from which Congress has yet to recover. Policymakers have not systematically evaluated the impact of this ruling on a whole body of law, preferring instead to rely on parliamentary gimmickry and legislative "ad hocery." Thus, in recent U.S. foreign policy disputes—debates over arms sales, covert aid, and the appropriate use of American forces in Beirut, Grenada, and the Persian Gulf—legislators have responded only to the specific crisis at hand. The more general underlying questions, which muddy the law and divide the institutions of Congress and the presidency, go unresolved. There has been a regrettable failure by Congress, executive branch officials, and the academic community to reexamine carefully the broader policy implications of changes that have occurred since the Capitol Hill revolution of the 1970s started waning under the natural forces of counterreformation.

This book is a modest attempt to meet that challenge. It is designed for the concerned citizen and the professional diplomat, the informed commentator and the confused policymaker. It is intended to guide—to explore behind the scenes even as it critiques the process by which U.S. foreign policy decisions are made in the real world. The book is divided into three parts. The first offers a critical overview of the history of competition between the executive and lesislative branches in making U.S. foreign policy. It focuses on the origins of the conflict and examines the lessons of the relatively brief and unique period of bipartisan consensus engendered by the consequences of World War II, and the nascent Soviet challenge. Part Two of this work examines how the institutions of Congress and the presidency function in the modern environment. The focus here is more on process than on personality: while the author has been involved in many of the policy disputes outlined, this is not another "kiss-and-tell" book. Part Three chronicles the key areas of controversy issue by issue, from war powers to foreign aid and human rights. Here the focus is on key procedural lessons, with succinct summaries of the broad areas of dispute.

This text is designed to be accessible, not encyclopedic. There are a few areas not assessed in which prominent Hill efforts have been made to challenge executive authority—most notably, in trade policy and oversight of the intelligence community. It has been the author's experience, however, that despite countless hours of debate, enduring congressional impact upon U.S. foreign policies in these areas has proven far more modest than upon policy in other areas. In the trade field, Congress has granted sweeping negotiating authority to the executive and has overwhelmingly embraced subsequent agreements. Beyond the rhetorical debates between free-traders and protectionists, most legislation advanced has been essentially a collection of export promotion measures with negligible impact on foreign relations. Similarly, Capitol Hill activities in the intelligence field have not markedly altered U.S. relations with most nations. Indeed, ever since the 1975 disclosures of CIA foreign assassination plots uncovered by the Church Committee led to the establishment of permanent House and Senate intelligence oversight panels, there has been limited congressional debate about the role of intelligence agencies in U.S. foreign relations. Such debates as have erupted—disputes about the proper CIA role in Angola or Nicaragua, for example—have really been arguments about foreign aid and about the best means of pursuing containment strategies, not about intelligence policy per se. The fact is that behind the rhetoric and the press releases, Congress is not presently a major player in setting foreign policy on key trade and intelligence matters.

This work concludes with a chapter designed to be both prescriptive and provocative. Clearly, the suggestions offered derive from some strongly held opinions. Here, as elsewhere, the author strives to rise above partisanship, both institutional and political. However, as one who participated as a legislative assistant in most of the Washington foreign policy controversies of the last decade, the author shares a significant measure of guilt. Like a discordant voice in a chorus singing out of tune, one must confess to being part of the problem and must strive to do better oneself, even as one proposes some possible solutions.

I THE HISTORICAL CONTEXT

1 FOREIGN POLICY UNDER THE CONSTITUTION
A Prescription for Conflict

> I do not hesitate to say that it is especially in the conduct
> of their foreign relations that democracies appear to me
> decidedly inferior to other governments.
>
> —Alexis de Tocqueville, 1835[1]

Throughout the hot Washington summer of 1987, senior officials of the Congress and the Reagan administration engaged in prolonged and very public combat. Ostensibly at issue was the propriety of executive branch actions in selling arms to the radical Iranian regime headed by Ayatollah Ruhollah Khomeini and then diverting sale profits to aid the Nicaraguan Contra forces. But simmering just beneath the surface—and occasionally erupting in tense exchanges—was an issue as old as the Constitution itself: what are the appropriate congressional limitations on the President's powers to execute foreign policies?

As witness after witness trooped before the unwieldy joint committee hearings, Americans viewed the televised drama with fascination. Few citizens who followed the Iran-Contra Committees' proceedings were left without a strong opinion on basic constitutional questions.

Had Congress gone too far in tying the President's hands? Wasn't it up to the President to lead in setting policy on relations with other nations? Can the President act unilaterally when national interests are at stake, or is he bound to adhere to both the spirit and the letter

3

of legislated restrictions? At what point is Congress obliged to step in to check excessive executive power?

The nationally televised exercise in self-examination has become a familiar part of the American political experience. Like the Army-McCarthy hearings of the 1950s and the 1973-1974 Watergate hearings on the abuse of presidential authority, the Iran-Contra hearings sparked widespread public discussion. At home, the Constitution itself once again became a topic for street-corner debate; abroad, the proceedings alarmed U.S. allies and confused adversaries. Why this American obsession with public revelation, many foreigners wondered? Americans could not easily appreciate the difficulty others had in understanding this interbranch combat: most of the world still lives either under authoritarian dictatorships that can ignore their legislatures or under parliamentary governments in which the leaders of the legislative and executive branches are one and the same.[2] Indeed, while the presidency of the United States remains the world's most powerful office, no legislature has greater foreign affairs prerogatives than the U.S. Congress.

Critics of the Iran-Contra investigation charged that the hearings dealt a blow to American diplomacy; they argued that the process of self-examination advertised Washington's indecision and ambivalence toward the nation's responsibilities as a global power. Others found in the committees' disclosures a salutary process of self-education for American voters. For better or worse, the proceedings were quintessentially American, in the oldest tradition of the U.S. government. They served to underscore the fact that the *process* by which Washington reaches foreign policy decisions is still evolving. The rules that govern the struggle to achieve consensus out of the foreign policy conflicts between Congress and the President are still subject to debate, still changing. That this contest should endure was, indeed, the design of the framers of the U.S. Constitution. An effective understanding of how American national security policy is made today must be grounded in an appreciation of this simple fact.

EARLY AMERICAN DIPLOMACY: MYTH AND REALITY

The contest between Congress and the President to shape American foreign policy was, from its very outset, intense and partisan. Collisions occurred almost immediately between the legislature and the executive. The fact is that each of the first three U.S. presidents left office amid bitter and divisive confrontations with Congress over international issues. And each of the first contested presidential campaigns was deeply affected by foreign policy issues. It is essential to appreciate these early experiences as we assess more recent confrontations between Congress and the White House.

During the last one and a half decades, partisans of the respective branches have perpetuated numerous myths about how American diplomatic practice has developed. These myths have become part of the popular consciousness. Unfortunately, their accumulation renders a clear understanding of U.S. foreign policymaking more difficult. For example, many commentators lament that "politics used to stop at the water's edge." It is suggested that the United States once had a "bipartisan tradition" whereby party differences were set aside by the White House and Congress when addressing crucial international questions. Patriots in distress, and politicians in hot water, repeatedly conjure up this notion.[3] But the regrettable fact is that such a consensus has rarely existed in American history, except in the midst of world war. The internationalist consensus that endured on most key issues from Pearl Harbor to the entry of U.S. combat troops into the Vietnam War thus warrants careful scrutiny as an *exception*, not as a norm.

Loss of institutional memory has propagated another myth—the absurd notion that congressional assertiveness on international matters was virtually unique to the post-Watergate era. It is suggested that initiatives during these years represented not simply an escalation of a familiar struggle but an unprecedented assault on "traditional" presidential leadership.[4] A more careful evaluation of the American experience, especially of the tribulations endured by the first several presidents, serves to dispel this illusion. It is true that the stakes are higher—because the latest round of legislative challenges is the first to take place at a time of American global leadership. Yet Washington has frequently witnessed congressional challenges that have weakened the authority of presidents late in their terms of office. "President-bashing" is not a new sport. Early U.S. history shows this clearly; the "imperial" presidency began neither with Richard Nixon nor with Franklin Roosevelt, and the relentlessly assertive congressional role is not a post-Vietnam novelty. It is essential to bear these facts in mind as we evaluate the experience of early

American administrations in wrestling with the challenge of governing the new republic.

From the very first Continental Congress, the experience of democratic government in the United States has been one of trial and
error. The constitution that governs the nation is the oldest living
government charter in the world. But it remains one of the most
revolutionary, offering an abundance of self-correcting mechanisms.
In its silences, as well as its explicit checks and balances, there is an
inherent tension, creative at times, troublesome on other occasions.
This inelegant division of authority provides a virtual guarantee of
conflict as Americans struggle to find their nation's place in the
world. Yet in an age of increasingly interdependent nations, in a
world with 50,000 nuclear weapons, America is now governed under
a document that was written primarily by isolationists.

The authors of the U.S. Constitution harbored deep fears of a
powerful executive. They worried that a single strong leader might
embroil the young nation in the endless intrigues of European monarchs. As a result, Americans wrote a governmental charter that, with
the exception of the Articles of Confederation, was unprecedented
in its limitations on executive freedom of action. Their efforts at
Philadelphia to define the proper role of the legislative and executive
branches were shaped by three distinct experiences of eighteenth-
century America.

A primary concern was the frequency of war. Four prolonged
conflicts had been prosecuted between the British and the French
during the eighteenth century. (Indeed, steering a safe course between this royal competition would preoccupy the first generation
of U.S. diplomats.) Battles had been waged across the European continent, on the high seas, and in many parts of the Americas. The motives for these grinding conflicts—petty jealousies and succession
struggles, religious differences, and contests for often minor overseas possessions—seemed spurious to Americans intent upon building a new order. But these European court intrigues inevitably embroiled the colonists, pitting local forces in the New World against
one another and taking their toll on soldier and taxpayer alike.
Strong executives were blamed for this readiness to make war. Thus,
after Americans won their freedom in six long years of armed struggle, they were determined to remove from the hands of the executive the sole power to commit the nation to hostilities.

A second phenomenon was the continuing effort to stabilize
commerce. Trade issues were a central preoccupation on the fron-

tier; as Thomas Paine observed, "America's plan is commerce."[5] The colonies had failed to establish customs unions, to set judicious tariffs, or to defend American trade rights. Individual colonies had made fleeting efforts to join together in trade agreements. When tensions with British authorities mounted, economic weapons were the first employed on both sides—the levying of higher tariffs and taxes against the colonists, the dumping of British tea in Boston Harbor, and the retaliatory closing of Massachusetts ports by the British. Trade woes also fueled the move toward a stronger federal union after independence. Dissatisfaction over the way the Articles of Confederation regularized interstate trade brought Virginia and Maryland together with other representatives of the sovereign states at Annapolis in 1786. These meetings led directly to the call for a constitutional convention the following spring. Indeed, in the absence of chronic trade disputes, there might never have been any federal constitution.[6]

The third experience that shaped the foreign affairs provisions of the Constitution was the persistent failure of the colonies—and later, of the nascent states—to forge alliances strong enough to secure their borders against foreign attack. For many years, individual colonies had pursued their own treaty arrangements, a practice ultimately outlawed in the Constitution.[7] The first serious attempt at union prior to the Continental Congress of 1775 had been designed to protect Americans against foreign danger. The Albany Plan of 1754 was an attempt to provide greater internal security for Americans against the manifold threats of the Spanish to the south, the French to the north and west, and the native Indian population everywhere. The ever shifting alliances of European princes had left Americans acutely vulnerable, subject to the vicissitudes of European court politics. The Articles of Confederation were too weak to secure the United States against the danger that European monarchs might move against the subversive American effort to establish a popularly elected democratic government. As Thomas Jefferson had written James Madison from Paris on the eve of the Constitutional Convention, it was essential for the nation to adopt a stronger federal charter, if only to convince Europeans to show Americans greater respect.[8]

THE CONSTITUTION AND NATIONAL SECURITY

The Constitutional Convention of 1787 opened with a number of conflicting objectives. The delegates were nearly unanimous in their

suspicion of executive authority.[9] Under the Articles of Confederation, Americans were ostensibly led by the titular President of Congress. But the United States had suffered from its lack of centralized
leadership. The delegates desired more secure and stable commerce
among the diverse states, and they sought a stronger customs union.
But they were reluctant to surrender to any executive the power to
start a war. They jealously guarded the exclusive authority of the
Continental Congress to negotiate treaties—affirmed under Article
IX of the Articles of Confederation. Indeed, Congress itself had negotiated the 1783 Treaty of Paris ending the War of Independence.
The delegates also were not eager to bind the young nation to any
foreign power for military alliance or trade cooperation. They shared
Paine's opinion that "it is in the true interest of America to steer
clear of European contentions. . . . Dependence on Great Britain
tends directly to involve this Continent in European wars and quarrels."[10] Thus, for a vast majority of the Constitution's framers, a
crucial element in any successful charter would be provisions to
make national involvement with the affairs of other countries extremely difficult. The "great rule of conduct" for the United States
in dealing with foreign nations, as George Washington later stated it
succinctly, "is, in extending our commercial relations, to have with
them as little *political* connection as possible."[11]

The proposals put forward in Philadelphia were very much the
product of the British experience. A civil war had been fought in
Britain in the 1660s to check royal powers in spending and diplomacy. Ever since the demise of Oliver Cromwell and the restoration
of the throne under Charles II, the British system had witnessed a
steady erosion of executive power—until the disastrous reign of
George III. Americans wished to renew and accelerate this British
trend in their own land. The British system of the 1780s still possessed a powerful executive; George III had overridden significant
opposition in Parliament to prolong the war with the colonies. Nevertheless, in the British system, powers over foreign policymaking had
come increasingly to be shared. "The British overlapped powers deliberately," a leading congressional analyst has noted, "especially in
foreign affairs. We have good reason to believe the Americans con-
sciously followed the pattern."[12]

The unifying principle of those at the Constitutional Convention
was the need to secure the new nation by strengthening federal authority, which was not simply the concern of diplomats like Jefferson, who complained about the indignities Americans had to endure

at the hands of Europeans. The Americans were beset by a failure to address domestic economic concerns, highlighted by an abortive uprising against debt collection—Shay's Rebellion—that shook the leadership of the young nation.[13] As a consequence of widespread criticism of the weak federal charter, virtually every major deficiency of the Articles of Confederation was remedied in the proposals adopted by the Constitutional Convention. In a sustained effort that appalled states' rights advocates, a strong federal system was created. The new government was granted authority in areas as diverse as road construction, the raising of armies, and the provision of postal services.

The document that emerged from the Philadelphia drafting sessions was tilted in favor of the legislature. Even the most assertive modern-day champions of executive power would concede that the framers' original intent was to provide an equal partnership in which Congress was first among equals. Congress predominated, especially in the Constitution's enumeration of foreign affairs powers. In Article I, Section 8, eighteen specific congressional powers were spelled out. Special note should be made of the fact that the legislature was given primary authority over the two international questions of greatest importance in the world of 1787—the regulation of foreign trade and the initiation of war. The Constitution specifies in great detail the authority given to the legislature. It vests the Congress with seven basic powers to govern the conduct of U.S. relations with foreign nations:

- the exclusive power to declare war;
- the exclusive authority to raise and support armies;
- the exclusive authority to regulate foreign commerce;
- the Senate's authority to consent to treaty ratification;
- the Senate's authority to confirm ambassadors;
- the sole right to issue letters of marque and reprisal; and
- the sole authority to define and punish piracies and other "offenses against the laws of nations."[14]

Arrayed against these explicit, unprecedented grants of legislative authority are far more vague and general powers that the Constitution provides to the executive. The independent executive branch and its president were new creations; it was left to the first generation of executives to define their parameters. In the Constitution, presidential powers were stated more briefly, almost grudgingly. These include the president's authority as the civilian commander-in-chief of U.S. military forces to direct combat operations—*after* the Congress has raised and funded military forces and has issued a declaration of war—as well as to receive foreign ambassadors. By implication, as well as subsequent practice, this latter procedural provision ensured presidential primary in the conduct of day-to-day diplomatic affairs—for there could be only one head of state. In the final days of the convention, the framers also moved to shift important authorities from the exclusive realm of Congress. The congressional authority to "make" (conduct) war was revised on August 17, 1787 to the power to "declare" war; the motion was made by James Madison and Elbridge Gerry just to clarify the executive's authority to repel sudden attacks. And after extensive debate regarding a prospective House role in ratification debates, treaty negotiating powers were shifted from the Senate to the president.[15]

The framers gave the president a veto power to temper the passions of a popularly elected legislature. But they granted Congress the ability to override an executive veto with a two-thirds vote. They gave the president the authority to conduct diplomacy and to prosecute a declared war. But they gave Congress the power to impeach a wayward executive and to cut off monies for any combat that the people no longer supported. They deliberately and systematically overlapped powers, united in their belief in the imperfection of man and the fallibility of individuals and institutions. The framers' religious beliefs upheld the popular notion that power unchecked would lead to despotism: they believed in original sin. Of the weak central government that existed between the Revolutionary War and the Constitutional Convention, George Washington noted, "We have probably had too good an opinion of human nature."[16] James Madison concurred, noting that "if men were angels, no government would be necessary."[17]

Throughout American history, these overlapping powers have presented unresolved contradicitons that remain a prescription for conflict. As noted presidential scholar Edward Corwin observed:

> What the Constitution does, *and all that it does*, is to confer on the President certain powers capable of affecting our foreign relations, and certain other powers of the same general kind on the Senate, and still other such powers on Congress; but which of these organs shall have the decisive and final voice in determining the course of the American nation is left for events to resolve.[18]

The struggle to resolve these conflicts did not occur in a vacuum. The debate began with the framers arguing constitutional theory in their proratification document, *The Federalist Papers.* Yet these lobbying tracts served only to underscore ambiguities in the division of foreign policymaking powers. They argued *against* a clean and tidy separation. Alexander Hamilton, later a champion of executive prerogative, wrote of the need to place legislative checks on presidential power:

> The history of human conduct does not warrant the exalted opinion of human virtue which would make it wise in a nation to commit interests of so delicate and momentous a kind, as those which concern its intercourse with the rest of the world, to the sole disposal of a magistrate created and circumstanced as would be the President of the United States. . . . The joint possession of the power in question, by the President and the Senate, would afford a greater prospect of security than the separate possession of it by either of them.[19]

But the debate over the appropriate balance would continue among the coauthors of *The Federalist Papers*, as well as the Constitution's detractors. Indeed, the framers of the Constitution were soon switching sides on key issues of executive versus legislative authority as practical experience and political needs clashed with theoretical abstractions. Soon after ratification, Madison, Hamilton, and John Jay would find themselves in bitter disputes over what the Constitution's shared foreign affairs powers meant; the ambiguities in the document itself were so great as to allow an effective champion of either branch of government to assert a significant degree of shared power. To this day, the Philadelphia debates offer protagonists a wealth of citations to support competing interpretations. As Justice Robert Jackson noted in the famous 1952 steel seizure case:

> Just what our forefathers did envision, or would have envisaged had they foreseen modern conditions, must be derived from materials almost as enigmatic as the dreams Joseph was called upon to interpret for the Pharaoh. A century and a half of partisan debate and scholarly speculation yields no net result but only supplies more or less apt quotations from respected sources on each side of the question.[20]

Beginning with a crucial 1801 Supreme Court test of the president's authority to determine the nature of diplomatic relations, the judicial branch of government has occasionally been called upon as an arbiter in the enduring dispute between Congress and the executive branch over foreign policymaking powers. The Court has upheld the president's authority to control diplomatic contacts and his right to sign or veto legislation passed by Congress. The Court has similarly defended the prerogative of Congress to establish policy through statutory intervention. Occasionally, overreaching dicta are offered to provide solace—and useful citations—to partisans of one branch or another. However, the Court has *not* played a central role in this dispute. In case after case, it has preferred instead to rule on the margin: the judiciary's legacy in the dispute between Congress and the White House is in fact quite thin. Repeatedly, justices have found that the contest to interpret the Constitution's division of foreign affairs powers is a fundamentally *political* dispute to be resolved by elected federal officials in the court of public opinion. But for a few instances where case law has been clearly established, justices have inevitably found that foreign policymaking tensions should be worked out by Congress, the president, and the voters.

These tensions are at the root of the contest for foreign policymaking primacy, which continues to erupt in our headlines. This work will consider a number of important examples of controversies that relate to the current policymaking environment. But let us begin this analysis by reviewing briefly the crucial experience of early U.S. diplomats.

CONGRESS VERSUS THE PRESIDENT: THE FIRST TESTS

The diplomatic history of the United States essentially begins with the Declaration of Independence. This elaboration of the rebels' cause was hailed at home for its inspirational value. Yet its design was primarily to aid American diplomacy by shaping European calculations.[21] Publication of the document was intended to aid the efforts of congressional representatives in foreign capitals. These ambassadors from the Continental Congress were desperately trying to impress upon would-be allies the colonists' determination to break with England once and for all. American envoys needed some proof to demonstrate that the breach was irreparable before they could begin to win foreign support for Revolutionary troops.

While American colonists fought to be free of the European courts, it proved ironic that they remained heavily reliant upon royal intrigue for the success of their revolution. A deliberate strategy of playing the royal courts against one another was central to American success.

At one point, the very fate of the United States seemed to hang on the resolution of a European dispute over the tiny Mediterranean outpost of Gibraltar—a dispute that could have united European courts against the insurrection in the American colonies.[22] Colonial military efforts were also highly dependent upon covert aid from France and Spain; it is estimated that some 90 percent of the gunpowder used in the early years of the Revolutionary War was smuggled from Europe. And of course eventual French military intervention, with the supply of naval forces and infantry, was central to the American triumph in the maneuvering at Yorktown.

American diplomacy suffered under the Articles of Confederation simply because Europeans did not take the colonial union seriously. Conversely, the success of the Constitutional Convention tremendously strengthened American diplomacy. Equally important was the accession of General Washington, who was much respected by British and French authorities, to the presidency. Washington took office with an enormous following in Congress as well. Indeed, the assumption that he would be the first president had led many in Philadelphia to be less squeamish in granting executive powers towards the close of the convention. As one delegate wrote, the executive's powers would have been far more modest "had not many of the members cast their eyes toward General Washington and shaped their ideas of the powers to be given to a President by their opinions of his virtue."[23] But these sentiments did little to prevent the lionized national leader from becoming embroiled in frequent combat with the new Congress over a host of foreign policy matters. Washington would ultimately leave office embittered by the capacity of foreign policy controversies to excite popular passions—a fate that ultimately befell many of his successors.

The President's first encounter with Congress on a foreign policy issue was almost comic. On Saturday, August 22, 1789, President Washington arrived at the Senate chamber (then still in New York) to receive the senators' advice and consent to consummation of a series of Indian treaties. As the drafts were read in the noisy chamber, it became apparent that the President—who was accompanied by his Secretary of War, Henry Knox—wished an immediate indication of senatorial approval. Though awed by the presence of their revered leader, the legislators balked. After some tentative discussion, Senator Robert Morris of Pennsylvania requested more time for study, to be followed by general debate the following Monday. "The President of the United States," one senator recalled, "started up in a violent fret. 'This defeats every purpose of my coming here,'" the exasperated Washington declared.[24] But he dutifully returned to the chamber two days later, where he witnessed a prolonged process of debate and amendment before finally receiving Senate consent. Forever shattered was his notion of the Senate as some type of executive council that would unthinkingly ratify executive diplomatic initiatives. The Senate had established itself as an independent body with its own review powers in treaty consideration. But never again would Washington return to the legislative chambers; it was his first and only attempt to solicit personally the Senate's views on treaty matters.

Trade and Indian matters were at the forefront of the foreign policy agenda in the first Congress convened after ratification of the Constitution. Many weeks in the first session in 1789 were consumed by a hotly debated tariff measure. Sectional divisions on international issues were clearly apparent. But soon the infant nation's tricky relations with France and England became the dominant international concern for both Congress and the Washington administration.

The French Revolution excited popular sentiment in favor of a stronger alliance with Paris. British delays in evacuating forts in the American Northwest fueled criticism from "anti-Federalists" in Congress. As tensions between the French and British grew and attacks on American shipping by British warships continued, there was pressure in Congress for a declaration of war. After hostilities broke out between France and England, President Washington responded unilaterally by issuing a proclamation of American neutrality. Secretary of State Jefferson had reservations about the constitutionality of the declaration, which was announced while Congress was in recess. Washington's views were challenged vigorously in Congress. But he ultimately prevailed because he had the executive's advantage of unity of purpose, while critics in Congress remained divided on procedural and substantive disputes. As a consequence, a vital precedent was established for executive initiative in foreign relations.

During the last three years of his presidency, Washington withstood pro-French sympathy and agitation in Congress for war with Britain. But his personal popularity did not prevent a prolonged conflict with the legislature over America's relations with the European belligerents. Congressional critics of Washington's policies employed tactics that have since been adopted by many opponents of executive actions in international affairs. Indeed, these first challenges became virtually a textbook manual for legislators looking to alter presidential foreign policies in the following areas:

Nominations: Republicans held up the nomination of John Jay to negotiate a permanent peace with London, subjecting the Jay Treaty to prolonged debate and pressing for a change in negotiating instructions.

Senate treaty consent: Repeated legislative efforts to scuttle the Jay Treaty were beaten back with no votes to spare.

Grass-roots lobbying: To build antitreaty sentiment, Republican clubs throughout the United States held rallies and bonfires, where Jay was repeatedly burned in effigy.

Challenges to "executive privilege": A party caucus in the House produced motions to secure all the President's documents relating to treaty negotiation.

Appropriations denials: Led by James Madison, the House sought to remedy its lack of a constitutional role in treaty consent by barring funds required to implement the Jay pact. Ultimately, the President prevailed, but with only a razor-thin margin of 51–48.

In the wake of the bitter confrontation with Congress, Washington declined to seek a third term. Weary of his battles over the Jay Treaty and related issues, he lamented that he had "been vilified as a Nero, or a common pickpocket."[25] Washington began in a fit of pique to draft a self-pitying farewell speech. Alexander Hamilton and others were enlisted to revise Washington's angry valedictory to the American people. Intended to summarize his hopes and fears for the young nation, his famous Farewell Address emerged as a landmark isolationist tract that has been cited innumerable times in our history to justify neutrality and noninterventionist policies. Washington offered grave warnings against international alliances and passionate attachments to foreign causes. "'Tis our true policy to steer clear of permanent alliance, with any portion of the foreign world," he wrote. "Why, by interweaving our destiny with that of any part of Europe, entangle our peace and prosperity in the toils of European ambition, rivalship, interest, humour or caprice?"[26]

Washington's Farewell Address was promptly used as a crucial campaign document in a presidential election that hung as much on the question of a closer alliance with France as upon any domestic issue. Emissaries from Paris clumsily sought to intervene in the election to gain support for the Republicans. Federalist leaders urged voters to "decide between the address of the President and the politicking of the French."[27] When the Federalist John Adams prevailed over Jefferson, the French displeasure was so great that relations between the two nations were virtually severed before the inauguration of the second U.S. president on March 3, 1797..

John Adams became the first, though certainly not the last, president to be inaugurated amid a clamor from "war hawks" in Congress. His entire presidency was bedeviled by passionate congressional divisions over the proper course to pursue in relations with London and Paris. So-called extreme-Federalists in Congress agitated for war with the French. But Adams and Hamilton resisted. Abortive negotiations with Paris led to another executive privilege fight with Congress over the secrecy of diplomatic negotiating records. Republicans critical of Adams's handling of French affairs demanded dispatches regarding talks with Parisian ministers. When these were ultimately revealed—suggesting ham-handed bribery attempts by the French—a new wave of support for Adams and hostility toward the French swept the nation. This "XYZ Affair" led Congress to adopt the notorious Alien and Sedition Acts: xenophobic measures curbing immigration and press freedoms that rank among the most repressive in American history. Still, Adams shied away from a momentous conflict with France. Ultimately, he split his own party over the wisdom of continuing to pursue a negotiated peace. Senate opponents used their power over nominations and treaty consent to grease the skids for the now unpopular president. Adams left office bitter and broken, another presidential victim of a prolonged effort to cool passions in Congress aroused by foreign policy issues. In departing, he wrote angrily that "we have no Americans in America. . . . A group of foreign liars, encouraged by a few native gentlemen, have discomforted the education, the talents, the virtues and the property of the country."[28]

Thomas Jefferson won election in an extraordinarily divisive presidential campaign that remained undecided in the House of Representatives until thirty-six ballots had been completed. Dark talk of secession and foreign intervention clouded the contested voting, which set in place the first transfer of government between the two major American political parties. Jefferson brought to the White House important diplomatic credentials—he was the second of four consecutive men who succeeded to the presidency with experience as secretary of state. As president, Jefferson initially remained suspicious of a strong executive. Yet Jefferson, the strict constructionist, became the first White House occupant to foray into the gray area of presidential war-making powers. Dispatching naval forces to make war on Barbary pirates off Tripoli, he waited nearly six months before he sought congressional approval—and then evaded the question of what instructions he had provided to U.S. commanders.[29] Jefferson also acted independently of Congress in defending U.S. territorial waters all the way to the Gulf Stream and authorizing military rearmament without congressional approval. Yet the crowning achievement of his presidency—the Louisiana Purchase—demonstrated his willingness to work with and respond to Congress on an international matter of great import. Troubled by the authority of the national government to extend its power over this vast area without a constitutional amendment, Jefferson ultimately dismissed such "metaphysical subtleties."[30] While this was *not* a foreign affairs dispute between the President and Congress, this type of creative flexibility on questions of constitutional authority would be emulated by many of Jefferson's successors.

Jefferson succeeded in keeping the United States out of European hostilities sparked by Napoleon's rise. But the Virginian did not fully escape the fate of his predecessors who had run afoul of the Congress over British-French issues. Continued mistreatment of American shipping by the European belligerents led an exasperated Jefferson to override his deep commitment to states' rights and to propose a trade embargo on both nations. Initially, Jefferson was able to blunt criticism in Congress, led by New England Federalists reliant upon trans-Atlantic trade. The President, who had become increasingly isolationist, actually extended the embargo against all nations, while calling for greater American industrial self-sufficiency. Bitter opposition mounted in Congress. As Jefferson's second term drew to a close, talk of secession was once again heard in a tumultuous presidential election. Ultimately, Republican election losses enabled the new Congress to repeal most of the embargo provisions before Jefferson had left the White House to be replaced by Madison. One historian summarized Jefferson's humiliating departure:

> If Washington's Presidency ended in anguish, Jefferson's ended in agony. Jefferson had remarked that Washington suffered during his second term "more than any person I ever yet met with" but Jefferson's own suffering in

the same cirucmstances was even greater. He came to regard each session of Congress as an unbearable ordeal; he repeatedly referred to the Presidency as his prison.[31]

Bitter struggles continued to mark the early exchanges between Congress and the White House in the realm of foreign affairs. The nation entered combat with Britain in 1812 far from united in war. Divisions fractured Congress along regional and party lines. Every single Federalist in Congress voted against the declaration of war. House speaker Henry Clay led war hawks in pressing the measure, and all but three Republicans supported President Madison's reluctant call to arms. A decade later, Congress split with President James Monroe on the issue of relations with the revolutionary governments in Latin America. Congressional leaders sympathetic to Latin Americans' uprising against Spain met with coolness from the Monroe White House. In response, activists led by Speaker Clay sought to open American diplomatic relations with the rebels on their own initiative. Congress went so far as to appropriate funds, which the President had not requested, for foreign missions. One outgrowth of these exchanges was an affirmation by the White House that the United States would oppose any attempt by European powers to reintroduce their forms of government into the hemisphere, the famous Monroe Doctrine.

EBBS AND FLOWS IN THE CONTEST
FOR SUPREMACY

The resolution of the United States' enduring conflict with Britain and the issuance of the Monroe Doctrine made it easier for Americans to turn their sights inward. Throughout the balance of the nineteenth century, diplomacy was only rarely of import to the average American. It occupied little of the federal government's energies, save as it related to westward expansion. The assertive American campaign to fill the continent prompted President James Polk to pick a fight with Mexico. Disputed territory was occupied at Polk's instruction; the President then called upon Congress to "recognize" the resulting state of war between the United States and Mexico.

From 1861–1865, the American Civil War brought only modest efforts at diplomatic maneuver. Ambassadors from the Confederacy sought to win European support. But Union prospects appeared too favorable to invite any foreign intervention before Federal primacy was restored. It would be a generation before Americans once again had much concern over international developments. Only after the continent had been explored and charted, after Americans governed from the Atlantic to the Pacific, did a new ideological crusade of "manifest destiny" begin to precipitate international forays into the Caribbean and the Far East.

The United States did not come to assume a global diplomatic role until its wealth and power—and the filling of the American continent—made it a rival to the imperial European powers at the end of the nineteenth century. Yet even during this most quiescent period of American diplomacy, a pattern was gradually established that characterizes American foreign policy to this day. This is the predictable cycle of American attitudes—and consequent congressional and presidential behavior—toward international matters as one generation is succeeded by the next. There has been a familiar ebb and flow in Americans' perception of the world: they have vacillated between isolationism and interventionism as one generation has offered its experience to the next, as one generation has reacted to the perceived excesses of its predecessors. These cycles in American history, most effectively analyzed by Arthur Schlesinger, Jr., extend deeply into the relations between Congress and the executive branch. They pervade national consciousness and substantially determine outcomes in the inevitable struggles between the Congress and the president. After a period of deep involvement in international affairs, America has quite naturally turned its sights to domestic matters. Military involvement and diplomatic entanglement have inevitably spurred voter reaction. A number of these cycles can be identified. For example, historian Frank Klingberg, writing in the 1950s, identified seven major periods: [32]

Introvert	Extrovert
1776-1798	1798-1824
1824-1844	1844-1871
1871-1891	1891-1918
1918-1940	1940-

What are the common characteristics of these alternating American cycles of relative isolation followed by global involvement? Clearly, they mirror periods of alternating congressional versus presidential dominance. The legislative branch has been relatively ascendant, assertive in its powers during periods of national retreat. Congress has succeeded in checking many presidential foreign policy initiatives during such eras. For example, from the close of the Civil War to the 1890s, a period of virtual government-by-Congress, weak presidents could pursue international matters such as tariffs and treaties only with the express approval of congressional leaders. As a vexed Henry Adams concluded at the time, the secretary of state existed only to recognize "obligations which Congress repudiates whenever it can."[33] Similarly, after the American commitment of troops to World War I helped yield an Allied victory, a new period of American isolationism set in. Presidential initiatives in foreign affairs were routinely checked. After Woodrow Wilson lost a prolonged struggle for American entry into the League of Nations, Senator Boies Penrose declared, "I do not think it matters much who is Secretary of State. Congress—especially the Senate—will blaze the way in connection with our foreign policies."[34] In the Depression years, Franklin Roosevelt faced similar skepticism. The White House was confronted with binding neutrality legislation and failed to gain substantial congressional support for aiding beleaguered French and British forces until more than two years *after* the Nazi invasion of Poland.

Conversely, in periods of expansion and conflict, Americans seem to welcome a strong executive. Congress quite readily acceded to President Abraham Lincoln's exercise of unprecedented powers when the Union was threatened. Similarly, public clamor for American expansion granted presidents like Polk and William McKinley tremendous support for military adventures against Mexico and Spain. In the same sense, the American anticommunist consensus gave President Harry Truman—and later, in the wake of the Gulf of Tonkin incident, President Lyndon Johnson—a very broad charter from Congress.

There is an important chicken-or-egg question here regarding the source of this phenomenon. Does the public mood, as reflected in Congress, shape presidential options? Or is a strong personality in the White House able to reshape the historical trend by force of his leadership? The American experience supports the former explanation. Even exceptionally strong presidents have been unable to swim far when attempting to pull against an isolationist tide in Congress. Franklin Roosevelt could not prevent—despite his domination of domestic affairs—congressional enforcement of strict American neutrality laws throughout the 1930s, whereas congressional expansionists virtually forced the Spanish-American War on an initially reluctant President McKinley. A nation weary of war checked Wilson's grandiose League of Nations scheme, while popular passions and congressional war hawks encouraged hostilities with Britain in 1812.

The foreign policy struggle between Congress and the White House has closely tracked the spiraling cycles between isolationism and interventionism experienced by the American people. Congress, for all its failings, is an extraordinarily representative body. It mirrors how power is held and which way public sentiment is leaning at any given moment. Thus Congress has reliably checked presidential initiatives during times of national introversion, when isolationist sentiment prevailed. By legislation and by inaction, congressional leaders have limited White House international options. In times of genuine national crisis or in times when voters have favored international involvement, no amount of legislative rope-tying by congressional Lilliputians has proved sufficient to restrain the presidential Gulliver. Therefore Lincoln could wield in the spring of 1861 what one of his contemporaries characterized as "more authority than any single Englishman [has had] since Oliver Cromwell."[35] And John Kennedy could deal with the Soviets, the Cubans, and Asian Communists with minimal involvement of Congress. But a popular and powerful leader like President Johnson could run afoul of the voters when the public mood finally turned inward and against unlimited commitments to combat the spread of Communist dictatorships.

No branch ever wins a final victory in this struggle. But the rules of the competition do sometimes change. New procedures are adopted, new options explored, and old precedents revived to ensure a continuing state of policymaking tension between Congress and the White House. Yet clearly there is an escalatory progression at work here. The experience of a previous president's war powers confrontation shades a successor's judgment. For example, Truman's decision to act unilaterally at the outbreak of the Korean War clearly was colored by memories of the failure of Wilson's League of Nations, as well as Franklin Roosevelt's struggles to overcome neutralist congressional sentiment in the 1930s to aid Europe before Pearl Harbor. As Truman described his decisionmaking process to the American people: "My thoughts kept coming back to the 1930s—to Manchuria, to

Ethiopia, the Rhineland, Austria, and finally to Munich. Here was history repeating itself. . . . If we let the Republic of Korea go under, some other country would be next, and then another, and the United Nations would go the way of the League of Nations."[36] Similarly, President Kennedy's aggressive responses at Berlin and in the Cuban Missile Crisis were grounded in lessons he drew from criticism of Allied passivity in the 1930s, which he had chronicled in his own book, *Why England Slept.* And Ronald Reagan's lightning strikes against Libya and Grenada were shaped, in good measure, by frustrations his predecessors endured when seeking congressional support for military actions at the close of the Indochina conflict in the 1970s.

As the overlay of legislative restraints accumulates, so too does the executive determination to resist. The process of change itself accelerates, making each cycle more dizzying. Cycles come more quickly now: introverted in the 1950s, extroverted in the 1960s, isolationist again in the post-Vietnam 1970s. Thus, the severity of recent foreign policy controversies between the White House and Congress is not simply a factor of the higher stakes attendant upon American world leadership. The struggle itself has become more intense as the legacy of past confrontations has provided new weapons for protagonists in the enduring policymaking competition.

NOTES

1. de Tocqueville, *Democracy in America*, p. 113.
2. Democratic Senator David Boren of Oklahoma summed up this difficulty during Lieutenant Colonel Oliver North's testimony: "When my constituents talk to me they say 'We don't understand; aren't you all working for the same people? When are you people going to stop being Democrats and Republicans or members of Congress and members of the Executive Branch, and work together as Americans?'" (Select Congressional Committee on Military Assistance to Iran and the Nicaraguan Opposition [Iran-Contra Committee], transcript of hearings, July 13, 1987, p. 85).
3. See, for example, the comments of President Reagan in his April 6, 1983 press conference: "We must restore America's honorable tradition of partisan politics stopping at the water's edge," or Dr. Zbigniew Brzezinski's assertion before the January 30, 1987 conference of the Georgetown Center for Strategic and International Studies that recent foreign affairs difficulties are attributable to "a collapse of bipartisanship."

4. Secretary of State George Shultz was arguing by 1984 that the relationship between Congress and the executive branch was "badly defective" (*New York Times*, March 28, 1984, p. 27). And Vice President George Bush argued in 1987 that "over the last twenty years we have witnessed a departure from the way we have conducted foreign policy for nearly two centuries. Congress has asserted an increasingly influential role in the micromanagement of foreign policy" (*Washington Post*, January 31, 1987, p. 16).

5. *Writings of Thomas Paine*, as quoted in DeConde, *American Foreign Policy*, vol. 1, p. 22.

6. See Smith, *Shaping of America*, vol. 3, p. 50.

7. Massachusetts joined with fellow colonies in Connecticut, New Haven, and New Plymouth in the 1643 Confederation of New England, which was a "perpetual league of friendship and amity for offense and defense, mutual advice and succor" (as quoted in DeConde, *American Foreign Policy*, vol. I, p. 17). Subsequent efforts to secure colonial union for international purposes included the Dominion of New England (1686) and the Albany Plan (1745).

8. Jefferson was in Europe during the Constitutional Convention; his principal contribution to the deliberations was a series of books and letters—pressing a staunch states' rights view—that he shipped to friends in the Philadelphia delegations (see Smith, *Shaping of America*, p. 50).

9. Elbridge Gerry of Massachusetts, who worried about an "excess of democracy" and eventually campaigned against ratification, was a dissenter. Alexander Hamilton also worried about too much legislative power; as a key adviser to President Washington, he would later do frequent battle with Congress. Yet at Philadelphia, both men firmly rejected the idea of unilateral presidential actions in the area of war-making powers.

10. *Writings of Thomas Paine*, as quoted in DeConde, *American Foreign Policy*, vol. I, p. 20.

11. George Washington, Farewell Address, as quoted in de Tocqueville, *Democracy in America*, p. 143.

12. Norman Ornstein, "The Constitution and the Sharing of Foreign Policy Responsibility," in Muskie, et al., *The President, the Congress, and Foreign Policy*, p. 37.

13. The uprising began in the Springfield, Massachusetts area when local farmers prevented a federal court from meeting for foreclosure proceedings. In their contemporary correspondence, future U.S. leaders such as Washington, Jefferson, and Madison debated the significance of the violent events that transpired. The libertarian Jefferson wrote Madison that "a little rebellion now and then is a good thing." A worried Washington wrote Henry Lee that "mankind, when left to themselves, are unfit for their own government" (as quoted in Smith, *Shaping of America*, p. 33).

14. Letters of "marque and reprisal" provided written authority to undertake retaliatory raids—or "limited wars." "Piracies" and "other offenses against the laws of nations" are—as Senator Charles Mathias has noted—terrorism, in modern parlance (see Senator Charles Mathias, testimony before Senate Foreign Relations Committee, Special Subcommittee on War Powers, August 13, 1988, p. 18). The Constitution clearly does *not* grant either power to the executive.

15. The original draft of the Committee of Detail provided that "the Senate of the United States shall have the power to make treaties." Gouverneur Morris and James Wilson wanted to include the House of Representatives in treaty review as well. (Farrand, *Records of the Federal Convention of 1787*, p. 392).

16. George Washington, as quoted in statement of Senator Robert Byrd, *Congressional Record*, October 23, 1987, p. S15030.

17. Federalist Paper no. 51.

18. Corwin, *The President: Office and Powers*, p. 171.

19. Federalist Paper no. 75.

20. *Youngstown Sheet and Tube Company v. Sawyer*, 345 U.S. 579 (1952).

21. See DeConde, *American Foreign Policy*, vol. I, p. 25.

22. Gibraltar became entangled in the fate of the American colonies when the French joined the Spanish struggle with England over this tiny Mediterranean outpost. The French pledged not to consummate a treaty with England until Spain recovered Gibraltar. British stubbornness on the issue helped ensure continued French military action in support of the rebellion being pressed by the American colonists.

23. Pierce Butler (a delegate from South Carolina), as quoted in Smith, *Shaping of America*, p. 118.

24. Senator William Maclay's journal of the first Congress (quoted here from Josephy, *American Heritage History of Congress*, p. 61) remains the best primary source on this incident. See also Senate Foreign Relations Committee, 1986, committee print, p. 2.

25. George Washington, as quoted in Josephy, *American Heritage History of Congress*, p. 108. As historian Forrest McDonald concluded, "The Presidency left Washington a broke and beaten man—embittered and given to almost insane rages . . . convinced that a conspiracy had undermined his Presidency" (Forrest McDonald, "A Mirror for Presidents," *Commentary* [December 1976]: 34).

26. George Washington, as quoted in Smith, *Shaping of America*, p. 247.

27. As quoted in DeConde, *American Foreign Policy*, vol. I, p. 67.

28. John Adams, as quoted in Smith, *Shaping of America*, p. 297. At one point late in his presidency, Adams was so exasperated with the pressure from war hawks that he threatened to resign, thereby leaving his office to his Republican vice president Jefferson—a prospect that horrified the

extreme-Federalists of Adams's splintered party (see Josephy, *American Heritage History of Congress*, p. 117).

29. Schlesinger, *Cycles of American History*, p. 278.

30. Thomas Jefferson, as quoted in DeConde, *American Foreign Policy*, vol. I, p. 76.

31. McDonald, "Mirror for Presidents," p. 41. See also DeConde, *American Foreign Policy*, vol. I, p. 87–88.

32. See, for example, Frank L. Klingberg, "The Historical Alteration of Moods in American Foreign Policy," *World Politics*, January 1952. See also, Schlesinger, *Cycles of American History*, p. 44. Alternative variants on this cycle are offered to explain periods of congressional versus executive dominance in Franck and Weisband, *Foreign Policy by Congress*, p. 6.

33. Henry Adams, as quoted in Schlesinger, *Cycles of American History*, p. 270.

34. Senator Boies Penrose, as quoted in Rubin, *Secrets of State*, p. 21.

35. James Bryce, *The American Commonwealth*, (1888), as quoted in Schlesinger, *Cycles of American History*, p. 279.

36. "Farewell Address to the American People," *Public Papers of the Presidents: Harry S. Truman, 1952–1953*, p. 1200.

2 FOREIGN POLICYMAKING IN THE NUCLEAR AGE

> We've junked the old Senator Taft practice that the duty of the
> opposition is to oppose. As a result, some people say I've been petti-
> coatin' around with Eisenhower. Well, that's not true. But I want
> to make absolutely sure that the Communists don't play one branch
> of the government against another, or one party against another. . . .
> I know where the basic responsibility for foreign policy lies [and]
> Mr. Eisenhower is the only President we've got.
>
> —Senate Majority Leader Lyndon B. Johnson, 1953[1]

The Second World War changed the character of American diplomacy more than any other event in U.S. history, producing for the
first time a consensus that the nation was obliged to fulfill a role of
global leadership. This consensus had profound implications for the
way foreign policy was made in Washington. It produced a golden era
of cooperation between the congressional leadership and the White
House. For the first two decades of the American experience as a
global superpower, a bipartisan tradition developed in support of
American initiatives like the United Nations, the Marshall Plan, and
the formation of the North Atlantic Treaty Organization (NATO). It
facilitated the establishment of new executive branch institutions
such as the Central Intelligence Agency (CIA), the National Security
Council (NSC), and the Department of Defense (DOD). It encouraged the development throughout the Congress of an internationalist

perspective, which insulated many key issues from the predictable partisan divisions of the past and dominated interbranch relations for a generation. And it led to a substantial expansion of presidential powers on key military decisions in the nuclear age.

The postwar era, to the surprise and dismay of most Americans, proved to be one of virtually continuous international crisis. And yet from 1945 to 1968, there were relatively few partisan foreign policy divisions within Congress or confrontations between Congress and the White House. Particularly with regard to U.S.-Soviet competition in Europe, an Atlanticist consensus in support of assertive presidential action reigned in Washington. Partisan eruptions were infrequent. By far the most debilitating was the "who lost China" debate; it colored U.S. policies in Asia for a generation and increased pressures for the United States ultimately to intervene in the Vietnamese civil war.[2] Most other disputes proved to have little enduring impact: the scattershot assaults of Senator Joseph McCarthy against alleged Communist influence in the executive branch and Senator John Kennedy's allegations of a "missile gap" during the 1960 presidential campaign had few major long-term consequences.

What were the unique circumstances of this era that produced such harmony between the legislative and executive branches? What changed to produce the generation of confrontation that has persisted since the late 1960s? A thoughtful review of this era offers insights that can help shape future policy options.

LESSONS FROM AN INTERNATIONALIST CONSENSUS

While the first generation of American diplomats had struggled to isolate the United States from the conflicts of Europe, the challenge facing U.S. politicians at the end of World War II was to sustain an enduring American commitment to Europe, to the Far East, and ultimately, to global responsibility. But the Congress and the electorate were ill prepared for this commitment to international leadership. Franklin Roosevelt had been hamstrung before Pearl Harbor by American voters intent upon noninvolvement in overseas disputes. Popular reaction against messianic Wilsonianism had persisted through the 1930s, when the electorate was bitterly divided about the wisdom of granting executive authority to stray from neutrality.[3] FDR won extraordinary powers to set *domestic* policy in the Depression years. Yet Congress was adamant—and effective—in preventing the exercise of greater foreign policy prerogatives by the White House. In 1936, Congress had blocked the President's efforts to impose an oil embargo against Italy, even though Mussolini's invasion of Ethiopia was imminent. Congress repeatedly extended neutrality legislation, even in the face of Japanese attacks on China and Nazi pressures on Czechoslovakia and Poland. It was not until March of 1941 that passage of the Lend-Lease Act marked the abandonment of isolationism as a majority policy on the Hill.

The legacy of this generation of isolationism—and suspicion of executive foreign affairs powers—was not easily overcome. After the burdens of World War II, Americans naturally pressed for demobilization of troops and attention to pressing domestic needs such as housing and education. Having vanquished the Axis, many voters were willing to once again retreat into a Fortress America perspective and, perhaps, to repeat the errors of the 1930s.[4] But for several key factors, Harry Truman could well have faced a renewal of crippling isolationist sentiment in Congress.

The primary factor in the rise of internationalism in the Truman years was the steady development of an anticommunist consensus that overshadowed long-standing partisan and institutional divisions in Washington. Americans were appalled to find that after defeating the Nazis and the Japanese, a new "red" menace lurked. At first, many voters were bitter. Suspicions about the renewed anti-Soviet rhetoric in Washington abounded for months after the end of World War II. There was considerable popular sympathy for Moscow, America's war-time ally of convenience; division persisted in Truman's cabinet well into 1946 on basic questions about the future of U.S.-Soviet relations. But then Soviet moves gave the President a stronger hand. Indeed, presidential initiatives in the postwar years— which might otherwise have met with strong congressional opposition—were invariably speeded along by provocative Soviet actions in Europe that spurred congressional outcries. Less than a year after V-J Day, anticommunism had become a unifying ideology in Washington. Anticommunism crossed party lines, united elites and average voters, and softened differences of approach between the legislative and executive branches.[5] Voters and their representatives in Congress became steadily more prepared for presidential initiatives in multilateral diplomacy and international security cooperation.

Americans strongly supported the United Nations, as they would back U.S. leadership in NATO. A generation after President Wilson had failed to win support on Capitol Hill for his League of Nations, the White House and Congress were in the hands of fervent anti-communists who warned of the potential costs of another U.S. retreat. The pendulum of American intellectual experience had swung against the isolationism of the interwar years, and voters gradually became convinced that the mistakes of the previous generation should not be repeated.[6]

A second factor crucial to the rise of American internationalism was the extraordinary effort at institution-building that followed on the heels of World War II. The federal government had experienced enormous growth through the war years. Patterns of bureaucratic cooperation that had developed spontaneously during the war were made permanent after its close. As Dean Acheson excitedly wrote from the State Department in 1946, the United States was "getting itself together" to address its new global responsibilities, rising to the challenge of the emerging Cold War in which new diplomatic tools would be required.[7] In a matter of months, the military command was reorganized and unified in a new Department of Defense. The entire national intelligence bureaucracy was reshaped, spawning new acronyms like DIA (Defense Intelligence Agency) and NSA (National Security Agency). The National Security Council was established to centralize White House day-to-day management of international activities. At the State Department, the nature of the Cold War challenge required coordination of new efforts in foreign aid, cultural exchange, and international propaganda. On Capitol Hill, a special joint committee of senior members was established to review all nuclear policy issues. Special committees were formed both in Congress and among leading private organizations to examine European needs and build support for the Marshall Plan (the same "blue ribbon" bipartisan commission model that was subsequently used with great success by Presidents Kennedy, Johnson, and Reagan). As during the war, the system for achieving congressional consensus was completely closed to junior members, who were cut out of the information flow and the decisionmaking process. There were but a handful of power brokers with whom the President needed to consult; these men could effectively deliver a majority vote once the White House gained their support.[8] Similar informal alliances prevailed among staff at the upper reaches of the executive bureaucracy.

Financiers like Averell Harriman, who had come to Washington as part of the war mobilization effort, joined in with the work of Ivy League-educated diplomats like Dean Acheson because they shared a common perspective on global problems. Opposition thinkers like John Foster Dulles—who was provided regular, thorough briefings by Truman administration officials—became committed to bipartisan internationalism. These so-called Wise Men ensured that while a novice diplomat in the White House steered the ship of state, a unified financial and academic "establishment" would help minimize any rocking of the boat. Foreign governments often brought opposition figures into war-time "national unity" cabinets. Truman—and later, both Dwight Eisenhower and John Kennedy—sought to emulate the practice. In international affairs, Truman continued FDR's war-time practice of deliberate consultation with senior members of the "loyal opposition." Truman made a concerted effort at "bipartisanship," what a recent national security adviser has defined as "the sharing of power with responsible members of the opposite parties with whom a certain degree of shared consensus exists."[9]

A third crucial element in the establishment of an internationalist consensus was the fact that the post-FDR leadership of the executive branch understood and was sensitive to Congress. Harry Truman was a creature of Capitol Hill. He knew its procedures and its egos, he had drunk with congressional leaders, and he had sat as vice president for long hours presiding over the Senate. In the crucial early months of his presidency, Truman's cabinet was joined by another leading Hill figure, Senator Jimmy Byrnes of South Carolina as secretary of state. Byrnes was succeeded first by General George C. Marshall, a masterful administrator who commanded enormous respect on Capitol Hill, and later by the brilliant Dean Acheson. Truman's team was soon forced to work with a Congress controlled by the Republican opposition—which won majorities in both houses in the 1946 elections. Bitter partisan differences persisted over many domestic policy questions. But President Truman offset these divisions by working effectively with the Republican leadership on Capitol Hill on most international matters.[10] Indeed, members of Congress who were willing, if not eager, to oppose the new president on domestic issues were prepared to give him virtually unqualified support on foreign policy matters, particularly as they related to European and Soviet policy. Members were sympathetic to the extraordinarily difficult situation in which Truman had landed, and many respected the

White House's superior sources of intelligence and military analysis in an unusually complex time. In the process, Truman steadily expanded presidential prerogatives in international affairs.

The most important example of cooperation between Congress and the White House was in the provision of massive American financial aid to Europe. The proposition faced its first key test after the abrupt British withdrawal from Greece and Turkey in early 1947, which threatened to leave an enormous power vacuum in the southern Mediterranean.[11] The question assumed broader implications with the promulgation of the Marshall Plan, unveiled by Secretary of State Marshall on June 5, 1947. Why would Americans, reeling from the burdens of their postwar domestic needs for housing and education, and suffering from an inflation-induced budget squeeze, want to initiate a massive program of foreign aid? Congress had every reason to reject these international initiatives. Yet because of the new internationalist consensus, these programs succeeded. Spurred by clumsy Soviet actions in Czechoslovakia and Berlin, they were successfully sold through impassioned anticommunist rhetoric employed by administration spokesmen like Acheson. Congress took the unprecedented step of establishing a joint Select Committee on European Aid to expedite the European recovery proposals. The ultimate passage of these measures, which brought more than $14 billion in aid to Europe, was attributable to shrewd leadership at both ends of Pennsylvania Avenue.

President Truman carefully involved congressional leaders in shaping these key programs. He included them, as a key Hill supporter Arthur Vandenberg noted admiringly, "in the take-offs" as well as "the crash landings."[12] A Michigan Republican, Vandenberg was central to the White House's success in increasing the broad international powers of the presidency. A convert from the isolationism of the 1930s, Vandenberg became chairman of the Senate Foreign Relations Committee in January 1947. A man of considerable ego, Vandenberg was deliberately encouraged by President Truman to place his imprimatur on the aid programs. After the White House unveiled new international proposals, Vandenberg would repeatedly propose supportive Senate resolutions and "perfecting" amendments symbolic of the partnership between the two branches. The White House got what it wanted, and the senior Republican got a major share of the credit. For example, Vandenberg did not make any major substantive changes in the Marshall Plan. But he did propose alteration of certain financing features. And he succeeded in placing his candidate, Republican Paul Hoffman, at the head of its administration. Truman overrode objections from his White House counselors to placate Vandenberg. In acquiescing, the President won essential Republican support.[13]

Such modest, public compromises represented perhaps the most enduring model for productive congressional involvement in foreign policy. It was a model that subsequent presidents would use with considerable success when they were willing to make the minor sacrifices necessary to proceed smoothly. Rules governing U.S. involvement in the emerging NATO regional security pact were reshaped in a similar fashion by Senator Vandenberg. Again, this process of gentle interbranch negotiation addressed substantive concerns while massaging egos. It succeeded in encouraging support on Capitol Hill for administration initiatives while keeping the basic policy decisions intact.

Co-opting the Republican leadership into supporting internationalist initiatives bore its costs for Truman. Republican stalwarts bristled at the obligation to back a president with whom they were doing such violent battle on domestic issues. President Truman had more than his share of personnel problems and management crises. Having finally won control of Congress in 1946, Republicans were eager to recapture the White House in the 1948 presidential election. Yet they were stuck *supporting* Truman on most foreign policy matters. Vandenberg wrote of how he proposed to resolve this ticklish political problem: "The Republican Party has this dilemma: if it does not cooperate in the world, it will be blamed for destroying the peace, as in 1920. If it cooperates too much with the Democratic Administration, it will be charged with having no policy of its own." Vandenberg resolved to back Truman on Europe "where we could lose everything" but to attack Truman's Asia policies "where there is no solution I can think of anyway."[14]

Vandenberg's formula anticipated both the assaults on Asia policy and the debilitating "who lost China" debate that gave rise to McCarthyism and the "red scares" of the 1950s. This GOP formula offered an outlet for backbenchers like junior Republican Congressman Richard M. Nixon from California, who employed divisive rhetoric to gain national prominence. Vandenberg's nuanced approach helped to ensure mainstream support for essential projects like the support of NATO—and ultimately, to woo Eisenhower into the GOP ranks.[15] But it was unable to satisfy some hard-line Republican colleagues. For example, Senator William Knowland of California complained that, under Truman's stewardship, European gains were more than offset by losses to communism in Asia.[16] Such observations foreshadowed efforts by GOP conservatives to place limits on bipartisan internationalism in the early 1950s.

Ironically, in the years immediately following World War II, as in the New Deal days of FDR, it was *liberal* commentators who advocated stronger presidential powers. (Indeed, Arthur Schlesinger, Jr. would publicly defend Truman's unilateral military action in Korea two decades before his indictment of the "imperial" presidency.) But so long as the internationalist consensus held, it was only the most conservative members of Congress who objected to the expansion of the President's international prerogatives. Senator Robert Taft was the most outspoken; he used arguments that would be echoed unconsciously during the later stages of U.S. involvement in the Vietnam War by liberal Democrats. The Ohio Republican retained an isolationist perspective and was deeply suspicious of presidential power. He deplored the alleged forfeiture to the White House in the NATO treaty of the right to declare war. But with Vandenberg securing the Republican center for the White House, Taft's arguments were soundly rejected. When the Senate approved the NATO pact on July 21, 1949, it was by a comfortable 82–13 margin.[17]

Just two days after Senate approval of the NATO pact, Truman stunned Congress with the bill for this and similar commitments. He requested a $1.5 billion package of military aid—not just to NATO partners but to such far-flung nations as Iran, South Korea, and the Philippines. This extension of the Truman Doctrine on a global scale promised to commit Congress and the nation for the first time to genuinely worldwide security obligations. Capitol Hill leaders balked. The request might well have been substantially reduced, or even shelved, but for the uncanny Soviet knack of rescuing Truman initiatives by undertaking actions that most Americans viewed as provocative. Just as the Berlin crisis had sped final approval of the Marshall Plan in the spring of 1948, the revelation in September 1949 that the Soviets had tested a nuclear weapon produced a wave of anticommunist sentiment in the United States. Amid a national mood of near panic, Congress overwhelmingly supported funding for the Mutual Defense Security Act. A web of American international security commitments was established that remains in place, largely unchanged, some forty years later.

THE RISE OF THE IMPERIAL PRESIDENCY

Anticommunism was the glue that united Congress and the White House in the postwar internationalist consensus. Its requirement for vigorous diplomacy provided cement for congressional backing of sweeping executive initiatives. But the advent of nuclear weapons—with their potential for virtually instantaneous, devastating international conflict—introduced a host of complications into the new relationship between Congress and the president.

Requirements of secrecy and swift military decision had always been arguments for a strong executive role in times of war. During the American Revolution, General Washington experienced the futility of conducting a war by congressional committee. Consequently, the Constitution gave the president clear control as commander-in-chief over battlefield manevuers. From Polk to Lincoln to Franklin Roosevelt, White House occupants had developed precedents for stretching these constitutional powers to the limit—and beyond, when the nation faced a diplomatic test. As historian Doris Kearns has noted:

> The presidential apparatus grew with the growth of military needs; the great steps forward in the expansion of presidential power were linked—whether as effect or cause—with the great wars: the Civil War, World War I, World War II, the Korean War. Time and again, the law of national self-preservation was seen to justify placing extravagant powers in the hands of the President.[18]

But the placement of such great trust in a peacetime president was different. Attributable not just to tensions with the Soviets, or to the new burden of international leadership placed upon Washington, this development was also a consequence of "The Bomb" itself. In the age of nuclear deterrence, military requirements inevitably enhanced the powers of the presidency. The need to act quickly, to understand the technology involved, and to maintain important secrets presented enduring challenges to the Congress's constitutional authority to declare war and to finance its prosecution.

In the months after Hiroshima and Nagasaki, Congress sought a meaningful role in nuclear policy questions. A principal goal was to inquire into the nearly $2 billion in funds that had secretly been siphoned off for the war-time Manhattan Project. Before Hiroshima, virtually no member of Congress knew about nuclear weapons. There was no insight on Capitol Hill into how these weapons worked or what they might portend. After the war, an unprecedented legislative body of senior House and Senate members, the Joint Committee on Atomic Energy (JCAE), was promptly established to review executive branch nuclear policies and funding recommendations.[19] But congressional involvement in the details of financing nuclear warhead production did little to offset the imbalance created by the military calculations these weapons forced upon the occupant of the White House.

Less than a decade after the surprise of Pearl Harbor, the Soviet nuclear test in 1949 raised the specter of massive U.S. devastation from a single bombing raid (just as the Soviet launch of Sputnik in 1957 would show that a few hours of preattack warning could be reduced to minutes by new technology). How could the president seek a declaration of war—or be expected even to consult with congressional leaders—under such circumstances? The existence of nuclear weapons placed a great premium on intelligence-gathering activities under the control of the executive, while raising the stakes of everyday diplomacy to such heights that the bias toward White House control of foreign policy was accelerated. As the months after V-J Day turned into years, the nation seemed to remain in a perpetual state of international crisis. Congress quite readily deferred on many security issues; the pendulum perceptibly swung toward greater presidential freedom in national security affairs.

When North Korean troops invaded South Korea on the night of Saturday, June 23, 1950, Truman was in Independence, Missouri. He did not consult with congressional leaders until an informal session on the twenty-sixth. By Friday the twenty-ninth, U.S. troops acting under the aegis of the United Nations had already been committed by the White House to the conflict. No declaration of war or authorization from Congress was sought by Truman. In fact, Truman followed the advice of Secretary of State Acheson, who maintained that debate on a joint resolution approving U.S. military intervention in Korea was unnecessary. Acheson insisted that the President did not need such approval, arguing that a debate on the Hill would only invite mischief—and implicitly limit the President's freedom of action. What Congress was required to give in the way of authorization, Acheson noted, could easily be withdrawn through legislative reversal.[20] There was precious little dissent in Congress for what hawks like Senator Knowland were quickly downplaying as a "police action" in Korea. Criticism from legislators was confined once again

to a few doctrinaire conservatives. Senator Taft deplored the "complete usurpation by the President of authority to use the armed
forces of this country."[21] And Senator Alexander Wiley, the senior
Republican on the foreign relations panel, warned that Congress was
surrendering "more and more of its authority and prerogatives" to
the White House. "If we are to sit by silently while the President
takes action which might lead us into a third world war," Wiley
argued, "the people will wonder whether the legislative branch has
continued strength and validity."[22]

There never was a formal declaration of war in the Korean conflict, even though more than 33,000 Americans died and the nation's
national security spending soared from $22.3 billion to $50.4 billion
in just two years. Indeed, as we shall explore in Chapter 6, there has
not been a congressional declaration of war since the Japanese attack
on Pearl Harbor brought a reluctant United States into World War II
against Japan and the Nazis. It was not until 1968 that sustained criticism of such unilateralism in a President's use—and alleged abuse—of
his war powers under the Constitution was heard across the political
spectrum. In the interim, President Truman stood up to criticism
when he relieved popular General Douglas MacArthur, just as President Eisenhower was given carte blanche on Capitol Hill in the 1956
Suez Crisis and the use of troops in Lebanon in 1957.[23] President
Kennedy weathered his 1961 fiasco at the Bay of Pigs, and Lyndon
Johnson was given a free hand to employ American forces against
North Vietnam after the Gulf of Tonkin incident. The 1962 Cuban
Missile Crisis seemed to exemplify the requirement for presidential
leadership in foreign affairs—to evaluate sensitive intelligence information and then to act decisively in the midst of a nuclear crisis.
Through most of this confrontation between Kennedy and Khrush-
chev—a confrontation that brought the nation to the brink of direct
combat with Soviet forces—Congress took a backseat to White House
leadership and most legislators remained completely ignorant of
essential details.[24]

Through these years, strong executives relentlessly expanded
White House prerogatives. As America's international relations grew
more complex and the executive bureaucracy swelled, the powers of
the chief executive inevitably increased. The roles of the president
as general manager of the administration, number-one analyst of a
raft of sophisticated new intelligence information, and chief television spokesman for the nation seemed to require this. Ever broader

discretion in the exercise of presidential foreign affairs powers became an accepted norm in the political culture. Indeed, when the cautious Eisenhower chose to come to Capitol Hill to request congressional backing for possible military moves in the Middle East, some legislators decried an alleged attempt to shift responsibilities. "The buck has been passed to us by the President," Congressman Abraham Multer complained at the height of the 1957 Lebanon crisis, maintaining that "under the Constitution, it is his duty and he has the power to make foreign policy."[25]

This expectation that America's new global role required broader exercise of foreign affairs powers by the president fed upon itself. As historian Arthur Schlesinger, Jr. observed, "In the decade after Korea, Congress receded not alone from the effort to control the war-making power but almost from the effort to participate in it, except on occasion when national security zealots on the Hill condemned the executive branch for inadequate bellicosity, i.e. versus Cuba."[26] But in exercising these ever broader grants of authority, successive executives employed constitutionally dubious methods—methods that would eventually meet with stern congressional opposition. Beginning with the years of FDR's assertive domestic leadership, sweeping presidential authority was exercised as the White House came to thoroughly dominate the conduct of America's international affairs. What were the tools with which executives effected this change? The three most extreme characteristics of this so-called imperial presidency have been cited as follows: abuse of the war-making power, excessive reliance on the use of secret diplomacy combined with assertions of executive privilege, and extensive resort in peacetime to the use of emergency authorities.[27]

Elements of such practices crept into the presidencies of virtually every chief executive after FDR. To a certain extent, these practices were deemed excusable at the time: predictable results of diplomacy in an age of unrelenting international tensions, when a crisis atmosphere prevailed year after year in Washington. But such practices eventually reached levels Congress would no longer tolerate during the presidency of Richard Nixon, when the strains of a sustained White House campaign to be free of congressional shackles erupted into bitter confrontation. As President Nixon himself came to define the scope of this showdown, it involved a struggle for control of the central process of government in the United States. Nixon believed

that moves to circumvent basic institutions of government were justified in time of crisis. He wrote tellingly in his memoirs of the rationale for employing extralegal means in pursuit of his ambitious
domestic and international goals:

> When all the leadership institutions of a nation become paralyzed by self-
> doubt and second thoughts, that nation cannot long survive unless those insti-
> tutions are either reformed, replaced or circumvented. In my second term I
> was prepared to adopt whichever of these three methods—or whichever com-
> bination of them—was necessary.[28]

JOHNSON'S CREDIBILITY GAP
AND THE NIXON LEGACY

If the seeds of the Nixon administration's confrontation with the Hill
were planted during the FDR years, when liberals favored a strong
presidency, the roots were sunk when Lyndon Johnson was in the
Oval Office. President Johnson enjoyed extraordinary powers over
Congress. He combined the tremendous clout he had developed as
the most powerful Senate majority leader in history with the 49-state
mandate he won in the 1964 presidential election. He applied these
powers, while marshaling the passions aroused by the horror of John
Kennedy's assassination, to push through a raft of social welfare and
civil rights legislation. These domestic "Great Society" programs
brought enormous growth in the executive branch bureaucracy and
in White House powers. But then, in 1965, President Johnson began
to lose the trust of several key members of Congress in his management of foreign affairs. A wound was slowly opened that ultimately
would sap the strength of the postwar bipartisan foreign policy consensus. Within a decade, any hope of regaining this consensus and
affirming a mutually acceptable division of foreign affairs powers
between the White House and Congress was lost.

Among some members, there was jelousy of Johnson's considerable power on Capitol Hill and silent anger at the way he repeatedly
intimidated members on Vietnam issues. The proximate cause of
Johnson's difficulties with Congress was, in fact, the misleading way
in which he described the unraveling situation in Vietnam—the
"credibility gap" between presidential statements and reality. But
the precipitating event that first started the Johnson presidency

down its slippery slope had nothing to do with Vietnam. The beginning of the end for interbranch trust in foreign affairs came over an
otherwise obscure series of events in the Dominican Republic.

When domestic disorders erupted in Santo Domingo in April
1965, the President swiftly dispatched troops to the Dominican
Republic, notifying congressional leaders only after the fact. Johnson
was uniformly applauded for the quick action, which he justified as
necessary to save American lives. Congressional liberals and conservatives alike praised the White House initiative. And there was no
Monday morning quarterbacking about the niceties of prior consultation, even after it became clear that the 5,000 U.S. Marines were
there to intervene on behalf of one faction in a domestic power
struggle. But with at least one key Hill figure, the credibility question
festered.

The chairman of the Senate Foreign Relations Committee, William
J. Fulbright, harbored a growing suspicion that his old friend Johnson was misleading the Hill on basic facts in order to aggrandize
presidential powers. Fulbright was torn. He was not only a fellow
Democrat and southerner and a longtime colleague of Johnson's,
but he was also an outspoken advocate of presidential leadership.
As recently as 1961 Fulbright had lectured that "the source of an
effective foreign policy under our system is Presidential power,"
while urging that the Congress "grant the Executive a measure of
power in the conduct of our foreign affairs that we have hitherto
jealously withheld."[29]

Fulbright had championed such a broad grant of authority when
he was floor manager for the August 1964 Gulf of Tonkin resolution,
which gave President Johnson carte blanche to pursue military action
in Vietnam. (Only two maverick senators—Wayne Morse of Oregon
and Ernest Gruening of Alaska—had risked the President's wrath by
opposing the resolution.) But as U.S. troop commitments to Vietnam
increased nearly tenfold over the next year—from 20,000 at the end
of 1964 to 185,000 in 1965—Chairman Fulbright began to have
gnawing doubts. He felt he had been snookered repeatedly by Johnson. His questions were not limited to Johnson's policy prescriptions;
they applied also to the facts the President gave to Congress when he
justified military commitments such as those undertaken in Vietnam
and the Dominican Republic. When Fulbright concluded after careful study that Johnson had lied to Congress about the Dominican
Republic, the Foreign Relations Committee chairman began a series

of broadside attacks on the credibility of the President's foreign policy pronouncements.

Fulbright's initial foray was a September 15, 1965 statement on the Senate floor decrying the "lack of candor" that had marked the April troop commitments in the Dominican Republic. But it was followed up by nationally televised hearings, which Fulbright convened, in the spring of 1966 on the conduct of the Vietnam War.[30] Fulbright suggested then that the Gulf of Tonkin incident might have been fabricated in whole or in part; but his evidence was not yet conclusive. (It was not until 1968 that evidence was publicly released suggesting that U.S. ships had not come under North Vietnamese fire in the Gulf of Tonkin.) But the questions Fulbright was raising in 1965 and 1966 legitimized attacks that other more junior legislators were beginning to make against the administration's conduct of the war. This criticism was originated by peace activists at the grass-roots level. But eventually the Congress responded to sustained public criticism and began to reflect voters' concerns. The President's foreign policies became fair game for attack within the Democratic Party and throughout Congress. The credibility issue opened the door wide to assaults on more executive branch foreign policy prerogatives. Consensus support for White House dominance of foreign policymaking ended.

It is essential to underscore the fact that it was not the war powers question per se that finally mobilized congressional opposition. Franklin Roosevelt had managed to send troops to Greenland and destroyers to Britain without congressional authorization, just as Truman had committed forces in Korea without any declaration of war by Congress. At issue in Washington in the late 1960s were more fundamental questions about facts, about basic trust between the two leading branches of government, about the sharing of information and policymaking power in an era of presidential dominance of the tools of government.

Johnson had enjoyed tremendous success on many domestic issues. But questions raised by those dissatisfied by the conduct of the Vietnam War, and by those who alleged that Johnson had repeatedly abused executive authority while stretching the truth, ultimately undermined the President's ability to govern. This challenge to presidential authority was by no means a new phenomenon. But with the election in November 1968 of Richard Nixon, the growing dispute between the branches of government was magnified. From early in his administration, President Nixon identified Congress as an adversary, an institution to be circumvented or overridden on all of the key issues of the day, both foreign and domestic. The battle with Congress was by no means confined to questions of international policymaking authority. Many months before the White House was linked to the series of criminal undertakings collectively known as the Watergate scandals, the President was engaged in an across-the-board battle to expand executive prerogatives. Again, Nixon's memoirs offer a candid description of the stakes:

> In this second term I had thrown down a gauntlet to Congress, the bureaucracy, the media, and the Washington establishment and challenged them to epic battle. We had already skirmished over the limitations of prerogative and power represented in confirmation of appointments, the impoundment of funds, and the battle of the budget.[31]

Indeed, with the beginning of his second term, it became clear that the struggle between President Nixon and the Congress was on a different order from that in which so many of the President's predecessors had engaged. It was different because of the President's professed willingness to undertake extralegal means to pursue his ambitious political and diplomatic agenda. It was different because of the President's methodical use of the instruments of government to assault the "enemies" that his aggressive policies engendered—particularly those in the press and on Capitol Hill who questioned his foreign policies. And it was different because of the vengeful determination of a bitter Congress to fight back relentlessly until Nixon was gone, a member of the Hill leadership who had never stood for national election had been appointed to the Oval Office, and the central foreign policy powers of the imperial presidency were undermined by dozens of legislative restrictions.

President Nixon's struggle to unburden the White House of certain constitutional checks and balances won him an extraordinarily free hand for a time. Nixon was a clever foreign policy strategist. During his first term, amid the turmoil of cultural upheaval in the United States, he boldly achieved some of the more significant diplomatic accomplishments the nation had made since the onset of the Cold War. These included the effective overture to the People's Republic of China (PRC), the SALT I and ABM treaties with the Soviet Union, and the beginnings of U.S.-Soviet detente. Nixon expanded U.S. support for Israel while advancing shaky security relationships with the "twin pillars" along the Persian Gulf, Saudi Arabia and Iran. But even such substantial accomplishments were oversold, leading to subsequent disappointments and reversals. And the President's procedural abuses sparked sweeping reform efforts on the Hill that were fraught with irony. It was liberals in Congress who moved first to check Nixon's excesses in foreign policymaking. But the revolution they began on Capitol Hill ultimately empowered arch conservatives, who moved in subsequent years to counter such Nixon-era initiatives as detente and arms control.

By January 1973, the struggle between the White House and Congress to control the policymaking process had become *the* dominant issue in Washington, overshadowing all specific policy questions. The President had defined the issue starkly while campaigning against Congress in his 1972 reelection bid. With Nixon's landslide victory, the congressional leadership responded with dire warnings. Senate Majority Leader Mike Mansfield called for a Hill counterattack, reminding his assembled Senate Democratic colleagues on January 4, 1973 that "the people have not chosen to be governed by one branch of government alone."[32] House Speaker Carl Albert similarly noted that Congress had to move against the "accelerating usurpation of power by the Executive branch . . . [and] these wholesale invasions of legislative powers and responsibilities." Albert warned that "what Congress has refused him, the President has undertaken to seize. What Congress has decreed, the President has circumvented."[33] Soon, a great many congressional leaders were pressing the same argument. Even conservative southerners like Gillis Long of Louisiana were sounding the alarm, claiming that "the President has overstepped the authority of his office. . . . He is risking retaliation from the Congress for his power grabs and support for the counteroffensive is found in the whole range of Congressional membership—old members and new, liberal and conservative, Democratic and Republican."[34]

It must be stressed that these sharp battle lines were formed *before* evidence came out establishing White House involvement in the June 1972 break-in at the Democratic National Committee headquarters in the Watergate building. And while liberals and conservatives alike were unsettled by Nixon's penchant for secret diplomacy and swift, unauthorized military actions, Vietnam was not the central issue in this showdown between Congress and the President. U.S. involvement in Vietnam appeared to be ending in early 1973. Foreign policy issues were not, at this stage, central to the debate on the Hill. Congress was most upset about Nixon's impoundment of appropriated funds, his refusal to heed Hill objections to government reorganization plans, and his cavalier assertion of ever broader forms of executive privilege to withhold information from Congress. The President, in turn, was piqued by endless Hill foot-dragging in spite of an inflation/recession squeeze, by what he perceived as partisan congressional meddling in his administrative decisions, and by continuing leaks of sensitive national security information—which Nixon blamed primarily on his own staff, and which had provoked widespread use of wiretapping on both Congress and executive branch staff.

It is true that antiwar members of Congress had been enraged by such actions as the temporary movement of U.S. forces into Cambodia in 1970 and the massive bombing of North Vietnamese targets during December 1972. But Vietnam War opponents on the Hill were still outnumbered. And in the winter of 1973, U.S. troops were being withdrawn from Vietnam. Thus, the executive-legislative struggle remained focused on control of the process of governing rather than a dispute over any single Federal policy.

The danger to the Nixon presidency ultimately lay in the fact that after picking an across-the-board fight with Congress over procedural prerogatives, certain White House officials chose to escalate the battle until it stumbled into the realm of criminal actions. Richard Nixon and his aides used the powers of the presidency indiscriminately to attack and spy upon his political enemies, while repeatedly lying to the American people about the White House role in illegal activities. The President systematically misled Congress on key issues of war and peace and engaged in schemes that included elaborate double bookkeeping to obscure massive U.S. bombing in Laos and Cambodia. Of course, the national security excuses employed by the White House *had* been used upon other occasions by presidents to stretch and strain their constitutional powers. Truman had acted unilaterally in Korea and illegally seized privately owned steel mills. Johnson had fudged on military facts and pored over FBI files on Hill opponents. But the Nixon administration cited national security justifications as a sweeping excuse to obscure from congressional review both controversial policies *and* criminal undertakings. The means employed by the White House in the Nixon years exceeded even the worst bare-knuckle tactics of the Kennedy and Johnson presidencies. In this respect, the Nixon administration's assault on the Constitution's balance of powers was by no means confined to the political crimes associated with the burglary of the Democratic National Committee headquarters; Watergate was not the sole source of President Nixon's downfall. Indeed, the break-in and cover-up were not the only charges for which the House Judiciary Committee considered impeachment.

Nixon was so aggressive in his use of presidential powers that even his most ambitious policy successes sowed the seeds for future reversals. In his wake, the presidency—and the authority to pursue his complex diplomatic strategies—was gravely weakened. The Nixon administration's rejection of most meaningful legislative restraints lay at the heart of his death struggle with Congress. Thus, by overreaching so dramatically, President Nixon opened the door to a horde of congressional initiatives that made his allegations of legislative micromanagement of foreign policy seem, in retrospect, quite timid.

CONGRESS CHANGES THE RULES

Congress began its assault on presidential powers well before the 1974 impeachment proceedings of the House Judiciary Committee. The fight to protect congressional prerogatives against Nixon administration challenges was under way in 1970 over the issue of presidential impoundment of appropriated funds. This dispute was the first of a series of congressional challenges to the constitutionality of administration actions. But it was not a substantial change in the relationship between the Congress and the White House that checked executive predominance. Rather, it was a sharp transformation within Congress itself that sparked legislative initiatives and ultimately altered the balance of policymaking power.

These internal changes were directly related to congressional divisions over the Vietnam War. As domestic criticism of the U.S. role increased, opponents in Congress sought ways in which to express concern and reshape American policy. But they were effectively blocked by the closed congressional system. Direct votes on how the war was being prosecuted were not obtainable. Key committees were in the hands of southern Democrats, who (with the exception of the gadfly Fulbright) supported the war. These veteran chairmen— elevated through the seniority system—firmly controlled committee

hearing agendas, subcommittee assignments, amendment opportunities, and staff appointments. Key meetings were held in secret.
House votes on the most divisive issues were rarely recorded. The
first antiwar challenge in the House—a 1967 motion by George
Brown of California to recommit a DOD funding bill with instructions that the committee bar funds for operations in or over Vietnam—was not even taken seriously. After brief debate, it was overwhelmingly rejected 372-18.[35] And it was not until the summer of
1970—after the spread of U.S. military operations to Cambodia—that
the Senate first addressed Vietnam War policy directly with a vote on
the Hatfield-McGovern measure to limit combat activities. Nearly a
decade after the first U.S. military personnel died in Vietnam, the
Senate still had not voted directly on the question of whether U.S.
military involvement in Vietnam should continue.[36]

As opposition to the war grew in the United States, junior members of Congress sought ways to register dissent. Intense media focus
had brought the war and the foreign policy debate into many voters'
living rooms. Hawks were questioning the tactics of fighting a "limited" war on the enemy's terms. They deplored high U.S. casualties
and endorsed escalation through more sweeping bombing efforts;
some even called for use of nuclear weapons in order to limit U.S.
ground casualties. Doves were questioning the premises of any U.S.
military presence in what they viewed simply as a Vietnamese civil
war; they favored either a tactical retreat or a complete withdrawal.
Thus, while there was declining support for the conduct of the war
under both the Johnson and Nixon administrations, there was no
congressional consensus on an alternative. The Democratic Party was
deeply split over the appropriate response to the enduring post-
World War II challenge of checking communist expansion in Asia.
But until Congress undertook internal reforms, dissent on the Hill
did little to alter U.S. policy. Congress reacted to, rather than led,
changes in public opinion on the war. With the notable exception of
Fulbright's Foreign Relations Committee hearings (and occasional
speeches by antiwar senators like Frank Church and Gaylord Nelson),
there was little discussion in Congress of policy alternatives. There
was no "great debate." The same closed system that had been of
such benefit to Truman during an era of consensus was employed to
stifle dissent through the first decade of U.S. involvement in the
Vietnam War. It was this congressional system that itself came under

assault, even before Congress legislated curbs on the U.S. war effort and presidential powers.

What ensued was a decade of turbulent change. The view that foreign policy must be entrusted to the executive had "gone down in flames in Vietnam," Arthur Schlesinger, Jr. observed in 1973. "Vietnam discredited executive control of foreign relations as profoundly as Versailles and mandatory neutrality had discredited Congressional control."[37] But before Congress could presume to challenge the White House, it had to reform itself. And reform it did: between 1970 and 1979, Congress enacted more than a dozen significant changes in its own rules, including changes in the seniority system, committee procedures, hearing requirements, voting practices, and campaign finance reform. These changes, which are explored in greater detail in Chapter 4, in turn facilitated a more aggressive assault on the powers of the executive, as they had come to be exercised in the early 1970s.

Congress did not succeed in barring funding for U.S. involvement in the ground fighting in Vietnam until long *after* the Paris peace accords of 1973 had been signed and U.S. soldiers were coming home. But in a sustained series of skirmishes, legislators did begin as early as 1969 to place limits on the flexibility of the White House in meeting the communist challenge in Southeast Asia.

The first time that a modern Congress barred funds for a looming White House military initiative was in 1969. At issue was concern that U.S. forces in Thailand and Laos might become involved in ground fighting. The CIA was involved in extensive operations in Laos, and Air Force bombing missions were operating out of U.S. facilities in Thailand. Leaks about contingency plans to commit ground troops in the event of any insurgency against Bangkok unnerved many on Capitol Hill. The Senate took the lead in pushing an outright ban on the use of U.S. ground combat troops in Thailand and Laos without congressional approval.

Critics were unable to place any curbs on funding Vietnam combat operations. But after President Nixon in May 1970 sent U.S. forces across the Cambodian border to assault guerrilla sanctuaries, a firestorm of domestic protest erupted. Despite the fact that the guerrilla bases were used to stage assaults on U.S. forces in South Vietnam, Senate opponents charged Nixon with expanding a conflict of which Americans were already growing weary. Administration defenders like Democrat Sam Ervin of North Carolina countered that "the Founding Fathers were not foolish enough to place the command of American troops engaged in combat operations in a Congress of the United States which is now composed of 100 Senators and 435 Representatives."[38] Republican leader Robert Griffin echoed the point, contending that Congress "cannot, and should not attempt to make battlefield decisions."[39] Nixon weathered the fury on the Hill; his supporters strung out the Senate debate until the day after U.S. forces had left Cambodian soil. Thus, the Senate move to bar Cambodian ground operations did not pass until after all U.S. combat troops had already been withdrawn. Meanwhile, U.S. bombing missions continued, with records falsified through a scheme of Pentagon double bookkeeping designed to keep elected policymakers on Capitol Hill ignorant of the facts. This proved to be a particularly subversive practice; executive branch bureaucrats were hiding illicit spending practices from elected representatives—those in whom the Constitution vests the appropriations power.

"Vietnamization" of the ground war and progress in Paris peace negotiations stemmed the tide of antiwar activism on the Hill during 1972. On the eve of the presidential elections, an elated Henry Kissinger proclaimed to the nation that "peace is at hand." But then to soften North Vietnamese negotiators and to conclude an accord for the return of U.S. prisoners of war, President Nixon chose to undertake massive bombing of Hanoi and the Haiphong port during Christmas time. When the new Congress convened weeks later, antiwar legislators lashed out in fury at the decision, undertaken in secret without even any token consultation with congressional leaders. Once again, however, the debate was moot: the U.S. bombing campaign had been halted and U.S. forces were accelerating their pullout from South Vietnam to meet a March 1973 deadline.

It was at this point that Congress finally began to muster majorities against *reintroduction* of U.S. forces. Suspicion of the White House ran extraordinarily high, and even conservatives were intent upon cutting U.S. losses. When it became clear in the spring of 1973 that the White House was still secretly directing air strikes against Cambodian insurgents, the Congress moved with determination to enact a prohibition. Here was another watershed event for the legislature: for the first time in the nuclear age, Congress cut off funds for an ongoing military operation. The White House, of course, resisted. But Nixon officials miscalculated. Administration witnesses before Congress were deliberately vague on questions of how long the Cambodia operation might continue and how much money was needed, suggesting that no congressional authorization was required to permit indefinite continuation of the bombing. Critics in Congress exploited the muddled White House position to expand vastly the scope of the funding cutoff under debate. Following the lead of Democratic Senator Thomas Eagleton of Missouri, the Hill extended the ban to cover all combat activities in or over both Cambodia and Laos. The prohibition was written to bar any use by the Pentagon of funds left over from other operations.

At this point, even the hawks rejected White House moves to block the measure. "We have got our prisoners of war out with honor," conservative Republican Milton Young of North Dakota explained. "What's the point of going on supporting a government that seems to have no will to fight and is corrupt?"[40] Nixon fought a desperate rearguard action, vetoing the measure. But the Senate put the funding cutoff on several "veto-proof" funding bills required to keep the federal government running. The stakes in the interbranch stare-down became ever higher as the summer of 1973 progressed: in a new version of the contested measure, opponents of U.S. combat operations anywhere in Indochina extended the prohibition to include combat operations in Vietnam. Scaled-down U.S. aid would continue until 1975. But with adoption of this legislation, direct U.S. involvement in the Indochina fighting was over. Congress had barred Nixon, and his successor Gerald Ford, from getting the United States embroiled once again in the conflict. Moot were President Nixon's secret assurances to the South Vietnamese of swift U.S. retaliation if the North Vietnamese violated the Paris accords. While Congress was completely ignorant of this private Nixon pledge, the commitment doubtless would have met with strident and sustainable objections from war-weary legislators in both parties. Henry Kissinger later sought to justify the Nixon administration failure to involve Congress in such a sweeping national commitment with the argument that "it would have struck us as inconceivable that the United States should fight for years and lose 45,000 men in an honorable cause and then stand by while the peace treaty, the achievement of their sacrifice, was flagrantly violated."[41] Yet contemporary critics dismissed Kissinger's claims: "The administration has intimated the Congress has reneged on 'commitments' and 'obligations' to the South Vietnamese government," hawkish Democratic Senator Henry Jackson of Washington complained in 1975. "The fact is that Congress is being accused of violating commitments and obligations it never heard of."[42]

Cutting American losses in Indochina was the specific cause that provoked a series of legislative restraints on executive foreign policy authorities in the early 1970s. But a newly assertive Congress was simultaneously advancing measures with more general procedural implications. The legislative branch was itself undergoing extraordinary change as the impact of the cultural upheaval of the 1960s weakened the importance of both party loyalty and the seniority system. Changes in the makeup of Congress in turn facilitated an assault on executive branch powers. In virtually every field of policymaking where President Nixon and his predecessors had asserted strong powers, Congress now moved with sustained legislative reaction. The body of law subsequently produced brought sweeping changes to the conduct of American foreign policy, altering the way the Congress and the executive branch interact to shape international policy. The struggle over this legislative legacy is the focus of the many policy disputes analyzed in Part III of this work. But in summarizing the precipitous decline of presidential powers in the 1970s, it is useful to note briefly the history surrounding these developments. Key changes occurred in seven areas during the tumultuous decade of procedural reform.

Executive Agreements/National Commitments. Beginning in 1969 (in the wake of revelations that parts of the Gulf of Tonkin incident had been fabricated by Johnson to enlist Hill support for a Vietnam commitment), the Senate moved legislation to define more clearly how national commitments could be made. In 1970, Congress repealed the Gulf of Tonkin resolution at the initiative of Republican Senator Charles Mathias of Maryland. But the problem extended beyond specific incidents in which a president came to the Hill at the outset of an international confrontation seeking an open-ended resolution of support. Going back to FDR's war-time diplomacy and the Yalta accords, the White House had adopted the habit of undertaking international obligations through executive agreements. Between 1945 and 1970, some 6,300 such agreements had been signed, while only 411 treaties had made their way to the Senate for approval. In 1972, the Congress blocked this backdoor treaty-making through adoption of the Case Act. Henceforth, executive agreements would have to be reported to Congress and be subject to review and possible disapproval.[43]

War Powers. With the White House continuing to insist that it needed no express congressional authorization for troop commitments, legislators groped to define the circumstances under which the president could send troops into battle without a congressional declaration of war. Beginning in 1970, legislation was advanced to clarify congressional authority—beyond its clear right to cut off appropriations—to participate in the decision to commit U.S. military forces. None of the war powers proposals in either chamber were designed to cover ongoing Indochina operations. Yet it took three years to reach a workable, if extraordinarily controversial, compromise between a strong Senate-passed measure and a weaker House version. On November 7, 1973, Congress passed the War Powers Resolution over President Nixon's veto.

Arms Sales. Congress also moved against the power of presidents to commit the nation to arms supply relationships. This effort was a logical outgrowth of concern over unlimited executive agreements and military deployments. In the 1974 Nelson-Bingham amendment to the Arms Export Control Act, Congress provided for a legislative veto of major U.S. arms sales. This measure afforded pro-Israel legislators a chance to block U.S. arms transfers to Arab belligerents; yet its immediate design was to respond more broadly to concerns over the U.S. security relationship with the Shah of Iran and other relatively unstable, dictatorial foreign rulers. Congress also cut all U.S. military aid to NATO ally Turkey after its invasion of Cyprus in 1974. Provoking a bitter confrontation with an utterly exasperated Ford White House, junior members of Congress overrode their own leadership to make the embargo stick.

Intelligence Activities. Consistent with the theme of curbing unauthorized foreign commitments by the executive branch, Congress sought to rein in the Central Intelligence Agency. Criticism had sprung from covert U.S. involvement in the 1973 overthrow of democratically elected socialist Salvador Allende in Chile. Beginning in the spring of 1975, and continuing through the extraordinary public hearings of the Senate Select Committee on Intelligence Activities (the "Church Committee"), Congress attempted to curtail certain

CIA covert operations. Funds for aiding anticommunist factions in Angola were barred in the 1975 Clark amendment, and permanent intelligence oversight panels were established on the Hill. In 1978, the Highes-Ryan Act was signed into law, placing strict conditions and reporting requirements on the use of foreign covert operations.

Nuclear Nonproliferation Policy. Congress moved also to curb the discretion of the executive branch to license exports of nuclear technology. The 1975 Zablocki-Findley amendment established new licensing requirements. Subsequently, the Glenn and Symington amendments were adopted, proscribing U.S. military aid to any new nuclear weapons states or nations that maintained sensitive nuclear facilities. Nonproliferation policy and nuclear export laws were then completely rewritten in the comprehensive Nuclear Nonproliferation Act of 1978. Important U.S. friends—including India, Pakistan, Argentina, and Brazil—were ineligible for U.S. nuclear trade or any form of U.S. military cooperation for a time; many of these prohibitions were subsequently waived by the Reagan administration.

Human Rights. With the weakening of executive authority came efforts from liberals and conservatives alike to elevate human rights considerations as an important determinant of Washington's international policies. The promotion of democracy abroad was made a central objective of U.S. foreign aid and military assistance efforts. Critics of detente with the Soviet Union moved in 1974 to pass legislation linking such trade benefits as most-favored-nation status and Export-Import Bank loans to the human rights practices of communist countries. Then, in 1975, Congress enacted curbs on military aid to consistent violators of human rights, a move targeted principally at anticommunist dictators like Ferdinand Marcos of the Philippines and Augusto Pinochet of Chile. The State Department Bureau for Human Rights was created by statute the next year, and the executive branch was required to produce an annual report on all nations' human rights practices.

Treaty Limitations. Throughout the decade, Congress presented severe tests to executive branch treaty-making initiatives. Congress placed important limitations on the 1972 SALT I Treaty with the Soviet Union. The 1974 U.S.-Soviet trade agreement was undermined by the Jackson-Vanik amendment on emigration policy. The

Senate came within one vote of rejecting the 1977 Panama Canal treaties; it nearly rejected the 1978 "package" sale of arms to Egypt, Israel, and Saudi Arabia; and it balked at ratification of the 1979 SALT II Treaty. Members of Congress also challenged President Carter's severance of diplomatic ties with the Republic of China (ROC) with lawsuits and adoption of the Taiwan Relations Act.

Virtually all of these congressional initiatives were opposed by the White House—under both Republican and Democratic administrations. Yet the majority of these measures were the direct consequence of perceived executive branch excesses in the area of foreign policy formulation. They grew from an environment in which confrontation between the branches had replaced consensus as the norm of the day. They were part and parcel of the "Vietnam syndrome": a neo-isolationist sentiment—shared by liberals and conservatives alike—that America needed to look with greater skepticism upon both "limited" military interventions and open-ended diplomatic commitments. Conversely, these measures demonstrated a new quasi-interventionist hunger on the part of some in Congress who sought to impose American values by statute upon foreign allies, clients, and treaty partners. They were also part of the social turmoil that changed the institution of Congress, changed the way members were elected, and changed the way they behaved once they arrived in Congress.

We shall consider the legacy of each of these reforms in later chapters. However, the greatest significance of the new foreign policymaking procedures will be lost if their historical roots are not fully appreciated. The congressional revolution of the 1970s needs to be seen as part of a recurring cycle, a process in which first one branch, then another, has gained ascendancy in shaping U.S. foreign policy. In the 1970s, there was an abrupt end to the unique era of bipartisan consensus that marked relations between the White House and Congress through the first twenty-five years of the Cold War. But the cycle from which the legislative assault of the 1970s grew was part of a continuum in the 200-year experience of American democracy. The body of law it produced was the result of an extraordinary time: a time of crisis, a time of sustained executive abuse of constitutional prerogatives, and a time of strident congressional counterassault.

The period that produced this legislation had no precedent in the modern American experience. As excess sparked reaction, insurgents on Capitol Hill sought first to foment revolution within their own institution. A reformed Congress then proceeded with vigorous authority to impose a new foreign policymaking structure upon an executive branch disoriented by its free-fall from the heights of extraordinary power. It is the legacy of this prolonged legislative assault with which current policymakers on both ends of Pennsylvania Avenue must struggle.

NOTES

1. Senator Lyndon B. Johnson, *Congressional Record*, February 15, 1953, p. S8046.
2. Conservative Republicans called for a more aggressive U.S. effort to aid the beleaguered forces of Nationalist Chiang Kai-shek, even though it was clear to most dispassionate observers by the late 1940s that his efforts to resist a Communist takeover were doomed. State Department personnel who reported this fact, or who were critical of the corrupt Nationalist regime, were subsequently purged. While this experience encouraged a readier application of U.S. military force to thwart communism in Asia, it should be noted that the conservatives' critique was not sufficient to justify committing U.S. forces to Vietnam in 1954 to aid the French.
3. Leftist historian Barton Bernstein offers a provocative explanation for the source of American divisions in the 1930s, maintaining that American industrial interests were inherently isolationist because they profited from trade with Axis nations. This thesis holds that the electorate was far readier to go to war than were elite policymakers, a point supported by many contemporary polls (see Bernstein, "America in War and Peace: The Test of Liberalism" in Bernstein, *Towards a New Past*, p. 29).
4. On the pressing postwar domestic needs, see O'Neill, *American High*, ch. 1.
5. Historian Daniel Yergin notes that the anticommunist consensus "existed first in the center, in the policy elite, before it spread to the nation" (Yergin, *Shattered Peace*, p. 171).
6. State Department officials often fretted that isolationist sentiment would return. The challenge, as Dean Acheson defined it, became "to prevent 140 million people from going back to worrying about 140 million other things" (as quoted in Rubin, *Secrets of State*, p. 61).
7. Dean Acheson, as quoted in Yergin, *Shattered Peace*, p. 56.
8. For an extensive discussion of the closed system that prevailed on the Hill immediately after the war, see Ornstein, "Sharing of Foreign Responsibility," pp. 50–53.
9. Brzezinski, *Power and Principle*, p. 11. The key leaders of the postwar bipartisan consensus are profiled in Isaacson and Thomas, *The Wise Men*.

10. Truman subsequently infuriated his internationalist GOP supporters, including Arthur Vandenberg, with his 1948 campaign assaults on the "do-nothing Congress."

11. A loan to the United Kingdom in 1946 met with little congressional opposition—especially after Winston Churchill's darkly anticommunist "iron curtain" speech in Independence, Missouri.

12. Senator Arthur Vandenberg, as quoted in *New York Times*, March 14, 1947, p. 1.

13. In *Presidential Power: The Politics of Leadership*, Richard Neustadt chronicles Truman's frequent fights with the executive bureaucracy and the partisan White House staff as he strove to maintain support from Capitol Hill Republicans for his international policies.

14. Senator Arthur Vandenberg, as quoted in Destler, et al., *Our Own Worst Enemy*, p. 18.

15. Eisenhower considered running as a Democrat because of his discomfort with the isolationist strain of some GOP conservatives. His crucial decision to run in 1952 as a Republican ensured that support for NATO and assertive internationalism would be enshrined as mainstream politics for a generation (see O'Neill, *American High*, p. 179).

16. Ibid., p. 43.

17. Josephy, *American Heritage History of Congress*, p. 378.

18. Kearns, *Lyndon Johnson and American Dream*, p. 291.

19. The JCAE wielded great power, but more in boosting commercial nuclear energy development than in controlling military programs. The JCAE would later fall under attack from Hill reformers, who criticized its extraordinarily close ties to industry. The panel was abolished in 1977 (see Chapter 8).

20. Acheson, *Present at the Creation*, pp. 414–15. Acheson wrote that while a congressional resolution might have afforded the President political support, "Congressional approval did not soften or divert the anti-war critics of Presidents Lincoln, Wilson and Roosevelt" (p. 415).

21. Senator Robert Taft, as quoted in Josephy, *American Heritage History of Congress*, p. 382.

22. Senator Alexander Wiley, *Congressional Record*, July 10, 1950, p. S9737.

23. Eisenhower's military experience made him extremely cautious in committing troops as president. (He also believed Truman had made a serious mistake in failing to gain congressional support for Korean deployments.) President Eisenhower came to the Hill for broadly worded resolutions of support during the Quemoy/Matsu incidents, the Suez Crisis, and the Lebanon peacekeeping efforts. And when, in April 1954, he received military counsel to call in air strikes to defend French forces besieged at Dien Bien Phu, Vietnam, Eisenhower refused to proceed without strong Capitol Hill support. But in a crucial meeting with congressional leaders on April 3, the proposal met with deep skepticism. Ironically, the leading critic of any

U.S. military commitment to Vietnam was none other than Senate Majority Leader Lyndon Johnson.

24. Congress was excluded in part because of White House fears that Hill pressures for more rapid escalation would have been intense. In fact, when congressional leaders were finally briefed, most felt that nothing short of American air strikes would suffice. Recent disclosures from the JFK Library indicate that President Kennedy was even more conciliatory toward the Soviets than originally believed; documents suggest that he explicitly linked withdrawal of Soviet missiles from Cuba with the removal of U.S. missiles from Turkey. For more on the very limited role of Congress in the Cuban Missile Crisis, see Allison, *Essence of Decision*, or Kennedy, *Thirteen Days.*

25. Congressman Abraham Multer, as quoted in Sundquist, *Decline and Resurgence*, p. 110.

26. Schlesinger, *Imperial Presidency*, p. 169.

27. Ibid., p. 8.

28. Nixon, *RN*, p. 763.

29. Senator William J. Fulbright, May 1961 speech at Cornell University, as quoted in Sundquist, *Decline and Resurgence*, p. 120.

30. LBJ returned Fulbright's personal scorn, telling contemporaries that "Fulbright's problem is that he's never found any President who would appoint him Secretary of State. He is frustrated up there on the Hill. And he takes out his frustration by making all those noises about Vietnam. He wants the nation to stand up and take notice of Bill Fulbright, and he knows the best way to get that attention is to put himself in the role of critic" (Kearns, *Lyndon Johnson and American Dream*, p. 328).

31. Nixon, *RN*, p. 763.

32. Senator Mike Mansfield, *Congressional Record*, January 4, 1973, p. S324.

33. Congressman Carl Albert, speech to *Time* magazine executives, January 1973, as quoted in Sundquist, *Decline and Resurgence*, p. 1.

34. Congressman Gillis Long, statement in the House of Representatives, April 18, 1973, as quoted in Franck, *Tethered Presidency*, pp. 6–7.

35. See *Congressional Record*, March 2, 1967, p. H2066.

36. While critics bemoaned the absence of a declaration of war by Congress, Johnson had framed requests for appropriations with explicit language. For example, on May 4, 1965, he sought $700 million to fund troop commitments, noting that "each member of Congress who supports this request is also voting to persist in our effort to halt communist aggression in South Vietnam. Each is saying that the Congress and the President stand united before the world." The request received House and Senate approval within seventy-two hours (as quoted in Sundquist, *Decline and Resurgence*, pp. 124–25).

37. Schlesinger, *Imperial Presidency*, pp. 282–83.

38. Senator Sam Ervin, as quoted in Sundquist, *Decline and Resurgence*, p. 251.

39. Senator Robert Griffin, *Congressional Record*, May 18, 1970, p. S15924.

40. Senator Milton Young, as quoted in Franck, *Tethered Presidency*, p. 19.

41. Kissinger, *White House Years*, p. 1373.

42. Senator Henry Jackson, *Congressional Record*, April 8, 1975, p. S9281.

43. See Lee Hamilton and Michael Van Dusen, "Making the Separation of Powers Work," *Foreign Affairs* 57 (Fall 1978): 21. The 1969 National Commitments Resolution was an initial response to the White House practice of making unilateral national commitments. The 1972 legislation was also meant to counter widespread use of "secret diplomacy," which served to shield national commitments from the eyes of Congress and the American people.

II | THE MODERN INSTITUTIONS

3 PRESIDENTIAL CONTROL OF FOREIGN POLICY

> Presidents hate Congress. Presidents view Congress as the enemy.
>
> —former Senator Tom Eagleton, 1988[1]

The modern presidency is predisposed to dominate foreign policy-making because it thrives upon international challenges. Nothing unites the American people and focuses media attention upon the commander-in-chief like a foreign crisis. Such tests inevitably afford presidents great freedom of action. Here, where secrecy and immediate access to intelligence are at such a great premium, presidents use their monopoly on diplomatic resources to move with fewer congressional restraints. Here, the president alone possesses the unity of purpose, the dispatch, and the ability to speak for the nation with a single voice. And here, most presidents strive to make their mark on history.

The fact that Washington has maintained an air of international crisis for the better part of the Cold War has facilitated a substantial increase in presidential power—just as the economic challenge of the Depression years enabled FDR to expand the domestic affairs prerogatives of the White House. These foreign crises of the modern era—both real and imagined—have invited a growth in presidential authorities that was by no means fully reversed by the congressional revolt of the 1970s. Presidents still must shoulder a unique burden to act "to preserve, protect, and defend" the nation. They alone possess the codes to launch America's 12,000 strategic nuclear warheads. They alone have the ability and the obligation to act decisively even while Congress divides over appropriate policy alternatives. The pursuit of American international interests remains a contest of geopolitical chess. And to the President's advantage, chess, as Senator John Tower has observed, "is not a team game."[2]

Of course, the federal government has far less control over international developments than domestic policy. And the executive branch is vulnerable to its own bureaucratic divisions—a diffusion of power has occurred here no less than within Congress. Yet to address a budget dilemma and advance a social program, the president must always face a formidable legislative gauntlet. Breaking ground for a new diplomatic course, however, requires the president to overcome far fewer hurdles on Capitol Hill. To pursue an international initiative, the president often need only telephone a general, or instruct one of his ambassadors, or contact one of his fellow chiefs of state abroad. Congress usually comes into the picture much later. The struggle to gain legislative support may be bruising. But consultation on international initiatives is often a formality undertaken only after the decision has already been made. "I do not have to unless I want to," President Truman remarked in 1951. "But of course I am polite, and I usually consult [Congress]. I don't ask their permission, I just consult them."[3]

These realities present the central dilemma of modern executive-legislative relations. Most chief executives prefer after-the-fact confrontations with the Hill to prior consultation. Soliciting congressional views before a decision has been made risks not only leaks of policy proposals but the initiation of timely opposition as well. When the president feels a need to act quickly, he is tremendously tempted to commit the nation first, then challenge the Congress with a fait accompli, knowing that details can be argued about later. A gambling president knows that once the nation is committed, the adverse consequences for national prestige of a subsequent legislative reversal will arm him with a compelling argument on Capitol Hill to sustain his course. This high-stakes game of "chicken" has been played repeatedly in cases ranging from Korea and the invasion of Cambodia to the Panama Canal treaties and the 1981 sale of advanced radar aircraft to Saudi Arabia. One of the unfortunate consequences of this confrontational approach is that foreign partners to agreements with the United States are often confused about the nature of a presidential commitment; questions are inevitably raised abroad by allies and trading partners deeply suspicious of the disunity tolerated by America's division of powers. And when the showdown on Capitol Hill results in a White House defeat—as in the Turkish arms embargo, or the failure to gain Senate support for SALT II ratification—the consequences for American diplomacy can be severe.

When the nation is engaged in an overseas challenge, the situation invites appeals to nationalist sentiment and calls for patriotic, bipartisan support. Foreign crises also afford significant opportunities for building the president's historical legacy. It is thus no coincidence that virtually every U.S. president since World War II has undertaken a major diplomatic initiative toward the end of his first term, acting with one eye on the polls and the other on his place in history. Indeed, Nixon as diplomat still evokes respect today for his efforts at rapprochement with the People's Republic of China and the Soviet Union, just as the unpopular Carter presidency is still credited for such bold diplomatic accomplishments as the Panama Canal treaties and the Camp David peace agreement. As Gerald Ford's White House chief of staff Dick Cheney has observed, "Our history praises those presidents who accumulated power and used it for the public good."[4]

Presidents also continue to turn to international issues in times of domestic political trouble. This is often part of a calculated White House strategy: Richard Nixon barnstormed the streets of Cairo on the eve of House impeachment proceedings, just as Ronald Reagan suddenly focused on arms control and peace in Central America when besieged by criticism of the Iran-Contra affair. In like manner, it is because of the president's relative freedom of action internationally that the idea of an "October surprise"—an election-eve foreign policy gamble—has become a campaign staple. Favor with voters has been curried through Johnson's abrupt halt to bombing of North Vietnam, the Nixon administration's October 1972 assertion that peace in Vietnam was "at hand," and the risky attempts by Carter and Reagan to secure the release of hostages in 1980 and 1984. Presidents have used their military and diplomatic prerogatives in efforts to change the voting climate just as readily as they have sought to pump-prime the national economy before the voters go to the polls. The presidency remains, as Theodore Roosevelt liked to observe, a "bully pulpit": an ideal platform for both leading and preaching.[5]

USING THE BULLY PULPIT

There is considerable truth in Senator Eagleton's observation that most presidents consider the powers of Congress in foreign policy to be a nuisance. Faced with seemingly endless and usually divisive legislative challenges, most recent White House occupants have been unable to accept a legitimate Hill role. As a consequence, they have often failed to use the opportunity that congressional involvement affords for maximum presidential benefit. Since the Kennedy administration, the White House has routinely resisted or tried to limit congressional involvement, apparently concluding that the national interests are better served when "diplomacy is the business of the prince," as the frustrated House majority whip, Democrat Thomas P. Foley of Washington, recently suggested.[6] Presidents have preferred to preach, to use their White House platform to lead the nation, and to then use political pressures and their powers of persuasion to bring Congress around to the executive branch point of view. In this important respect, American foreign policymaking in the television age has developed an important bias toward the presidency, an advantage that has been only partially altered by recent congressional assertiveness.

Today the president wields foreign policy influence through the use of at least six key tools:

Media Access. The president retains an unparalleled ability to set the agenda, to appear on national television, and to change the focus of national debate. The opportunity to present a unified message—which requires internal discipline within the cabinet and the executive branch bureaucracy—can be the president's single most effective weapon in any struggle with the 535 members of Congress. This power to persuade is, as scholar Richard Neustadt has argued, the key to effective presidential governance.[7] When legislators disagree with a White House proposal, they do so for a variety of reasons; their dissent is no guarantee of majority support for a practical alternative. A persistent president can press a media campaign—through "fireside chats," stump speeches, and weekly radio addresses, or through surrogates on the weekend talk shows—to make the legislature look like so many second-guessers. A president who can effectively communicate with the electorate "over the heads" of Congress can often prevail in confrontations over even the most controversial policies. Indeed, it is the mastery of media skills that makes many think of John Kennedy and Ronald Reagan as "successful" presidents despite their relatively modest diplomatic records, while denigrating the accomplishments of Presidents Johnson, Nixon, and Carter—which, in fact, were far more significant.[8]

Intelligence Access. The president enjoys immediate access to a wide array of intelligence information. At his disposal are satellites that can produce minutely detailed photographs, as well as direct reports from ambassadors and agents-in-place in foreign capitals. A good deal of this information merely confirms what is publicly known. In addition, much is available to congressional leaders in a timely fashion through the *National Intelligence Daily*, the intelligence community's morning summary of international developments, which is widely circulated in Washington. But American ambassadors serve at the pleasure of the president and report to him first. And intelligence agencies rarely volunteer great insights to Capitol Hill unless legislators know precisely what to ask—and are able to pursue the truth when, upon occasion, they are lied to.[9] The president can effectively use the mystique surrounding his intelligence resources to intimidate members of Congress and press commentators who argue for a different policy course. In the nuclear age, the White House can awe even the most determined Hill dissenters by making dark references to highly classified intelligence reports. It is difficult to debate such information in public. And of course the White House can selectively leak details favorable to its case to rally opinion behind its approach. Indeed, most experienced Washington observers conclude that the vast majority of intelligence leaks come from executive branch officials who are seeking to either win an internal policy struggle or shape the Hill debate. For example, on the eve of key Hill votes on Contra aid, Reagan administration officials repeatedly "leaked" information about Soviet arms shipments to Nicaragua, or about alleged Sandinista cooperation with Salvadoran guerrillas. These carefully planted bits of raw intelligence data appeared in favored publications, such as the conservative *Washington Times* and the Evans and Novak syndicated column, and helped shape subsequent debate.

Military Authority. The Constitution's grant of powers to the commander-in-chief is extremely modest; it was designed simply to ensure unity of command and civilian control over wars to which only Congress could commit the nation. Yet as the head of the armed forces, the president has the ability to use force to protect U.S. citizens abroad and to defend against perceived threats to American interests. Notwithstanding disputes over the use of troops in undeclared wars, the president's authority to direct military operations in war time is unchallenged. And it is clear to all that with Soviet submarine-launched missiles now always less than ten minutes from Washington, military decisions in a nuclear confrontation will have to be made by the president without any consultation whatsoever with Congress. These realities give added weight to appeals from the commander-in-chief even in peacetime debate over diplomatic policy and arms procurement priorities. As the embodiment of national power, the president will always be able to "wrap himself in the flag" to help win backing for his policies.[10]

Bureaucratic Administrator.   The president sits astride an enormous national security bureaucracy, employing substantial staff resources with which to wear down even the most determined legislative protagonists. Divisions within this bureaucracy—an especially notable example being the recent confrontations between the National Security Council and the State Department—can devastate the president's efforts. But when it functions in a disciplined manner, the executive branch bureaucracy can be a formidable force. Cabinet members are available to coordinate their testimony and lobbying efforts. Intelligence agencies from the National Security Agency to the Defense Intelligence Agency can produce a common analysis and, particularly when politicized by White House pressures, present the Hill with a united front that leaves little room for public dissent. While Congress divides over alternatives to presidential proposals, a unified executive branch can press ahead. Unilateral White House moves like the Persian Gulf naval deployments of 1987–1988 inevitably spark criticism on Capitol Hill. But the ranks of Hill opponents behind a consensus alternative are rarely unified. At the end of the day, the decision—and the ultimate responsibility for such risky efforts—usually comes to rest in the Oval Office.

Party Leadership.   While there has been a severe erosion of discipline in American political parties during the last two decades, the president still retains substantial powers to reward those who back him in the pinch and to punish those who vote with the opposition. This is not simply a matter of securing federal funding for a bridge or dam in the district of a key legislator; nor is it simply a question of offering other familiar White House perquisites like dinner invitations, use of the president's box at the Kennedy Center, and foreign diplomatic missions. The president's role in prospective campaigns has become a key issue in recent strong-arm lobbying efforts by the White House. During the 1981 effort to win approval of the Reagan administration's Saudi arms sale package, White House aides promised the enormous draw of presidential fund-raising appearances to senators who backed the package. Similarly, to help win votes for Contra aid, White House officials contacted home-state supporters of undecided senators in an effort to generate grass-roots pressure to back President Reagan. In other instances, White House officials have pledged not to work for the defeat of an opposing party senator if he would help the White House.[11] Recent presidents have also sought to impress upon a loyal senator or congressman the extent to which their political fortunes might be linked; if their party were to lose a string of Hill tests on key issues, this argument goes, neither would fare well in the next election. Thus, most members of the president's party have been loathe to oppose him on more than one major foreign policy issue in a given Congress—and to demonstrate their independence, have often picked a single issue on which their defection is less costly. An important corollary is that presidents must choose carefully where to use their political capital; by lobbying so hard to win the Panama Canal treaties in 1978, President Carter found that he had less influence to call upon when lobbying Democratic senators in 1979 for votes on the SALT II Treaty. And key Republicans who had gone with the White House on Panama—like GOP Senate leader Howard Baker—were unswayed by presidential lobbying in the subsequent SALT II battle, which became enmeshed in the politics of the 1980 presidential elections.[12]

Few of these presidential powers are unique to the modern era. Several have been undercut by advances Congress has made in developing its own resources. But these remain the basic tools with which recent presidents have sought to advance America's position in the world while attempting to dominate the Washington debate over U.S. foreign policy. As such, these tools have played a central role in almost every recent foreign policy dispute between Congress and the

White House. The common ingredient in each of these White House weapons is the essential presidential power of initiative. The president can lead—and potentially dominate—the Congress because he can act, and act alone. Theodore Roosevelt bragged about this power when he explained his Panama initiative: "I took the Isthmus, started the Canal, and then left Congress—not to debate the Canal, but to debate me!"[13] This ability to force the action is unique to the president and empowers those who heed Napoleon's maxim that "the tools belong to the man who can use them."[14] The Constitution gives the president important powers in the conduct of diplomacy, if not in the establishment of a policy course. As the Supreme Court ruled in a decision quoted with relish by champions of presidential authority: "In this vast external realm, the President alone has the power to speak or listen as a representative of the nation. [He] alone negotiates. Into the field of negotiation, the Senate cannot intrude; and Congress itself is powerless to invade it."[15]

A sage chief executive can use the opportunity for initiative to resist engagement with Congress altogether, to virtually ignore the institution. For example, President Reagan repeatedly undertook military moves without looking to Congress for authorization or advice. Similarly, in Richard Nixon's domination of policymaking throughout his first term, he often viewed Congress as an adversary to be avoided at all costs. Trying to fight Nixon initiatives was thus, as one analyst of the period has written, "like pushing a string. There was no resistance. Instead, Nixon tried to run things without Congress. Impounding funds, deferring the spending of them, shifting money from one purpose to another. . . ."[16]

The courageous use of the initiative power helped make several presidents' places in history when they were willing to pursue unpopular stands. Truman had the guts to rein in, and then to fire, General MacArthur during the Korean War. Eisenhower pressed the British, French, and Israelis to back off from the Suez. Carter pressed the Panama Canal treaties, and Reagan stood by El Salvador and the Contra cause despite weak voter support on these issues. Conversely, presidents who sense an issue slipping from their grasp have been more than willing to set up Congress as the scapegoat. Sometimes these developments were after the fact, as when Nixon claimed that the United States would have won the war in Vietnam but for congressional timidity, or when Carter assaulted the Hill for footdragging on SALT II. In other instances, proposals were pressed on the Hill with little chance for success but with an eye toward shifting the blame for subsequent disappointments. President Ford and Henry Kissinger pressed for covert operations in Angola long after there was any realistic prospect of success. And Reagan administration officials pressed unrealistic "Star Wars" schemes and Contra aid plans long after such ambitious proposals began to appear less than promising. Thus, the power of initiative has come to include the ability to "pass the buck" as well.

THE EXECUTIVE BRANCH PERSPECTIVE

The principal source of tension between the Congress and the executive branch is the fact that the world looks far different from the White House than when viewed from Capitol Hill. The president is responsible for day-to-day relations with 147 different nations. He has direct responsibility for officers who maintain the U.S. nuclear deterrent twenty-four hours a day. In the Oval Office, there is a sense of imminent accountability that is simply not present in most legislative deliberations. Congress can express its "reservations" about a risky venture like the 1983 Beirut troop deployments. Members can hedge their bets and provide themselves political cover by going on record with their concerns—in case something goes wrong. But the ultimate responsibility for the lives and safety of U.S. military forces is felt most deeply by the president alone. In most foreign policy debates, the ultimate credit for success—or the blame for failure—will rest with the nation's chief executive.

The president is also obliged to consider individual foreign policy initiatives as part of a complex strategic puzzle—the geopolitical chess game. He must weigh how one policy will affect another; the consequences of miscalculation can be grave. For example, President Carter had to consider in 1978 how recognition of the People's Republic of China might affect the conclusion of arms treaty negotiations with the PRC's adversaries in Moscow. The subsequent Carter "tilt" toward Beijing not only stalled the SALT II negotiations but activated conservative Hill opposition to such a detente-like initiative. Presidents must also decide which foreign policy initiatives most warrant expenditure of precious resources. This was a challenge that President Ford faced when grappling with Congress simultaneously over the Turkish arms embargo, Indochina policy, the

Vladivostok arms accord, and investigations of the CIA. Political capital must be conserved for the most important tests; dissipation of strength entails the risks of sequential setbacks for the White House.

The four-year cycle of the presidency provides its own distinct sense of timing. Risks can be taken early in the term with the full knowledge that several years will pass before the president must face the voters again. For example, President Carter chose to press the unpopular Panama Canal treaties at the outset of his incumbency. Similarly, Ronald Reagan proposed the controversial sale of arms to Saudi Arabia in 1981—immediately after his first major budget test, but a full three years before he stood for reelection. Conversely, presidents returned for a second term and aware that they will never again have to face the voters have repeatedly gotten into trouble.

Integration of the president's foreign policy agenda has become the province of the national security adviser, who competes with other members of the National Security Council to manage the president's program. Conflict with the Hill—where broader ideological goals are often at issue—seems inevitable. This divergence in global outlook is most acute between career foreign service officers in the State Department and the professional politicians on Capitol Hill. The State Department must juggle dozens of bilateral relationships and interests with multilateral institutions. Congress is far more responsive to individual nations and their domestic supporters—what one critic, Republican Senator Daniel Evans of Washington, branded "the adopt-a-country approach to foreign affairs."[17]

The State Department manages specific issues in day-to-day diplomacy, such as a Soviet request for an export license; Congress is deeply concerned with general, philosophical causes, like anticommunism. The State Department operates with a hierarchical chain of command; the modern Congress rewards insurgency—junior legislators win recognition and power by challenging established authorities. Foggy Bottom relishes quiet diplomacy and bipartisan cooperation; Capitol Hill operatives often seek out opportunities for confrontation and the media attention it attracts. The executive branch rewards unity; legislators curry favor with voters by stressing their independence. Analyst Stanley Heginbotham brilliantly summarized these conflicting institutional perspectives:

> [Executive branch officials] consider members of Congress and their staffs to be insensitive to the need for privacy and confidentiality in foreign relations. They view the legislators as predisposed to grandstanding, prone to

disrupting important incremental day-to-day shifts in relations with other countries, dilatory and unpredictable in their legislative actions, ignorant of basic foreign policy realities, and parochial in their approach to global issues. Members of Congress and their staffs are often just as firmly convinced that foreign policy officials are unquestioning in their advocacy of administration policies, obsessed with the minutiae of ritualized diplomatic exchanges, insensitive to broad patterns of American interests, more concerned with the interests and needs of foreign counterparts than with the democratic processes of their own government, arrogant in their belief that their academic training and field experience give them a monopoly on foreign policy wisdom, hypocritical in their claim exclusively to represent the national interest, and skilled primarily in staunching the flow of meaningful information to Capitol Hill.[18]

The traditional State Department perspective has invited challenges not only from Congress. Beginning with Franklin Roosevelt's presidency, America's professional diplomats have come under sustained assault from White House staff. FDR was one of the first to consistently use personal emissaries to bypass State Department professionals and his own political appointees. His reliance upon backdoor channels that reported directly to the Oval Office—men like Harry Hopkins and Averell Harriman—considerably weakened his secretaries of state. (Similarly, President Wilson had served as his own negotiator at Versailles and delegated considerable authority to his chief of staff, Arthur House.) Franklin Roosevelt found, as many subsequent presidents have complained, that the State Department was inherently conservative and cautious, prone to dealing with the status quo rather than undertaking risky efforts to change it. Roosevelt was frustrated by the fact that the State Department of the 1930s was so violently anticommunist as to be "soft" on the Nazi threat. FDR had to constantly press State to work more aggressively against the Axis in the years before Pearl Harbor—and then had to keep pressuring the department to accommodate Washington's war-time allies in Moscow when that alliance of convenience was formed.[19]

President Truman relied heavily upon State Department professionals in his early months. But the President's frustration with challenges to his foreign policymaking primacy led to a higher profile for White House diplomacy. Secretary of Agriculture Henry Wallace was fired in 1946 for giving what was then deemed an excessively pro-Soviet speech—a text that supposedly received inadequate White House clearance. Secretary of State Jimmy Byrnes, who saw himself as the rightful heir to the Roosevelt legacy, was eased out for acting too independently of Truman. Each year that Truman grew in office, foreign policymaking increasingly came to be centered in the White House.

Dwight Eisenhower's military experience gave him great respect for the counsel of professional diplomats. He was deferential to, if not dominated by, his formidable secretary of state, John Foster Dulles. But under President Kennedy, there was a renewed reliance upon less formal lines of authority. Use of private channels to pursue diplomatic goals through ad hoc procedures became a common practice. A former member of the Senate Foreign Relations Committee, Kennedy often vented his frustration over the slow, deliberate fashion in which State proceeded. His chief of staff, Ted Sorensen, wrote that Kennedy

> was discouraged with the State Department almost as soon as he took office. He felt that it too often seemed to have a built-in inertia which deadened initiative and that its tendency toward excessive delay obscured determination. It spoke with too many voices and too little vigor. It was never clear to the President . . . who was in charge, who was clearly delegated to do what, and why his own policy line seemed consistently to be altered or evaded.[20]

Under President Nixon, this process of dissipating the State Department's authority rapidly accelerated. Throughout his career as a member of the House and Senate, Nixon had demonstrated intense distrust of State's professional diplomats. Indeed, Nixon had first gained national attention in 1948 when he implicated senior State official Alger Hiss in a Communist spy scandal. Upon his election to the presidency in 1968, Nixon moved swiftly to curb State's powers by establishing White House control over all major foreign policy decisions through his national security adviser, Henry Kissinger. Meanwhile, Nixon's first vice president, Spiro Agnew, kept up a steady barrage of public criticism of the State Department, dismissing it in one memorable 1972 speech as a "Cowardly College of Communist Containment" populated by "whining, whimpering and grovelling diplomats."[21]

White House staff loyal to Nixon and accountable only to his political appointees played a central role in diplomatic planning and execution. For example, throughout the SALT I negotiations, Nixon maintained a back channel of communication with the Soviet leadership through Kissinger. Foggy Bottom officials from Secretary of

State William Rogers to Arms Control and Disarmament Agency (ACDA) head Gerard C. Smith were kept in the dark.[22] This distrust of State and other agencies, together with an obsessive fear of news leaks, led Nixon and Kissinger to adopt a secretive style of operation dubbed "Lone Rangerism." Secrecy became almost an end in itself—with severe consequences on the Hill when disclosures were ultimately made about the secret annexes to the Paris accords on Vietnam, or about secret U.S. involvement in the overthrow of Chilean President Salvador Allende. The White House used ruses and back channels to pursue a breakthrough in relations with the People's Republic of China. An internal security unit was established in the White House basement that directed wiretaps and break-ins in a futile attempt to trace leaks of diplomatically sensitive and politically embarrassing information. This "plumbers" unit ultimately produced the Watergate break-in and led to the unraveling of the Nixon presidency.

MANAGING THE PRESIDENT'S BUREAUCRACY

Modern presidents have struggled mightily with adversaries in the legislative branch to steer the ship of state. Yet internal struggles within the executive branch itself have made management of the national security system a key challenge to effective presidential foreign policymaking. In theory, foreign policy is the area where presidents retain the most control. But in practice, it is in the diplomatic area that internal control of the bureaucracy has proven most difficult. Here the president's struggles have so often been not with Congress but with forces within his own branch of government. As a lame duck, Harry Truman summarized this frustration in his famous comments on how President-elect Eisenhower would find governing the bureaucracy: "He will sit here and he'll say, 'Do this! Do that!' And nothing will happen. Poor Ike. He won't like it a bit."[23]

Many of these internal tensions are attributable to the changed nature of the State Department. There was a time when the secretary of state was almost always an experienced politician. Many of the early American diplomats—Jefferson, Adams, and Madison included—used the State post as a stepping-stone to the White House. The State Department post was often given as a consolation prize for senior party leaders—men like William Seward and Jimmy Byrnes—who had fallen short in their own presidential bids.[24] But in recent years, the slot has often been filled by less flashy academics and career diplomats—men like William Rogers, Dean Rusk, or Cyrus Vance—who have become vulnerable targets for political appointees at the NSC and the Pentagon. Consequently, recent U.S. diplomatic history has been littered with the carnage of clashes between secretaries of state and national security advisers. These have not been simple clashes of ego or policy perspective. There is a fundamental institutional conflict between the two jobs as presently defined—a basic question regarding who is to be the number-one operational strategist for the president on international security questions. Natural rivalries of senior administration officials have been exacerbated by the intense media focus of investigative journalists in recent years and the cavalier use of leaks by bureaucrats in order to gain an upper hand in interagency competition. Both factors have encouraged greater use of the NSC staff under White House control for sensitive international missions. The NSC has moved from a coordinating role to an operational one. And the temptation for the president to "privatize" foreign policy by employing personnel who are independent of the bureaucracy has become great.

Tensions within the executive branch became extreme under Richard Nixon, when the NSC was used repeatedly to implement White House diplomatic strategies, humiliating State Department officials in the process. Under President Carter, the wars between National Security Adviser Zbigniew Brzezinski and Secretary of State Cyrus Vance reached epic proportions, spilling out into the news with numerous leaks of Cabinet Room battles. The problem continued under President Reagan, who had very little turnover elsewhere in his cabinet during the first six years of his administration but had six different national security advisers and two secretaries of state during this time. This sorry Reagan record was but a continuation of an alarming pattern, as former diplomat Richard Holbrooke has noted:

> Every Administration begins with high-sounding rhetoric about the primacy of the Secretary of State and orderly procedures, but as the President and his staff grow impatient with what they often view as the State Department's leisurely, domestically insensitive, bureaucratic approach to policy, the White House starts to get involved. At first, it tries to get results through second-guessing and prodding the Department, and then, sometimes, it takes matters

directly into its own hands . . . [leading] to large-scale political problems and erosion of public confidence in the President's ability to govern.[25]

The enduring problem presented by such instability reflects the two advantages every national security adviser has in bureaucratic competition. The first is proximity; the national security adviser is always there. The secretary of state is across town, or up on the Hill, or out of the country. But the national security adviser remains at the president's elbow; his desk is just footsteps down the hall from the Oval Office, and he is ready to greet the president every morning with a daily world roundup briefing. While it is technically the national security adviser's responsibility to coordinate the executive branch bureaucracy, his constant presence in reality invites a short-circuiting of the process. Alone, the national security adviser can get things done with greater dispatch, less public accountability, and more loyalty to the president than he could adhering to any department or bureaucratic tradition.

The second advantage the national security adviser enjoys over the secretary of state derives from the complexity of most recent foreign policy decisions. The State Department is no longer the only lead agency in international matters. Since World War II, charters have been granted not just to the National Security Council but also to a new Department of Defense, the Central Intelligence Agency, the U.S. Information Agency, the Agency for International Development, the Defense Intelligence Agency, and the U.S. Mission to the United Nations, among others. Other cabinet-level agencies, including Agriculture, Energy, Treasury, and Commerce, maintain large staffs with international responsibilities. The missions of these different agencies often escape State Department coordination and control. Particularly worrisome for a chief executive intent upon centralized control and internal unity is the fact that different parts of the intelligence community compete with each other every bit as much as the Pentagon competes with State to shape international options. This dilemma has led to the grooming of a host of challengers to State Department diplomacy, as one analysis concludes:

> Presidents who mistrust State—as too careerist, stodgy, slow, unimaginative, and too eager to appease foreigners—seek other agencies to do the job. Each succeeding administration has expanded the number of challengers to State's primacy. Eisenhower elevated the CIA; Kennedy, his White House staff; Johnson, the Defense Department; and Nixon, the national security advisor.[26]

Little wonder that recent presidents have set up their own "mini-cabinet" operations under their hand-picked NSC men.

A predictable champion of a strong national security adviser is Zbigniew Brzezinski, who held the post under President Carter. Brzezinski has argued for a lead NSC role in developing—and explaining to Congress in monthly meetings—an administration's strategic approach to the world. And what of the secretary of state? Brzezinski concludes that

> the Department of State does not shape national security policy. The Department of State too often confuses diplomacy with foreign policy, forgetting that diplomacy is only one aspect of foreign policy: military power and intelligence and covert activity and financial power and threats are all part of the process of making a national security policy, for which diplomacy is but one component.[27]

The State Department has the advantage of its enormous, highly trained staff of foreign policy professionals—career officers less susceptible to the political whim of the moment. Yet State Department diplomats are readily challenged from within the executive branch, from Pentagon officials who believe them naive about military matters, from intelligence officials who believe them insensitive to security issues, and from commercial interests who find them ineffective in promoting American economic interests. And even champions on Capitol Hill of the foreign service criticize the department as simply "too remote, too old-fashioned, too isolated from the blunt common sense of constituents," as Congressman Lee Hamilton has argued. The Indiana Democrat adds a familiar populist charge that "the executive branch's greatest weakness is that its foreign policy bureaucracies are inaccessible to the people."[28]

There have been deliberate efforts to shore up the State Department by reducing NSC to a coordinating role. Shifting Kissinger from NSC to State accomplished this purpose immediately in 1973, and the tenure of Brent Scowcroft on Ford's NSC was marked by smooth intrabranch relations. Again under Colin Powell in 1987 and 1988, NSC took a backseat to a State Department effectively dominated by George Shultz, who called the shots on most Reagan administration international policy questions late in the second term. Scowcroft and Powell followed the design of the authors of the NSC statute: to establish a bureau "wherein the complex and now uncoordinated problems of bringing foreign policy into harmony with the military means to enforce that policy may be brought to light and resolved."[29] Yet the experience of most other recent NSC incumbents has demonstrated that the White House agency today remains part of the crippling problem of diffused executive branch policy-making authority—that it is not yet a reliable contributor to that problem's resolution. Every president since John Kennedy has approached this problem, and then run away from it, by using ad hoc procedures and awkward, parallel structures to operate through independent means. Frustration has led even a highly organized man like Jimmy Carter to end-run executive branch procedures as well as legislative requirements. President Carter sent Hamilton Jordan off for secret negotiations with the Khomeini government on the hostage issue; Ronald Reagan authorized similar moves by his national security adviser Robert McFarlane, who showed up in Teheran with a cake shaped like a key and a Bible signed by the President. To maintain secrecy and to stifle bureaucratic dissent, president after president has privatized certain sensitive diplomatic operations. In the process, they have systematically alienated legislators and increased Capitol Hill suspicions of "secret White House diplomacy." Americans' natural tendency to favor what President Wilson championed—"open covenants openly arrived at"—has only been reinforced by White House efforts to resist. Thus, the internal tensions of the executive branch have become a guarantee of trouble not only in implementing U.S. foreign policy but in selling policy proposals to Capitol Hill as well.

WHITE HOUSE MANAGEMENT OF CONGRESSIONAL RELATIONS

No recent president has established a steady, reliable relationship with Congress on foreign affairs policy matters. And every recent president has come up with all sorts of creative excuses and strategies for avoiding a congressional role, despite repeated warnings from executive branch officials that "consultation is a sacred principle."[30] Indeed, the failure to consult often becomes the principal focus of opposition, supplanting the controversial policy initiative as a lightning rod. In this manner, process overtakes substance as the key source of conflict. As a summary of three major Congressional Research Service (CRS) studies on consultation concludes, the most sustained Capitol Hill opposition to executive branch positions is often generated by "the disdain and insensitivity with which executive branch officials treated Congressional participants rather than by the specific policies the officials espoused."[31] Of course, the problem works both ways: many congressmen revel in the pleasure of browbeating administration witnesses on unpopular proposals and coming up with procedural complaints about substantively responsible positions.

How does a willful president exploit congressional weaknesses to prevail on the Hill? Numerous devices have been resorted to. Sometimes, in order to mute criticism and to avoid a critical mass of opposition, controversial moves are deliberately timed for a congressional recess, when members are absent from Capitol Hill. For example, Reagan administration officials delivered to Capitol Hill notice of a controversial May 1987 Saudi arms sale at 5:57 p.m. on a Friday afternoon before the start of a ten-day recess. Upon other occasions, the president has pursued an overload strategy—lumping controversial policies that might be targets for opposition in with a string of announcements, hoping that opposition will be overwhelmed and unable to coalesce against any one proposal. Both President Nixon and President Carter chose to keep a number of diplomatic balls in the air simultaneously—and to then argue with the Hill that the complexity of White House strategy obliged the Congress to avoid "meddling." Sometimes a select group of senior congressional leaders are brought into the picture, but the president implores them not to share the information with their colleagues for fear that national interests will be harmed. Men like Richard Lugar and Sam Nunn—senators who can deliver the votes of dozens of their colleagues when they resolve to take a public position—are attractive targets for early administration efforts at co-optation. And sometimes the administration chooses to keep Congress completely in the dark, gambling that adverse reaction once the initiative is found out will be less severe than a premature disclosure, which might mobilize opponents on the Hill. Regardless of its strategy for selling its policy on the Hill, the executive branch benefits from the fact that many foreign policy issues—at least at the formative stages—move too quickly to allow a prompt and decisive congressional response.

The challenge of maintaining Hill support for controversial initiatives has been accentuated since the reforms of the 1970s. It is indicative of the institutional nature of this conflict that some of the most serious executive branch setbacks on Capitol Hill occurred under the administration of Jimmy Carter, when both branches were controlled by the same political party. True, many of President Carter's difficulties were attributable to his populist rhetoric and his innate suspicion of the Washington establishment. Jimmy Carter had run against Potomac politicians and bureaucrats—his campaign manager Hamilton Jordan had even commented that his efforts would be a failure if establishment figures like Vance and Brzezinski came to control the foreign policy machinery. It was thus inevitable that the Carter White House would have trouble with proud Washington figures like House Speaker Thomas ("Tip") O'Neill and Senate Democratic Majority Leader Robert Byrd. These problems would only be compounded by the divergent policy lines of Vance and Brzezinski, and by the bureaucratic feuds they inspired between State and the NSC.

Carter's problems with Congress and his own bureaucracy extended beyond personality clashes, however. Carter was idealistic in pursuing a risky and ambitious diplomatic program while battling the Hill on several domestic fronts—from energy policy to funding dams. Carter's activist approach to the presidency and his own insistence on involvement in even the smallest details of policy implementation led to acute difficulties in setting priorities. No presidency can succeed if clear priorities are not set for the use of its political capital. What were the Carter administration's foreign policy priorities in its early years? The administration was simultaneously talking about withdrawing troops from Korea, solving the international energy crisis, completely rewriting nuclear export laws, recognizing China and ending relations with Taiwan, bringing peace to southern Africa, ratifying the Panama Canal treaties, embarking on a global human rights crusade, selling arms to the Saudis and Egypt, calling a multinational Middle East peace conference, scrapping the Vladivostok accords, canceling the B-1 bomber, pushing the MX missile, and cutting U.S. and Soviet nuclear weapons with a substantial new SALT II treaty. Poorly consulted Hill supporters were naturally confused, divided, and overwhelmed by the string of naive White House declarations. Opponents had a field day as the President demonstrated ineptitude and inconsistency in pursuing competing objectives.

Under pressures that were often self-imposed, President Carter set what in hindsight appear to have been questionable priorities: shelving the nearly completed Ford administration effort on SALT II—

thereby delaying ratification—and putting the Panama Canal treaties first on its plate of major Hill tests. Political capital used to sway key Senate moderates like Howard Baker was not available for subsequent tests. A similar question of priorities can be raised on the decision to incur the wrath of conservatives in Congress—and the Soviets—by establishing formal ties with the People's Republic of China before completing SALT II and gaining Senate consent to its ratification. This pushed SALT into 1979, while raising howls from critics in both the Senate and the Kremlin.

By the end of the Carter administration, the President appeared to be reacting to events rather than holding the initiative. The Iran hostage crisis, especially, limited the President's ability to pursue new initiatives. Yet even then there were significant accomplishments beyond Panama and the Middle East peace treaty produced at Camp David. An all-out assault on the energy crisis left the Reagan administration with a reduction in the real price of oil, whereas Carter had been saddled with a more than 200 percent increase during his tenure. The Carter administration laid the groundwork for the Reagan-Gorbachev treaty on intermediate-range nuclear forces (INF) in Europe by securing in 1979 the crucial NATO two-track decision to commit to deployments of intermediate range missiles while pursuing INF negotiations. In 1980, Carter made the first of what would become a series of dramatic increases in defense spending. He continued to press for the Trident II submarine, the D-5 missile, the MX, and cruise missiles—which would form the backbone of a decade of U.S. military buildup. But President Carter remained bedeviled by problems over which he exercised little control—OPEC price gouging, the radicalism of Khomeini's Iran, and the Sandinista overthrow of Nicaraguan dictator Anastasio Somoza. On these issues, Carter was unable to fashion policies that enjoyed the support even of his own party in Congress, much less that of the opposition. (And he was unable to free the Teheran hostages before the voters went to the polls in November 1980.) To the extent that his presidency was deemed a "failure," it was in good measure because he was constantly feuding with a Congress dominated by members of his own Democratic Party. Here his ineptitude was so great that even many of his considerable accomplishments in the fields of energy and defense improvements were credited not to his administration but to his successors.

On the eve of the Reagan administration, Vice President Mondale lamented the unending challenges the ambitious Carter agenda had faced on the Hill:

> One of the most grievous inadequacies of our present system is that the President of the United States, who has to conduct foreign policy, is left enfeebled in terms of . . . crucial foreign aid and military assistance. I could give you a hundred examples. It took us a year to get the little help we got in Nicaragua. . . . A president should have a chance to be a president for four years. For crying out loud, let a president govern.[32]

Like so many of his recent predecessors, Ronald Reagan chose to reject much of what had come before him. The new president was determined to make sharp breaks with past policy, to make sweeping personnel changes, and to alter swiftly the nation's diplomatic course. Elected in part out of reaction to the perception that White House leadership had been lacking, Ronald Reagan was combative in his relations with Congress from his first day in office. The Reagan administration repeatedly criticized the role of Congress in reviewing such presidential commitments as the sale of arms to Middle East nations and the deployment of troops in Lebanon. And when things went wrong—when 241 Marines were killed in Beirut, when no basing scheme for the MX missile could be devised, when no START treaty could be achieved—the President publicly alleged that Congress was responsible for raising doubts in the minds of U.S. adversaries about America's staying power. From the specifics of arms sales policy to the more general area of foreign aid conditions, the Reagan administration was committed to a wholesale assault on nettlesome congressional restrictions. President Reagan often spoke against "the rash of Congressional initiatives to limit the President's authority" adopted in the 1970s. As he bluntly complained in a April 4, 1984 press conference:

> The Congress has imposed about one hundred and fifty restrictions on the President's power in international diplomacy, and I think that the Constitution made it pretty plain way back in the beginning as to how diplomacy was to be conducted. And I just don't think that a committee of 535 individuals, no matter how well intentioned, can offer what is needed in actions like the Beirut troop deployments.[33]

Secretary of State Shultz weighed in as well during this campaign-year counterattack against Hill restraints. He told the Senate Appropriations Committee the same week that Congress was overreaching its foreign policy powers. "There has to be a capacity for decisiveness under certain circumstances. There has to be an ability to go along without being constantly undercut, or surrounded by so many conditions that you don't have much room for maneuver."[34]

This combative Reagan administration stance succeeded for a time in arresting the erosion of presidential powers in foreign policy. Indeed, the power of initiative was regained by the assertive executive branch team. In his first term, President Reagan prevailed on a host of issues. Military aid to El Salvador was vastly expanded, and arms began to flow to the Nicaraguan Contras. The President pressed ahead with the B-1 bomber and the Strategic Defense Initiative (SDI, or "Star Wars"), while nearly doubling defense spending. He pushed through the Saudi AWACS sale and escaped virtually any criticism for his handling of the Beirut disaster. In contrast to the Carter years, there were virtually no major diplomatic successes in the first four years of Reagan's tenure, save for maintenance of the INF deployment schedule. But President Reagan was enormously successful in articulating general ideological principles, then sticking firmly to them. For example, the President committed early on to a strategy of stressing economic issues and rearmament while directing a steady stream of critical rhetoric at the Soviet Union and putting arms reductions negotiations on hold. While the Soviets stumbled through a succession of leadership crises and worry mounted in Moscow about the Pentagon's weapons-buying spree, the White House took increasingly bold risks in Central America and the Middle East. The President demonstrated a desire to "go it alone" internationally. Unilateralism reached new heights at the United Nations and in the World Court, where the administration dismissed anti-U.S. votes and unfavorable opinions. If its international accomplishments were modest, however, the Reagan administration's bullish nationalism delighted the U.S. electorate. As one commentator summarized this "feel good" approach to diplomacy:

> It is foreign policy by public opinion poll, and in many ways it works. The country is happy. . . . The problem is that the undisciplined and ad hoc style of the Reagan Administration makes it hard to achieve any breakthroughs. It's surprising, in fact, how little this strong and popular president has been able to accomplish.[35]

Eventually, President Reagan's problems on Capitol Hill began to mount. Despite efforts to involve selected congressional leaders in bipartisan commissions, criticism from legislators soon became severe. The usually restrained and relatively conservative Senate Majority Leader Byrd was by 1984 pointedly accusing the administration of shattering hopes for genuine partnership and bipartisan cooperation:

> They just don't accept the fact that Congress has a constitutional role in the formulation and implementation of foreign policy. You have top people in the administration denigrating the role of the Congress, questioning the patriotism of those in Congress who would differ. . . . I've never seen an administration so partisan, so political, so arrogant.[36]

Such bitterness ensured that the opportunities for bipartisan cooperation with Congress were limited by the end of the first term—well before the Iran-Contra scandal shattered White House credibility and weakened the President's ability to conduct diplomatic initiatives. The administration did enjoy some success with conservative southern Democrats (so-called "boll weevils") on Central America issues. Staunchly anticommunist, members of this bloc provided reliable support in a series of crucial Contra aid funding requests. But waning support for the Contras and internal Democratic Party politics eventually shattered this modest bipartisan alliance. On key defense and arms control issues, the administration benefited for a time from the support of key Democrats like Byrd and Nunn, whose support for funding of programs like SDI ensured that opponents would remain in the minority. But Pentagon obstinance on issues like Star Wars funding, SALT II compliance, and ABM Treaty interpretation finally led these key Democrats to break with the administration in 1986 and to support legislative initiatives against White House policies. The severe blow of the Iran-Contra affair foreclosed other opportunities for legislative-executive cooperation, leaving the administration to address each major foreign policy issue on an ad hoc basis. When the administration finally did begin in its last months to make breakthroughs with the Soviets on INF negotiations, few reliable lines of communication with the Hill remained open. And there was little basis for building on the bipartisan support this modest treaty gained.

The Reagan years saw an increased resort to procedural gimmicks designed to win Hill support for diplomatic initiatives. The President nurtured his winning image by doing whatever was necessary at the last minute to avoid defeat. "What you read in the papers is that Reagan won on 'x' vote," explained Reagan's White House aide Kenneth Duberstein during one battle. "What you don't read in the headlines—or watch on network news—are the conditions Congress incorporated in the Reagan win."[37] Time after time the White House would seem to pull a rabbit out of the hat. There was a last-minute presidential letter on the 1981 Saudi AWACS sale. There was an executive order implementing limited antiapartheid sanctions on the eve of a 1986 Senate vote to override the President's veto of an anti-apartheid measure. There were the bipartisan commissions hastily assembled when MX funding and Contra aid faced congressional defeats. Several operational principles governed here. The White House was determined to do whatever was necessary to avoid the "loser" tag, to give undecided members a public justification for coming down on the President's side, and to put results and public opinion ahead of any concerns about the purity of the policymaking process.

The elevation of political expediency to an art form won the Reagan administration many legislative victories. Throughout its early years, the Reagan team succeeded in forcing members of Congress to balk when confronted with determined and imaginative executive branch adversaries. President Reagan was forced to compromise on a number of foreign policy issues. But rarely were his proposals rejected outright on the Hill. This strategy ensured that great violence would be done to the process by which policy is made. Foreign partners were often at a loss to predict how proposals would emerge from the legislative gauntlet. And the jerry-built structures erected by the administration's congressional lobbyists offered little certainty for subsequent Hill tests; one could never be confident of their staying power. It was a method of presidential governance that invited renewed conflict with each legislative cycle. The fact is that issues like the MX, SDI, SALT limits, Contra funding, and Middle East arms sales were fought bitterly on Capitol Hill almost every single year of the Reagan presidency. Few lasting victories were won. And the battle lines along Pennsylvania Avenue became as entrenched as ever.

These recent experiences ably demonstrate both the virtues and the limitations of procedural expediency. They serve also to demonstrate the importance of the president maintaining unity within the executive branch while securing a winning reputation on Capitol Hill—key aspects of successful White House diplomacy. Compromisers can prosper where ideological purists meet with frustration. And as we shall see in both our analysis of the modern Congress and our subsequent review of key policy disputes, tolerance for imaginative winning strategies is just as important as the definition of clear priorities. Recent history suggests that the president can benefit significantly from both legislative flexibility and the establishment of a modest, realistic agenda. Only then can the White House manage change adroitly—only then can the president respond to the complex international crises of the modern era with two feet on the ground.

NOTES

1. Senator Thomas Eagleton, testimony before Senate Foreign Relations Committee, Special Subcommittee on War Powers, July 13, 1988, p. 15.
2. John Tower, "Congress Versus the President," *Foreign Affairs* 60 (Winter 1981-1982): 34.
3. "President's Press Conference of January 11, 1951," *Public Papers of the Presidents: Harry S. Truman, 1951-1952*, p. 20.
4. Dick Cheney, as quoted in *Washington Post*, September 2, 1984, p. 17. Cheney was elected to the House as a Wyoming Republican after serving in the executive branch.
5. Theodore Roosevelt, as quoted in *Works of Theodore Roosevelt*, p. 57.
6. Congressman Thomas P. Foley, as quoted in Brzezinski, *Power and Principle*, p. 7.
7. See Neustadt, *Presidential Power.*
8. The television can also be unforgiving: President Ford's awkward comments suggesting that Poland was free of Soviet domination, viewed by millions of voters during the 1976 presidential debates, may have cost him the election. Exploitation of the medium for political purposes has been blasted even by senior executive branch officials. Secretary of State Alexander Haig complained in 1981 of the proclivity of Reagan officials "to view the presidency as a public relations opportunity and to regard Government as a campaign for reelection" (as quoted in Destler, et al., *Our Own Worst Enemy*, p. 13).
9. During the months the Iran-Contra scheme was unfolding, Congress received false testimony from a host of officials, including CIA Director William Casey and national security advisers Robert McFarlane and Admiral John Poindexter.

10. See Arthur Schlesinger, Jr., speech to January 30, 1987 conference of the Georgetown Center for Strategic and International Studies.

11. Democrat Dennis DeConcini of Arizona was one senator who complained publicly about such tactics.

12. As a GOP moderate, Baker faced a familiar problem of trying to win Republican primaries while advocating improved relations with the Soviets. He chose to take a hard line against SALT II as he geared up for the 1980 campaign, singling out the treaty's tolerance of a Soviet advantage in the subcategory of heavy missiles.

13. Theodore Roosevelt, as quoted in Franck, *Tethered Presidency*, pp. 47–48.

14. As quoted by Justice Robert Jackson in *Youngstown Sheet and Tube Company v. Sawyer*, 345 U.S. 579 (1952). See also Josephy, *American Heritage History of Congress*, p. 3.

15. *United States v. Curtiss-Wright Export Corporation et al.*, 299 U.S. 304 (1936).

16. Ralph Huitt, as quoted in Mann and Ornstein, *New Congress*, p. 231.

17. Senator Daniel Evans, speech to January 30, 1987 conference of the Georgetown Center for Strategic and International Studies, p. 6. Former Senator William J. Fulbright similarly complained in 1979 that "it is not easy for us to decide upon and follow a foreign policy consistent with our own national interest when so many of our people and our legislators have deep emotional attachments to other countries which have interests different from ours" (William J. Fulbright, "The Legislator as Educator," *Foreign Affairs* 57 [Spring 1979] : 721).

18. Stanley J. Heginbotham, "Dateline Washington: The Rules of the Game," *Foreign Policy* 53 (Winter 1983–1984): 157–58.

19. Rubin, *Secrets of State*, p. 34.

20. Sorensen, *Kennedy*, p. 322.

21. Spiro Agnew, as quoted in Destler, et al., *Our Own Worst Enemy*, p. 147. Agnew termed this strategy of attacking even members of Nixon's own executive branch "the politics of positive polarization."

22. See Gerard C. Smith's book *Doubletalk* about the SALT I negotiating experience. After SALT I was ratified, the ACDA bureaucracy was thoroughly purged by the White House staff, which feared it was "soft" on the Soviets.

23. Harry Truman, as quoted in Miller, *Plain Speaking*, p. 84.

24. Neither Seward nor Byrnes fared particularly well at State. Seward never enjoyed Lincoln's full confidence—though he was attacked by the Booth assassins, who feared that Seward would assume governing power upon Lincoln's death. Byrnes was edged out of the State post by Truman, who found his proud independence intolerable.

25. Richard C. Holbrooke, "Stop the Ruinous Turf Wars Over Foreign Policy," *New York Times*, August 2, 1987, p. 23.

26. Rubin, *Secrets of State*, p. viii.

27. Brzezinski, *Power and Principle*, p. 5.

28. Hamilton and Van Dusen, "Making the Separation of Powers Work," p. 32.

29. Senator Lister Hill (D-AL), *Congressional Record*, July 9, 1947, p. S8506.

30. Douglas Bennet (Assistant Secretary of State for Congressional Relations), "Congress in Foreign Policy: Who Needs It?" *Foreign Affairs* 57 (Fall 1978): 45.

31. As cited in Heginbotham, "Dateline Washington," pp. 165–68. The key case studies forming the basis for conclusions on consultation failures were the Turkish arms embargo, the Rhodesia chrome ban, the 1979 withdrawal of recognition of Taiwan, and the 1981 Saudi arms sale.

32. Walter Mondale interview of January 20, 1981, *Washington Post*, September 2, 1984, p. 17.

33. *Presidential Documents: Ronald Reagan*, week of April 2, 1984, p. 13.

34. George Shultz, as quoted in *Washington Post*, March 29, 1984, p. 6.

35. David Ignatius, *Washington Post*, September 14, 1986, p. F4.

36. Senator Robert Byrd, as quoted in *Washington Post*, September 2, 1984, p. 17.

37. Kenneth Duberstein, as quoted in ibid.

4 LEGISLATING FOREIGN POLICY
The Congressional Challenge to Executive Authority

The imperial presidency, in the wake of Vietnam and Watergate, seems to have fallen as fast as it rose, while those of us [in Congress] who prodded what seemed to be a hopelessly immobile herd of cattle a decade ago now stand back in awe in the face of a stampede.

—Senator William J. Fulbright, 1979[1]

Post-Watergate Congressional bravado had a way of sputtering out in the face of a crisis. . . . It was Congress that turned out to be helpless. In foreign policy, the inclination is to let the Presidency have the responsibility—and the power.

—Arthur J. Schlesinger, Jr., 1986[2]

As the debate rages over whether the authority of the modern Congress in foreign affairs has grown too strong or too timid, a popular misunderstanding persists at the heart of the dispute. There is a widespread failure to appreciate the distinction between policy *formulation* and policy *implementation:* the difference between defining a national objective and executing instructions to achieve this goal. The latter function is purely administrative. Here the responsibility is entirely the president's, as even the most assertive legislators would concede. For as Thomas Jefferson, the great skeptic of presidential powers, noted, "The conduct of diplomacy is a function altogether executive."[3] But diplomacy—the management of day-to-day direct communication with foreign governments—must be differentiated from policymaking. The debate over the U.S. course in foreign affairs is an essentially political dispute. Policy is to be thrashed out by members of both the executive and legislative branches, who must struggle in the political arena to define the national purpose. The Congress has an obligation to be centrally involved in determining the American role in the world. The assertion of this right, however, has proven a difficult and inelegant task throughout American history—especially as the modern Congress has struggled to keep pace with expanding presidential powers in an age of U.S. global leadership.

Most members of Congress bear a chip on their shoulder when it comes to foreign affairs. Presidents are the nation's leading diplomats. They go to summits and sign treaties. Presidents give the prime-time speeches, prosecute the wars, and earn credit for keeping the peace, giving rise to tremendous jealousy on the Hill as they fly about on Air Force One with its princely trappings.[4] Congress usually must act more like a review board that remains open to the charge of obstructionism while it evaluates executive initiatives. Out of frustration, members push to involve themselves in micromanaging implementation. "Congress is still far too deeply into policy execution," Congressman Lee Hamilton has conceded. "This has come about because of a hangover of frustration over having not been adequately consulted."[5] Yet traditional and practical restraints on the legislative conduct of diplomacy leave Congress with a fundamentally reactive role in international matters. As a consequence, most congressional input on a given foreign policy controversy smacks of the second-guessing of a Monday morning quarterback.

Constitutional scholar Louis Koenig summarized this dilemma brilliantly in his discussion of the Constitution's "invitation to the struggle." Congress is so often relegated to "followership" because "in the interbranch struggles over the concurrent powers, advantage most often lies with the branch that outraces the other in taking the initiative; whoever gets there first prevails. Generally, the President has run faster than the Congress and therefore usually occupies a far greater sector."[6] This question of initiative lies at the heart of the interbranch dispute. The weak efforts of the Continental Congress to conduct a dialogue-by-committee with foreign leaders made clear the importance of having a single voice for the nation in international affairs. The presidency was originally conceived under the Articles of Confederation as a sort of ambassadorship to represent the Congress and the nation in the conduct of diplomacy. But the Constitution gave the president greater responsibility for initiative in negotiating treaties, appointing ambassadors, requesting appropriations, and commanding troops. With these powers of initiative in the executive, it has fallen to Congress to review and ratify, to alter on the margin, or to obstruct—but not often to lead in charting the course for U.S. international relations.

Contrast the nature of the foreign policymaking battle with domestic affairs. On all sorts of national issues, Congress takes the lead. In recent decades, Capitol Hill has been far ahead of White House initiatives in such areas as civil rights, health policy, space exploration, and environmental protection. Yet unlike debate over domestic programs, Congress rarely succeeds in initiating new departures in American foreign policy. Rather, the institution is prone to react to presidential initiatives already under way. True, there is a bit of a chicken-or-egg problem here: often the president seizes an idea that has long been advocated in Congress and makes it a cause of his own. For example, President Kennedy made establishment of the Peace Corps and the Arms Control and Disarmament Agency important elements of his White House legislative agenda. Yet these were ideas long propounded on Capitol Hill by Senators Hubert Humphrey and Clairborne Pell, among others. In this sense, Congress is an incubator, providing a fertile environment for developing and testing ideas. Yet when these ideas are successfully marketed, the political payoff often flows to the man in the Oval Office.

Congress finds itself on the defensive especially in matters relating to treaties and troop deployments, where its powers are essentially those of the veto. Since the last congressional declaration of war in December 1941, Congress has reviewed major U.S. troop deployments only after the fact. Similarly, the Senate receives treaties to which the president has already committed his signature and the nation's prestige. There is then tremendous pressure on the Senate, for it can block the presidential initiative only by withdrawing what most foreign partners are led to believe is already a national commitment of the American people. The Senate has not been hesitant to challenge treaties and to offer reservations to resolutions of ratification. But presidents consistently choose to present treaties to Congress as fait accomplis—and then to dare the Senate to dissent from this new reality.[7]

In confrontations over war powers, it has proven far more difficult to vote against the White House. Such a vote is too easily characterized as a vote for retreat, for surrender of ground that has already been won under presidential initiative. As the late Senator Richard Russell liked to explain, "Once the troops are committed, the die is cast. The flag is there. You don't vote to bring the flag back once the boys are in the trenches."[8] Congress is more likely to ratify a military or diplomatic decision after some nibbling at the margins. The pressures against "cutting and running" or withdrawing under fire limit congressional reservations. For example, Congress avoided any decisive votes for months after President Reagan deployed troops in Beirut, and later, warships in the Persian Gulf. No matter how great the misgivings on Capitol Hill, Congress has proven unlikely to force the president's hand. Yet Hill debates have certainly raised questions at home and abroad about American staying power.

In key matters of war and peace, the congressional role remains a strikingly awkward one. Brinksmanship is a poor way to shape policy options: it elevates procedure at the expense of substance and makes policy disputes more a battle of wills than a search for wisdom. And there is still no consensus on which branch is exceeding its limits. A former legislator like Fulbright could argue in 1979 that Congress was being excessive in tying the president's hands; less than a decade later, a former champion of executive power like Arthur Schlesinger, Jr. complained that legislators were too weak and timid.[9] Indeed, virtually every recent U.S. foreign policy controversy has been accompanied by some background noise about who is usurping whose prerogatives, about the alleged restoration of the imperial presidency, or about the dangers, as one exasperated senator put it in the 1987 Persian Gulf debate, "of the Senate acting like 535 secretaries of state, not to mention 535 commanders in chief."[10] Americans still cannot argue the substance of foreign policy without resorting to debate over the process by which it is decided.

THE LEGISLATIVE GAUNTLET

Presidents come and presidents go. But Congress remains as a living institution—many of its members serving alongside five or six different administrations. It is these senior members who are ultimately most skilled at assaulting executive branch initiatives and prolonging the legislative gauntlet. The number of procedural tools with which Congress can wield influence at times seems infinite, and Congress itself an endless maze full of traps and delays. The system that results is anything but efficient. This, however, was the constitutional design. "The doctrine of separation of powers was adopted by the convention of 1787, not to promote efficiency," Justice Louis Brandeis explained, "but to preclude the exercise of arbitrary power."[11] There was never any guarantee or requirement that this shared authority would function smoothly. Indeed, as Alexander Hamilton, a champion of a strong executive, explained, "In the legislature, promptitude of decision is oftener an evil than a benefit. The differences of opinion, though they may sometimes obstruct salutary plans, yet often promote deliberation and circumspection, and serve to check excesses."[12]

Congress asserts influence over foreign policymaking by a number of means. Congress can press specific concerns to the forefront, forcing them onto the president's negotiating agenda—as when pressure in the early 1970s from champions of Soviet Jewry forced linkage of the emigration issue to improvement in U.S.-Soviet trade relations. Congress can initiate debate on alternatives to the president's prescribed course of action—as when legislators' support for the 1987 Arias/Contadora peace plan in Central America undermined support for Reagan administration Contra aid funding requests. And Congress can reflect popular sentiment that the president should initiate a new diplomatic campaign—as when the nuclear freeze movement prodded the Reagan Administration to resume U.S.-Soviet arms reduction talks in the 1980s.

Congress has a vast number of opportunities for altering presidential initiatives. It is very rare that Congress rejects a White House foreign policy initiative outright. Yet legislators are determined to have an effect on White House proposals—to alter them on the margin, if only to assert their jurisdiction and exercise their prerogatives. "A favorite word in Congress is 'conditionality,'" White House congressional lobbyist Kenneth Duberstein explained in 1984. "Congress likes to always have a little bit of a hedge, a little bit of a hook, to keep their jurisdiction."[13] A sage executive branch strategy is thus anticipating these changes and ensuring that they are advanced by legislators who will be able to command a majority position for the essence of the president's proposal. How exactly does Congress work such conditions into U.S. foreign policy initiatives? Following is a summary of the key tools with which legislators can place their imprimatur on American foreign policy.

Authorization and Appropriation of Funds. The power of the purse remains the most potent weapon available to legislators, and it is in the authorizing and appropriating process that most legislative forays are made against executive branch proposals. Congress can add money for a program it favors, cut it, or "zero it out" altogether. And legislators get several different cracks at an issue because of the telescoping of the process, which the many-layered Hill budget review system ensures. For example, the 1981 Reagan administration proposal for a new $3.6 billion aid program for Pakistan required first a waiver of prohibitions on aid to the Pakistanis that had been established on nuclear nonproliferation grounds. The request then had to secure favorable votes to authorize the spending program in both the House and Senate foreign affairs committees. The authorization bill then faced debate in both the full House and Senate and a prospective conference committee to iron out differences; votes on the conference report in both chambers followed. Then the entire process had to be repeated through the appropriations panels and the full House and Senate in order to secure funds for the program. At any step of the way, a majority of legislators could have voted to change the entire nature of the program and a willful minority could have stalled it—perhaps killing it altogether.

Legislative Riders. Only a small fraction of the thousands of bills introduced each Congress are brought to a vote.[14] But many of the rest enjoy new life as "riders": amendments to spending measures destined for the president's desk. The slow movement of an enormous foreign aid authorization or appropriation bill through Congress leaves it vulnerable to amendment. Members often attach provisions the White House may not favor but chooses to accept because the absence of a line-item veto means that a bill signing is an all-or-nothing proposition. Legislators thus offer unwelcome riders on the most certain vehicle available—a "sure train" unlikely to be vetoed because it contains funding for programs desperately sought by the White House, like an end-of-the-fiscal-year, catchall appropriations measure. Thus do Congress and the president often engage in a game of legislative chicken; many times in the past decade the government has technically run out of funds as the Hill and the White House argued over riders to an emergency continuing resolution (CR) which continues funding of government agencies at the previous year's levels. The most prominent example was the Boland amendment to the 1984 CR, which barred any U.S. government funding of the Contras. If the measure had been freestanding, it would have been vetoed—and there was not a two-thirds majority in Congress to override. But as part of an emergency CR, the amendment survived because of the President's reluctance to bring U.S. government operations to a halt.

Reviewing Arms Sales and Nuclear Exports.   Congress acted in the 1970s to provide itself a major role in approving export licenses for sensitive nuclear technology and military hardware. The threat of a resolution disapproving a specific export proposal gives members considerable power over key security and trade relationships. The Arms Export Control Act (AECA) affords any single member the power to obtain a record vote on approving any major arms sale. And there are safeguards to prevent delaying tactics in the Senate, such as filibusters. But Congress no longer has the power to block exports by a simple majority vote on a concurrent resolution. The 1983 Supreme Court decision *INS v. Chadha* struck down this legislative veto provision.[15] Now Congress must adopt a joint resolution to oppose an arms sale—a resolution that will be presented to the president and presumably vetoed. Then Congress must override the veto by a two-thirds majority in both houses in order to bar an export.

Legislative Initiatives.   Congress does have the power to accomplish many objectives independent of executive branch proposals. And legislators are by no means timid in advancing their own ideas: some 8,404 separate bills were introduced in the 99th Congress. Those foreign policy measures that survive the legislative process and become law are often reduced to exhortations only—statements of U.S. hopes and concerns that have no binding effect, no legal bite. Senator Fulbright even created a special vehicle for legislators to vent such ideas—the State Department authorization bill. Yet some Hill legislative proposals do survive largely intact. For example, the 1986 South Africa sanctions measure was a creature of Congress and was ultimately passed over President Reagan's veto. Such a measure follows a direct legislative track from committee hearings and "markup" (a line-by-line consideration and vote) to floor action in both chambers. The process is never simple, however, as measures are subject to delay both in the House Rules Committee and on the Senate floor, where there is an omnipresent threat that the bill will be talked to death—a filibuster can be broken only by a vote of sixty senators. And legislation is often delayed by referral to more than one committee. The banking committees played a major role in the South Africa issue because of their jurisdiction over export restrictions; the Senate Armed Services Committee had a major impact upon the 1979 SALT II Treaty debate; and the 1987 trade bill was handled by more than a dozen separate committees of the House and Senate— everything from agriculture to judiciary to government operations.

Senate Powers on Treaties and Ambassadors. The Senate jealously guards its authority to consent to treaty ratification—and the House has been consistently assertive in trying to define its role in funding treaty implementation ever since the Jay Treaty. But also of considerable importance is the Senate's influence over the appointment of ambassadors to negotiate overseas. In some nomination challenges, the personal qualifications of the president's appointee are genuinely at issue and senators become investigators. More often, the debate is really about policy and the unfortunate nominee in the hot seat is merely a pawn in a political game.[16] Senators seek White House concessions on policy as the price of confirmation votes. Senators suspicious of White House policies will use confirmation hearings to issue very public warnings or to recommend policy alternatives. "Sending a message" was the primary motive of challenges to the nomination of Charles Bohlen in 1953 as ambassador to the Soviet Union, of Paul Warnke as SALT negotiator in 1977, and of Leonard Woodcock as ambassador to the People's Republic of China in 1979. In the cases of the 1981 nomination of Ernest W. Lefever to be assistant secretary of state for human rights and the 1982 nomination of Kenneth Adelman as head of the Arms Control and Disarmament Agency, critics of White House policies questioned both the nominees' qualifications and the administration's sincerity in supporting the missions of the two agencies. Bitter personal confrontations erupted on the Hill. Adelman was opposed by the Senate Foreign Relations Committee, but rescued by the GOP-controlled Senate on a narrow 57–42 vote. Lefever was rejected 13–5 in committee and chose to withdraw. And even under a Republican president, Senate conservatives pressed their own agenda in challenging Reagan nominees: Senator Jesse Helms used his position as senior Republican on the foreign relations panel to delay numerous ambassadorial nominees, holding their approval hostage to administration concessions on a broad array of policy and personnel issues.

Congressional Resolutions. The legislators can "go on record" with foreign policy concerns—without bargaining for the president's signature—by pressing a concurrent resolution. These provide members with political cover at home (going on record on an issue) while, ideally, having considerable impact in foreign capitals. A congressional resolution opposing a beleaguered dictator in Panama, or another in support of a nascent democratic regime in the Philippines, often become front-page news overseas, even though such "motherhood" resolutions usually sweep through the Congress with great dispatch and a minimum of discussion. In rare instances, congressional resolutions have been provided for by law as a means of revisiting a legislative controversy. For example, when Congress became bogged down in a series of contentious debates in the early 1980s over the basing mode for the MX missile, parties to the controversy agreed that future funding requests would be reviewed with a simple up-or-down vote on a resolution with "expedited procedures": provisions ensuring that no delaying tactics would be permitted. In such a procedural maneuver, monies are often "fenced," that is, set aside for later use, subject to congressional approval by resolution. Such fencing tactics were used repeatedly to defer Hill confrontations over Contra aid and the MX missile in the latter part of the Reagan administration.

Consultation and Oversight. Adept use of the gavel affords committee chairmen many opportunities to influence policy short of proposing new statutes. Hearings by Congress to monitor existing programs or to review administration policies can substantially alter the debate on policy alternatives. The Senate's Watergate Committee hearings of 1973 and the joint hearings of the Iran-Contra committees had no legislative proposals before them, instead, these committees pursued investigations designed to fulfill the Hill's oversight responsibilities. Such proceedings afford important opportunities to shape future options and educate the public while scoring points for or against administration initiatives. Advance consultation provides another opportunity for key legislators to weigh in with their views; when the president does choose to consult with Congress, an important process of negotiation takes place. A key legislator can alter policy by threatening to oppose it unless one element is changed. A lawmaker can make a preemptive strike by building public opposition to a proposal before it is announced—or, as is so often the case in bureaucratic disputes within the executive branch, by leaking the most extreme version of the proposal to the media and then manipulating the ensuing public outcry to ensure that the initiative is still-born. Senior legislators also retain total control over scheduling of Hill debates. A chairman of a foreign affairs committee who is intent on aiding Greece can fast-track his proposals; an opponent of a nuclear freeze resolution might bottle up the measure in his committee indefinitely. And timing in considering a Hill initiative can be decisive. For example, a majority leader determined to force a South Africa sanctions measure upon the White House might wait until the morning after a new crackdown in Pretoria to schedule a Senate floor vote; or a House Speaker might block a rule for floor consideration of a Contra funding measure until after a wave of anti-Sandinista furor sparked by news developments out of Managua dies down. Legislators remain greatly influenced by the daily headlines; in efforts to win a close vote, timing is often everything. Thus, threats, concessions, and scheduling delays become part of the bargaining process between the White House and Congress.

CONGRESS AND THE ELECTORATE

The procedural tools that the modern Congress has perfected are used with great effect to shape policy. But no single procedure is more important in forging American foreign policy than the central characteristic of the legislative institution itself. Simply put, Congress is an extraordinarily representative body. With uncanny precision, Congress reflects the way power is distributed in the American electorate—not the ideal way that power would be distributed in a perfect democracy, but the way it actually is in contemporary America. Congress mirrors the underrepresentation of women and most ethnic minorities in American society. It reflects the passions, the prejudices, and the parochial instincts of those who wield influence in the United States, from the grass-roots organizer to the "fat cat" fund-raiser, to the faceless "swing voter" who computer projections predict will sway the next election.

Far more than the executive branch, Congress serves as a barometer of public opinion. While some members seem to stay forever—incumbents handily win more than 95 percent of elections—the policy views of members seem to change more rapidly. The veterans on Capitol Hill are survivors who have proven remarkably adaptable to changes in public sentiment. By contrast, the White House often has more rigid, short-term goals. In recent years, each president has tended to cite his election as a specific mandate for every policy from A to Z—ignoring the fact that the quadrennial poll comes down to just an either-or choice under the two-party system. The White House view of the executive power at times approaches an electoral kingship, with the president acting as some type of a national sovereign free to lead in any direction, subject only to a single plebiscite after a four-year term. By constitutional design, Congress is a far more representative and responsive institution. Elections every two years for House members and the modern requirements for virtually nonstop fund-raising by senators keep legislators in remarkably close touch with voter sentiments.

The conventional wisdom is that Americans vote their pocketbooks; political scientists often argue that economic issues play a far more central role in shaping election results than international concerns. But this is true only to a limited extent. Foreign policy issues are of such great volatility that they can overwhelm pedestrian debates over familiar domestic issues. Indeed, international issues like Vietnam, Central America, and U.S.-Soviet relations have fueled many recent presidential primary campaigns—including challenges to incumbents from within their own parties. The emotional intensity of questions regarding war and peace and patriotism is crucial to campaign activists. Issues like support for Israel and aid to the Contras help raise funds. Issues like arms control get out the volunteers and bring voters to the polls. And for all the domestic concerns about the economy, the environment, and social issues, a foreign policy crisis can have an electrifying effect on voters on the eve of an election. At such times, a private decision in the polling booth or a public declaration at a campaign rally provides voters a most tangible way to express their sentiments. Congress thus remains very close to the voters on emotional foreign policy issues.[17]

Congressional involvement in shaping U.S. foreign policy has thereby produced a central truism: no presidential foreign policy initiative can succeed over the long term unless it garners the support of the American people through their elected representatives in Congress. Or, as Averell Harriman stated the proposition, "No foreign policy will stick unless the American people are behind it. And unless Congress understands it the American people aren't going to understand it."[18] In this sense, the Congress holds not just the practical veto power of controlling military expenditures or reviewing treaties, but a substantial power to shape national thinking. Ideally, the public airing of views in Congress provides an important opportunity for public education and construction of the solid base of support essential to the long-term success of any policy initiative—as occurred, for example, in the debate over the Panama Canal treaties, when a wildly unpopular proposition was sold to the American people by convincing their representatives in Washington. In a related manner, private consultation affords what one senior official has called the "scrubbing of options," which is crucial to sound policymaking.[19] Indeed, Congress has offered the common sense necessary to avoid a number of potential fiascos, from Dien Bien Phu to the "dense-pack" plan for MX basing.

When they work together, Congress and the president can use each other to their mutual benefit. The president can use the obligation of congressional review to make legislators complicit in a controversial policy decision—as with, for example, the 1981 arms sale to Saudi Arabia—thereby reducing the heat on the White House for pursuing a risky course. The same is true of troop deployments pursuant to the War Powers Resolution: involving Congress can deepen the national commitment while spreading political accountability in case something goes terribly wrong.

Conversely, Congress can make its approval of presidential initiatives contingent upon compromise. Congress employed this model in the early 1980s to sharply curtail the MX missile construction program while winning White House support for more aggressive arms reduction negotiation efforts and research on the new Midgetman missile. This process can work for those on both ends of Pennsylvania Avenue. It is only when Congress is misled by the president, or when Congress fails to produce a clear and consistent position, that the process inevitably breaks down.

Sage leaders in Congress recognize that sometimes they do not want to win every confrontation, that sometimes they do not want to succeed when they challenge a presidential initiative. They understand the value of prevailing over one aspect of policy—of trimming the policy on the margin and introducing new conditions on its execution while they may be "losing" the key vote. "Congressional victory is achieved when restrictive legislation loses," one analyst explains, "but Congress extracts some policy compromise."[20] For example, in 1980 the Hill's lead advocate of strict nuclear export controls, Democratic Congressman Jack Bingham of New York, narrowly lost a vote to bar new nuclear fuel shipments to India. But in the process, Bingham exacted a pledge from the Carter administration to renegotiate its nuclear fuel supply agreement with India—while serving notice on the Indian government that there was stiff opposition on the Hill to business as usual. This type of "good cop, bad cop" routine requires the maturity to understand that losing is winning if a message is delivered. It is essential to recognize in this respect that since adopting the new laws in the mid-1970s, Congress has yet to enact any measure barring a proposed arms sale or nuclear export. Yet legislators have had a chilling effect on numerous proposals and have profoundly altered the direction of executive branch policy and diplomatic negotiations. Without formally blocking anything, Congress has completely changed the nature of the debate on sensitive exports.

Genuine leadership requires action that sometimes moves against popular sentiment. Government by referendum has its limits. No nation can afford, as Cyrus Vance once declared, to have a "foreign policy which is hostage to the emotions of the moment."[21] Voter education and a sustained effort to change national sentiments are sometimes required. Congress does not do this well; thus, such unpopular efforts usually fall to the executive. It is the White House that has repeatedly identified a compelling national interest in pursuing unpopular measures and produced what many consider the presidency's finest hours. The White House has demonstrated courage in pursuing controversial initiatives—ranging from FDR's efforts to curb the spread of Nazism to President Nixon's efforts to forge a new U.S. relationship with the People's Republic of China, to Jimmy Carter's effort to secure use of the Panama Canal through the 1978 treaties. Ronald Reagan demonstrated similar persistence and commitment to his principles in pressing for aid to the Nicaraguan opposition, even though it was never a cause embraced by the majority of American voters.

Congress has often challenged such bold initiatives because the legislature provides a reliable picture of a populace uncomfortable with world leadership. With infrequent exceptions, American voters and their representatives in Congress have tended towards isolationism. True, legislators have clamored for war upon occasion—against England in 1812, against Spain in 1898, or against Cuba in 1962. And some of America's most senseless, least defensible battles were ignited by war hawks in the Congress. But the electorate has been reluctant in most instances to make a sustained commitment of resources overseas. Thus, the challenge of maintaining a consensus behind international engagement has been a prolonged one. "Although a great power," Senator Dan Evans notes, "we have been dragged kicking and screaming into an active role in the international community."[22]

Congress has responded to this caution by carving up foreign aid requests, by shying away from support of U.S. military intervention overseas, and by virtually rejecting proposed multilateral arms reduction measures. In the mid-1980s, congressional aversion to international programs remained so substantial that even a publicly acclaimed budget-cutter like Ronald Reagan had to castigate Congress for slashing foreign aid funding requests. While piling on to the national deficit enormous Pentagon spending programs, Ronald Reagan had to defend against the inclination of Congress to hack away at requests for foreign military assistance, State Department operational funds, and multilateral development bank contributions.

While Congress has been alternately belligerent and isolationist over the years, it has also provided a crucial element of restraint. Few can argue that Reagan's Beirut troop commitments or MX deployment schemes did not warrant scrutiny, or that the unremitting anti-Soviet rhetoric of his early tenure was not open to question. Few can make the case that Carter's Korean troop withdrawal proposals did not deserve critique or that his Panama Canal treaties and SALT II proposals did not justify serious debate. Congress has also shown an admirable ability to reverse itself—curbing pressures in the 1970s for pulling troops out of NATO, or restoring aid to Turkey in order to secure U.S. access to valuable military facilities. And sometimes Congress does resist a wildly popular proposition advanced by the White House, showing wisdom and courage in the face of a heavy presidential selling campaign. For example, despite the enormous popularity of the idea of a "peace shield" against nuclear weapons, Congress in the mid-1980s voted a number of curbs on President Reagan's heavily sold Strategic Defense Initiative. Conversely, Congress fought to keep the B-1 bomber alive. And Congress has maintained U.S. support for multilateral diplomacy at the United Nations, despite assaults against the institution from a variety of quarters.

Congress has proven strikingly effective as a brake on many dubious international initiatives, as the Constitution's authors clearly intended. Its checking and balancing function is inherently conservative. It counsels caution against new foreign policy departures. To the frustration of many, the process often produces indecision, delay, or deferral. More rarely, it results in the rejection or abandonment of a presidential initiative—Wilson's League of Nations pact, Ford's Turkish aid proposals, Reagan's Jordan arms sale. But Congress will always be handicapped by its basic infirmity: its inability to put forward a coordinated foreign policy program to supplant those advanced by the executive. Bicameralism, fragmentation, and the diffusion of power remain formidable enemies of comprehensive planning. When Congress tries to address a host of international issues simultaneously, it ends up weighing one bill down with so many contradictory amendments that the U.S. Capitol resembles a modern Tower of Babel: "We are a cacophony of confusion," Senator John Danforth lamented as the chamber completed action on the heavily laden 1987 State Department authorization bill.[23]

THE MODERN CONGRESS: A SELF-"REFORMING" MAELSTROM

The continuing foreign policymaking struggle between the White House and Capitol Hill has been markedly altered by reforms made during the past two decades within the institution of Congress. Congress has changed more in the past twenty years than it did during the previous 180. While these changes affect issues across the board, their impact has been greatest upon the process of shaping international policy. The unique post–World War II years of relatively bipartisan consensus thrived upon a closed, hierarchical congressional system—a system that enforced unity on diplomatic issues. Yet in recent years, systemic change has made foreign policy an area where dissent affords individual legislators their best opportunity for publicity and policy impact. International affairs afford even the most junior member a chance to make his or her mark.

The breakdown of the closed congressional system began as an assault by the Kennedy White House on the anti-civil rights House Rules Committee—during a period when liberals controlled the White House and the Supreme Court but were faced with more conservative entrenched powers heading up key House committees.[24] Liberals were again at the forefront of efforts in the early 1970s to obtain more open deliberation and recorded votes on Vietnam War issues. Following President Nixon's August 1974 resignation under threat of impeachment, liberals put forward a series of amendments to the House and Senate rules. In December 1974, the Democratic caucus of the incoming 94th Congress undertook a series of internal reforms of the seniority system that set the pace for future colleagues. From that point forward, reform efforts developed a momentum of their own. Rank-and-file members clamored to make their own imprint on internal change—to continue the reform process—with almost every new Congress. "Reform" became an unquestioned virtue, an end unto itself.

But many of these efforts to open up the Congress proved a mixed blessing, bringing new problems even as old ones began to be resolved. For while the reforms have undoubtedly made congressional procedures more democratic, they have made the process of government infinitely more complicated. By the end of the 1980s, the legislative process had become so burdensome that many members—even the younger ones—began to look elsewhere for more satisfying work. Men like Paul Trible, Charles Mathias, Bill Brodhead, Lawton Chiles, Daniel Evans, and John Cavanaugh left Congress for a variety of professional and personal reasons. But each expressed a common complaint about the Byzantine maze that the legislative process has become. "Much of the important work of the nation doesn't seem to get done," explained Republican Senator Trible of Virginia, who stepped down at the age of forty-one. "The committee hearings, debates, filibusters and roll call votes go on and on and on."[25] Senator Evans underscored the difficulty in his valedictory; "We've gone from a Senate where power was concentrated in a few leaders to where there are 100 different power centers, and you can't accomplish much."[26] Suggestive of the depth and breadth of these changes on the Hill are the following figures:

Growth of Personal Staff. In the past three decades, staff in members' personal offices and congressional committees has grown from approximately 2,000 to more than 18,000. This has meant an increase in resources for combating executive branch initiatives, which is especially important in the foreign policy field, where congressional expertise had previously been lacking.[27]

Expansion of Research Capabilities. The creation of the Congressional Budget Office (CBO), the Congressional Research Service (CRS), and the Office of Technology Assessment (OTA) has augmented resources of the General Accounting Office (GAO) and provided Congress with another 10,000 support personnel to pursue investigations and draft policy initiatives.[28]

Increase in Recorded Votes. Changes in the congressional process led to many more recorded votes. The total number of House and Senate roll calls—most of which last at least fifteen minutes each—soared from 600 in the 1959–1960 session of Congress to a peak of more than 2,300 in 1979–1980.[29]

Proliferation of Subcommittees. Between 1960 and 1980, the total number of committee and subcommittee meetings more than doubled, from just over 5,000 in the 86th Congress to nearly 11,000 in the 96th.[30] New subcommittees were created with chairmen enjoying far more extensive powers than before. The explosion of subcommittees and the duplication of committee jurisdictions in the 1970s prompted a modest counterreform effort to spur consolidation. Yet today seventeen of twenty-two committees of the House still deal with some aspect of foreign policy, as do sixteen of nineteen full Senate committees.

Cost of Elections. While sessions of Congress have grown much longer and the volume of legislation has become much more burdensome, far more time must be spent away from Capitol Hill to raise campaign funds. CRS figures show the average House race cost $50,000 as late as 1974; in 1986 the average contested race ran closer to $260,000. Comparable Senate figures were $440,000 in 1974 versus $2.7 million in 1986.[31]

As a consequence of all these changes, today's Congress is a more fractured body, in which consensus on any issue is far more difficult to achieve. Party discipline has been shattered by the increasing freedoms offered junior members. The retirement rate has increased rapidly, despite the fact that incumbency has become an ever more certain guarantee of reelection. Institutional memory, while still superior to that of the political appointees in the executive branch, has been severely compromised. And the attention span of a typical member has grown ever shorter.[32] The explosion of staff resources has had a particularly fragmenting impact on members as aides have competed to gain attention. Endless legislative initiatives are proposed, but in some measure they are designed to justify staff salaries during those slow periods when Congress is in recess. As a result, members sense a loss of control. It seems everywhere there is "staff, staff, staff driving you crazy," Democratic Senator Ernest Hollings of South Carolina laments, "Nutty whiz kids!" The explosion reminded one-time White House aide Bryce Harlow of "millipedes crawling up the walls, coming out of every drawer."[33] An inevitable consequence is that more work has been created and less coordination is possible. Assertive Hill forays against executive branch diplomatic initiatives are now aggressively manned. Staff are "spilling off the Hill," alleges conservative commentator Patrick Buchanan, "and many see as their purpose in life the enfeeblement of the President of the United States in the conduct of an anticommunist foreign policy."[34]

Two new technological factors have accentuated the centrifugal forces at work on the legislature: the pervasiveness of television coverage and the obligations of virtually nonstop fund-raising. A savvy campaigner can build a week of speeches around one 16-second exchange in a televised hearing—which makes an ideal "bite" for television news coverage. For example, Senator Joe Biden's bid for the 1988 Democratic presidential nomination reaped substantial dividends from coverage of one sharp exchange he had with Secretary Shultz in July 1987 over the issue of how best to oppose apartheid. Similarly, when Senator Robert Dole engaged Sandinista dictator Daniel Ortega in a shouting match in Managua in late 1987, Dole was careful to ensure that his campaign aide captured the moment on film for political use back home. These crisp exchanges with unpopular adversaries can reap enormous dividends for computer-targeted, direct-mail fund-raising programs. Some legislators are therefore eager to cross swords with a bête noire of their particular constituency, be he Ted Kennedy or Jesse Helms. Members are also prone to give extended floor speeches—even to near empty chambers—so that they can use elaborate Republican and Democratic Party facilities to beam the footage back home by satellite for free publicity by local television stations.

A similar distraction from the process of consultation and cooperation on divisive international issues is the ever increasing demand for member travel—usually by air. Where thirty years ago a California legislator might return home from Washington once or twice a year, now a senator like Pete Wilson, faced with a tough reelection campaign, will cross the country and return at least once every *week*. Fund-raising requirements also bring members to states far from their home precincts; Los Angeles, Chicago, New York, and Miami have become required destinations for fund-raisers in most contested campaigns. Such travels have the benefit of sensitizing members to the views of more wealthy and politically influential voters. But they do little to contribute to coherent, consensus policymaking in Washington. Rather, the policymaking process has been skewed in favor of a handful of the most effectively organized lobbies—such as defense contractors, union bosses, and supporters of a handful of American allies abroad. In addition, the door has been opened to repeated scandals—from Koreagate to Abscam—in which members have been found guilty of taking money in return for pressing proposals beneficial to selected foreign governments. And it is now much more common for U.S. government officials who have enjoyed long access to U.S. military and diplomatic secrets to turn around and become lobbyists for such foreign clients as Saudi Arabia and Japan.

New resources have doubtless made members of Congress better informed and more effective politicians. Yet legislators are also more susceptible to interest group pressures, which make it harder to discern American objectives on international issues. Legions of lobbyists have descended on the Capitol in the 1980s in what one analyst has termed a "political gold rush."[35] At last count, there were more than 23,000. The resulting dilemma has been ably summarized by former Senator Fulbright:

> The modern legislator, with some admirable exceptions, has discarded the
> role of educator in favor of performing services for his constituents—and not

really his constituents as a community, but rather the best organized, best funded, and most politically active. . . . There has been a reversal of priority between policy and politics. The responsible legislator will begin with a policy or program that he believes to be in the national interest and may then resort to technique and salesmanship to win its enactment. The new breed of Congressperson seems more inclined to test the market first to ascertain what is in current demand, and then to design a program to fit the market.[36]

THE CAPITOL HILL PERSPECTIVE ON THE WORLD

The renewed assertiveness of the modern Congress—together with the explosion of news production—has reaped a publicity windfall for legislators. This increased scrutiny has in turn rendered members ever more jealous of their constitutional role in foreign policymaking. But Congress has not always risen to that challenge. Often, Congress chooses to avoid a tough decision, such as whether the wildly popular invasion of Grenada was consistent with the War Powers Resolution. Sometimes Congress takes sharply contradictory positions, as when it reversed itself twice in an 18-month period on the question of funding the Contras. On other occasions, Congress has backed down altogether, as when legislators failed after months of debate to take a clear stand on the wisdom of naval deployments in the Persian Gulf. The Congress is ever more insistent that its views be considered, however. "Consult with Congress first" has become a unifying refrain among modern legislators.

When Congress finally does address an international question, its perspective may be entirely different from that of executive branch officials. On Capitol Hill, goals are often more thematic and doctrinaire—opposing communism, promoting human rights, combating nuclear proliferation. Rhetorical objectives are often long-term. For example, there was much less concern in 1980 about souring U.S. bilateral relations with India over a nuclear fuel shipment than there was about advancing global efforts at nuclear nonproliferation. Similarly, congressional support for the proposition that it is unwise to arm the enemies of your allies has been a potent argument for pro-Israeli legislators in sinking Arab arms sales.

In the majority of recent foreign policy debates, there have been a host of legislators who relish confrontation. The press and the fund-raising community reward showdowns. The troublesome international consequences of the pitched interbranch battles that inevitably ensue fall in the lap of the executive. For example, in 1978 freshman Senator Dennis DeConcini insisted that Panama accept U.S. military defense of the Canal in the event of an emergency. Had insistence on this reservation ended up scuttling the treaties and leading to violence in the Canal Zone, it would have been the President's responsibility to address the resulting crisis and to act to protect American citizens. The handful of treaty critics would have had little immediate accountability for their actions; this is a luxury Congress enjoys to the great discomfort of the executive.

It is rare that a legislator is forced to bear consequences at the polls for thwarting an executive foreign policy initiative. In fact, the converse is true. A number of members have been successfully targeted for defeat because they *supported* an unpopular executive branch initiative. Senate Foreign Relations Committee Chairman Frank Church of Idaho backed the unpopular Panama Canal treaties and then lost his 1980 reelection bid. Church's committee successor, Charles Percy, championed President Reagan's 1981 Saudi arms sale and then was successfully targeted for defeat by supporters of Israel in his 1984 campaign. A similar fate befell Senator Roger Jepsen, a one-term Republican from Iowa. In 1981, he was an original author of a resolution opposing the sale of AWACS aircraft to Saudi Arabia. When the White House needed the vote of this Reagan loyalist, they called him down and threatened to withhold support for Jepsen's reelection unless he backed the White House. The resultant uproar over Jepsen's reversal was masterfully exploited by his Senate opponent, who made the question of Jepsen's flip-flop and lack of independence a major issue.[37] Today, independence from the White House—even when led by a president of one's own party—is quite often a virtue, not a handicap, in the polls.

THE LEGACY OF REFORM

Two hundred years after the ratification of the Constitution, Congress's role in U.S. foreign policymaking is as inexactly fixed as ever. Today the institution itself, especially the Senate, is ripe for new attempts at internal reform. Such efforts face formidable opposition. Yet it is noteworthy that virtually all candidates for Senate leadership posts in November 1988 made pledges to change the institution.

New reform efforts could have a substantial impact on its foreign policymaking role. Congress still muddles through on foreign policy. It rarely speaks with one voice, and it rarely resolves a controversial issue with finality. Reform has opened the process and ensured that differing views and minority opinions are fully aired. But changes in the way members are elected to Congress and lengthening of legislative reviews have made the process far less reliable.

The greatest difficulty confronting would-be reformers has been to ensure that congressional involvement in shaping foreign policy is both coordinated and timely. There has been increased reliance on expedited procedures to ensure prompt floor votes on controversial issues like arms sales and Contra funding. But prolonged policy reviews have too often made Congress not only uncertain of its position but too late to make a difference in any event; important policymaking prerogatives have thus been forfeited entirely to the executive branch. To be sure, delays can have merit. They allow time for passions to cool, for facts to become clear, and for new options to develop. But delays also diminish the relevance of Congress. For example, Congress has repeatedly balked at pressing war powers challenges in a timely fashion. Similarly, the repeated failure of the House and Senate foreign affairs committees to gain floor consideration of the annual aid authorization bill has diminished the influence of those committees. Since 1978, only two foreign aid bills have been signed into law. Because of opposition to foreign aid, because of controversial provisions adopted by the committees, and because these measures have developed a reputation as legislative "flypaper"— to which all sorts of mischievous and controversial foreign policy initiatives are attached—the measures have languished. Committee actions on controversies like aid to Pakistan, nuclear nonproliferation policy, the Greece-Turkey dispute, human rights conditions, and Philippine assistance have been rendered irrelevant by delay and lack of consensus. When foreign affairs–related legislation is finally put to debate in the House and Senate chambers, it often sinks under the weight of amendments proffered. The 1988 State Department authorization bill was pummeled in the Senate for four days, during which time a total of ninety-two amendments were advanced.

Some of these developments are a direct result of the fact that the once prestigious Senate Foreign Relations Committee has had its star tarnished. Increasingly, this historic panel is bypassed. The Senate Appropriations Committee has become the key source for funding international programs and defining program guidelines. Together with the Armed Services panel, the Appropriations Committee has been successful in repeatedly invading the jurisdiction of Foreign Relations. The Foreign Relations Committee has also suffered from a high turnover rate, having had six different chairmen in the past fourteen years as Senate control has twice switched parties and three foreign relations chairmen have lost reelection bids. Today the panel is larger than ever before, but its membership is more junior. And the committee has stumbled in recent tests ranging from Persian Gulf war powers to the handling of the Threshold Test Ban and Peaceful Nuclear Explosives treaties, to the failure to seize the Iran-Contra issue. Effective work on the INF Treaty did little to recoup these losses.

The House Foreign Affairs Committee has also lost some of the clout it gained from its assertiveness on funding issues during the 1970s. In the Reagan years, executive branch officials so strongly opposed amendments adopted in the House committee on issues like arms control and aid to Turkey and Pakistan that the administration opposed passage of any authorization bill. On other international security issues, like controversial arms sales or nuclear arms policy, Reagan administration lobbyists chose to write off the House altogether and to work exclusively with Republican forces in the Senate to sustain the President's position. Throughout this period, most of the foreign policy legislation in Congress has not come from the foreign affairs committees. Rather, it has been incorporated as part of the omnibus continuing resolution on appropriations that rolls disparate legislation into a $500 billion spending measure considered on the last night of the fiscal year by bleary-eyed legislators.

Reform has had another side effect unintended by its liberal, progressive proponents. There has been a marked rise in the number of conservative challenges to executive branch initiatives in foreign policy. At times the issues have been constitutional—as in 1979 when Senator Barry Goldwater and others challenged the legality of President Carter's withdrawal from the mutual security pact with the Republic of China. Sometimes conservatives have focused on military security, as when Senators Malcolm Wallop of Wyoming, Dan Quayle of Indiana, and others, tried to force the Pentagon to respond to alleged Soviet violations of the SALT I and ABM treaties. On other occasions, right-wing criticism has been more crassly political: in the mid-1980s, Senator Jesse Helms of North Carolina held up dozens of ambassadorial appointees, questioning their anticommunist credentials while pressuring the Reagan administration to place favored Helms personnel in senior posts.[38]

Empowering conservative dissenters has also led to repeated floor votes in recent years on such issues as cutting funding for the United Nations, multinational development banks, and international population control efforts. It is more difficult for congressional leaders to sidestep such uncomfortable issues. Special interest groups of widely ranging views, from the National Conservative Political Action Committee to the liberal Council for a Livable World and the American Civil Liberties Union, are often poised to make fund-raising mailings that grade legislators' votes days after such roll calls. Senator Helms and his colleagues in the informal Senate Conservative Caucus have had substantial impact upon Senate procedures, if not national policy. They have challenged the internationalist, pro-detente, pro-arms control wing of the Republican Party establishment as effectively as left-wing interest groups have pushed Democratic campaigners away from the more centrist positions of Democrats like "Scoop" Jackson, Hubert Humphrey, and Sam Nunn. More open debate in Congress has accelerated centrifugal forces that have divided the membership of both the Democratic and Republican parties. In the process, these debates have made a governing consensus on international issues ever more difficult to achieve.

Today the greatest challenge Congress faces in meeting its international policymaking responsibilities remains in war and peace issues. This is altogether appropriate. Here is where Congress's constitutional responsibilities are greatest, here is where its proximity to the electorate is most significant. Congress has struggled unsuccessfully to clarify its role. But it seems clear that legislators' success in asserting their prerogatives will be as much a product of the mood of the times as a consequence of constitutional precedent. In most cases, strong legislative leadership will restrain an executive only when the voters clamor for restraint. An assertive president will enjoy a strong hand only so long as he maintains popular backing.

The advent of a more democratic process for foreign policy debate has served a clear need by increasing executive branch accountability while reducing the opportunities for abuse of power by both cabinet officials and senior committee chairmen in Congress. It has checked presidential adventurism and trimmed policy excesses on the margin. It has injected a healthy sensitivity to the concerns of the electorate into State Department deliberations. And it has encouraged the creation of new mechanisms for calculated cooperation between the legislative and executive branches—the "good cop, bad cop" routine, the congressional resolutions intended to send public messages overseas, and the compromises on conditional U.S. assistance used to provide leverage in pursuing American goals abroad. Yet it is clear that the procedures of the modern Congress have created headaches all around. On balance, has the more determined role Congress has recently taken in setting international policy proved to be a success? Or have these reforms weakened the American decisionmaking process? Has legislative restraint in foreign policymaking been excessive, or too timid? How can this system be made to function in a manner more beneficial to the national interest? These are the fundamental questions of our inquiry; they warrant responses that are necessarily value-laden, answers that reflect one person's reading of U.S. history and fundamental political principles. We shall turn to these questions once again at the conclusion of this work, after carefully evaluating the key case studies of the last two decades of struggle in the making of U.S. foreign policy.

NOTES

1. Fulbright, "Legislator as Educator," p. 726.
2. Schlesinger, *Cycles of American History*, pp. 277, 291.
3. Thomas Jefferson, as quoted in Ornstein, "Sharing Foreign Policy Responsibility," p. 38.
4. During the Vietnam years, Senator Edmund Muskie regularly lambasted the characteristics of the "royal court" in the White House, "the ceremonial trappings . . . the immunization of foreign affairs question from Congressional debate . . . the moral certainty . . . the temper of monarchs," which Muskie attributed to the Nixon administration (*Congressional Record*, January 18, 1973, p. S1394).
5. Hamilton and Van Dusen, "Making the Separation of Powers Work," p. 27.
6. Ornstein, "Sharing Foreign Policy Responsibility," p. 48.
7. Senators have occasionally been made observers on U.S. negotiating teams, with mixed results. In the case of the INF Treaty, the effort helped to develop a cadre of supporters, both liberal and conservative, who were well versed in treaty details. In other instances, senators' presence at the negotiating site has been disruptive to progress and a distraction to executive branch negotiators, at best.

8. Senator Richard Russell, as quoted by Senator Thomas Eagleton, testimony before the Senate Foreign Relations Committee, Special Subcommittee on War Powers, July 13, 1988, p. 15.

9. See Schlesinger's "After the Imperial Presidency," in *Cycles of American History*, pp. 278–336.

10. Senator John Danforth, *Washington Post*, October 22, 1987, p. 23. Vice President George Bush echoed the criticism of Capitol Hill, complaining: "You got 535 secretaries of state up there with their own briefcases and their own agenda. The American people see that . . . the world outside observes and loses faith. Our chaos does not go unnoticed" (*Washington Post*, January 12, 1988, p. 18).

11. See *Myers v. United States*, as quoted in *Congressional Record*, October 23, 1987, p. S15028.

12. Federalist Paper no. 70.

13. *Washington Post*, September 2, 1984, p. 10.

14. An *authorization* bill legally establishes a spending program, sets policy guidelines, and places conditions on expenditures; the foreign aid authorization originates in the House Foreign Affairs and the Senate Foreign Relations committees. An *appropriations* measure allows federal agencies to obligate funds and draw checks from the Department of the Treasury; for foreign aid, it originates in the House Appropriations Committee's Subcommittee on Foreign Operations.

15. Congress typically passes only 5 percent of the bills introduced. In the 99th Congress (1985–1986), 8,404 bills were introduced, yielding just 389 public laws.

16. *INS v. Chadha*, 462 U.S. 919 (1985). A *concurrent* resolution is an expression of Congress that does not require the president's signature. A *joint* resolution must be presented to the president and, if vetoed, has binding effect only if passed again by a two-thirds majority in each house.

17. Senate Republican Whip Alan Simpson of Wyoming explained this phenomenon in greeting one controversial nominee: "Welcome to the Stygian pits of clamoring Congress-persons, jaudiced journalists, crafty staffers, lachrymose lobbyists and low-flying and silent missiles that seek out and create their own targets that are always sensitive to heat but rather impervious to light" (as quoted in *Washington Times*, November 17, 1987, p. 1).

18. See Hughes, *Domestic Context of Foreign Policy*, or the excellent publication of the Chicago Council on Foreign Relations, "American Public Opinion and U.S. Foreign Policy, 1987." The latter offers an interesting insight into the question of whether Congress has too much influence in foreign policy: 77 percent of executive branch officials said yes, as compared to only 28 percent of business and academic leaders.

19. Averell Harriman, as quoted in Schlesinger, *Cycles of American History*, p. 311.

20. Bennet, "Congress in Foreign Policy," p. 45.
21. Heginbotham, "Dateline Washington," p. 170.
22. Cyrus Vance, as quoted in Tower, "Congress Versus the President," p. 245.
23. Evans, speech to CSIS conference (see ch. 3, note 17), p. 7.
24. Senator John Danforth, *Washington Post*, October 22, 1987, p. 23. See also James J. Kilpatrick, "Four Days of Merriment," *Washington Post*, October 22, 1987, p. 23. Note that the State Department authorization bill was first created by Senator William Fulbright when, as chairman of the Foreign Relations Committee in the 1960s, he sought a place to deposit all the amendments he did *not* want on his foreign aid bill.
25. For an excellent description of the closed House procedures before the 1970s reforms, see Congressman Richard Bolling's *House Out of Order*, written in 1965.
26. *Washington Times*, November 17, 1987, p. 4. Some House leaders even took to blaming the Senate for harming the reputation of Congress. See comments of Democratic House Ways and Means Committee Chairman Dan Rostenkowski of Illinois, as quoted in *Washington Post*, February 14, 1988, p. 21.
27. *Washington Times.* November 17, 1987, p. 4. See also Evans's remarks in *Washington Post*, January 4, 1988, p. 1.
28. Ornstein et al., *Vital Statistics on Congress (1986)*, p. 120.
29. Ibid. These figures compare with more than 1,500 in the president's Executive Office, 26,000 in the State Department, and some 3,000,000 in the entire executive branch.
30. Ibid.
31. Ibid., p. 148.
32. Watergate-era reforms put strict limits on the amount of money individuals can contribute to a single campaign—making it necessary to have many more donors than before to finance expensive contests.
33. On Senate working conditions, see Democratic Senator David Pryor of Arkansas, *Congressional Record*, August 7, 1987, pp. S11601-3. Pryor observed that "the Senate is approaching procedural 'gridlock.' Over the past twenty years there appears to have crept in a decided inability to successfully complete the business of the Senate." Pryor noted that filibusters increased from sixty-two between 1841 and 1968 to sixty-two since 1968—more in the last nineteen years than during the proceeding 127.
34. Bryce Harlow, as quoted in Smith, *Power Game*, p. 281, 290.
35. *Washington Times*, November 23, 1987, p. D1. Buchanan alleges that a liberal bias exists throughout government bureaucracy, asserting that "like the universities and civil service, Capitol Hill is one of the beaches upon which the flotsam of the '60's washed up."
36. Smith, *Power Game*, p. 216.
37. Fulbright, "Legislator as Educator," p. 723.

38.   White House officials exacerbated Jepsen's problems by bragging to his home-state paper about their clout: "We just called him in and beat his brains out. We showed him his political grave" (as quoted anonymously in the *Des Moines Register*, November 2, 1981, p. 1.

39.   Senator Helms also took the extraordinary step of soliciting endorsements for his 1984 reelection campaign from sitting U.S. ambassadors—who, although mostly political appointees, would have to pass before the committee again for confirmation to any subsequent diplomatic posts. This practice was denounced by a number of professional foreign service officers and former secretaries of state.

III THE NEW POLICYMAKING REALITIES

5 THE POWER TO MAKE WAR

> The exigencies of modern warfare are far beyond the imagination
> of those who drafted our fundamental law. Today the Commander-
> in-Chief can move whole divisions half-way across the globe in a
> matter of hours, complex military alliances seem to commit us far
> beyond our borders, [and] we can destroy ourselves and the rest
> of the world at the press of a button.
>
> —Senator Tom Eagleton, 1973[1]

On the morning of April 24, 1980, senior congressional leaders were urgently summoned to the White House Cabinet Room for a meeting with President Jimmy Carter. The night before, a military disaster had befallen the United States; forces secretly sent to Iran by the President in a risky attempt to overwhelm Teheran's defenses and free American hostages had failed to accomplish their mission. Lives had been lost. Valuable intelligence assets had been compromised. And the nation had been embarrassed by a disastrous predawn collision of U.S. military aircraft at the Desert One staging area.

In preparation for the Hill leaders' after-the-fact meeting with the President, several congressional aides had armed their bosses with memoranda analyzing the provisions of the War Powers Act.[2] The aides argued that basic requirements of the law had been violated by the clumsy White House move. While they granted that the American people were desperate for any type of action to free the hostages,

119

who had been abused for over a year, Carter's provocative election-year effort to end the national trauma seemed unlikely to succeed from the outset and had invited open war with Iran. Hill aides maintained that the President's failure to consult with congressional leaders before the military operation was under way could not be excused by the "traditional" presidential authority to act to rescue American citizens in distress and that the requirements for secrecy were not a sufficient excuse for keeping Congress in the dark. More than 2,000 Department of Defense personnel had been involved in preparing for the raid, and dozens of executive branch political appointees knew of its details. There was no security justification, Hill staffers insisted, for excluding the most senior elected officials of the U.S. Congress.

There was every reason to believe that the legislators summoned to the White House would embrace this forceful critique. While there was considerable pressure on the White House from Capitol Hill to take some type of military action against the Khomeini regime, explicit warnings about prior consultation with the Hill had been issued. On the eve of the ill-fated military strike against Iran, the chairman and ranking Republican member of the Senate Foreign Relations Committee had together written senior administration officials reminding them of the legal obligation to consult with Congress on military moves contemplated to implement the President's recently enunciated Persian Gulf Doctrine. "The consultations called for [by the law] do not necessarily signify at all that a decision has been made to introduce United States Armed Forces into hostilities," Senators Frank Church and Jacob Javits wrote. "On the contrary, the advance consultation provisions of the War Powers Resolution are intended to come into play *before* any such decision has been made, in order to ensure that any such decision, if made, is a national decision jointly entered into by the President and the Congress."[3]

But when the congressional leaders held their press conferences throughout the day on April 24, none of these arguments were heard. Carter won the full backing of Foreign Relations Committee Chairman Frank Church—who just hours before had been insisting that the President had violated the requirements in the War Powers Act for prior consultation.[4] "The President would have been a hero if it had worked," observed Alan Cranston of California, a strong defender of the letter of the law. "He should be supported. I think it was not a military action; I'll accept the President's definition—it was humanitarian action."[5]

It was the same with others. No senior member of Congress was eager to press the war powers issue after meeting with the President—even after it was revealed that planning for the military strike against Iran had been under way for *five months* without any briefing offered to congressional leaders, and even after Secretary Vance resigned to protest a unilateral White House gamble that he had believed to be indefensible. Sheepish Capitol Hill aides filed their memos. In the national disappointment over the tragedy, there was no stomach for pursuing questions of legality.[6]

Of course, had the Iran hostage rescue attempt miraculously succeeded, there would not have been much legal debate either. As the Grenada invasion of 1983 would later demonstrate, the satisfaction of a popular victory dismisses most second thoughts about the president risking war without involving Congress in the gamble. Jimmy Carter *would* have been a hero if he had pulled off a military rescue; no Monday morning quarterbacking from a gang of congressional lawyers would have been tolerated by the American people.

In this respect, the Iran hostage rescue attempt illustrates a basic truth: the moment American forces are engaged, the moment American soldiers' lives are on the line and the commander-in-chief repairs to the Situation Room, the instinctive reaction of members of Congress is to "rally around the flag." Their every political and patriotic instinct tells them to back the president—the embodiment of national will—in a crisis. Even liberal senators like Cranston, who had serious reservations about the wisdom of the military strike against Iran, or like Church, who had insisted on prior consultation, chose to back Carter unequivocally once he had committed the nation. President Carter contorted the English language in a time-honored White House tradition, denying that the armed forces were engaged in a "military" action. White House lawyers, led by special counsel Lloyd Cutler, dismissed requirements for involving Congress in the commitment of forces to hostilities against Iran.[7] But no one on Capitol Hill rose to press a successful challenge to these legally dubious assertions. This has been the reaction time and again since the adoption of the controversial 1973 War Powers Act. From the *Mayaguez* fiasco to the Grenada triumph, from the Beirut disaster to the clumsy air raid over Tripoli, presidents have tolerated few congressional restraints on their ability to make war.

DEBATING THE WAR POWERS ACT:
WHO SHALL COMMIT THE NATION?

The central American foreign policy challenge of the post–World War II era has been to contain the spread of communism without engaging in a direct superpower military confrontation. This challenge has required both creative diplomacy and presidential flexibility in the application of force. It has invited the arbitrary use of executive branch authority from Korea to the Bay or Pigs and the Dominican Republic, to Vietnam. It was to check this inexorable expansion of executive authority—to end perceived abuses like the unilateral decision by President Nixon to move U.S. forces into Cambodia—that war powers legislation was drafted in the early 1970s. The popular cry was, "No more Gulf of Tonkins." The legislature was determined that never again would a prolonged commitment of troops be made to a war that Congress had not formally agreed to prosecute. "Undeclared war," Senator Jacob Javits of New York explained in 1971, "has meant presidential war. Prolonged engagement in undeclared presidential war has created a most dangerous imbalance in our constitutional system."[8]

The war powers debate of the early 1970s saw congressional critics of White House powers using the provisions of a 190-year-old constitution as their essential argument. The modern presidential practice of committing troops first and notifying Congress only after the fact cannot be squared with a strict construction of the Constitution, which clearly grants the war-declaring power to Congress. In the 1780s, the Constitution framers were determined to deny the chief executive the arbitrary power to commit the nation to war. The issue was at the heart of the fight for independence from the British king. It was central to the struggle for representative democracy and for noninvolvement in European intrigues. Even those at the Philadelphia convention who most vigorously championed executive powers explicitly denied the president the right to act alone in initiating military commitments. On this point there was virtual unanimity. It was to be the "exclusive province of Congress, when the nation is at peace, to change that state into a state of war," Alexander Hamilton explained. "It belongs to Congress only to go to war." The president's commander-in-chief powers, Hamilton underscored, would consist of "only the occasional command of such part of the militia of the nation as by legislative provision may be called into actual service of the union."[9] The Constitution thus vested Congress alone with the power to declare war and to raise and regulate the nation's fleets and armies. The much-noted change in the last week of the 1787 convention—giving Congress the power "to declare war" instead of "to make war"—was designed simply to clarify executive authority to repel sudden attacks and to ensure unity of command once Congress had approved military action. Under the Constitution, the authority for the United States to initiate a military conflict "is fully and exclusively vested in the legislature," James Madison explained. "The executive has no right, in any case, to decide the question."[10]

Presidents from Washington to Reagan have swept such restraints aside under the pressure of swift-moving diplomatic and military confrontations. The United States has been involved in more than 200 separate incidents in which the president has ordered armed forces into combat.[11] Congress would likely have approved most of these engagements if asked prior to the commitment of U.S. forces. Yet only five times has the Congress committed the nation to hostilities with a formal declaration of war. It was in response to this legacy—and to renewed concern over the escalation of U.S. involvement in the Vietnam War stemming from the May 1970 incursion into Cambodia—that Congress finally sought to check executive branch authority in the War Powers Act of 1973.

Revisionist historians frequently attribute the genesis of this landmark legislation to the decline of President Nixon's popularity, that is, to "the combined pressures of Vietnam and Watergate."[12] This argument maintains that war powers legislation was an aberration that would never have been pressed had not the powers of the Nixon presidency been diminished. It is certainly true that Nixon's veto of the measure might have initially been sustained had his standing among mainstream Republicans not sunk so low. Yet the implication of this argument is false. The war powers debate did not arise and advance because Nixon was weak or unpopular. The war powers legislation was originally drafted in early 1970 by a member of Nixon's own party, Senator Javits. Versions first passed both houses in *1972*—when Nixon's powers were greatest and hopes for an end to American involvement in the war were at their highest. Cosponsored by such Vietnam War supporters as Senator John Stennis of Mississippi and Congressman Clement Zablocki of Wisconsin, both the

House and Senate versions of 1972 were prospective in their application. They explicitly "grandfathered" the commitment of U.S. troops to Indochina combat, making it clear that the legislation would not restrict the President's authority to continue Vietnam operations.

The final steps toward an override of the President's veto were indeed marked by the conviction that Nixon's governing authority was suddenly diminishing. While the war powers legislation was co-sponsored by many Vietnam War supporters, the revelations in July 1973 that the Nixon administration had falsified military reports in order to conduct a secret air war over Laos and Cambodia, involving more than 3,500 B-52 sorties, damaged the legitimacy of White House leadership.[13] Similarly, the resignation under indictment of Vice President Spiro Agnew and the "Saturday Night Massacre"—the October 31, 1973 firing of Watergate special prosecutor Archibald Cox and Attorney General Elliot Richardson—enhanced the prospects of a veto override substantially. The President's credibility with even his most stalwart GOP defenders had plummeted to new lows by November 1973. Yet the battle lines had long since been drawn. The Senate had passed a strong version of war powers legislation on April 13, 1972 by a 68-16 vote—the same year Nixon won forty-nine states in his landslide reelection, the same year the Paris peace talks were bearing fruit and curbing U.S. military involvement in Indochina, and a full year before revelations of White House involvement in the June 1972 break-in at the Democratic National Committee headquarters in the Watergate office building. The fact is that the war powers debate moved forward as part of a sustained process that had begun as early as 1969 with hearings on the National Commitments Resolution, and that continued for more than three years before Nixon's popularity waned.

Ironically, through the months that the authority of the Nixon White House was declining, the strong Senate version was weakened in the legislative process. In marked contrast to current practice, the Senate was then much more aggressive than the House in challenging executive foreign policy powers. The Senate bill sought to circumscribe the president's unilateral power to commit the nation to war to only three carefully defined emergency situations. But Senate leaders were repeatedly confronted with the necessity of compromise with House conferees who were more deferential towards the White House. An effort to reach agreement in the House-Senate conference on a consensus bill stalled in 1972 because of recalcitrance on the part of some representatives who were still reluctant to cross President Nixon.

The original Javits-Stennis-Eagleton bill was passed again in 1973; it provided explicit prohibitions on virtually any injection of military force by the president unless prior approval of Congress was obtained. The House version began as little but a reporting requirement. It was strengthened as the legislative process continued, ultimately becoming as strong as to limit unauthorized troop deployments by the president to not more than ninety days. The Senate consistently passed legislation with more than the two-thirds margin necessary for a veto override. But House leaders could not muster a two-thirds majority behind any bill until the veto override test in November 1973. In the end, Javits caved in to pressure from House conferees; his desire to put some legislation on the books in this crucial area led him to accept the bulk of the weaker House version as a compromise to break the conference committee deadlock.[14]

The relative weakness of House support for the final version of the act was somewhat misleading; a split had developed among backers of a strong measure. More than a dozen liberals—representatives like John Culver of Iowa, Bella Abzug of New York, and Ron Dellums of California—joined conservatives in opposing the compromise because they viewed it as conferring upon the president powers he did not already possess under the Constitution. These Democrats heeded the counsel of Senator Eagleton, who consistently maintained that the House version granted a unilateral war-making power to the president that the Constitution had denied him. As Congresswoman Elizabeth Holtzman summarized this critique moments before passage of the House version on July 17, 1973: "The bill instead of limiting Presidential war powers enshrines the unilateral war-making power on the part of the President for 120 days."[15] But Eagleton was alone in the Senate in pressing for a stronger measure. A coauthor of the original resolution, the Missouri Democrat voted to sustain Nixon's veto of the conference report, calling the compromise "a horrible mistake: every president of the United States will have at least the color of legal authority, the advance blessing of Congress given on an open, blank-check basis to take us to war."[16] Yet the misgivings of most legislators were set aside by intense lobbying from critics of the White House, who were intent upon some action being taken, and from liberal groups like Americans for Democratic Action, which maintained that it was an improvement over the status quo.[17] Enough House members switched to ensure a two-thirds majority for the November override. The final tally in the House was 284-135; in the Senate, it was a more comfortable 75-18 vote.

The final version of the 1973 act provided strict procedures for Congress to force withdrawal of U.S. troops from a hostile situation—a requirement Congress could press either by a swift vote to pull back or by failing to vote to authorize continuation of troop deployments. The law limited unauthorized wars to ninety days, while requiring prior consultation and prompt reporting in the event of emergency action by the executive. The legislation sought to prevent presidential commitment to military actions without express congressional approval. In one sense it succeeded: since its passage, the United States has engaged in military hostilities for more than ninety days only in Beirut and the Persian Gulf, and fighting in those two instances proved sporadic. The decade and a half since passage of the War Powers Act thus marks the first time since the 1930s that the United States has gone more than ten years without a major war. But the act places a great premium on quick strikes and proxy wars— actions often undertaken at a greater risk of superpower involvement.[18] And the efforts of successive presidents to avoid strict compliance have clearly made the attainment of a domestic consensus behind such perilous deployments as those in Beirut and the Persian Gulf even more difficult. In this most important respect, the act clearly failed to accomplish its goal. It was only a matter of time before Eagleton and other original cosponsors were calling for a return to the measure's stronger Senate version. As one Senate critic complained at the height of the Lebanon crisis, the act "does not stop a President from sending troops into hostilities whenever and wherever he chooses."[19] Indeed, the one time that Congress has acted forcefully to bar any U.S. military commitment, it was in a rider to a Department of Defense bill—the Clark amendment prohibiting covert involvement in the Angolan civil war—that tied up appropriations, and not through use of procedures established by the War Powers Act.

What went wrong? Why has the controversial measure failed to fulfill its intent? The war powers debate has become so clouded by overheated rhetoric that it is important to take a hard look at the actual text of the measure before assessing the unhappy experience

THE POWER TO MAKE WAR

of governing under its provisions. The following is a summary of what Public Law 93–148 actually says.

Definition of Presidential Authority.   Relegated by the Senate-House conferees to the nonbinding "purpose and policy" section of the act—a preamble statement of interpretation that does not have the full force of law—provision 2(c) declares that the authority of the president to act unilaterally is limited to only three instances: (1) pursuant to a declaration of war, (2) under specific statutory authorization, or (3) in response to a national emergency created by an attack on the United States, its territories, or its armed forces.

Consultation.   Section 3 of the War Powers Act requires that the president shall consult with Congress "in every possible instance" before introducing U.S. forces into a hostile situation. The exception was intended, according to the law's legislative history, only to cover actions for which such speed was required that congressional leaders literally could not be contacted in time to secure legislative approval before military action was required.

Reporting.   Under Section 4(a)(1), the president is required to report within forty-eight hours the introduction of armed forces "into hostilities or into a situation where imminent involvement in hostilities is indicated by the circumstances." The president can also choose to report a deployment of forces "equipped for combat" into foreign territories or airspace under 4(a)(2)—an oft-used loophole because only a "4(a)(1) report" triggers the requirement for Congress to approve continued deployments under Section 5. It is left to the president to define under which category a Section 4 report should be filed.

Termination of Military Deployments by Congress.   One of the most controversial provisions ever legislated by Congress, Section 5(b) forces the withdrawal of troops to begin sixty days after a report under section 4(a)(1) is required, unless Congress acts to approve the deployments. (The time for orderly withdrawal can be extended for thirty additional days—thus the "90-day clock.") This means that a failure by Congress to act requires the president to initiate a forced retreat. Section 5(c) provides for a "legislative veto" of troop de-

ployments at any time, permitting Congress to attempt forcing withdrawal of troops whenever it wishes by a simple majority vote of
both houses to adopt a concurrent resolution. Many scholars maintain that this provision is invalidated by the *Chadha* decision, but the
issue remains in dispute.[20]

Inferred War-Making Authority. Section 8 makes it clear that no
defense authorization bill, no vague Gulf of Tonkin-style resolution
or mutual security treaty, can be inferred to grant authority for the
president to unilaterally commit troops to war without express congressional approval.

Separability. Section 9 states that if one provision of the act is
ruled unconstitutional, all the other provisions of the act still stand
as requirements of law. The applicability of this provision is not in
dispute; even the act's harshest critics in the Reagan administration
recognized that rejection by the Supreme Court of the legislative
veto did not render the entire act unconstitutional.[21]

THE WAR POWERS ACT IN PRACTICE

Governance under the War Powers Act has a deeply troubled history.
Since the very day of its enactment, the measure has been assailed as
either too weak or too strong. It has been skirted, twisted, and successfully confronted. Executive branch officials—especially in the
Reagan years—have so often made the political argument that the
act overreaches that its provisions are assumed by many to be a dead
letter. The law has successfully been discredited. Compliance with its
terms has become an option, and flouting its provisions has become
an action applauded in many quarters. Today most policymakers
have concluded that the measure is an abject failure. In the heat of
recent debates, legislators have bemoaned its weaknesses, describing
it variously as "a eunuch," "a nullity," and a statute that is "de
facto dead."[22] Some lawmakers recognize that the act has facilitated
timely debate on important policy choices; they cite the restraining
influence it had on White House officials who might have committed
U.S. forces more freely in El Salvador, Nicaragua, and Iran. "The
practical effect," Senator Charles Mathias has argued, "is that whether

the President likes the War Powers Act or not, he is always thinking about it. . . . We have forced upon the consciousness of the Administration the whole idea that he cannot act with total disregard for the law—he has to pay some political consequence."[23]

There have been at least twenty-two instances where U.S. troops were committed to hostile situations since the war powers measure was enacted.[24] In virtually every case, the executive branch has successfully devised a strategy to avoid meaningful congressional restraints. A total of thirteen reports have been filed, yet only two triggered the 90-day clock as a result of reporting under the crucial Section 4(a)(1). Each of these thirteen reports has been sent "consistent with" or "taking note of"—but never "pursuant to"—the act's provisions. These reports have usually been designed not to trigger any specific section of the act, but rather to provide an after-the-fact supplement to token "consultations." It is worth briefly reviewing the history of these reports before turning to more detailed consideration of the two most important cases, Beirut and the Persian Gulf.

Vietnam Evacuation

Ironically, the first reports submitted to Congress pursuant to the act pertained to withdrawal of U.S. forces and Vietnamese loyalists from Da Nang and Saigon. After the U.S. evacuation began in earnest on April 4, 1975, Congress failed to move in a timely manner to provide the statutory authority for military movements requested by President Ford. (The Congress was in recess, with members of the leadership as far away as Beijing, when the Da Nang airlift began.) At the time that President Ford reported troop movements to Congress "consistent with" Section 4(a)(2), there was an absolute prohibition in law against any Indochina combat operations. The White House was also confronted with the fact that the War Powers Act conferees had expressly sought to deny presidential authority to engage in sweeping "rescue missions."[25] Nevertheless, President Ford proceeded boldly, acting unilaterally to save lives even as debate in Congress droned on. The failure of Congress to complete action on a law to authorize these essential military operations before the fall of the South Vietnamese government on April 29 forfeited an opportunity to establish an important precedent.[26]

Cambodia—The Mayaguez Incident

Less than two weeks after the Vietnam withdrawal was completed, the United states was again involved in fighting in Indochina. On May 12, 1975, when a Khmer Rouge unit off Cambodia seized a U.S. registered merchant ship, President Ford chose to ignore statutory prohibitions on combat operations in Cambodia and to launch a rescue mission and retaliatory attack. Public opinion rallied strongly behind him—even when the costly raid continued after the ship and its crew had been released unharmed. The President called in air strikes against a Cambodian military base and a Marine landing against heavily guarded Koh Tang Island. Forty-one U.S. military personnel lost their lives, though the *Mayaguez* crew was safe. A report submitted by President Ford on May 15, after hostilities had ended, "took note" of Section 4(a)(1)—but the question of whether the 90-day clock had started was moot.[27]

The Iranian Hostage Rescue Attempt

President Carter filed a report "consistent with" the War Powers Act on April 26, 1980, two days after U.S. forces had pulled out of Iran. Terming the mission "humanitarian," the President refused to specify which section of the act applied, although he cited his "powers under the Constitution as Chief Executive and Commander in Chief of the United States Armed Forces" and referenced Section 8(d)(1) of the act, which notes that nothing in the measure "is intended to alter the constitutional authority" of the president.[28] The report also asserted that the president had the right to decide when security considerations overrode his legal obligations to consult with Congress.

Sinai Observer Force

On March 19, 1982, President Reagan reported the deployment of U.S. forces to help monitor Sinai withdrawal provisions of the Camp David peace treaties. The report was submitted "consistent with" Section 4(a)(2); but the deployments already had their own statutory authorization under a resolution enacted by Congress in December of 1981 after considerable debate.[29]

The Grenada Invasion

Just hours after 241 Marines were killed in a suicide attack on their Beirut barracks, President Reagan launched a full-scale invasion of the tiny Caribbean island of Grenada. Ostensibly undertaken to "rescue" U.S. medical students, the October 25, 1983 operation was not deemed complete until a government more favorable to Washington was installed in place of the group of pro-Havana thugs who had terrorized the island in the days immediately prior to the U.S. invasion. Reagan administration officials told Congress that the lives of U.S. students had been threatened, air links with Grenada had been severed, and the United States was obliged to respond to a request for aid from the Organization of Eastern Caribbean States. In time, each of these assertions proved to be false. But crushing the outlaw regime proved wildly popular among Americans still mourning the Beirut disaster; Capitol Hill questions about the consistency of the invasion with the War Powers Act were muted in the wake of this success. Both houses of Congress did manage to pass resolutions demanding a Section 4(a)(1) report. But the issue was deemed moot by the time the conference report was considered on November 17; the administration had pledged to remove all remaining U.S. troops from Grenada within ninety days, thereby conveniently avoiding a showdown over war powers issues.[30]

The Libya Raid

An entirely new type of conflict arose on April 14, 1986 when President Reagan, citing his obligation to defend American citizens, directed a deadly air raid against targets in the Libyan capitol of Tripoli. The President informed Hill leaders of the action just minutes before the bombs began falling—in a raid that was broadcast live on prime-time network news in the United States. While European leaders had been widely consulted in advance, Congress was not consulted—a decision that incensed a number of lawmakers.[31] The administration refused to cite any specific provision of the War Powers Act in submitting its after-the-fact report, which used a vague, anti-terrorist justification. Maverick Republican Senator Lowell Weicker of Connecticut deplored the raid, claiming it was "no different than what Qadaffi had done" in allegedly spearheading a series of murders of U.S. military personnel in Western Europe.[32] But Democratic leaders like House Speaker Tip O'Neill backed the Libya raid, warning that "we're just not going to let Americans be terrorized around the world."[33] Senate Majority Leader Bob Dole took the issue a step further. An original cosponsor of the War Powers Act, Dole proposed in the aftermath of the Libya raid that the President be granted blanket authority to take any military steps necessary to combat terrorism. The Dole bill did not advance, but it served to illustrate how concern about terrorism had changed thinking on the Hill.[34]

El Salvador

There have also been several occasions since 1973 when U.S. troops have been introduced into hostile situations but no war powers reports have ever been filed. The most important case is El Salvador—where anticipation of congressional assertion of war powers restrictions noticeably restrained executive branch actions.[35] The Reagan administration was pressing in the early months of its tenure for a substantial increase in grant aid to the Salvadoran military. Congress insisted as a condition that a ceiling of fifty-five be placed upon the number of U.S. military advisers in the country at any given time; the option of more direct U.S. assistance to Salvadoran Air Force bombers and counterinsurgency troops was foreclosed, and a series of human rights conditions was attached to future Salvadoran aid funds.

The debate over the applicability of the War Powers Act to deployments in El Salvador also produced the most important court test of the measure to date. In *Crockett v. Reagan*, several determined members of the House Foreign Affairs Committee insisted that the President violated the law by not submitting a Section 4 report on U.S. military activities in El Salvador.[36] Eventually, twenty-nine members of Congress joined as plaintiffs—with another two dozen colleagues filing briefs *against* Congressman George Crockett's

suit, arguing that Congress had already passed on a number of opportunities to curb funding for U.S. military activities in El Salvador.
But the U.S. district court ruled that the issue of presidential non-
compliance fell to Congress to address first, concluding that the
"subtleties of fact-finding in this situation should be left to the
political branches."[37] This, indeed, seems likely to be the bottom
line on war powers adjudication, short of a Supreme Court test of
any attempt by Congress to force troop withdrawals by concurrent
resolution. This "political question" doctrine throws the war powers
dispute back in the laps of Congress and the president; there is no
eagerness in the judiciary to step in and referee.[38]

PROCESS OVERSHADOWS POLICY: BEIRUT AND THE PERSIAN GULF

The two key tests of the War Powers Act both arose when the United
States sought to combat Middle East terrorists with a show of conventional military force. In both the 1983 Marine deployments in
Beirut and the 1987 convoying of Kuwaiti oil tankers in the Persian
Gulf, the U.S. military became bogged down in complicated and
unfamiliar situations where old rules of engagement did not apply.
By and large, Congress was supportive of these presidential initiatives. Yet, as we shall see upon closer examination, both experiences
showed how easily disputes over procedural options can undermine
consensus on national policy.

The Marines in Beirut

U.S. forces returned to Beirut for the third time since World War II
on August 25, 1982. The brief deployments of peacekeeping forces
under Eisenhower (1957) and Ford (1975) proved much less complicated. The Marines were originally sent in 1982 as part of a multinational force with a clear and distinct mission—to secure withdrawal
of disarmed Palestine Liberation Organization (PLO) fighters. The
mission was completed, and U.S. forces withdrew within weeks. But
a force of 1,500 Marines was back in Beirut again on September 29,
after the assassination of President-elect Bashir Gemayel and the
massacre of civilians at the Sabra and Shattila refugee camps. There

the Marines remained month after month in a futile attempt to restore public order in a nation ravaged by a seemingly endless civil war.

Congress was initially supportive of the Marine deployments, though Senate Democrats sought to limit the duration of their stay. The administration reported on the move, "consistent with—but not "pursuant to"—the War Powers Act. President Reagan agreed in signing the April 1983 Lebanon Emergency Assistance Act to "obtain statutory authorization from Congress" in the case of "any substantial expansion" of the Marine contingent. But as the months went by, the Marines' vague and ill-defined mission began to shift. In time, they could no longer claim to be a neutral force. They became participants in the Lebanese civil war—acting militarily in support of one of several warring factions. The American forces thus became inviting targets for those suffering under the status quo—as well as for anyone wishing to deliver a symbolic blow against U.S. influence in the Middle East.

After several Americans were killed in an August 29, 1983 attack on Marine positions near the Beirut airport, the United States began returning fire more deeply into the city and suburbs. On September 14, the United States began shelling targets in Suk al Gharb, east of Beirut, using the refurbished battleship *New Jersey* anchored offshore. For the first time since World War II, the U.S. Navy was attacking targets in the Mediterranean. Even though the rules of engagement for U.S. forces remained unchanged, the Reagan administration could no longer maintain the fiction that the troops were not in a position where "hostilities were imminent." Indeed, U.S. troops in the area were drawing combat pay.

Congressional leaders insisted that Section 4 of the War Powers Act be invoked and the Marines' mission be clarified. U.S. troops had been in Beirut for twelve months already, with no end in sight. It was clear to most observers that the United States was now viewed as a direct participant in Lebanon's civil war. Proceeding with any further commitment warranted a joint decision by the legislative and executive branches. But Congress was deeply divided on the basic policy questions. Senate Republicans sought to maximize White House flexibility in responding to a dangerous and fluid situation. Senate Democrats wanted a strict timetable for the deployments— six months was the minority's position—and a clearly defined mission set for U.S. forces. The minority nearly won a key committee test before Majority Leader Howard Baker pulled Republicans back to prevail in a party-line vote. House Speaker O'Neill, commanding a forceful Democratic majority in the House, pressed for a bargain with the President. In return for the procedural "concession" of invoking the limitations of the War Powers Act, the administration won from House leaders substantive support for a longer stay with a less precise mission. The cosmetic compromise was a face-saver for lawmakers who were still ready to grant the White House the flexibility it requested for military and diplomatic maneuver.[39] President Reagan paid obeisance to the war powers process by signing legislation authorizing his deployment of troops—which thus implicitly gave Congress control over their possible redeployment. In return, Congress gave him a free hand by authorizing the Marine presence in Beirut for at least another eighteen months.[40]

A sigh of relief was heard from many quarters; the lengthy time frame was designed to postpone divisive debate until after the 1984 elections. It would sidetrack the legal dispute over Reagan's non-compliance with the War Powers Act, while defending Democrats against the charge—already floated by the White House and echoed by Senate Republicans—that they were isolationists who wanted the United States to "turn tail and retreat under fire." In signing off on the deal, President Reagan explicitly rejected any binding requirements of the 1973 act. Yet he was uncharacteristically lavish in his praise of Democratic bipartisanship in hammering out the deal.

Then tragedy struck. Early on the morning of October 22, 1983, a truck loaded with explosives destroyed the Marine barracks at the Beirut airport, killing 241 Americans. With the U.S. mission in the Lebanese civil war so unclear, the Marines now appeared to many Americans to be sitting ducks. Political support in Washington for a continued U.S. military role dissolved overnight. Secretary of Defense Caspar Weinberger aired the Pentagon's long-standing reservations to the deployments (which had consistently been defended by Secretary Shultz, in a familiar State-Defense split on the issue of using military force).[41] On Capitol Hill, legislators sought a graceful way to hasten the departure of the remaining U.S. forces in Lebanon. But the President had gone so far out on a limb insisting that the United States had "vital interests in Lebanon" and that U.S. forces would remain until public order was restored, that there was no easy way out.

There ensued a remarkably bitter round of recriminations. Democratic calls for a more specific mission and a shorter time limit for the Marine deployments were met with accusations from the President that Congress wanted to "cut and run."[42] President Reagan—to whom legislators had given a free hand to pursue his Beirut mission—sought to make Congress the scapegoat after the barracks disaster. Secretary of State George Shultz took up the charge against Congress; he claimed that the public debate necessary to obtain the 18-month authorization "totally took the rug out from under" administration efforts in Lebanon. He quite astonishingly asserted that the U.S. role "was hamstrung by legislative inhibitions."[43] Administration loyalist Charles Percy, the Republican chairman of the Senate Foreign Relations Committee, spoke for many in rejecting the clumsy administration campaign to blame Congress for the Beirut disaster: "The joint resolution that authorized the commitment of American marines to Beirut provided the Administration with ample opportunity to help bring about lasting peace in Lebanon. . . . It is not accurate to assert that the Lebanon resolution impeded the President's ability to carry out effective diplomacy."[44] Percy's House counterpart, Chairman of the Foreign Affairs Committee Democrat Dante Fascell of Florida, was blunter, dismissing the administration finger-pointing campaign as election-year politics.

In the end, few policymakers were satisfied with how the Beirut episode was handled. Senate Democrats were angered by the acquiescence of House leaders to the open-ended commitment sought by the White House. And they fumed when Reagan then made it clear—even after obtaining the support of House Democrats—that he would not be bound by war powers strictures. GOP lawmakers were angry at being made scapegoats by the administration, while the White House was genuinely irritated by the requirement for prolonged debate over how long the United States should remain in Lebanon. Secretary Shultz invested tremendous personal prestige in Lebanese efforts to forge a disengagement pact—the one and only peace treaty negotiated during the first Reagan term. With its collapse, Reagan and Shultz turned on the Hill with a vengeance. Hindsight suggests that congressional skepticism was amply justified; Reagan himself found it necessary to withdraw under fire. Yet Congress can be criticized for failing to press its concerns more forcefully so as to help avoid an American disaster. In the round of recriminations that ensued, the War Powers Act took its lumps as well. As America withdrew again from the Beirut quagmire, the dispute over war powers *procedures* overshadowed debate on the *substance* of a very risky, and ultimately tragic, U.S. policy course in Lebanon.

U.S. Naval Deployments in the Persian Gulf

A similar experience unfolded in the lengthy debate surrounding U.S. naval deployments in the Persian Gulf during the Iran-Iraq war. By the fall of 1987, the United States had amassed in the Gulf the largest armada the world had seen since the height of the Vietnam War, a force crewed by more than 15,000 U.S. military personnel. But the mission of these U.S. forces—and their rules of engagement—lacked clarity, consistency, or any time limitation. Once again, the State Department and the Pentagon were split over the wisdom of expanding U.S. involvement. (Navy Secretary James Webb was particularly outspoken in his criticism of the Navy's vague and ever shifting mission.) The 100th Congress was deeply divided, too. Lawmakers questioned the wisdom of U.S. intervention in the Iran-Iraq war and were loathe to see American forces acting as an international "coast guard" in the troubled Gulf waters. Yet despite two years of often heated debate, Congress failed to achieve a consensus not only on the question of whether to support or oppose administration policy but also on the question of whether or not to invoke the War Powers Act.

Much of the difficulty confronting policymakers stemmed from the fact that the Reagan administration was both unwilling and unable to be frank about the objectives advanced by the massive naval deployments. The mission was initiated at a time when U.S. relations with the Arab states of the Persian Gulf had been shaken by revelations that the Reagan White House had secretly been selling missiles to Teheran. The purpose of U.S. naval deployments was said to be defense of neutral shipping in international waters. Yet the majority of attacks against oil tankers were undertaken by *Iraq*— the nation that benefited from Washington's desire to mend fences with the Arab states—while the United States sought to defend tankers against attacks only when they were perpetrated by *Iran*. The U.S. buildup in early 1987 began as a consequence of Kuwaiti requests for escorts for its shipping. The pro-Iraqi Kuwaitis brilliantly played the United States against the Soviets by soliciting assistance from both nations, a move that invigorated U.S. efforts to step in and avert any Soviet security role. The United States was determined to reassure Iraq's Arab allies in the wake of the "arms to the Ayatollah" scandal. Reagan administration officials were also driven by a desire to check Iranian war gains; Teheran was mounting a promising ground offensive in early 1987. The administration thus told Congress that, as a great power, the United States was obliged to help Kuwait by putting U.S. flags on its oil tankers. The mission was quickly expanded to that of keeping the international waters of the Gulf open for all (non-Iranian) oil traffic. The administration ignored the fact that the majority of Persian Gulf oil is moved overland by pipeline and that the United States today imports relatively little oil from the region. Checking Soviet influence remained the driving justification; but recouping from the Iran arms debacle was a crucial subtext.

Assistant Secretary of State Richard Murphy offered classified briefings on the original reflagging scheme to the foreign affairs committees—in the House on March 31, 1987 and in the Senate the next day. At this point, there was remarkably little interest on the Hill. Few legislators recognized the possible pitfalls at the outset because the original mission was confined to the protection of Kuwaiti ships and the Congress was more focused on questions about an imminent Saudi arms purchase.

On May 17, 1987, a devastating attack on the U.S.S. *Stark* abruptly changed the Hill's focus. This assault by a wayward Iraqi Mirage F-1 killed thirty-seven crewmen, fueling a new concern in Congress about the U.S. effort on behalf of the Kuwaitis and their allies in Baghdad. Faced with a mid-July deadline before the first reflagged convoy began transiting the Gulf, many in Congress sought to delay implementation of the plan. Provisos urging a delay were attached to unrelated House and Senate measures.[45] They probably would have faced a sustainable veto in the Oval Office. But these provisions did not even reach the President's desk in time to attempt a delay of the convoys. And once the reflagging commenced on July 22, a step-by-step acceleration ensued. Iran mined waterways and U.S.-flagged tankers were damaged. U.S. forces sank Iranian patrol boats engaged in military operations, Iranian aircraft traded fire with U.S. planes, and the United States blasted Iranian oil platforms that were supporting Teheran's sabotage efforts.

Congressional reservations about the expanding U.S. military involvement in the Persian Gulf did not translate into a consensus behind any alternative. Through the summer and early fall of 1987, Republican Senators Lowell Weicker and Mark Hatfield sought to force the President to submit a Section 4(a)(1) report. But they were confronted by a successful, GOP-led filibuster. In October, Democratic Majority Leader Byrd sought to compromise the War Powers Act by moving a resolution, together with Republican Senator John Warner of Virginia, that would have deferred the issue for months but would have guaranteed a later vote on Gulf policy. However, Byrd faced a revolt led by liberals like Patrick Leahy of Vermont and Joe Biden of Delaware. In an embarrassing setback, senior members of Byrd's own party joined Republicans to reject his proposal to sidestep the War Powers Act, provoking the voluble Democratic leader to berate his colleagues: "The Senate looks terrible. Senators want to have a voice in formulation of policy in the Persian Gulf, but the Senate is musclebound. It can't do anything."[46] Byrd later reversed the vote. But House leaders were reluctant to fall into the trap of invoking war powers and then being forced to either confront a presidential veto or support a policy fraught with peril.

Only the White House was happy with the result of the prolonged Hill wrangling. The harder Congress tried to achieve a policy consensus, the more deeply it became entangled in procedural questions. By the end of 1987, the very mention of another war powers debate brought groans from Republican and Democratic cloakrooms alike. The law itself had become an embarrassment to a majority in Congress. Thus, legislators chose to do nothing rather than choose between challenging the White House on Gulf policy or forcing a legal showdown over the War Powers Act's provisions.[47]

Further escalation occurred in 1988. Repeated incidents involving Iranian speedboats laying mines led the Reagan administration to expand its military rules of engagement even further. The United States was now committed to defending international traffic throughout the Gulf and to initiating combat and rescue efforts even if no assistance was sought by foreign ships. The rules put American forces on a hair-trigger alert in the midst of a commercial crossroads and an international war zone. The almost inevitable accident that followed proved tragic: 290 civilians were killed on July 3 when the U.S.S. *Vincennes* launched missiles against a commercial Iran Air flight. If ever there was a situation in which the 1973 law applied, surely it was an ongoing, open-ended deployment of 15,000 troops in the midst of a war zone that drew them into frequent combat. But there was no consensus behind an alternative and no hunger to confront the procedural issues. By the time the Iran Air tragedy occurred, the Gulf war was winding down and the U.S. naval armada was widely seen as having served its purpose. Reagan administration officials asserted that the armada's presence hastened the war's conclusion, while Congress remained unwilling to confront the war powers issue. And for many months after a tentative Iran-Iraq truce was set in August 1988, U.S. forces continued to patrol the Gulf without any authorization from Congress. In the Persian Gulf, as in Lebanon before, Ronald Reagan was given a free hand.

THE WAR POWERS ACT RECONSIDERED

The Persian Gulf debates represented the nadir of the 1973 act. These divisive procedural disputes subjected both the War Powers Act and the Congress to continuing ridicule. As the chairman of the Joint Chiefs of Staff (JCS), Admiral William Crowe, lectured one Capitol Hill panel in the aftermath of the Persian Gulf episode: "Too many members of Congress were content to debate about the war powers process and were happy to avoid being held accountable for approval or disapproval of the policy [of U.S. intervention]."[48] Yet from these bitter debates a consensus did emerge. Champions of both a strong White House role and an assertive Congress united behind the proposition that the terms of the 1973 act should be systematically reexamined. Conservatives pressed for outright repeal; the Republican presidential ticket of George Bush and Dan Quayle made scrapping the act an important element of their national security platform. Liberals called for restoration of the act to its original, Senate-passed version and for the addition of binding requirements for presidential consultation and reports. Few witnesses believed the act was working under existing terms.[49]

The Senate began a thorough review of these issues when it convened the Special Foreign Relations Subcommittee on War Powers in the summer of 1988. The original focus of these hearings was a bill, put forward by outgoing Majority Leader Byrd, to abandon key provisions of the 1973 measure while establishing a supercommittee of House and Senate leaders empowered to "fast-track" joint resolutions designed to cut off appropriations for unauthorized presidential war-making. Ironically, the Byrd proposal so unnerved liberals advocating a stronger role for Congress that it inspired efforts to prolong hearings and ensure that the Byrd measure would never be put to a vote in the full Senate.[50] The principal criticism of Byrd's proposal was that it would gut the key Section 5 provisions of the 1973 act: empowering Congress to halt unilateral presidential war-making, Section 5 permitted the president a free hand so long as he could maintain support from the minority that is necessary to sustain a veto— one-third plus one in a single chamber of Congress. Yet the Byrd bill—which enjoyed cosponsorship from respected Senate national security experts like Nunn of Georgia and Warner of Virginia—was also opposed by executive branch spokesmen, who maintained that Congress had no authority to legislate itself any powers on such constitutional disputes.

The far-reaching inquiry of the Senate's special war powers subcommittee offered a clear analysis of the tortured legacy of the 1973 act. Witnesses involved in every phase of drafting and implementing the measure—former cabinet officials, generals, congressmen, and legislative aides—presented testimony offering vivid contrasts in perspectives on what had gone wrong. Why had the act failed to achieve its twin objectives of facilitating interbranch consensus while limiting unilateral presidential war-making? The simplest explanation was offered by the special panel's chairman. "The War Powers Act has not failed," Senator Biden observed. "It has not been tried."[51] Indeed, the record demonstrated that with the exception of the Lebanon case—when President Reagan ultimately sought to make Congress the scapegoat for U.S. failure—no president has tried to employ the terms of the measure to achieve interbranch unity and an explicit grant of authority. As one witness argued convincingly, "The refusal, or inability, of the executive branch to comply with the law [rather than any inherent flaws in the law itself] is the reason for the disappointing result."[52] The determination of successive Oval Office occupants to resist the idea that Congress could circumscribe presidential war-making powers ensured that the full promise of the measure has yet to be realized. State Department counsel Abraham Sofaer summarized this executive branch view: "In our system of government, explicit legislative approval for particular uses of force has never been necessary, and the War Powers [Act] cannot and should not be permitted to make it necessary."[53] Witnesses from the military were even blunter. A distinguished panel headed by General Brent Scowcroft offered the astonishing notion that the only constitutional role of Congress in making a decision to commit the nation to war was the formality of recognizing "that a state of war does, in fact, exist" by responding favorably to a White House request for a declaration of war.[54]

As the sweeping war powers debate continued on Capitol Hill through the end of the 100th Congress, several weaknesses in the law stood out, deficiencies that can be traced directly to the 1973 dispute accompanying the original House and Senate versions of the law. The most serious weakness of the measure remains quite simple. The determination of Congress to get the act adopted never proved sufficient to overcome misgivings about the right of members to legislate such provisions in the first place. Passing one controversial law over a president's veto has exacerbated, not resolved, a 200-year-old debate. The War Powers Act was intended to "insure the collective judgment of both the Congress and President" in a national commitment to war. But while it is true that since the act's adoption the United States has not been engaged in any sustained ground conflicts, every president since 1973 has circumvented its central requirements. The White House has proven both effective and imaginative in this bipartisan effort. Justifiable questions raised about the constitutionality of individual provisions like the legislative veto have deliberately been expanded into an assault designed to undermine the legitimacy of the entire act. Many contemporary critics still insisted that President Nixon was correct in the central argument of his veto message. They maintained that the entire law was invalid because "the only way in which the constitutional powers of a branch of the government can be altered is by amending the Constitution—and any attempt to make such alterations by legislation is clearly without force."[55] Former Senator Barry Goldwater continues to argue for repeal of the measure:

> Those members of Congress who contend that Congress is empowered under the "necessary and proper clause" to define the President's powers over the conduct of military hostilities . . . are dead wrong. That there does exist some ultimate area of unshared independent power of the President in the conduct of foreign affairs and preservation of our national security is the cornerstone on which the survival of our nation rests.[56]

Congressional champions of the 1973 act counter this broadside by restating the act's central purpose: only to *clarify* powers and procedures. It does not purport to grant any new authority to either branch. If Congress's exclusive constitutional power to declare war is to have any meaning, laws are required to restrain the executive from unilaterally committing the nation to sustained hostilities. But citation of the Constitution's explicit grant of authority to Congress to "make all laws necessary and proper" for implementing the charter has proven ineffective in overcoming doubts. And it has not been backed by meaningful legislative action to enforce the terms of the 1973 law. In this dispute, liberals who champion a strong congressional role have a strict construction of the Constitution on their side. But legal right has not been translated into political might. Legislators have been unable to muster strong majorities to make their interpretation of law stick. As Defense Secretary Frank Carlucci chided advocates of a strong war powers role for Congress in the fall of 1988:

> Schemes to inhibit the Constitutional powers of the President . . . obscure the real source of many members' frustration—namely their inability to persuade their own colleagues to agree with them and vote with them. When the American people overwhelmingly and strongly believe that the President's policy must be reversed, the Congress will reverse it.[57]

Unable to overcome their own misgivings about the authorities reserved to Congress under the 1973 act, a key swing bloc of legislators in the center of the political spectrum has deferred to executive leadership, their constitutional responsibilities notwithstanding. Amid such divisions, the debate over war powers has transcended the purely legal realm and drifted into an almost theological debate about institutional prerogative. In this environment, successive presidents have been able to act militarily first and argue legalisms after the fact. The White House's power of initiative has overwhelmed the Congress's ability to hold the White House to the letter of the law. The persistence of executive branch objections—objections to timely consultation, to timely reports, and to honest descriptions of wartime situations—has ensured that consensus is ever more difficult to achieve.

An inherent weakness of the current war powers statute stems from the compromises Senate leaders were forced to make to win House conferees' support. The reporting and consultation requirements of the law are, as one key study notes, "riddled with loopholes"; the executive can quite readily evade strict compliance simply by contorting the English language and failing to acknowledge that U.S. forces are in fact engaged in "hostilities."[58] The conferees' decision in 1973 to relegate definitions of situations under which the president can deploy troops to a nonbinding declaration has also invited executive circumvention of key limitations. In no time at all, the White House had its lawyers arguing that there were all sorts of situations under which the president was justified in acting unilaterally to commit the nation to combat.[59] And the original proposal to bar troop commitments unless prior approval was first obtained from Congress has been viewed as simply too revolutionary in light of modern practice. Here the sanctity of the original intent of the Constitution's framers has been of little concern to conservative champions of a strong president—strict constructionists all.[60] The compromise of the Senate version, as critics predicted, has proven debilitating to efforts to curb arbitrary use of power by the White House. Congress has been reluctant to even *consider* withdrawing American troops once they have been deployed—no matter if their deployment appears open-ended, poorly justified, or inconsistent with the War Powers Act.

Today, the very power of Congress to challenge executive compliance with key terms of the 1973 act is open to question. The subject of the 1983 *INS v. Chadha* decision of the Supreme Court was unrelated to war powers. But this decision rejecting use of the legislative veto when Congress has explicitly granted an administrative power to the executive has raised basic questions about Sections 5(b) and 5(c) of the act.[61] Can Congress force such a momentous decision as the withdrawal of troops merely by failing to act on an authorization request? The legality of Section 5(b) remains unclear. But deep divisions remain over the wisdom of this provision, which could force an American retreat while Congress ducks a vote. "In any question as important as the life and death of American servicemen," Republican Congressman Charles Whalen of Ohio noted during the 1973 debate, "the Congress should decide yes or no as to whether or not these troops should be committed to that possible fate."[62] Defenders of Section 5(b) insist that the president has no authority to engage in sustained acts of war without express congressional approval. But the provision runs afoul of the same presentation clause of the Constitution that the courts found decisive in the *Chadha* case.

A stronger case can be made for the constitutionality of the legislative veto in Section 5(c) of the War Powers Act. In *Chadha*, the Court rejected concurrent resolution vetos—but only when Congress has expressly granted an administrative power to the executive. Thus, legal experts who defend the 5(c) provisions, including Senate Judiciary Committee Chairman Biden, maintain that its use here remains a legitimate exercise of power: "The legislative veto does not undermine the principle of separation of powers. It does not accompany a delegation of law-making authority to the Executive Branch, and it does not attempt to interfere with the administration of law."[63]

The central dilemma of the enduring war powers dispute has become the question of enforceability. The exhortations of successive commanders-in-chief have effectively intimidated legislators, in whom the Constitution vests the power to write policy instructions. Lawmakers continually flinch when confronted with presidential obstinance on troop deployment issues. What *should* Congress do when the president fails to consult them before committing the nation to battle? How *should* Congress respond when the president fails to comply with the provisions of the law of the land? Some representatives have gone to court, pressing legal claims against the president. Others have fallen back on face-saving compromises, gaining White House cooperation on procedure in return for congressional acquiescence on the substance of military and diplomatic policy.[64] Yet as one key Hill aide notes, "Congress should not have to pass a new law in order to enforce a law already on the books."[65] And even if such a move succeeds and a new measure forcing compliance is adopted, this strategy begs the question. "What do we do," one Senate leadership aide asks. "Send the Sergeant-at-Arms to the White House to wrestle with the President?"[66]

Congress and the White House deserve strong criticism for their handling of war powers disputes. Important opportunities have been lost, opportunities to establish a policy consensus that could make American force and diplomacy more effective, opportunities to bring American voters behind a commitment to a clear and unified policy. Today, interbranch harmony on war powers issues is as far away as ever. Some promising ideas were tabled during the lengthy 1988 hearings of the Special Senate War Powers Subcommittee. But no consensus is yet in sight on how Congress and the White house might chart a more promising course in the future. The basic question remains one of political will. As the courts have thus far concluded, the dispute over application of the War Powers Act to a U.S. military engagement is not one that the judicial branch can properly decide. These are issues to be thrashed out between the Congress and the president, between politicians and the voting public. Like most vital public policy questions engaging Americans, these disputes must be resolved in the political arena.

NOTES

1. Senator Thomas Eagleton, testimony before House Foreign Affairs Committee, March 7, 1973, p. 5. Eagleton observes that the introduction of the atomic bomb "has forced us to consider contingencies that were beyond the wildest dreams of Thomas Jefferson and Alexander Hamilton."

2. President Carter had called Senate Majority Leader Robert Byrd down to the White House on the evening of April 23, for a vague conversation after U.S. forces were already in the air, bound for Iran. In the aftermath, few argued seriously that this discussion constituted the prior consultation required by the War Powers Act.

3. Senators Jacob Javits and Frank Church, letter of April 24, 1980 to Secretary of State Cyrus Vance (sent before the Iran raid was under way), reprinted in Senate Foreign Relations Committee, "The Situation in Iran," May 8, 1980.

4. Earlier that morning—before he had met privately with the President—Church had chastised Carter on the war powers issue in a nationally televised interview. Douglas Kiker of NBC had asked Church on "The Today Show," "Do you think he [the President] violated the law?" "Yes," Church replied, "I think he disregarded this [consultation] section of the War Powers Act."

5. Papers of Senator Alan Cranston, transcript of White House press comments, April 24, 1980 (see Chapter 6, note 3).

6. The Senate Foreign Relations Committee did eventually convene hearings to evaluate the hostage situation in the wake of the rescue attempt and to discuss the implications of President Carter's new Persian Gulf Doctrine—which held that a challenge to Gulf security represented a threat to the security of the United States and would be met with force.

7. Cutler's widely assailed central argument was that it was "impractical" for the President to consult with leaders of Congress because the deployments depended on "speed and surprise"—which would have been compromised by such conversations because, he believed, those conversations would have been subject to foreign surveillance and eavesdropping. "Technology," he asserted, "rather than Presidential usurpation has removed Congress from this life-and-death exercise of the war-making power" (see Lloyd Cutler, "The Constitutional Sharing of the War Power," *Center for National Priorities Newsletter* [March 1988] : 5–6).

8. Senator Jacob Javits, as quoted in *National Journal*, May 19, 1984, p. 289.

9. Federalist Paper no. 69. It should again be emphasized the framers' writings offer internally contradictory interpretations. Thus, Hamilton warned against excessive executive powers in Federalist Paper no. 75, noting that "the history of human conduct does not warrant that exalted opinion of human virtue which would make it wise in a nation to commit interests of so delicate and momentous a kind as those which concern its intercourse with the rest of the world to the sole disposal of a magistrate, created and circumstanced, as would be the president of the United States." Yet in Federalist Paper no. 23, Hamilton rejected detailed limitations on war powers, asserting that "the circumstances that endanger the safety of nations are infinite, and for this reason no constitutional shackles can wisely be imposed on the power to which the care is committed."

10. James Madison, as quoted by Senator Thomas Eagleton, testimony before House Foreign Affairs Committee, March 7, 1973, p. 6.

11. Even in the eighteenth century, formal declarations of war were becoming less frequent than before. All five U.S. war declarations—the War of 1812, the Mexican War, the Spanish-American War, World War I, and World War II—were made by Congress after they had been requested by the president (see "Background Information on the Use of U.S. Armed Forces in Foreign Countries," published periodically by the Congressional Research Service).

12. Eugene Rostow, "Repeal the War Powers Resolution," *Wall Street Journal*, June 27, 1984, p. 34.

13. The revelations of the Senate Armed Services Committee established that under White House orders, the Pentagon had established a system of double bookkeeping to hide the conduct of this secret war from those in Congress who appropriated military funds. This abuse of power gave rise to an article of impeachment, framed by members of the House Judiciary Committee in August 1974 but not adopted.

14. See Sundquist, *Decline and Resurgence*, p. 258.

15. *Congressional Record*, July 17, 1983, p. H24098.

16. Senator Thomas Eagleton, as quoted in *1973 Congressional Quarterly Almanac*, p. 3. In a bitter floor exchange with Senator Javits on November 7, 1973, Eagleton also attacked the conferees' compromise relegating the definition of circumstances under which the president could use force—Section 2(c)—to the nonbinding "purpose and policy" preamble (see Eagleton, *War and Presidential Power*, pp. 207–223).

17. Senator Eagleton testified in 1988 that he had lobbied Senator Gaylord Nelson with the argument, "You can't vote for this 90-day unilateral war making. It is probably unconstitutional!" He quoted Nelson's reply: "Tom, I love the Constitution, but I hate Nixon more!" (Senator Thomas Eagleton, testimony before Senate Foreign Relations Committee, Special Subcommittee on War Powers, July 13, 1988, p. 35).

18. Graham Allison argues this latter point in "Making War: The President and Congress," in Tugwell, *Presidency Reappraised.*

19. Senator Alan Cranston, *Congressional Record*, September 29, 1983, p. S2087.

20. See Senator Charles Mathias, testimony before Senate Foreign Relations Committee, July 13, 1988, p. 6.

21. "The Supreme Court's decision does not affect any of the procedural mechanisms contained in the War Powers Resolution other than that procedure specified in section 5 (c)," according to the July 20, 1983 testimony of Deputy Attorney General Edward Schmults before the House Foreign Affairs Committee, as quoted in Ellen M. Collier, "The War Powers Resolution: A Decade of Experience," *Congressional Research Service*, February 6, 1984, p. 10.

22. Comments of Senators Paul Sarbanes, Paul Trible, and Lowell Weicker, as quoted in *New York Times*, October 6, 1987, p. A32.

23. Senator Charles Mathias, testimony before Senate Foreign Relations Committee, Special Subcommittee on War Powers, pp. 29–30.

24. Figures are through the fall of 1988. They do not include repetitious reports regarding Persian Gulf deployments.

25. See remarks of Senator Jacob Javits, *Congressional Record*, November 7, 1983, p. S3411.

26. Speaker Carl Albert called the House floor from the White House on the morning of April 29 asking that final action on the bill be delayed in view of the collapse of the South Vietnamese government. The measure was shelved on a 162–246 vote on May 1, 1975.

27. See Franck, *Tethered Presidency*, p. 45. For a detailed chronology of these events, see Michael J. Glennon, "Strengthening the War Powers Resolution: The Case for Purse-Strings Restrictions," *Minnesota Law Review* (November 1975).

28. Lietenant Colonel Andrew M. Egeland discusses the Carter report in "The Legal Limitation on the Use of Military Forces Under the War Powers Resolution," *Air Force Law Review* 25, no. 2 (1985): 150–51.

29. The Multinational Force Observer Participation Resolution (P.L. 97–132).

30. The House vote was 403–23; the Senate vote was 64–20 (see Collier, "The War Powers Resolution," p. 17).

31. The State Department legal adviser, Abraham Soafer, sought to defend the President's position in subsequent House Foreign Affairs Committee hearings by attacking Congress:

     The need some members of Congress feel to defend the Resolution's viability, even in situations well beyond those contemplated at the time of its adoption, causes Congress to shift its concern, deliberations, and political leverage away from evaluating the merits of military actions to testing their legality, and to focus on formal institutional issues rather than on the substance of our policies.

THE POWER TO MAKE WAR

Chairman Dante Fascell's rejoinder was, "You are telling us that we are wasting our time worrying about the Constitution" (as quoted in Jeremy J. Stone, "Libya and the War Powers Resolution," *Federation of American Scientists Bulletin* [June 1986] : 11).

32. Senator Lowell Weicker, as quoted in *New York Times*, April 16, 1986, p. 17.

33. Congressman Thomas P. O'Neill, as quoted in *New York Times*, April 16, 1986, p. 17.

34. The raid apparently was in part an attempt to assassinate Qadaffi. While the Libyan leader survived, the attack succeeded in stilling Qadaffi-sponsored terrorist attacks against Americans (see Thomas Campbell, "An Understanding of the Constitution's Foreign Affairs Powers," Heritage Foundation Lectures, October 6, 1986, p. 5.

35. See War Powers Resolution amendments of 1982 (S. 2179), introduced by Senator Byrd of West Virginia.

36. *Crockett v. Reagan*, 558 F. Supp. 893 (D.D.C. 1982).

37. As quoted in Collier, "The War Powers Resolution," p. 22.

38. No president has sought to challenge the constitutionality of the War Powers Act through adjudication, and no Congress has sought to force a troop withdrawal under Sections 5(b) or 5(c). Some members have unsuccessfully sought an advisory opinion to get around the unwillingness of courts to hear cases that are moot.

39. Another factor was the desire of Democrats to duck the issue while leaving ultimate responsibility for an unpromising situation to the President. "His fingerprints are all over it," several Democratic colleagues advised Senator Eagleton at the height of the Lebanon war powers debate. "Let's not get ours all over it" (Senator Thomas Eagleton, testimony before Senate Foreign Relations Committee, Special Subcommittee on War Powers, July 13, 1988, p. 36).

40. The Senate vote on the 18-month authorization was along party lines, with the measure passing 54–46.

41. Shultz consistently proved readier to use American forces in unconventional combat situations than Weinberger—who was always reluctant to allow U.S. involvement in unpopular conflicts because it could diminish support for his military buildup. The Shultz-Weinberger split on Lebanon ultimately fueled Hill debates. The Pentagon had been "opposed to the Lebanon policy from the beginning," as a Senate Democratic aide noted after the President turned on the Hill. "They're the ones who triggered the debate" (as quoted in *National Journal*, May 19, 1984, p. 993).

42. Ronald Reagan, as quoted in *National Journal*, May 19, 1984, p. 993.

43. George Shultz, testimony before Senate Appropriations Subcommittee on Foreign Operations, March 2, 1984, as quoted in Jacob K. Javits, "Congress' Crucial War Role," *New York Times*, March 16, 1984, p. 25.

44. Senator Charles Percy, as quoted in *National Journal*, May 19, 1984, p. 993.

45. The House vote on July 8 was 222–184 to prohibit reflagging for at least ninety days. The Senate voted later that month on a nonbinding measure urging that alternatives to reflagging be pursued.

46. Senator Robert Byrd, as quoted in *Washington Post*, October 22, 1987, p. 1.

47. Several members of Congress filed suit alleging that the facts of the situation in the Gulf required that the 90-day clock of the War Powers Act be triggered. "The whole purpose of the War Powers [Act]," plaintiff Congressman Bruce Morrison of Connecticut explained, "is not to have to pass a new law every time we have a Vietnam or a Cambodia." But the U.S. district court ruled in favor of the administration, agreeing with the assertion of Justice Department lawyers that the issue was "a quintessentially non-justiciable political question" (see "War Powers Battle Goes to Court," *Washington Times*, March 1, 1988, p. 4).

48. Admiral William J. Crowe, testimony before Senate Foreign Relations Committee, Special Subcommittee on War Powers, September 23, 1988, p. 5 (prepared statement).

49. The warmest praise for the act came from former White House and Defense Department aide and former Secretary of State Cyrus Vance, who observed that the act "reinforces presidential self-restraint and serves as a constant reminder that policies involving the use of force overseas must garner support beyond the short term" (Cyrus Vance, testimony before Special Subcommittee on War Powers, September 16, 1988. p. 6).

50. See S. J. Res. 323, 100th Congress. The hearings were also delayed by the serious illness of the subcommittee's chairman, Senator Biden.

51. Senator Joseph Biden, Special Subcommittee on War Powers hearing September 7, 1988, pp. 90–91.

52. Albert Lakeland, testimony before Special Subcommittee on War Powers, September 7, 1988, p. 1 (prepared statement). Lakeland was legislative assistant to Senator Javits, the principal sponsor of the 1973 act.

53. Abraham Sofaer, testimony before Special Subcommittee on War Powers, September 15, 1988, p. 5 (prepared statement).

54. General Brent Scowcroft, Special Subcommittee on War Powers, September 7, 1988, p. 93.

55. *Weekly Compilation of Presidential Documents: Richard Nixon (1973)*, p. 1286.

56. Barry M. Goldwater, "The President's Constitutional Primacy in Foreign Relations and National Defense," *Virginia Journal of International Law* 13, no. 4 (Summer 1973): 487–88.

57. Frank Carlucci, testimony before Special Subcommittee on War Powers, September 23, 1988, p. 14 (prepared statement).

58. Daniel Paul Franklin, "War Powers in the Modern Context," *Congress and the Presidency* 14, no. 1 (Spring 1987): 90.

59. In 1975 House hearings, State Department legal adviser Monroe Leigh suggested a number of other instances beyond those stipulated in Section 2 (c) in which the president could unilaterally commit U.S. troops to combat. Leigh's list included rescuing U.S. citizens abroad, defending U.S. embassies, suppressing civil insurrection, implementing cease-fires, and carrying out security commitments pursuant to treaty obligations (see Glennon, "Strengthening the War Powers Resolution," note 22).

60. Professor Robert Scigliano notes that "the resolution's opponents seem to address the constitutional issues with some embarrassment, as well they might, in view of the insurmountable evidence against them on this [war powers] question. And its supporters often cite that [constitutional] evidence with the enthusiasm of recent converts, as indeed many of them were, having been until a short time before advocates of a powerful presidency in the manner of Franklin Roosevelt" (Robert Scigliano, "The War Powers Resolution," in Bessette and Tulis, *Presidency in the Constitutional Order*, p. 262).

61. *INS v. Chadha* was an immigration case in which the authority of Congress to veto executive branch regulations was held to violate the presentation clause of the Constitution. This decision invalidated legislative veto provisions contained in nearly 200 separate laws under a practice that dated back to the Hoover administration (see Franck, *Tethered Presidency*, pp. 78–80).

62. Congressman Charles Whalen, as quoted in 1973 *Congressional Quarterly Almanac* 29, p. 7.

63. Joseph Biden, Special Subcommittee on War Powers hearing, September 16, 1988, p. 58. See also Senator Charles Mathias, testimony before Senate Foreign Relations Committee, July 13, 1988, pp. 46–47.

64. Introduction of the Byrd bill was cited by several senators as justification for deferring war powers disputes surrounding the Persian Gulf deployments of 1987–1988. But one Democratic senator continued to press for repeated roll calls on the application of the act to the Gulf situation: "We can't evade the obligations created by the law just by introducing legislation designed to fix it," Senator Brock Adams of Washington insisted. "The law is the law and we took a sacred vow to uphold it" (as quoted in *New York Times*, June 7, 1988, p. 13).

65. Richard P. Conlon (executive director of the Democratic Study Group), as quoted in *New York Times*, October 6, 1987, p. 32.

66. As quoted in ibid.

6 THE TREATY-MAKING POWER

A treaty entering the Senate is like a bull going into an arena: no one
can say just how or when the final blow will fall—but one thing is
certain—it will never leave the arena alive. . . . One third plus one of
the United States Senate can be counted upon to vote upon the black-
guard side of any question.

—John Hay, 1900 [1]

Politics makes for strange bedfellows. But rarely in recent American
political experience has such an unusual alliance been formed as that
which assembled on October 29, 1987 in Room S-148 of the Capitol
Building. The challenge of defeating an antitreaty Senate coalition
of one-third-plus-one had brought these men together to advance
the emerging treaty on intermediate-range nuclear forces in Europe.
The INF pact offered no reductions in U.S. and Soviet *strategic*
arsenals. But it represented a significant breakthrough in the troubled course of superpower relations. And it looked to be the first
U.S.-Soviet arms treaty the Senate might ratify after fifteen years of
disappointment.

Gathered in the ornate Senate Democratic whip's office that
gray October afternoon were men who had dominated opposing sides
of the Washington arms control debate for a generation—men now
prepared to join in a coalition of convenience to work for swift rati-

fication of the INF Treaty. There was Paul Nitze—the brilliant law-yer had led the fight against the SALT II Treaty as a private citizen, only later to become President Reagan's special ambassador for the INF negotiations with the Soviets. There were arch-conservatives present from the Senate Republican leadership—party whip Alan Simpson, Ted Stevens from the Defense Appropriations Subcom-mittee, and Richard Lugar from the Foreign Relations Committee. They were joined by Secretary of State Shultz, who had shepherded the INF negotiations through the shaky second Reagan term, but who even then was engaged in a nastry confrontation with Senate Democrats over compliance with terms of the 1972 ABM Treaty and the unratified SALT II pact.

On the Democratic side were veteran arms control champions like Dale Bumpers of Arkansas, Paul Sarbanes of Maryland, and Joe Biden of Delaware. The host of the meeting, California Senator Alan Cranston, had convened, in that very room, dozens of sessions of legislators determined to prevail in pushing through such arms con-trol measures as SALT II. His SALT working group had done battle with the likes of Nitze and Shultz and their Republican Senate col-leagues for more than a decade. A number of the senior Democrats present remained bitter over Ronald Reagan's many years as a stri-dent critic of all arms control treaties. "If political justice were the measure," one critic summed up their sentiment, "the Senate would throw the INF treaty back in [President Reagan's] face. In his time as a presidential candidate in the 1970s, nobody did more to make life difficult for presidents trying to move treaties through the Sen-ate, and nobody was more irresponsible in doing so."[2]

The legacy of these old disputes weighed heavily upon those pres-ent. Yet forging an alliance to press for swift Senate approval of the INF pact—without any weakening amendments—was not difficult. The senior Reagan administration officials recognized that White House credibility still suffered from the Iran-Contra affair. With Department of Defense officials damning the INF pact with faint praise, Senate leaders would have to carry the ratification fight. Con-versely, arms control advocates from the Democratic ranks under-stood that it was their Republican colleagues who would prove most effective in countering Senate conservatives who were deeply sus-picious of Reagan's eleventh-hour conversion to the cause of U.S.-Soviet detente. The formal treaty ratification fight would not begin until late January. But with a new Reagan-Gorbachev summit on

strategic arms already scheduled in Moscow for the spring of 1988—
a summit that would prove unproductive, if not acrimonious, if the
Senate was still picking over the INF pact—the ratification fight
became a battle against time. Could the complicated and unprecedented pact be carried over the many looming hurdles? Could advocates prevent the resolution of ratification from being loaded down
with hostile amendments that might kill the pact? Would the Senate
finally overcome enduring partisan divisions and, for the first time
in fifteen years, give its blessing to a treaty advancing U.S.-Soviet
relations?

The divergent perspectives brought to the discussion in Cranston's
Capitol office readily coalesced behind a determination to achieve
these goals. There was not an ideologue among the liberals and conservatives, Democrats and Republicans, present. Thus, an elaborate
strategy began to take shape that would guide meetings of the informal group in subsequent months. It served well to avert dangerous
delays, to overcome numerous obstacles, and to reject any killer
amendments. From October through the following May, these senators worked together on an informal, though remarkably productive,
basis. With two days to spare—and in spite of clumsy and ineffective
White House intervention—the INF ratification job got done.[3]

Both the INF and the SALT II debates—which we shall revisit
shortly—illustrate a central irony of the reforms of the 1970s. Liberals in the U.S. Congress led the Vietnam War-era challenge to the
president's prerogatives in foreign policymaking. Senate progressives
were at the forefront of this effort, revitalizing old procedural tools
and forging new ones. Yet it has been *conservatives* who have oper-
ated most effectively in the resulting environment. By pressing a consistent ideological agenda, conservatives have shaped the terms of
American treaties on security, commerce, and peace. Conservatives
have built upon the long-standing tradition of Senate skepticism in
treaty matters, giving new resonance to a familiar refrain of isolationism in the conduct of America's international affairs. In so doing, the
forces of the political right have had a significant impact upon the
conduct of American relations with both the Soviet Union and
China, as well as the lesser developed nations of the Third World.

Few constitutional provisions have had a more profound impact
upon U.S. diplomacy than the granting of a treaty veto to a Senate
block of one-third-plus-one. This revolutionary empowerment of a
legislative minority has confounded chief executives throughout

U.S. history. From President Washington's first awkward encounter in the Senate chamber to the League of Nations disaster, to the SALT II debacle, this constitutional check has proven a formidable deterrent to executive initiatives in treaty affairs. In the modern era, the Senate's power to veto treaties has enjoyed heightened significance as America has struggled to reconcile its enduring suspicion of "entangling foreign alliances" with its new global responsibilities as an economic and military superpower.

While the INF debate produced a modest victory, other recent tests have limited White House diplomatic options on key international security questions of the day. The presidency has suffered major setbacks on such issues as strategic arms limitations, U.S.-Soviet trade, and relations with China. Even the one celebrated ratification battle that Senate conservatives lost in the mid-1970s—the Panama Canal fight—yielded important benefits for the political right. Of the thirty-eight treaty supporters who faced the voters in 1978 and 1980, fully twenty were defeated, including the floor manager for the ratification fight, Foreign Relations Committee Chairman Frank Church.[4]

Repeated Senate challenges to treaties have lent uncertainty to modern U.S. diplomacy, confounding foreign friends and foes alike. This lament is a familiar one. Yet there is a striking contrast when one compares the repeated failures of congressional challenges to the commander-in-chief in the war powers area to the relative success of a Senate minority in circumscribing treaty-making options. It often seems easier for Congress to acquiesce in commitments to war than to approve the ratification of treaties of peace. Why have Senate treaty-making challenges succeeded when so many other international initiatives of Congress have failed? Is it the enduring legacy of isolationism? Is it the fervent post–World War II commitment to anticommunism of a determined Senate bloc? Or is it simply institutional jealousy, the unremitting suspicion popularly elected legislators hold for State Department negotiators and "secret White House diplomacy"? These are crucial questions to weigh as we consider recent U.S. practice in negotiating and ratifying treaties. We shall begin with an examination of important general principles before turning to the specifics of two key debates—the troubled course of U.S.-Soviet treaty relations since the advent of detente, and the watershed battle over Senate ratification of the 1978 Panama Canal treaties.

THE SENATE AND THE TWO-THIRDS REQUIREMENT

The Constitutional Convention of 1787 only grudgingly gave the president the power to negotiate treaties. Early drafts of the charter vested in the Senate the exclusive right to conduct actual negotiations and to assess the adequacy of international compacts. Authority was provided for the Senate to confirm the president's ambassadors—and thereby to review the ambassadors' negotiating instructions—prior to their departure on a mission. The practice during the eighteenth century was to send American ambassadors overseas only for the conduct of a specific negotiation. Thus, the confirmation power granted the Senate broad control over the conduct of diplomacy. So great was the framers' suspicion of a powerful executive that the Constitutional Convention seriously considered a proposal by James Madison that separate rules be established for Senate control over the negotiation and ratification of peace treaties. Madison argued, with considerable initial support from delegates, that "the President would necessarily derive so much power and importance from a state of war that he might be tempted, if authorized, to impede a treaty of peace."[5] Madison retreated from his proposal in the closing days at Philadelphia. But the new Senate proved to be assertive in defending its treaty review authority.

We have previously recounted the bitter foreign policy disputes that President Washington and his ambassador John Jay had with the Senate. The crucial treaty precedents established in these divisive struggles remain with us today. The Senate has protected its right to reject a treaty to which the executive has committed the nation—a genuinely revolutionary development in eighteenth-century diplomacy that shattered the existing doctrine of obligatory ratification.[6] Yet the Senate does not usually become directly involved in treaty negotiation, rarely going beyond token representation in U.S. delegations. Even in the INF case, the Senate Arms Control Observer Group was just that—a bipartisan delegation of legislators who occasionally visited the Geneva talks. They had no impact on the course of negotiations. And while the observer group did develop a certain amount of expertise that might have proved useful in the Senate's review of the INF pact, members had no special role in treaty ratification efforts.

The Senate does reserve the right to challenge ambassadorial nominees and to alter the negotiators' handiwork with unilateral amendments to treaty texts. Nominations have often served as a lightning rod for senators determined to "send a message" to the White House and to seek changes in administration policy. Senators have also developed considerable skill in exacting compensatory policy changes as a price for their consent to treaty ratification. In some cases, this has required adoption of countervailing policy initiatives to balance the thrust of a treaty; for example, new White House commitments to make negotiated reductions in Soviet conventional arms a top priority in negotiations were won in return for some senators' support for INF ratification. In other cases, the political wheeling and dealing has been cruder. Democratic Senator Herman Talmadge of Georgia withheld his vote for the Panama pacts until he won White House concessions on a $2.3 billion program of agricultural subsidies, while Senator Dennis DeConcini bargained for a $500 million federal purchase of surplus copper to aid economically depressed Arizona miners.[7] House members witness such scrambling and try to carve out a treaty role of their own. Indeed, in both the Jay Treaty and the Panama Canal debates, the House sought to bar funds for implementing treaties that were opposed by many of its members. The House votes in both instances proved extremely close; President Washington and President Carter were each forced to fight a second battle in the lower body after having already prevailed on the treaty ratification question in the Senate.[8]

The statistics on treaty debates suggest a heavy bias in favor of the executive. The United States has ratified more than 1,500 treaties. Only seventeen have been rejected outright by Senate vote. While nearly 600 treaties have been ratified since the failure of the Versailles agreements, only three relatively minor treaties have been formally rejected by roll call votes in the U.S. Senate since 1920.[9] However, unless examined more carefully, these totals can serve to obscure rather than enlighten. Just as the most essential treaty of early American diplomacy (the Jay pact normalizing relations with Great Britain) narrowly escaped defeat on Capitol Hill, two of the most important pacts of this century—the League of Nations compact and the SALT II Treaty—failed to gain timely Senate consent. The Senate has on numerous occasions checked international treaty initiatives that presidents have deemed vital to the nation's security. As many as 117 treaties have been stalled in the Senate either through

the attachment of amendments unacceptable to foreign treaty partners or because of Senate refusal to put the measures to a final up-
and-down vote.

The greater than 90 percent success rate for treaty ratifications
also gives no indication of security compacts that were stillborn
because of congressional hostility—as when FDR sought to aid the
British people while they were under Nazi siege in 1940. The numbers give no indication of initiatives checked because of potential
Capitol Hill objections—as when Jimmy Carter shelved two U.S.-
Soviet nuclear testing accords, the Threshold Test Ban Treaty and
the Peaceful Nuclear Explosives Treaty, and decided against concluding a comprehensive test ban treaty. The statistics give no indication
of pacts approved by the Senate only after substantial alterations
were made in their terms—as in the Panama Canal debate. And the
numbers do not include treaties that sunk under the weight of
"killer" amendments adopted by the Senate to gut key provisions—
as happened to the League of Nations Treaty before the heavily
amended compact fell short of a two-thirds vote on a 49–35 roll call.

Senate opportunities for scuttling treaties are indeed numerous.
But most still arise through assault by indirection. Lying before
the Senate during a treaty ratification debate is not the text of
the treaty itself, which is contained in the presidential message held
at the presiding officer's desk. Rather, the Senate technically votes
on a resolution consenting to the ratification of the treaty by the
president—a resolution open to amendments that can condition presidential ratification upon other actions, including renegotiation of
treaty provisions. Technically, the Senate does not "ratify" treaties;
it merely grants the president the authority to do so through the
exchange of ratification instruments with foreign treaty partners.
Under the Constitution, the Senate gives its "advice and consent" to
this presidential act, but can place all sorts of conditions on its execution. It is principally through the addition of such conditions in a
resolution of ratification that the Senate can alter the course of U.S.
diplomacy, setting the parameters for acceptable policy departures
without confronting the president with outright rejection of a treaty
he has already signed. Such maneuvers have gone beyond mere procedural skirmishes to strike at the heart of basic U.S. foreign policy
objectives, even when treaty ratification appears to be a foregone conclusion. These battles have given policymakers the opportunity to
fashion a host of unique procedural weapons with which to wage com-

bat over the course of American diplomacy. Understanding how to use these tools is the key to success in treaty-making confrontations.

PROCEDURAL ALTERNATIVES TO TREATY RATIFICATION DEBATES

Faced with an often uphill fight to obtain the support of two-thirds of the Senate for treaty ratification, presidents have proven remarkably adept at devising end-run options. The easiest method for avoiding the slippery slope of a ratification debate is to conclude an international accord as an executive agreement instead of a treaty. By asserting that a particular agreement is not central to security and commercial relations with a foreign people, the president can unilaterally commit the United States to an executive agreement between governments. Such an agreement can only be blocked by timely passage of a joint resolution through both houses of Congress and the subsequent override of the inevitable veto. The criteria for choosing between a treaty and an executive agreement are entirely arbitrary and can be readily exploited by the White House. When Jimmy Carter was under assault during the course of the controversial SALT II negotiations—with the prospect of strong Senate opposition growing each month—he openly mulled submitting this momentous pact to Congress as an executive agreement. SALT supporters in the Senate, including Majority Leader Robert Byrd, promptly warned Carter that the move would ignite a formidable protest on procedural grounds; the protest would severely damage efforts to win votes on the substance of the emerging treaty. Carter backed down. But he did choose in 1977 to extend the terms of the expired SALT I accord by exchange of diplomatic notes with the Soviets. He did not seek any formal Hill support whatsoever for this move—which was tantamount to an executive agreement, though not legally binding on the parties.

The rise of America's international role since the beginning of World War II has brought an explosion in the number of executive agreements. Where there were less than 1,000 between 1789 and 1939, there were more than 9,500 in the subsequent forty-five years: from the 1945 Yalta agreement to the Vietnam peace agreement of 1973, to the Iranian hostage pact of 1981. Congress reacted to this phenomenon as early as 1970, when it adopted the Case Act. This measure (as further refined in 1978) requires notification and transmittal of all executive agreements to Congress. In some instances—agreements for nuclear cooperation, for example—Congress provided for expedited review of resolutions by which it can bar entry into force of a new accord. But even with such procedural restraints, executive agreements still grant the White House far greater initiative and latitude than is available through the treaty route because they do not require affirmative Senate action before entering into force.

The converse of the White House executive agreement maneuver is Congress's recent approach of adopting legislation to force U.S. compliance with certain treaty terms, so long as the Soviets do likewise. This tactic is primarily a feature of the Reagan years before the INF accord, a period when many in Congress viewed the White House as hostile to arms accords. The effort began in 1982 when Congress pushed a nonbinding resolution urging that the President negotiate with Soviet leaders a bilateral freeze on the number of nuclear weapons deployed by the two superpowers. But the President had made a deliberate commitment to belligerent anti-Soviet rhetoric throughout his first term. Aided by a suspect Soviet record on compliance with past treaties, the White House campaign led eventually to U.S. renunciation of the numerical ceilings on arms deployments contained in the SALT II accord. The President was intent on deploying weapons in excess of these ceilings as a means of burying the treaty once and for all. Congressional advocates of U.S.-Soviet arms negotiations, including House Armed Services Committee Chairman Les Aspin and Senator Dale Bumpers, pressed opposition. They pushed for binding legislation to force the United States to comply with the SALT II ceilings unless the President certified that the Soviets had already breached these numerical limits.[10] Similar provisions were adopted halting U.S. tests of antisatellite (ASAT) weapons so long as the Soviets refrained from such testing.

These legislative efforts proved extraordinarily controversial, for they were tantamount to Congress making proposals directly to the Soviet Union and bypassing the executive branch. Defenders of the efforts maintained that they were a legitimate exercise of the Congress's right to determine what military systems would be funded. But SALT II opponents were genuinely outraged that liberals would seek to force selective compliance with the terms of an unratified treaty. Senator Robert Dole threatened at one point to call up the resolution of ratification for the SALT II pact and to seek its repudiation. "They don't have the votes for it," Republican Senator Dan Quayle observed. "That's why this is such a perversion of the Constitution. [SALT II proponents] are trying a backdoor treaty ratification by having a majority vote in the House and the Senate." [11]

The clash over U.S. adherence to SALT II limitations escalated through several sessions of Congress. Each year, the Hill would move toward adoption of binding legislation, using the argument that existing limits should remain in place while the sluggish START (strategic arms reduction talks) negotiations continued. Each year, Reagan administration officials would prevail upon legislators to back down at the last minute. Often the White House would use the charge that the proviso would "tie the President's hands" in imminent meetings with Soviet General Secretary Mikhail Gorbachev. It seemed to many Hill critics that negotiations were *always* "at a crucial point"; this White House strategy was used once too often, infuriating critical swing votes like Sam Nunn in the Senate and Jim Wright in the House, who had their own political agendas to consider. [12] In November 1987, Congress adopted binding provisions in the Department of Defense authorization bill conference report. On the very eve of the Reagan-Gorbachev Washington summit, this House-Senate compromise forced the President to reduce the number of deployed U.S. strategic nuclear systems. The measure had only a modest impact on U.S. nuclear forces. But the precedent it set clearly had a significance that would outlive the specific issue of U.S. force structure.

Related debates on treaty issues have broken out on several fronts in recent years. A summary review of these important interbranch confrontations illustrates the great variety of devices the two branches of government can employ for one-upmanship in defending treaty-making prerogatives. Three particular devices have proved crucial.

Reinterpretation of a Treaty. The protracted dispute between the Reagan administration and Congress over the 1972 antiballistic missile (ABM) accord threatened to undermine the Senate's treaty-making role and deprive the ratification process of much of its meaning. The stakes of this confrontation over Senate understanding of executive branch representations became higher and higher, until the interbranch dialogue on arms treaty issues reached what one contemporary analyst termed "the point of near political paralysis." [13] The policy issues were clear. The Reagan administration was committed to the Strategic Defense Initiative, the testing phase of which violated the consensus definitions of the ABM Treaty. So administration lawyers prepared a legal brief attempting to reconcile testing with the ABM treaty restraints. Obscure in-house documents from the treaty's negotiating record were used to construct an argument that a reinterpretation of treaty provisions could permit SDI tests. This new interpretation was disputed by virtually all members of the U.S. negotiating team for the 1972 pact.[14] But the argument extended far beyond the immediate issues of Star Wars testing. Its broader implications on constitutional treaty issues were even more profound, raising central questions about the Senate role in ratifying the imminent INF pact. To what extent is the president committed to explanations given to the Senate by a predecessor? Is the executive branch bound by a Senate interpretation even if a foreign treaty partner is not? What meaning does Senate treaty review have if the executive branch may later "reinterpret" its terms at will? These legal questions were overshadowed by a fundamental political reality: when the executive branch attempts a procedural end-run, the Congress can always respond by using its power of the purse. When State Department counsel Abraham Sofaer continued to insist that the administration could test Star Wars systems and still be in compliance with the ABM Treaty, Congress moved to bar funding. Democratic Senator Carl Levin of Michigan pressed a measure preventing any Star Wars tests that violated the traditional interpretation of the ABM Treaty. When conservative Democrats like Nunn rejected the Sofaer Doctrine and joined with Levin to forge an Armed Services Committee majority against "reinterpretation," the Reagan administration's position was doomed.[15] A bar to testing under the new interpretation was enacted. And then specific language was attached to the INF resolution of ratification guarding against any reinterpretation of treaties in the future.[16]

Presidential Abrogation of a Treaty. A corollary to the reinterpretation issue is found in the threat of unilateral White House treaty abrogation. If treaties are the "law of the land" and if the Senate is part and parcel of their making, what happens when the president chooses to abandon an international treaty commitment? Jimmy Carter confronted the issue head on when, as part of the 1978 move to establish full diplomatic relations with the People's Republic of China, he exercised the withdrawal clause in the U.S. mutual defense agreement with the Republic of China. This time liberals defended presidential prerogative, while conservatives were outraged by the denial of any Senate role. Senator Goldwater pursued the issue with a lawsuit. But he and other friends of Taiwan were hampered by the fact that President Carter's action was not inconsistent with treaty terms. The President was merely exercising—without consulting the Senate—the U.S. prerogative to withdraw from the treaty. The Supreme Court held for the executive branch, concluding that the President was within his rights and that the question was a "political dispute" that it was inappropriate for the Court to resolve.[17] Congress did manage, however, to find a legislative means of manifesting members' concerns about abrogation of the pact with the ROC. Lawmakers drafted amendments to the Taiwan Relations Act offering assurances to Taipei on future arms sales and "nonofficial" relations with the Nationalist regime. Senate liberals like Edward Kennedy and Alan Cranston succeeded in preempting the issue of continuing security ties with the ROC authorities on Taiwan by offering a nonbinding commitment to support Taiwan in the event of attack from the Communist Chinese on the mainland. President Carter threatened to veto the measure if stronger amendments were added. But after much negotiation over final terms, he signed the bill.[18]

Secret Addenda to Peace Accords.   Another fundamental question about the executive-legislative partnership on treaty issues was prompted by the private assurances of continuing American support that President Nixon gave to South Vietnamese leaders in 1973. To what extent are legislators bound by personal commitments the president makes in order to secure an international agreement? The issue weighed heavily upon legislators when Hanoi violated the Paris peace accords after U.S. forces had accelerated their withdrawal from South Vietnam. In the abstract, the constitutional question was clear. Congress could not be bound by commitments it had not reviewed. The U.S. government cannot be obliged to fulfill treaty obligations to which the legislative branch has not been a party. But in the case of the Paris peace accords, the political impact of this debate struck more deeply. President Nixon had given secret assurances to the Saigon leadership as an added inducement to accept the Paris accords. Months later, when Communist aggression proved unrelenting, a Congress weary of American involvement refused to send substantial aid to beleaguered South Vietnamese forces. Few in Congress had knowledge of the Nixon pledge, and there was no enthusiasm for

committing new U.S. forces to a lost cause. War opponents successfully resisted "throwing good money after bad." But critics of Congress were appalled. Soon revisionist historians were at work pressing
the argument that the United States would actually have *won* the
war in Vietnam if only Congress had not cut funding. The assertion
was disputed by many legislators, who were convinced in 1974 and
1975 that new aid could have done little to save the disintegrating
Saigon regime. But the image of Congress undermining a vital presidential commitment has endured. The political questions involved—
as well as the constitutional issues at stake—persist today.

THE ROCKY PATH OF U.S.-SOVIET TREATY RELATIONS

Since the advent of detente during the Nixon-Brezhnev years, the
U.S.-Soviet treaty relationship has weathered a difficult course.
Treaties negotiated have not been consummated. Treaties signed have
not been ratified. Treaties ratified have been reinterpreted, violated,
or allowed to expire. And those agreements that have been imple-
mented—the limited test ban, the hot-line accord, SALT I, and the
INF pact—have been modest in scope and have done nothing to cut
strategic arms levels.

Throughout this troubled experience, Congress has played a crucial
role in shaping treaty relations. The availability of numerous procedural options has empowered congressional critics of White House
strategy to press their own priorities. Detente opponents have successfully linked concerns on issues like Soviet human rights violations
and the brutal Soviet invasion of Afghanistan to accords on nuclear
arms issues. Each U.S.-Soviet treaty has become a target for legislators intent on pressing broader concerns. Critics in Congress have
thus helped to widen the parameters of debate while redefining the
U.S.-Soviet bilateral agenda.

The Senate has thrown up a number of impediments to strengthened U.S.-Soviet ties. Congress blocked realization of the 1974
U.S.-Soviet trade pact by placing conditions on its implementation
that proved unacceptable to the Soviets. Conservatives also looked
askance at the 1979 SALT II accords, assailing the agreement through
months of hearings in the Senate committees on armed services and
foreign relations and setting conditions for approval of the pact that

might well have proved unattainable. Yet in the Reagan years, progressive forces in the Senate successfully pressured the White House to be more energetic in pursuing U.S.-Soviet arms accords. Congress repeatedly pushed the White House to negotiate reductions and to conclude agreements on strategic arms and testing limitations, as well as the INF pact. Indeed, in this topsy-turvy Washington struggle, the only constant has been a deep and enduring dispute between Congress and the White House over how best to proceed with the Soviet relationship. There simply has not been an enduring interbranch consensus on a strategy for treaty relations with Moscow. The intramural struggle has thus forced presidents to negotiate with congressional critics and Soviet adversaries simultaneously, in a most clumsy and awkward process. President Carter was pressed by conservatives in Congress, just as Reagan felt the heat from liberals on Capitol Hill.

Divisions on strategy have not only divided Congress from the White House. The executive branch itself has remained sharply divided over the desirability of U.S.-Soviet detente. Internal administration disputes have played a key role in hamstringing U.S. efforts to achieve consistency in Soviet policy. These arguments are as old as the Cold War itself. President Truman sacked Henry Wallace for being too soft on Moscow, while right-wingers in Congress led by Joe McCarthy sought to purge the State Department of any pro-Soviet sympathies. In recent years, Cabinet-level disagreements have repeatedly erupted in public. In one almost comic episode during the Carter years, the Brzezinski-Vance debate on detente strategy became so entrenched that the President made clumsy efforts to reconcile both perspectives. For a major address at Annapolis, President Carter blended paragraphs from two drafts submitted by his feuding aides, weaving together hawkish and dovish statements in an incoherent mix. A similar celebrated dispute raged in the Reagan years between the "two Richards"—Perle of Defense and Burt of State, who headed the efforts of their respective departments to shape strategy on U.S.-Soviet relations. The persistence of such disputes has created a cumbersome, three-cornered treaty-negotiating process. The administration must hammer out an internal consensus and then is obliged to negotiate with Congress before it even begins to approach the Soviets. As a consequence, internal cohesion suffers and there is a temptation to bypass the Hill. "The process of reaching a decision within the executive branch is frequently so laborious," Brent Scowcroft has explained, "that there is little inclination to start the process over again with Congress."[19] Furthermore, the losers of an internal administration dispute inevitably feed their briefs to critics of administration policy on the Hill. Ammunition is thus provided from within the secret councils of the executive branch to assault administration policy. This type of networking by policy dissenters can make the effective conduct of negotiations well nigh impossible at times.

It is therefore not surprising that in the forty-four years of the nuclear age, the United States and the Soviet Union have never negotiated and ratified a strategic arms reduction agreement. And in the twenty-five years between the Limited Test Ban Treaty of 1963 and the 1988 Euromissile accord, only the ABM Treaty and the SALT I agreement were concluded. The latter two pacts were key building blocks in the Nixon-Kissinger grand strategy of detente. The SALT I interim accord enjoyed substantial congressional support—despite its implicit acknowledgment that the United States no longer possessed nuclear superiority over the Soviet Union. It gained Senate approval with a strong bipartisan majority in an election year. Only with the Jackson Amendment—requiring that subsequent treaties provide for precisely equal numbers of strategic systems on both sides—did the Senate leave its mark.[20]

The ABM Treaty enjoyed similar support. In fact, this accord halting deployment of nuclear defenses was in many ways a direct result of congressional agitation. Senate skepticism of ABM technology was a major impetus to Nixon's desire to conclude a treaty banning a futile ABM competition. An August 1969 vote of 51–49 to continue ABM funding was won in the Senate only after last-second vote switches on the Senate floor.[21] Three years later, the Senate endorsed the pact virtually barring ABM deployments. Both hawks and doves embraced the treaty's concept of mutual assured destruction (MAD): the notion that effective defenses were not feasible and that an assured retaliatory capability for both superpowers was essential to deterrence and stability in the nuclear age.

Nixon and Kissinger oversold the modest U.S.-Soviet accords, raising the expectations of American voters to an unrealistically high level. SALT I merely capped the total number of strategic weapons, establishing a framework to govern future arms deployments. It did nothing to slow modernization or fractionization ("MIRV-ing") of missile warheads. And a parallel U.S.-Soviet agreement on preventing the outbreak of misunderstandings in the Third World proved entirely hortatory. The pact was utterly unenforceable and thus proved to be a prescription for disillusionment. Indeed, within months of the conclusion of these major Nixon-Brezhnev pacts, Washington and Moscow were on the brink of a direct confrontation in the Middle East. When Soviet-backed forces in Egypt and Syria attacked Israel in the fall of 1973, U.S. troops were placed on worldwide alert.

Efforts to broaden the U.S.-Soviet treaty relationship beyond pacts regularizing arms competition foundered. The White House saw promise in a U.S.-Soviet trade pact that would expand Soviet reliance on Western grain and technology while promoting American exports. During President Nixon's 1972 visit to Moscow, a deal was struck. Soviet goods would be offered most-favored-nation treatment and the Soviets would be eligible for Export-Import Bank credits in return for payment of $700 million in World War II—era lend-lease debts and greater U.S. access to Soviet markets. The trade opportunities held great promise for Americans; in 1973, the United States enjoyed a more than $1 billion annual trade surplus with the Soviets.[22] But congressional leaders were eager to link these desirable goals with attainment of another—improvement of the deplorable Soviet practices on emigration, particularly toward Jews wishing to move to Israel or the United States. Together with Democratic House Ways and Means Committee Chairman Charles Vanik of Ohio, Senator Henry Jackson pressed the issue effectively. They pushed an amendment to the Trade Reform Act of 1974 that would place major roadblocks in U.S.-Soviet trade unless substantial improvements occurred in Soviet emigration practices.[23]

Secretary Kissinger pleaded with congressional leaders to avoid binding legislation. He sought and received private Soviet assurances that offensive practices, such as the levying of "exit fees" or "education taxes," would end. President Nixon had received private assurances in Moscow that emigration of Soviet Jews would remain as high as the 32,000 permitted to leave in 1972. And Kissinger was able to extract similar pledges in private eleventh-hour negotiations with Soviet officials. But Senator Jackson, who was gearing up for a presidential bid backed in part by strong support in the American Jewish community, hardened his position in response. Jackson believed that binding legislation was the only way to guarantee Soviet compliance with emigration promises. Like many in Congress, Jackson was skeptical of detente and less willing than State Department diplomats to accept pledges from a Communist power with a legacy of deceit. Jackson therefore upped the ante. He insisted on an annual level of at least 60,000 Jewish emigrants—twice the 1972 numbers.

Kissinger desperately tried to save the U.S.-Soviet trade pact, warning legislators that linking emigration policy to it "would do serious and perhaps irreparable damage to our relations with the Soviet Union."[24] But Jackson-Vanik was enacted—as was a parallel Stevenson amendment limiting Soviet access to Export-Import Bank assistance. Nixon administration officials were furious, accusing legislators of playing domestic politics with a crucial foreign policy objective. Critics of detente on the Hill countered that the White House took a naive approach to Soviet relations and was unwilling to press human rights concerns by applying real pressure for improvement. There the division on strategy remained. Even when a surge of visas for Soviet Jews took place during the course of SALT II negotiations (the numbers exceeded 51,000 in 1979), Congress failed to embrace calls for a temporary waiver of the curbs on Soviet trade. The determination of Congress to spell out specific details of accords with sovereign powers—as well as legislators' insistence on linking the achievement of one desirable goal to the accomplishment of several others—had a profoundly chilling effect on improved U.S.-Soviet relations.

By the time of the 1976 Republican presidential primaries, "detente" had become a dirty word in American politics. In the fall of 1975, President Ford reached agreement with Soviet leaders on a framework agreement for a follow-on to SALT I, the Vladivostok accord. This agreement represented an important opportunity for continuity in U.S.-Soviet treaty relations. But it went unratified when Ford caved in to right-wing pressures raised by Ronald Reagan's primary challenge. Ford shelved the draft treaty for the duration of the campaign. This retreat was later compounded by the March 1977 decision of President Carter to set aside the progress made at Vladivostok and to pursue a different course. The newly elected chief executive wanted a treaty that made far deeper cuts in the superpowers' arsenals. Carter aides wanted a treaty that bore their imprimatur. And having run as an anti-Washington candidate, the new president was eager to take a different approach. So Carter decided not to press for conclusion and ratification of a Ford-era treaty that would make only token reductions.

Carter's calculation was based upon the reality of mounting Hill opposition to arms accords with the Soviets. Congressional critics of detente were now led by Henry Jackson. The senior Democrat shrewdly decided to send a shot across the Carter administration's bow by exploiting the Senate's prerogative to ratify ambassadorial appointments. Jackson forced a major battle over confirmation of Paul Warnke as Carter's SALT negotiator. Though Warnke's confirmation prevailed 58–40, the Jackson effort succeeded in sending an unmistakable message: the more than one-third-plus-one total against Warnke could readily be fashioned into an anti-SALT veto in the Senate. Carter would have to appease Jackson's forces if he wanted a SALT II accord ratified.

Despite the challenge to Warnke, Congress would probably have ratified the modest Vladivostok framework if it had been put forward in treaty form. Momentum could have been achieved for deeper cuts. Instead, Carter advanced a sweeping arms reduction proposal that caught the cautious Soviet leadership off guard. Brezhnev rejected it outright. Then when Carter doubled back to a Vladivostok-type proposal, hard-liners in Congress savaged the White House retreat. "The Soviet Union bluffed and we folded," one key critic fumed.[25] While tedious negotiations ensued in Geneva to realize a more modest strategic arms treaty, Carter decided against sending the Hill two minor Nixon-Ford–era accords with the Soviets limiting nuclear testing. The President also decided to postpone efforts to negotiate a comprehensive ban on nuclear testing, concluding that he should not squander precious political capital to achieve a modest goal, but rather should await SALT II ratification. Once again, the White House decision delayed Senate action that might have brought new U.S.-Soviet accords into practice.

In the interim, Soviet proxy intervention in the Third World took a newly aggressive turn. Conflicts in Ethiopia and Angola heated up. While waiting for SALT negotiations to be completed, the President was forced to use all his persuasive powers to gain ratification of the Panama Canal treaties. Then in the fall of 1978, the White House managed to infuriate both the Kremlin *and* Senate conservatives by establishing full diplomatic relations with Beijing, to commence the following January. Valuable time was lost. When the Senate Foreign Relations Committee finally received the SALT II accord after Carter and Brezhnev's June 1979 summit in Vienna, the Hill atmosphere had become poisonous. Senator Jackson attacked the agreement as "appeasement" naively advanced "in a misty atmosphere of amiability and good fellowship."[26] Republican Minority Leader Howard Baker announced his unequivocal opposition. And within days, amendments were proliferating that, if adopted, would require substantial renegotiation of the treaty.

Treaty criticism was orchestrated by the political right. An effective lobbying coalition was assembled by conservatives like Paul Nitze, Eugene Rostow, and Kenneth Adelman. Their Committee on the Present Danger assailed the SALT II pact's acceptance of a Soviet advantage in heavy land-based missiles—which critics alleged would leave the United States vulnerable to a first-strike attack. Their case was bolstered by the resignation on June 30, 1979 of Lieutenant General Edward Rowny, who had served on the SALT II negotiating team. Rowny promptly joined SALT opponents as a staff member of the Senate Foreign Relations Committee.

On the left, Senators George McGovern, William Proxmire, and Mark Hatfield threatened to oppose the pact because it failed to make meaningful reductions in superpower arsenals. McGovern asserted that he would "not vote for the illusion of arms control."[27] SALT II called for the destruction of several hundred Soviet systems and required the retirement of aging systems before new forces could be added; but, as Carter administration witnesses explained repeatedly, the agreement would not impede any planned U.S. nuclear force improvements. Programs like the MX, the Trident II submarine, and the cruise missile were free to move forward. Indeed, the President made a public commitment to substantial defense spending increases as an inducement to gain support from a group of key treaty critics led by Senator Nunn. Nevertheless, most arms control activists were willing to enlist in the SALT II campaign. And the State Department worked with liberal groups to launch a team of "SALT-sellers" nationwide. At the height of the ratification debate, military officials and administration diplomats were blanketing the country, addressing Rotary clubs and lobbying small-town newspapers in swing states for editorial endorsements of SALT II.

Throughout the summer of 1979, Senate Democratic whip Alan Cranston kept a running tally of how he expected his colleagues to vote. By the end of the long committee process, his tally showed sixty senators inclined to support, thirty against, and ten undecided. Ratification was still winnable, though it appeared to be very much an uphill fight that might involve heavily amending the treaty and sending it back to the Soviets for renegotiation. Several southern Democrats had joined with presidential candidate Baker and many Senate Republicans to oppose the treaty. And the Armed Services Committee—under Senator Jackson's prodding—was savaging the agreement; Jackson ultimately won a committee vote to issue a report assailing pact terms. But as the August recess neared its end, the treaty remained alive. The argument that its ratification would lock the U.S. land-based nuclear missiles into a position of inferiority while lulling the Western alliance into a false sense of security had not yet sunk the pact.

Then a grievous blow to treaty prospects was struck by a misleading revelation by a politically pressed Foreign Relations Committee member. On August 29, the committee chairman, Frank Church—whose reelection was endangered by a right-wing challenger—disclosed the existence of a Soviet troop "brigade" in Cuba. Treaty critic Richard Stone, a Florida Democrat facing his own tough reelection fight, demanded that the Carter administration press the Soviets for its removal. Carter himself termed the presence in the Caribbean of this Soviet force "unacceptable"; the White House heightened its call for substantial defense budget increases. But the public relations damage had been done. While the brigade was not a new deployment, public discussion of its presence struck a raw nerve on Capitol Hill.[28]

Soviet proxies were already causing the United States grief in a number of countries. The Soviets were expanding their intermediate-range nuclear forces targeted on Europe and introducing a provocative new system with multiple warheads, the SS-20. Senators were deeply concerned about what message would be sent if a strategic arms accord was ratified in such an environment. The SALT II resolution of ratification thus became the vehicle for a sweeping debate about the future of U.S.-Soviet relations, and the treaty text a "whipping boy" upon which legislators could vent their frustrations.[29] Linkage of other concerns on the American agenda to the emerging arms deal became an unavoidable fact of life.

The Foreign Relations Committee proceeded to attach all sorts of provisos to the SALT II resolution of ratification in its fall 1979 markup. The committee broke proposals into three categories. The first was amendments to the text of the treaty itself, all of which would require renegotiation with the Soviets. Second were reservations to the Senate's consent to ratification; added to the resolution of approval, these bound the President to take certain action as a

condition of ratification. Finally, there were nonbinding understandings—unilateral declarations of the Senate's views on such matters as
Soviet human rights abuses. The resolution of ratification was loaded
up with eighteen separate understandings and two key reservations
before the committee reported it to the full Senate on November 9.
The weak 9–6 vote to report was well short of the symbolic two-
thirds margin.

The prospects on the floor were for further delay and the attachment of more substantial weakening amendments. And the administration still did not have sixty-seven votes. While awaiting the
beginning of the full Senate debate, the administration induced
NATO allies to commit to a "two-track" response to the Soviet's
INF deployments of SS-20s—that is, the alliance would back both
deployments of new Pershing II and cruise missiles and efforts to
negotiate reductions. But the Soviets apparently wrote off the prospect of any arms accord with the Carter administration. On December 27, apparently concluding that SALT II was dead and American
political reaction was of little consequence, the Soviets launched a
full-scale invasion of Afghanistan. It was left to Majority Leader
Byrd to impress upon President Carter the necessity of shelving the
unratified SALT II pact. A partisan move to formally reject the
treaty and send it back to the White House was tabled on January 22, and for more than half a decade the unratified strategic arms
pact remained pending on the Senate's executive calendar.

The Reagan years brought little progress on the basic strategic
arms issues presented by the SALT II pact. The Soviet Union stumbled through three successive leadership crises, showing little flexibility in its approach to strategic arms talks until Mikhail Gorbachev
was firmly in place. The Reagan administration aggressively funded
the Carter-era nuclear programs, while directing a steady stream
of anti-Soviet rhetoric at the Kremlin. The subsequent Reagan-
Gorbachev summits produced a good deal of utopian rhetoric, but
not a single agreement on strategic arms or nuclear testing curbs.

The one modest arms control pact produced during the eight years
of the Reagan military buildup was the INF pact—which covered less
than 4 percent of U.S. and Soviet nuclear systems capable of striking
each other's territory. When the Soviets first moved towards acceptance of the American INF proposal in 1987, the prospects for Senate approval seemed bright. Surely a Republican president with
credentials as a virulent anticommunist could gain swift Senate con-

sent. But as the Capitol Hill debate neared, numerous hurdles to timely ratification were erected.

The principal challenge was to deal with a dozen or so right-wing senators—led by Helms, Wallop, and Quayle—whose efforts might have delayed ratification until after the Mosocw summit of 1988. Liberals and conservatives alike viewed strategic arms reductions as the "main chance." The battle over INF thus became an important preliminary in which skeptics sought to block any progress on START. A related concern was that arms control champions, chagrined and cynical about the belated Reagan conversion to their cause, would condition INF approval on achievement of other key objectives. There was serious debate, for example, about the wisdom of conditioning INF ratification upon continued compliance with SALT II ceilings or the traditional interpretation of the ABM Treaty barring SDI tests. Senators Biden and Bumpers insisted that the INF pact was of little value if strategic arms arsenals were free to grow. Absent some type of interim restraint agreement on strategic arms pending the conclusion of START, the Kremlin could simply add hundreds of new ballistic missiles and retarget them on Europe, undermining the whole objective of the INF pact. Suspicion of White House motives in pressing the INF agreement as a political cure-all for its Iran-Contra ills abounded on all sides. And the legacy of a decade of bitter parliamentary warfare between arms control supporters and critics was difficult to overcome—even with the alliance forged between party whips Simpson and Cranston and key policymakers like Secretary Shultz, Ambassador Nitze, and Senators Stevens and Lugar. Compounding these strains was a bungled Reagan administration effort to dodge the treaty reinterpretation issues presented by its ABM-SDI gambit. Led by Senators Nunn and Biden, arms control supporters made it clear that any possibility of future "reinterpretation" of the INF Treaty would have to be foreclosed or treaty ratification would be held up.

In the end, the bipartisan leadership coalition which emerged in the Senate systematically defeated critics of the pact. This coalition succeeded in keeping the resolution of ratification free of confrontational language that would have inhibited further progress on U.S.-Soviet relations. Liberals were persuaded to drop linkage to SALT, START, or nuclear test bans. Conservatives were isolated on efforts to delay the INF pact until U.S. concerns about Afghanistan and conventional force imbalances were resolved. And White House efforts to fudge the reinterpretation issue were rejected outright. In approving INF ratification, the Senate adopted consensus language that upheld its role in determining treaty meaning, language that utterly buried the troublesome Sofaer Doctrine.[30] The resolution of ratification passed on May 27, 1988 and was flown directly to Moscow just hours before President Reagan's first meeting with Soviet leaders.

THE PANAMA CANAL BRAWL

The struggle to shape Washington's policy toward the Soviet Union has spanned a generation. But perhaps the most bitter treaty fight during these years erupted on an entirely unrelated issue, the relinquishing of U.S. control over the Panama Canal Zone. The fight to gain Capitol Hill support for the Panama Canal treaties produced the longest Senate debate ever for a pact that ultimately prevailed.[31] More than two months of maneuvering took place on the Senate floor in the winter of 1978—from February 6 to April 18—before the Senate gave its conditional consent to ratification by a one-vote margin. Senate Foreign Relations Committee deliberations were equally contested, involving some ninety witnesses and 2,500 pages of testimony. Even after the Senate approved ratification, a series of bitterly fought House votes continued for more than a year on challenges to the passage of the legislation that was necessary to implement the Canal transfer. And for years later, candidates who backed the treaty were subject to retribution at the polls.

The fight over the Canal treaties was remarkable in several other respects. It was the first treaty ratification battle fought by Congress and the White House under the new post-Nixon rules. President Carter had to fight from beginning to end from a weakened executive branch position. The closeness of the Senate vote also produced an extraordinary muddying of roles between the two branches. Senators negotiated directly with foreign heads of state. Members of the Carter cabinet rolled up their sleeves to pen legislative language in late-night drafting sessions. Senators blatantly exploited their leverage over the vulnerable president to wring concessions on a host of unrelated domestic spending issues. Nevertheless, President Carter prevailed on a wildly unpopular measure in the face of highly organized nationwide opposition.

Certainly the Panama dilemma was one that nobody in Washington relished. Jimmy Carter had known the fight was coming even before his inauguration. At one of his first meetings as president-elect, he had summoned Democratic leaders to Georgia and asked for their help on the Panama issue. Particularly troubling was a preemptive move under way by Republican Senator Strom Thurmond of South Carolina to introduce in the new Congress a resolution co-sponsored by a treaty-threatening bloc of thirty-four senators. Thurmond's effort was parried by Byrd and Cranston, who pleaded with Senate colleagues to hold off the antitreaty resolution and to give the new administration a chance. Yet Carter—the foreign policy novice who had run against the Washington establishment—was left with a commitment to proceed to complete a Panama pact that his predecessors had ducked and that a vocal majority of American voters opposed. It was an unenviable task that even the most skilled politician could have fumbled.

Carter prevailed for two principal reasons. First, he showed a keen sense of timing, making the Panama test his first major foreign policy battle on the Hill. He used to great advantage the desire of senators not to "break" another presidency at its outset.[32] Second, after several initial setbacks, President Carter and his staff relied heavily on the Senate Democratic leadership to navigate the pacts through their rough Hill passage. Senate leaders controlled the parliamentary process effectively, freezing action when trends went against ratification and pressing ahead once hurdles had been reduced.

The basic question before legislators was quite simple. The United States had exercised sovereignty over the Canal Zone ever since Teddy Roosevelt conspired with French investors in 1903 to provoke Panama's secession from Colombia.[33] By the 1960s—at the height of the age of nationalism—the American presence astride the isthmus was a source of shame for most Panamanian generals and politicians. First Lyndon Johnson and then Richard Nixon had committed the United States to negotiating effective Panamanian sovereignty over the American-built canal and the narrow zone strip. But many Americans simply did not want to go through with this commitment. As then-candidate Ronald Reagan repeatedly intoned: "We bought it, we paid for it, we built it, and we intend to keep it." To turn this strategic asset over to the unstable Panamanian regime was unacceptable—"a dangerous step," Senator Robert Griffin noted, "a gamble for the security of the United States."[34]

Treaty proponents demonstrated sensitivity to Latin American nationalism, with the President speaking of a "determination to deal with the developing nations on the basis of mutual respect and partnership."[35] Senate floor manager Frank Church similarly decried opponents' "vain attempt to preserve the past, to perpetuate an American colony against the wishes of the Panamanian people."[36] But these noble proclamations obscured the central argument, which proponents preferred to address more obliquely: better a Panamanian canal accessible to Americans than an American canal exposed to the hostility and sabotage of Panamanian nationalists. Secretary of Defense Harold Brown diplomatically stated this proposition in a rare public comment on the danger: "The treaties offer the firmest and most practicable guarantees obtainable that the canal will remain operational, secure, and available to the United States."[37]

An extraordinary lobbying campaign unfolded even before Senate Foreign Relations Committee hearings opened on January 13, 1978. Opponents targeted the states with key swing votes in the Senate—including Louisiana, Kentucky, Georgia, and Arizona—launching a nationwide tour of conservative lawmakers to drum up criticism of the pacts. They relied heavily for their effort upon the opposition of many veterans groups. The State Department countered with an effective nationwide campaign that included traveling "truth squads" headed by Secretary of State Vance and televised "fireside chats" by President Carter.

The White House proved less effective in lobbying the Hill. In the Senate, the President's only major contribution was his success in gaining treaty support from Republican Minority Leader Howard Baker—without which the treaties might well have been doomed. But subsequent White House efforts were poorly coordinated with State and Defense. They invited individual senators to up the ante in negotiating with the administration on the conditions under which they might vote for ratification. Negotiations with a host of individuals on their distinct personal agendas became so complex and contradictory that the White House, as one NSC official lamented, "almost ended up with a treaty between the President and Congress, instead of between Panama and the United States."[38] Success on the Hill was ultimately produced by Senate Democratic leaders, men like Byrd, Cranston, Church, and Sarbanes. It was these senators who could best stare down their colleagues, who crafted the language and cut the deals necessary to get that essential sixty-seventh vote.

Indeed, as one postmortem noted, "Carter's lobbyists were so poorly regarded on Capitol Hill that they were virtually barred—for their own good—from the Senate's bartering and bargaining process. Finally, the treaties were only put over the top by an appeal to the Senate's conscience."[39]

The key to success thus became adept management of the ratification debate by the Senate leadership. Treaty proponents agreed to defer votes on any and all amendments until the treaty was before the full body. Byrd instructed the Foreign Relations Committee to forgo the usual procedure of adopting amendments, reservations, and conditions in committee. This afforded members the opportunity to find some political cover on the Senate floor. More senators could take credit for altering the treaty on the margin with a showy floor effort—and thereby justify an "aye" vote on final passage. But this strategy also encouraged the proliferation of amendments to the resolution of ratification. Nearly 200 were offered for debate, with even the most junior members encouraged to hold out for concessions. Before the two-month floor debate was over, the troublesome specter of a senator not two years in the chamber negotiating with a foreign head of state was presented to America's allies and adversaries abroad.

At no time before the final roll was called did the Senate leadership have confidence that a two-thirds majority was in hand. Indeed, as senators traveled to the Canal Zone and back for study and direct negotiations with Panamanian leaders on the terms of possible treaty amendments, problems seemed to multiply rather than diminish. And even after endorsement of the first of the two pacts in a dramatic 68–32 vote on March 16, the neutrality pact was still in jeopardy. The attachment to the first treaty of a reservation by Senator Dennis DeConcini was objected to so strenuously by the Panamanian government that this damage had to be addressed in the second pact.[40] The Senate leadership was forced to devise a means of undoing the DeConcini provision (which the White House had accepted) without losing votes for adoption of the neutrality pact in the process. With the President fully exposed, the Senate leadership had to negotiate, first with DeConcini, and then with a host of other legislators in order to obtain the necessary two-thirds vote. Senator James Abourezk, a maverick South Dakota Democrat, threatened to oppose the pact unless concessions were obtained on the deregulation of natural gas. Senator Talmadge held out for more lavish benefits in the farm bill. And freshman Republican S. I. Hayakawa of California extracted a humiliating pledge in a one-on-one meeting with Carter that the President would consult closely with him on all major foreign policy decisions in the future.

The image of the President being nickle-and-dimed by senators taking advantage of his diplomatic exposure appalled many observers. But it was a price the White House had to pay in order to gain the Senate's approval, which finally came on April 18. Then a full year of after-the-fact skirmishing began. House opponents tried relentlessly to block adoption of implementing legislation, insisting that only the full Congress was authorized under the Constitution to dispose of American property. Indeed, the Carter administration had confronted this question early on, preferring to look for a Senate vote of two-thirds and a favorable court ruling rather than try to get a simple majority vote in the House. As Attorney General Griffin Bell explained the calculation:

> [voters] would oppose any proposal to transfer the Canal to Panama. The House of Representatives was close to the people, and if the proposal were submitted to the House, the members would be forced to vote on it in an election year. The chance of a favorable vote in the House was very small indeed. In contrast, the Senate was a peculiar institution in which two-thirds of the members were always at least three to four years from the next election. . . . Senators took pride in their detachment, their judgment, and their expertise in the field of foreign affairs.[41]

This choice proved a wise one. After the Senate approved ratification and pressed ahead with legislation to execute the pacts, the House voted repeatedly against funding their implementation. When this ploy failed, several members sued, but this effort proved unsuccessful as well.[42]

When the dust stirred up by the Panama fight finally settled, the bottom line was that the President could prevail in gaining ratification of an unpopular treaty. In the Panama dispute, the system worked. The prolonged Senate debate was used to systematically educate legislators—and through them, the American people—about the necessity of doing something a majority of voters were not eager to see done. Legislators modified the pacts, protecting some important American interests in the process. Some took advantage of the vulnerable president, virtually blackmailing the White House to obtain benefits for voters back home. Others took a politically fatal step in order to secure ratification. But in the end, the case for the treaties prevailed.

The fight to ratify the Panama Canal pacts, like the struggle to shape U.S.-Soviet treaty relations, demonstrates the fragility of the power balance between the president and Congress. To be successful in diplomacy, the United States needs a coherent strategy for pursuing new initiatives and building upon old ones. The president is best equipped to take the lead both in defining a complex policy and in executing the diplomatic initiatives necessary to broaden treaty relations. Congress provides an important brake, a popular forum for the public scrubbing of policy options. Legislators will always demand that the best deal possible be achieved, that key national interests be protected, that popular goals be advanced. At times, the Senate can offer nothing but trouble. Legislators often cannot resist the temptation to turn a resolution of ratification into a vehicle for pressing a broad ideological agenda. But at its best, the Senate can be an arena for enlightenment, educating voters while serving as a forge in which a new consensus can be hammered out. A Senate test offers both a heavy dose of common sense and a healthy sense of the common good. History suggests that when the president chooses to work effectively with the Senate leadership, the positive aspects of their shared treaty-making power can prevail and the job of conducting diplomacy in a complex world can get done.

NOTES

1. John Hay, letter to Samuel Mather, September 28, 1900, as quoted in *Life and Letters of John Hay*, vol. 2, p. 254. Hay's diplomatic career spanned an era of particularly strained White House relations with Congress. Between 1860 and 1900, the Senate rejected eleven different treaties, including four important pacts with Great Britain.

2. Stephen S. Rosenfeld, *Washington Post*, January 29, 1988, p. 23.

3. Notes on the meetings of the INF working group are from the private papers of Senator Alan Cranston.

4. See Crabb and Holt, *Invitation to Struggle*, p. 84. Voter hostility to the "Panama giveaway" had caused several of Jimmy Carter's White House predecessors to balk at concluding the pact. And even before the pacts were concluded, they provided a devastating election issue. For example, in 1976 California Senator John Tunney was upset in his reelection bid

by S. I. Hayakawa—a candidate who maintained the United States should keep the Canal "because we stole it fair and square."

5. James Madison, as quoted in "Treaties and Other International Agreements: The Role of the United States Senate," *Congressional Research Service*, June 1984, p. 36.

6. The King-Hawksbury Convention of 1803, a U.S.-Great Britain accord, became the first treaty torpedoed by Senate action when the British rejected amendments attached during the ratification debate. The head of the British Foreign Office at the time, Lord Harrowby, attacked the legislative practice as "new, unauthorized and not to be sanctioned" (as quoted in ibid.).

7. Upon learning of his colleagues' tactics, Senator Dole, a treaty opponent, commented that he was holding out for a naval base in Kansas before he would endorse the Panama Canal treaties (see Franck and Weisband, *Foreign Policy by Congress*, p. 278).

8. In 1976, the House had voted 246–164 to bar any effort to "give away" the Panama Canal. In 1978, the Panama enabling legislation was defeated on several occasions in the House—including a 192–203 vote on September 20—before the Democratic leadership finally prevailed in passing a compromise measure. The effort to withhold funds for implementing the Jay Treaty was overcome in the House by only a 51–48 vote.

9. Treaties rejected included a pact with Turkey (1927), the St. Lawrence Waterway agreement with Canada (1932), and the International Court of Justice accord (1935). A Law of the Sea protocol (1958) and the Montreal Aviation Agreement (1983) failed to win a two-thirds majority; but motions to reconsider the votes were entered, so they technically remain pending on the Senate's executive calendar.

10. Many argued that the Soviets were in violation of selected provisions of SALT II regarding the encoding of missile flight test data and limitations on new missile types. But the assertion that the Soviets had already breached the treaty's numerical limitations was a minority view. Thus, proponents of the "SALT II ceilings legislation" were pressing for selective enforcement on both parties of the terms of the unratified treaty,

11. Senator Dan Quayle, as quoted in *National Journal*, June 27, 1987, p. 1648.

12. Nunn, the key Democratic vote on many security issues, was gearing up for a possible 1988 presidential bid in which he would need the support of more progressive party members. Arms controllers' passion for SALT II had a similar impact upon Wright, whose campaign to succeed House Speaker Tip O'Neill needed liberal votes, and House Armed Services Committee Chairman Les Aspin, who was held in deep suspicion by the left because of his support for the MX missile.

13. *National Journal*, June 27, 1987, p. 1644.

14. Indeed, one of the only opponents of the ABM Treaty was Republican Senator James Buckley of New York, who voted against it on the grounds that it would bar testing of futuristic space-based defense systems that the United States might invent after the pact was signed.

15. Under the terms of the ABM Treaty, the administration could simply have given advance notification of intent to withdraw. A strong case could have been made for the move in light of Soviet violations of treaty terms through the construction of an inland early warning radar at Krasnoyarsk. But the Reagan administration chose the prolonged battle with Congress over "reinterpretation" rather than the simpler—though politically and diplomatically riskier—decision to withdraw from the ABM Treaty altogether.

16. See Joseph Biden and John B. Ritch III, "The End of the Sofaer Doctrine: A Victory for Arms Control and the Constitution," *Arms Control Today* (September 1988): 3–8.

17. See the Supreme Court finding in *Goldwater v. Carter*, 444 U.S. 996 (1979).

18. See Senate Foreign Relations Committee, hearings on the Taiwan Relations Act, November 15, 1979.

19. General Brent Scowcroft, Special Subcommittee on War Powers, September 7, 1988, p. 64.

20. Note that SALT I was an election-year executive agreement, not a treaty. This "interim accord" was designed to set a stable ceiling from which to negotiate substantial reductions. After much debate, President Nixon chose to submit it for a majority vote in both houses. Debate on the Jackson amendment, which was ultimately adopted 56–35, delayed Senate endorsement. The final Senate vote on SALT I was 88–2 on September 14, 1972.

21. On the ABM debate, see Frye, *Responsible Congress*, pp. 15–47.

22. See Sundquist, *Decline and Resurgence*, p. 279.

23. The Jackson-Vanik amendment covered all non–market economy countries and had a profound impact on U.S. trade with such Warsaw Pact nations as Romania. But its principal target was clearly the Soviets and their reprehensible emigration practices.

24. Henry Kissinger, as quoted in Sundquist, *Decline and Resurgence*, p. 281.

25. Lieutenant General Edward Rowny, as quoted in *1979 Congressional Quarterly Almanac*, p. 415.

26. Senator Henry Jackson, as quoted in ibid., p. 411.

27. Senator George McGovern, as quoted in ibid., p. 413.

28. Destler, et al., *Our Own Worst Enemy*, p. 76.

29. Ibid., p. 145.

30. See "INF Treaty Mired in Controversy," *Washington Post*, May 1, 1988,

p. 1; "Slow Lift-off for the INF Pact," *National Journal*, April 30, 1988, p. 1136; "Shultz, Dole Attack INF Treaty Delays," *Washington Post*, May 24, 1988, p. 1.

31. The Panama debate actually involved two treaties. One, the Panama Canal Treaty, governs operation of the Canal and U.S.-Panamanian cooperation on its transfer. The other, the Permanent Neutrality Treaty, ensures that the Canal will remain permanently neutral and secures important U.S. rights of access.

32. As Henry Kissinger warned the Senate Foreign Relations Committee on September 14, 1977, "Defeat of the Panama Canal treaties would weaken the President's international authority at the beginning of his term." Kissinger was expanding on his perennial argument that congressional activism—and criticism of Watergate-era abuses—had crippled diplomatic efforts under Nixon and Ford (as quoted in *1978 Contressional Quarterly Almanac*, p. 383.

33. The United States paid a French company $40 million for the right to revive their failed canal construction attempt and negotiated the treaty granting perpetual U.S. rights to the Canal Zone with Frenchmen purporting to represent the new Panamanian state.

34. Senator Robert Griffin, as quoted in *1978 Congressional Quarterly Almanac*, p. 380.

35. Jimmy Carter, as quoted in ibid.

36. Senator Frank Church, as quoted in ibid.

37. Harold Brown, as quoted in ibid.

38. As quoted in Franck and Weisband, *Foreign Policy by Congress*, p. 285.

39. Barry Rubin, "Panama Canal Retrospective," *Contemporary Review* 234 (February 1979): 84.

40. The DeConcini reservation gave the United States the right to unilateral military action to defend the Canal. It was adopted March 16 by a 75–23 vote—then undercut by language adopted during debate on the second treaty.

41. Griffin Bell and Miles Foy, "The President, the Congress and the Panama Canal," *Georgia Journal of International and Comparative Law* 16 (Spring 1986): 635.

42. *Edwards v. Carter*, 580 F. 2d 1055 (D.C. Cir. 1978).

7 CONGRESS AND ARMS SALES
A Familiar Battleground

> The debate over diplomatic policy normally takes place only in the
> context of debate over arms sales and not on its own merits.
>
> —Harold Saunders, former Assistant Secretary of
> State for the Near East and South Asia, 1986[1]

Selling arms to the Middle East has become one of the most controversial presidential foreign policy initiatives on Capitol Hill. In recent
years, arms export proposals have proved every bit as divisive as arguments over war powers and treaty-making prerogatives. These arms
sales disputes have frequently paralyzed American diplomacy in the
Middle East, becoming a symbol, if not a substitute, for more vigorous efforts to advance the peace process. And debates over the
export of sophisticated American weaponry have not been confined
to the Middle East; they have embroiled Washington in disputes as
diverse as the rivalry between Greece and Turkey along NATO's
southern flank, or the rift between the People's Republic of China
and the Kuomintang authorities on Taiwan. Indeed, as veteran State
Department adviser Harold Saunders suggests, arms export controversies have replaced executive-legislative consultation as the basis for
dialogue on the broader framework of diplomatic strategy. Process
has eclipsed policy. The executive branch practice of presenting arms
sales proposals to Congress as fait accomplis has heightened inter-

branch tensions considerably. Arms sales debates have also exacerbated parochial divisions within the electorate, encouraging the growth of several dozen foreign affairs–oriented political action committees (PACs) that funnel millions of dollars to candidates primarily on the basis of a handful of arms export votes. While the vast majority of congressional export reviews result in routine approval, it is the few controversial proposals that make the legislative prerogatives so very contentious.

To be sure, an assertive congressional role in arms sales has produced some valuable interbranch cooperation. It has introduced new safeguards and some important restraints into security assistance programs. It has also helped curb several imprudent sales, making it more difficult to repeat spectacular mistakes like the sale of U.S. weapons to the terrorist Khomeini regime, or risky proposals like the provision of deadly Stinger missiles to unstable Middle East regimes. But congressional activism on arms exports has also greatly complicated executive branch diplomacy, while tightening the not always constructive linkage between U.S. foreign policy and domestic politics.

That the arms sales struggle has become so intense is in some respects surprising. Relatively few Americans criticize the fact that more than a generation after World War II and the Korean War the United States still pays to keep more than 500,000 soldiers in Europe and East Asia. Yet just a handful of arms sales to U.S. friends and allies abroad have produced prolonged Washington donnybrooks—struggles that have threatened to seriously impair more than one president's ability to conduct foreign policy.

Since 1975, virtually every executive branch proposal to sell arm arms to pro-Western Arab nations or to Iran has triggered combat with Capitol Hill. Controversy has also surrounded sales to nations as diverse as Pakistan, Honduras, and China. But the vast majority of non-Arab applicants—as well as Egypt since the Camp David peace treaty—have been granted with a minimum of congressional debate. A peculiar ritual has developed in the wake of Middle East arms requests, a ritual not unlike an elaborate mating dance. The Pentagon and commercial American arms manufacturers serve as matchmakers, seeking out export opportunities and pressing the White House to consummate a deal. The White House then courts the Congress. Congress spurns the initial approach, objecting loudly. The executive branch then doubles back, proposing a cosmetic comprom- ise while pressing its case. Congress ultimately yields, claiming a moral victory.

But this procedural dance satisfies few participants. Certainly in the case of would-be purchasers of American arms, the exercise has become humiliating in the extreme, as sovereign nations are placed in the congressional docket to be pilloried in drawn-out debate. Pro- posed weapons sales, advanced to secure allies and extend American leverage, have ended up alienating foreign clients. Legislation designed to lend greater certainty to the arms export licensing process has sown confusion. And subsequent refinements in this export review process, designed to enhance executive-legislative cooperation, have produced bitter confrontation among the very officials charged with its implementation. Finally, in the wake of the 1983 Supreme Court decision undercutting the legislative veto, the arms sales equation has been significantly altered, returning important advantages to the president. The dance itself has changed, and the partners seem to be making up new steps as they go round and round.

SELLING ARMS: A FORCE
PROJECTION SUBSTITUTE

The arms sales imbroglio has become equated in most policymakers' minds with the Arab-Israeli dispute. It is a fight in which the real agenda—access to oil, sympathy for Israel—is often a hidden one. The struggle to guide America's Middle East diplomacy has in turn been portrayed by cynics as a fight pitting State Department "Arabists" and Pentagon "cold warriors" against pro-Israeli legislators eager for campaign support. However, this caricature obscures several crucial facts about the congressional review process and its origins. Indeed, at the outset of this struggle, arms sales to Israel and its Arab neigh- bors were not the central issue.

The roots of the recurring interbranch conflict over arms sales lie in the requirement for new means to project power in the Cold War era, particularly since the withdrawal of U.S. ground troops from Vietnam. Just as "Vietnamization" of the Indochina conflict re- quired massive transfers of U.S. weapons to Saigon's army, the earlier withdrawal of European powers from Africa and the Middle East had left a power vacuum that U.S. diplomats and military officials rushed to fill with American arms. The 1950s saw the crest of nationalism as a force in international relations. In the 1960s, newly independent nations rapidly chose up sides in the Cold War. This in turn brought massive infusions of U.S. and Soviet arms into hot spots around the globe as client states insisted on the latest weaponry from the respective superpowers.

Congress was initially comfortable with this executive branch strategy, which was most clearly enunciated in the Nixon Doctrine. This was a somewhat isolationist declaration that while the United States would uphold its treaty commitments and maintain its "nuclear umbrella" deterrent against potential Soviet aggression, the strength of U.S. friends abroad would be enhanced primarily through foreign aid and arms sales: "We shall look to the nations directly threatened to assume the primary responsibility of providing the manpower for its defense," President Nixon declared.[2]

The strategy was popular because it greatly diminished the requirement for U.S. troop deployments abroad. A member of Congress was always more willing to sell weapons than to send troops overseas. This export strategy was a key to containment; it helped to check the expansion of Soviet influence. It was also good business—foreign governments buying U.S. arms, or receiving dated weapons from Pentagon stocks, inevitably meant more manufacturing jobs in congressional districts throughout the United States. This in turn brought down unit costs for domestic military production, while delighting U.S. arms manufacturers who aggressively peddled U.S. weapons overseas with virtually no restraint. But early in the 1970s, when President Nixon's powers and popularity were at their zenith, Congress began to balk at repeated arms export proposals.

The initial concern expressed by Hill leaders was simply that Pentagon and State Department bureaucrats, through arms transfer programs, were making extraordinary international commitments with virtually no input from the elected representatives of the American people in Congress. (The criticism was not unlike that provoked by FDR on the Hill when he sought to buck prevailing isolationist sentiment to help defend England against German aggression through the provision of surplus U.S. weapons.) The challenge Nixon faced in Congress was a natural outgrowth of the unceasing debate over U.S. involvement in the Indochina conflict. In Vietnam, deployment of technical advisers and arms transfers had led to a step-by-step infusion of American ground troops. Except for the vague Gulf of Tonkin Resolution, there never was an explicit legislative authorization for this commitment of troops.[3] Congress pursued the arms sales question because less than ten years after the Gulf of Tonkin debate, policy decisions and binding commitments were being made in secret by Nixon administration officials, who often denied legislators even after-the-fact notification. Nixon's repeated surprises—the Kissinger visit to China, the Cambodia invasion, and the Christmas-time bombing of Hanoi—unnerved congressional leaders. These unilateral actions by the President invited legislative restraints on foreign commitments like arms sales.

U.S. military export programs in the early 1970s stood in marked contrast to the early post–World War II U.S. arms assistance programs, which were grants, not sales. The security assistance portions of the Marshall Plan and the emergency package for Greece and Turkey had first been sent to Capitol Hill for approval as foreign aid requests. Congress had ample opportunity to amend and approve these commitments *before* they went forward. Indeed, Congress retained a legislative veto over the 1947 Mediterranean aid program. Subsequent arms transfers to treaty partners in NATO and elsewhere became an accepted routine. But in the Nixon years, Cold War realpolitik required the increasingly risky use of arms sales to new security partners as a foreign policy tool. And as the price of oil rose and OPEC gained new strength, the wealth of petrodollars brought orders for top-of-the-line weapons from nations to whom the United States was less than eager to sell. Congress began to voice general concern about the proliferation of arms around the globe and the diversion of Third World resources away from development and into weapons. The continuing India-Pakistan conflict heightened this dilemma: here were two poverty-stricken nations battling each other with American-made arms employed on both sides. Members of Congress reacted in disgust, adopting several hortatory resolutions and calling for new White House initiatives "to work actively with all nations to check and control the international sales and distribution of conventional weapons of death and destruction." However well intended, these sense-of-the-Congress resolutions had little effect.[4]

The abrupt withdrawal of British influence from the Persian Gulf in 1971 spurred a massive U.S. program to shore up the Saudi and Iranian military—the so-called "twin pillar" approach to Gulf security. At the same time, the United States was tilting towards Pakistan and paving the way for a substantially expanded military assistance program for that southwest Asian nation. With the program of steady Vietnamization of the civil war between Saigon and Hanoi, the United States was also required to accelerate military aid grants and cash sales to secure nervous U.S. allies in the Philippines and South Korea.[5] The Nixon-Kissinger strategy was consistent. It reduced pressures for U.S. military deployments by building up bulwarks of anticommunist strength in global hot spots. Friendly regimes were armed with advanced American weaponry. If these foreign rulers did not meet democratic standards, it was too bad: better an authoritarian regime friendly to the United States and able to resist communist influence than a totalitarian government spreading Marxist dogma.[6]

By 1973, it was inevitable that clashes would occur between the White House and Congress over arms transfer policies. A legislature empowered by the sudden, Watergate-induced weakening of executive authority was determined to reassert its prerogatives in reviewing international commitments. With Washington increasingly utilizing arms sales as a substitute for more traditional methods of force projection and diplomacy, the heavy administration reliance on arms exports was open to second-guessing. And for proponents of intellectual consistency, Nixon's zero-sum strategy of arming the enemies of U.S. adversaries produced a host of ideological contradictions. For example, the unswerving White House commitment to anticommunism brought an ever firmer embrace of antidemocratic rulers like the Philippines' Marcos and the Shah of Iran. It also appeared that the increasing sophistication of the U.S. military technology being exported ensured that other friends and allies would look to the United States more and more for increasing amounts of aid and armaments to keep up. Washington was fueling a Third World arms race that American taxpayers were being called upon to help finance.

Critics in Congress charged that the United States was becoming less and less the "arsenal of democracy" and more and more the dispenser of "dollars for dictators" and "planes for potentates." Liberals in Congress viewed human rights and democratic reform as essential elements of an effective anticommunist strategy. They questioned how unrestrained sales and grants of weapons helped. Legislators were also angered by Pentagon salesmanship—the fact that military officials and defense contractors often stimulated arms requests from impoverished foreign governments. At the same time, many critics ignored the role that internal security often played as a precondition for democratization: many a foreign ruler sought to keep his military morale high by importing fancy American weapons, lest he face an antireform coup. It proved unrealistic to expect some foreign governments, confronted by regional warfare and domestic insurrection, to remake themselves promptly in the image of American democracy.

Early in Nixon's second term, reformers in Congress tried to check executive branch arms export powers. Legislators sought to curb mounting international arms traffic while carving a new congressional role in reviewing export commitments. Their concerns were both procedural and substantive. But in the early 1970s, the Arab-Israeli dispute was not yet the central issue in arms export debates. It was only later in the decade—after President Sadat had expelled the more than 10,000 Soviet advisers in his country, and after King Hussein of Jordan had turned to the United States for weapons to defend against the disparate threats of the PLO and Syria—that the struggles in Washington over arms sales policies became synonymous with debate over the U.S. approach to the Arab-Israeli dispute. Indeed, it was not until the middle of the Yom Kippur War in October 1973 that a major U.S. program of weapons assistance to Israel even began.[7]

THE ARMS EXPORT CONTROL ACT

Members of Congress sought a procedural handle to curb the president's power over weapons transfers. The design was to give Congress a lever to force meaningful White House consultation *before* commitments were made, to elbow legislators' way into the decisionmaking loop early in the process. Many on the Hill were alarmed by spiraling sales to the petrodollar-rich Shah of Iran (which continued despite the Shah's participation in the crippling 1973 OPEC oil embargo against the West). Yet legislative initiatives advanced on Capitol Hill were not directed against any particular country. Similarly, while the legislative veto over arms sales was advanced at the same time that Congress was moving to suspend military cooperation with Turkey in reaction to its 1974 invasion of Cyprus, the generic measure had no direct impact on that specific dispute. For in blocking aid to Turkey, Congress was simply upholding existing legal requirements in the foreign assistance bill that limited the use of American-supplied weapons to defensive actions only.

Clearly, the Turkish arms embargo was part and parcel of the same emotional debate. The embargo resulted from a prolonged impasse between legislators determined to hold Turkey to the letter of American law and professional diplomats in the executive branch who feared that an arms embargo would alienate a key NATO treaty partner. The United States had explicitly warned the Turks against using American arms on Cyprus. The violation of this legal bar—and the fervent desire of Greek-American legislators to punish Turkish aggression—obliged Washington to respond. Secretary Kissinger sought to deflect Hill concern, suppressing a State Department legal study that concluded Ankara had violated U.S. laws. Many in Congress sought simply to use the *threat* of a cutoff as leverage against the Turks. But a back-bench revolt led by junior members undermined the ability of congressional leaders to contain passions. Despite extraordinary administration lobbying efforts—and two consecutive Ford vetoes of embargo legislation—the cutoff was ultimately enacted.[8] However, this traumatic move was an after-the-fact, punitive measure, attempting to pressure the Turks to reverse their invasion and partition of Cyprus. It was advanced as a human rights measure, designed to uphold American laws while encouraging the new democratic government in Athens. It was not designed by any means as a model procedure for congressional review of other arms transfers.

The generic remedy proposed by Congress to address major arms sales was a simple legislative veto over export licenses. Authored by Democrats Senator Gaylord Nelson of Wisconsin and Congressman Jonathan Bingham of New York, the 1974 proposal backed a congressional veto over arms exports on "good government" grounds. The bill was resisted by the White House—which was still reeling from the 1973 war powers debate—as yet another unconstitutional encroachment on executive authority.[9] But the Nelson-Bingham provision was debated at the height of the impeachment crisis. With White House credibility at a low ebb, the legislators won support for the view that Congress had an essential role to play in these international commitments. As Senator Nelson observed: "The Department of Defense is consulted. The manufacturers of weapons and providers of military services are consulted. The foreign purchasers are involved. But Congress is hardly informed of these transactions, much less consulted as to their propriety."[10] Bingham echoed these sentiments in arguing for House passage, noting that the legislative veto on arms sales would "enable Congress for the first time to exercise effective oversight and control over [these sales]."[11]

The measure passed as part of the 1974 Foreign Military Sales Act. Its principles were subsequently incorporated into Section 36(b) of the revised International Security and Arms Export Control Act of 1976 (AECA). This measure was initially vetoed by President Ford, who continued to maintain that it was unconstitutional. But an accord was ultimately reached. Capitol Hill leaders worked with administration officials to establish a two-step process whereby the Pentagon would informally notify Congress twenty days prior to a "36(b)" notification. An export license for the arms covered in that notification could then be vetoed through House and Senate adoption of a concurrent resolution within thirty calendar days. The legislation has repeatedly been tinkered with over the last decade; reporting requirements have been added and the scope of sales subject to congressional review has been broadened. But the essential features of the 1974 proposal remained in place until virtually all uses of the legislative veto were barred in the 1983 Supreme Court case, *INS v. Chadha.*[12]

There were good arguments to be made for the stronger congressional role in 1974. The legislative branch *did* need to play a part in such important national undertakings—especially if these commitments were to be sustained over time. The proliferation of sensitive U.S. military technology to often unstable and antidemocratic nations was worrisome. Weapons could easily fall into Soviet hands (as ultimately occurred when the F-14 fighter aircraft and Phoenix missile technology were compromised after the Shah of Iran fell). But the new legislation promptly subjected the least popular of American security partners to a gauntlet of congressional criticism. From the date of its enactment, security cooperation with the United States entailed higher costs for foreign partners and would-be arms purchasers.

In reviewing the most noteworthy of these controversies, three central points should be borne in mind. First, it must be recognized that the vast majority of arms exports are noncontroversial. And even the controversial sales are usually approved in the end. Indeed, Congress has never prohibited a single arms sale through the adoption of a resolution of disapproval under the terms of AECA. On the other hand, it should be understood that by threatening to oppose some exports, Congress has forced the executive branch to make substantial alterations in the terms of several controversial sales. Equally important, Congress has had such a chilling effect on some sales that they have been scrapped without even being formally proposed by the executive branch. Finally, it should be noted that the very process by which these interbranch debates have unfolded has taken on a life of its own. Thus, arms sales disputes are worthy of detailed study for the insights they offer into the confused state of current relations between the branches. They provide valuable illustrations of both the best and the worst that this partnership has to offer for the pursuit of U.S. national security interests.

A DECADE OF ARMS SALES FIGHTS

The Kingdom of Jordan was the first nation to have its request for American arms vetted through the new "36(b)" congressional review procedures. In 1975, King Hussein sought to purchase advanced mobile Hawk air-defense systems to be deployed against potential threats from the substantial air forces of Syria, a Soviet client state. While Jordan technically remained in a state of war with Israel, the King had met secretly on numerous occasions with Israeli envoys to explore possibilities for peace. While Jordan had fought Israel—and suffered severe losses—in 1967, Jordanian forces had not joined in the 1973 surprise attack by Egypt and Syria against the Israelis. Therefore, the Ford administration backed the 1975 Jordanian request. The White House argued that it should be met in order to reassure King Hussein of American support and to discourage him from accepting Soviet offers of assistance. American arms could provide Hussein a measure of security that might encourage him to pursue peace with Israel more vigorously, while maintaining the morale of the King's troops in the face of the constant threat of internal rebellion.

But Congress balked. With a logic that would become familiar in years to come, critics on Capitol Hill argued that it was imprudent for the United States to arm nations still in a state of war with Israel, America's only reliable, democratic ally in the Middle East. Would not arming enemies of the Jewish state require more Israeli arms purchases—and more U.S. taxpayer contributions to foreign aid—in order to maintain Israel's technological margin of safety?[13] True, Jordan was far less likely than other Arab belligerents to strike at its immediate neighbor. But deployment of a sophisticated air-defense system would surely make it more difficult for Jordan to resist pan-Arab calls to join in yet another "holy war" against Israel. It would be far better, Hill critics concluded, to await a general peace in the region before proceeding to arm both sides of the Arab-Israeli dispute. "We are building the biggest powder keg in history," Democratic Congressman Robert Drinan of Massachusetts warned, noting that nearly 80 percent of U.S. arms sales in the mid-1970s were going to the Middle East and the oil-rich nations of the Persian Gulf.[14] Congressional supporters of Israel rejected administration arguments, maintaining that Jordan's refusal to establish diplomatic relations with Israel and forge a peace agreement should not be rewarded.

The administration worked secretly with Jordan on the details of the sale for nine months—from November 1974 until July 1975—before informing Congress of the proposal. There was no advance consultation whatsoever; the export license was sent to the Hill for review on the eve of the August recess. But the attempt to present harried legislators with a fait accompli backfired spectacularly. The end-run effort provoked a fight in which procedural objections served to reinforce congressional reservations about substantive policy; the error has since become a familiar one in executive branch relations with Congress. Strong opposition formed on Capitol Hill behind resolutions of disapproval in the same week that Congress was formally notified of the proposed Jordan sale. The House version was sponsored by Congressman Bingham; in the Senate, it was pressed by Republican Clifford Case of New Jersey. Critics of spiraling U.S. arms sales were joined by supporters of Israel in the first test of the legislative veto provisions. The American Israel Public Affairs Committee (AIPAC) effectively pressed the argument that Arab arms sales should be shelved until the peace process moved forward. But legislators needed little urging. Before another week had passed, a House Foreign Affairs Committee majority had endorsed a resolution to prohibit export of the arms—making it clear that the sale would go down to defeat if Congress was forced to vote before the upcoming recess.

What ensued established a routine for many subsequent arms sales controversies. The administration withdrew the formal notification

in order to stop the action-forcing "30-day clock." Senior administration officials then began to negotiate in earnest. But the negotiations had to proceed .on two tracks—first with leading congressional
opponents, to ascertain under what conditions a majority could be
obtained on Capitol Hill behind a scaled-down package for Jordan,
and only then with Amman, to ascertain whether King Hussein was
still interested in buying American weapons under new restrictions.
As a result, a handful of congressional leaders were able to use leverage to place restrictions on how Jordan's sovereign territory could
be defended.[15] President Ford formally notified congressional leaders
on September 17, 1975 that the Jordanians had agreed to deploy the
Hawk missile batteries in a fixed, nonmobile mode (that is, sunk in
concrete and facing north toward Syria, not west toward Israel). In
return, Bingham and Case agreed to shelve their resolutions of disapproval. The administration succeeded in persuading even Israel's
strongest supporters on the Hill of the wisdom of some U.S. arms
sales to an Arab nation still technically at war with Israel. Indeed,
the final compromise was partially brokered by AIPAC officials, who
acquiesced in the sale. But the costs to administration diplomacy and
interbranch relations were considerable. Because of the capitulation
by the Ford White House, serious questions were raised in the United
States and abroad about the credibility of executive branch commitments.[16] And the Jordanians, whose goodwill the sale was intended
to produce, were embittered by the humiliation they had endured at
the hands of a foreign legislature.[17]

The next major Washington arms sales contest, in September of
1976, produced a similar result: all parties emerged with an ability
to claim victory, but none felt particularly good about the process.
In this instance, the Ford administration sent the Hill a whole series
of requests on the eve of Congress's preelection adjournment. Among
the proposed sales were several for Iran, including top-of-the-line
F-16 fighter aircraft. The proposals also included an unprecedented
request for sales of advanced Sidewinder and Maverick missiles to
the Saudis for their air force.[18]

Senator Nelson was so disturbed by the dollar volume of these
thirty-seven different requests that he introduced individual resolutions of disapproval for each one. But this protest was largely symbolic; sustained opposition focused on but a handful of the proposed
exports. A bid by Democratic Senators Dick Clark and Joe Biden to
block the Iran sales failed on a close vote in the Foreign Relations

Committee. Subsequent lobbying on the Hill focused almost exclusively on the Saudi missile request. Bargaining between administration officials and the Senate Foreign Relations Committee staff produced a compromise under which the Saudis would get 650 Mavericks instead of the 1,500 they sought. Yet a resolution proposed by Senator Case to disapprove this compromise passed the committee 8–6 on September 24. A floor fight loomed—a debate that would pit Case, the ranking Republican, against Democratic Foreign Relations Committee Chairman John Sparkman of Alabama, who supported the sale. But Sparkman went to extraordinary parliamentary lengths to stall the opponents' resolution. Then an eleventh-hour intervention by Henry Kissinger averted further battle. Kissinger met with Foreign Relations Committee members in a lengthy executive session on the eve of congressional adjournment. In one of his final Hill appearances as secretary of state, Kissinger argued passionately that rejection of the scaled-down Saudi request would be a grave setback for hopes of improved U.S.-Saudi ties.[19] The dire warning in the classified briefing worked. Sparkman succeeded in shelving the resolution of disapproval. The prospect of no Senate vote made any question of House action in 1976 moot; a showdown on sales to America's "twin pillar" friends in the Persian Gulf was postponed until the next Congress.

In early 1977, the incoming Carter administration sought to address the problem of surging U.S. arms exports to the Middle East and the Persian Gulf by advancing a global policy of both qualitative and quantitative restraints. In May, the President proposed bilateral negotiations with the Soviets (the conventional arms transfer [CAT] talks). The President pledged to reduce the total dollar volume of U.S. arms exports each year, while curbing sales of high-tech, top-of-the-line weapons outside NATO. But the President then promptly exempted an imminent Iranian request for $1.2 billion worth of sophisticated AWACS aircraft. Concern about the vulnerable Persian Gulf regimes overrode the commitment of the Carter White House to the broader objective of restraining weapons proliferation.

The debate in Congress on the Iranian AWACS request involved several issues. None was more important than questions about the Shah's stability, and hence, the danger that the sophisticated U.S. technology employed by the AWACS might be compromised. Legislators questioned how AWACS could help the Shah against his greatest immediate threat, which was posed by domestic opposition. Was

this not precisely the type of profligate spending on military hardware that the Carter arms policy was designed to curb? The opponents' hands were strengthened by a July General Accounting Office
report that challenged much of the White House justification for the
sale, and by reports that the CIA was deeply worried about the prospect that the technology might ultimately be compromised as a
result of the rising internal challenge to the Shah's rule. Once again,
executive branch divisions were exploited effectively by the President's opponents on Capitol Hill. Internal dissents from within the
executive branch review process found their way to critics in Congress, who used these leaks to great effect.

With opposition growing, Senate Majority Leader Robert Byrd
recommended that the White House withdraw the sale proposal. The
advance was at first rejected by President Carter. But after a disapproval resolution passed the House Foreign Affairs Committee, the
President heeded Byrd's counsel. As in the Jordan case, the immi-
nence of a congressional recess was hastening a showdown vote that
the White House might lose. So the White House "stopped the clock"
and began to work with key swing votes on the Senate Foreign Relations Committee—Hubert Humphrey and Clifford Case—to cut a
deal.

The delay strategy worked. The White House finally focused on
the legitimate concerns Hill critics had, especially on the technology
security issue. Senators exacted agreement on six strict conditions
to govern the future delivery and use of the airborne radar aircraft
by Iran. And President Carter agreed to withhold the most sensitive communications and encoding equipment from the proposed
AWACS sale. As a result, further opposition was blunted. The now
conditional sale was cleared when the Senate failed to adopt a resolution disapproving it in September. (Providentially for American
security interests, the AWACS planes had not been sent to Iran
before the Shah fell in 1979. Thus, the AWACS technology was not
compromised, as other U.S. weapons systems were when members of
pro-Soviet factions gained access to them in the Khomeini coup.)

By placing conditions on proposed arms sales, Congress demonstrated the importance of compromise in this first trio of arms
export challenges. These tests also showed how interbranch bargaining could serve U.S. national security interests. But continuing controversy in 1978 over the sale of planes to Egypt, Israel, and the

Saudis showed how deep the divisions over basic arms sales policy remained. The debate over the 1978 "package sale" demonstrated unequivocally the danger that institutional differences over *procedural* prerogatives could be exploited by arms sales critics to exacerbate divisions over the *substance* of weapons transfer policies.

What the Carter administration did in 1978 was to "package" sales to Israel and her Arab enemies for presentation to Congress on an all-or-nothing basis. The scheme advanced by national security adviser Brzezinski initially looked like a nonstarter. The heavy-handed effort to silence pro-Israel legislators by threatening to withhold sales to Jerusalem if Congress balked at the request to arm Egypt and the Saudis almost backfired. Pro-Israel legislators resented a process that placed Israel's military needs on the same terms as weapons for Arab states. Opponents of the Arab arms sales joined with defenders of the integrity of the congressional review procedures to cry foul. The process itself became the issue. Had it not been for rapidly moving developments in the Middle East, the package approach might have resulted in disaster for the executive branch.

The key factor working in favor of the Carter administration was the courage of Egyptian leader Anwar Sadat. Rejecting the American call for a multinational peace conference, which would have involved the Soviets, Sadat flew directly to Jerusalem in November 1977. A dialogue began that would evolve less than a year later into the face-to-face negotiations at Camp David among Carter, Sadat, and Israeli Prime Minister Menachem Begin. But in the interim, Sadat sought U.S. arms to placate his own military and to replace aging stocks of Soviet-supplied weapons. The Saudis were also waiting in line, holding a 1976 promise from the lame-duck Ford administration that a sale of F-15 aircraft to Riyadh would follow the September 1976 missile sale. The Saudis had been put off until after the grueling AWACS-to-Iran fight on the Hill. But executive branch officials were nearly unanimous in the belief that U.S. efforts to moderate the Saudi role in the Arab world could not survive a Carter reversal of the Ford administration pledge.

Thus, the Carter White House approached the Hill in February 1978 with anything but eagerness. The administration's dilemma was that without linkage to the Israeli planes, there was no reason to believe Congress would approve sales of fighter aircraft to Egypt, not to mention to the Saudis. Yet a rejection on Capitol Hill would humiliate Sadat and probably scuttle the whole Middle East peace effort. This provoked the gamble of a take-it-or-leave-it package offer to the Hill.

It is true that these sales might never have been approved without the package approach and the hardball tactics. And yet, as Carter policymaker Harold Saunders lamented, the procedural gimmickry obscured the fact that the proposals were indeed substantively linked. Congress focused only on the specific arms sale at hand, overlooking the broader diplomatic strategy involved. The initiative to provide potential allies a measure of security was, as Saunders noted, a key part of efforts to induce Egypt and Saudi Arabia to take risks for peace:

> The executive branch failed to force debate over the basic issue that it needed to develop the relationship with Saudi Arabia and other Arab states in order to broaden the position of the United States in the Middle East—and could do so without diminishing its support for Israel. That was the basic substantive point behind packaging the three sales, but the Administration allowed the packaging to be seen only for its tactical purpose.[20]

Three tactical decisions early in the debate advanced the administration's case. First, the administration toned down its confrontational rhetoric about an all-or-nothing deal. The point had been made. Legislators understood that the Israeli sales might offset the dangers posed by new planes for the Saudis and that Egypt might need new arms to be more forthcoming in peace negotiations. And it had always been clear that the President was under no obligation to conclude *any* of the sales, even if the export licenses were authorized by Congress. Thus, it was worthwhile to cool the rhetoric and thereby diminish the threat that procedural critics could strengthen the hand of opponents of the substance of the policy.

Secondly, the administration wrote off the House, establishing a precedent that was to be followed in virtually all subsequent Arab arms sales disputes. Representatives were simply too vulnerable to the pressures of biannual elections. Why should a junior congressman from Topeka incur political risks for Riyadh? Abandoning the fight in the House freed up administration officials to focus on the senior body, where the handful of swing votes could be more easily counted and worked one by one. Crucial to this strategy was President Carter's personal success in enlisting Republican Senate Minority Leader Howard Baker and senior Democrat Abe Ribicoff of Connecticut, a leader in the American Jewish community, whose support for the package insulated the President from the charge that he was insensitive to Israel's security needs. A vote for the sales became a respectable option—even for Republican's—and the strong opposition of AIPAC was somewhat neutralized.

Finally, the administration—with Sadat's help—was able to isolate Senate opposition and to focus almost exclusively on the Saudi component of the package. The White House then proceeded to deal effectively with questions about the propriety of arming the Arab nation with America's best fighter aircraft. President Carter played a key role in defending the Egyptian component of the package; he wrote each senator a letter stating that a rejection of Cairo's planes would constitute a "breach of trust" with Sadat who "has turned away from a relationship with the Soviet Union to work with the United States in the search for peace."[21] Defense Secretary Harold Brown focused in turn on the package's Saudi element, which was drawing so much fire. AIPAC's information packets shed a great deal of light on the offensive capabilities of the Saudi aircraft; if deployed against Israel, they could pose a grave threat in the event of any future Arab attack. Sale critics also pilloried the Saudis' dismal role in the 1973 oil embargo—which cost hundreds of thousands of U.S. jobs—as well as the Saudis' status as principal patrons of the PLO. Secretary Brown provided senators with essential political cover by providing a series of written pledges regarding where the Saudis would base the U.S.-built planes and what add-on technology the United States would provide to augment the F-15's capabilities in future years. The 1978 Brown letter specifically ruled out future U.S. sales to Saudi Arabia of bomb racks, advanced air-to-air missiles, or aerial refueling equipment—all of which would enhance the Saudis' ability to attack Israel, which might require offsetting Israeli weapons purchases. In addition, the Saudi Embassy and Riyadh's Washington lobbyist, Fred Dutton, enlisted U.S. business leaders to back the sale. They pointed to the instability confronting the Saudis in the Gulf region, as well as to the fact that if the United States refused to sell, the Saudis would turn to European suppliers.

Critics in the Senate continued to object to the package sales on the grounds that they provided an unwelcome infusion of arms into the peace process. As Democratic Senator John Glenn of Ohio argued: "At this delicate stage of negotiations to inject a public arms sale debate on the Mid-East with all that entails cannot but hurt our efforts toward peace."[22] Yet it was a White House compensatory move to send still *more* warplanes to the region—another twenty F-15s for Israel—that, together with the Brown letter, clinched the deal in the Senate. Executive branch officials worked together as an effective team, providing senators with tangible evidence of improvements in the package that legislators could cite to justify their support. This was essential for political cover. After an emotional floor debate, the Senate voted on May 15, 1978 against a resolution to disapprove the entire package. The 54–44 vote meant that the arms export licenses were cleared. With this obstacle removed and the door to improved U.S.-Egyptian relations opened, the Carter administration pressed ahead on the Middle East peace process. Less than four months later, in a moment of great personal triumph for Jimmy Carter, a framework for an Israeli-Egyptian peace treaty was hammered out at Camp David and signed at the White House.

THE 1981 SAUDI SALE:
STATE-OF-THE-ART LOBBYING

Each of these early arms sales disputes offered echoes of previous debates. And each contained the seeds for subsequent controversy. The height of these enduring struggles was the case of the 1981 debate over a bundle of Saudi arms requests—a dispute that was fought over the same divisions featured in the 1977 and 1978 debates and that laid the groundwork for another decade of dissension of America's Middle East arms sales policies. At issue in 1981 was the security of U.S. technology sent to a shaky desert kingdom, as well as the crucial 1978 pledge to the Senate by Defense Secretary Harold Brown that the Saudis would not be provided with the advanced equipment necessary to turn the F-15 squadrons into a potent offensive force. Less than three years later, the nascent Reagan administration scrapped the Brown pledges in their entirety. And in 1981, there was no compensatory offer of an Israeli component or an ongoing Saudi-Israeli peace process to soften the blow. Thus, the 1981 White House request for a mammoth new Saudi arms package threw gasoline on the still smoldering embers left by the previous Hill arms sales battles.

The Saudi arms fight is a crucial case study because it starkly illustrates the lobbying techniques that both sides use in debating Middle

East arms sales proposals. In the prolonged 1981 struggle—fought over the course of seven months—these tactics were heavy-handed and highly public.

The Reagan administration assembled an effective lobbying team in support of the sale. It extended beyond the usual senior officials of the White House and the State and Defense departments. The CIA was brought in to make the point with selected senators that security cooperation with the Saudis brought important corollary benefits.[23] The manufacturers of the $8 billion worth of arms at issue—especially Boeing, maker of the AWACS—were involved effectively, as were U.S. oil refiners like Mobil Corporation, which had close business links to the Arab world. A number of former government officials on retainer to Arab governments also lobbied the Hill in favor of the sale. These included former Senators Fulbright and Abourezk, as well as former Kennedy administration aide Fred Dutton, who worked on an annual $200,000 retainer from the Saudi Embassy. Dutton's firm produced elaborate advertising brochures lauding U.S.-Saudi ties. The administration also brought Saudi Prince Bandar bin Sultan to the Hill to lobby key senators; the Saudi prince in fact ended up negotiating directly with members of the legislative branch over the final terms of a conditional approval resolution. Senator Baker even provided Bandar with a private Hill office from which to work.[24]

Ranged in opposition to the sale was the full machinery of AIPAC, then nearing the height of its power on the Hill. AIPAC lobbyists were supplemented in due course by a host of groups friendly to Israel, ranging from the Anti-Defamation League to the American Jewish Committee. Prime Minister Begin also lobbied senators directly in opposition to the AWACS proposal. But AIPAC took the lead in building grass-roots support for the Senate resolution of disapproval advanced by Senators Packwood, Cranston, Jackson, and Jepsen. The senators personally approached colleagues on the Senate floor and in the cloakrooms, signing up several dozen original co-sponsors against the sale. AIPAC was particularly useful in pressuring swing votes—junior senators, often Republicans from the Midwest, who were torn between supporting the President and going with the potent pro-Israel lobby, as well as their own inclinations to reject the sale. AIPAC worked to increase the pressure from campaign contributors and opinion leaders in these senators' home states. Key grass-roots supporters were called from AIPAC headquarters and urged to press senators to join against the Saudi sale. Morrie Amitay, the former executive director of AIPAC, described how this process typically works:

> A lot of these [uncommitted] Senators are from the Midwest, West, down South. . . . The Jewish constituents from sparsely inhabited states are typically teachers, they are doctors, they have invariably been involved some way in politics. They are usually respected people in the community, so you do not have to pitch it at the level of, "I contributed ten thousand dollars to your campaign—unless you do this you will make me unhappy and I will contribute to your opponent next time." At most it's implicit.[25]

When pressed for votes, the White House was far more blunt. Reagan aides explicitly threatened to withhold President Reagan's fund-raising support and to cancel campaign appearances for GOP senators who failed to support the sale. The White House also worked the same ground as AIPAC. The White House used its own computerized campaign lists to contact dozens of supporters and key opinion leaders in the home states of key senators. Reagan aides urged these grass-roots leaders to pressure swing votes in the Senate into not abandoning the President.

There were strong substantive reasons for taking a position for or against the sale quite apart from these lobbying pressures. The march of international events provided the White House with a strong case. The Gulf situation had changed markedly since the 1978 Pentagon pledge to the Senate not to upgrade the Saudis' air capabilities:

- Iran had fallen into the hands of Islamic fundamentalists, leaving the Saudis as a lone pillar of moderation in the Gulf.

- Afghanistan had been invaded by the Soviets, and the Saudis were supporting the Moslem freedom fighters there, exposing themselves to potential Soviet threats.

- Iraq had attacked Iran and become mired in a vicious war along the northern shores of the Gulf.

- Camp David had brought peace between Israel and Egypt, but there was an urgent need to broaden the peace process and to encourage some Saudi risk-taking on America's behalf.

The sale opponents had a logical case as well. The Saudis remained in a state of war with America's only stable, democratic ally in the region—Israel. Saudi Arabia still spearheaded the effort to strangle Israel economically through the Arab boycott. The Saudis were the principal bankrollers of the terrorist PLO. The authoritarian, utterly antidemocratic Saudi kingdom was also subject to the same internal instability that had led to the overthrow of the Shah—which would have compromised American AWACS technology had it been delivered to Teheran. Many Senate critics objected to the Saudi sale on technology security grounds alone; for these legislators, Israeli interests were not central to the question. There were also the 1978 Brown assurances. It helped the opponents' case that the executive branch—albeit under a different administration—was proposing to exploit precisely those weapons that the Senate had less than three years before been assured would not be sold to Riyadh. Where would these spiraling sales end, critics demanded, noting that the Saudis had contracted to purchase more than $40 billion in U.S. military services and weapons since 1950. The AWACS would enhance the capabilities of the entire Saudi air force, providing an extraordinary "force multiplier" effect in any future Arab-Israeli conflict.

In the face of these concerns, the administration campaign for the sale got off to a disastrous start. Less than one month after taking office, Reagan officials were on the Hill calmly briefing members on the President's intention to enhance the Saudi F-15's capabilities with AIM-9L air-to-air missiles, range-extending conformal fuel tanks, and aerial tankers. Included in their briefing was an allegation, later withdrawn, that the lame-duck Carter administration had made a commitment to the Saudis to propose such a sale. A decision on AWACS was imminent, the Hill was told in late February, and the Brown assurances were no longer relevant due to the changed circumstances in the Gulf. On March 6, the White House announced the sale proposal—still minus the AWACS planes.

Led by Bob Packwood and Alan Cranston, Senate opponents immediately responded with floor speeches and a series of public letters to the White House. A series of twenty-one separate Senate speeches against the sale were made on March 24. Yet at this point, the administration still did not face full-force opposition. For while the government of Israel had repeated boilerplate criticism of this (and any other) proposed sale of weapons to a belligerent, Jerusalem was not fully engaged against it. "What good will it do us with Ronald Reagan," one Israeli diplomat explained, "if our first encounter is a fight?"[26] And Senate critics of the proposed sale were engaged in a heated behind-the-scenes battle to enlist AIPAC, which had decided to mute its opposition if AWACS were not included. This initially cautious AIPAC strategy was part of a deliberate decision to court the incoming executive branch. In 1981, AIPAC hoped to win over the "Arabists" at State and DOD, while using its traditional support on the Hill only as an "insurance policy" in the event of a breakdown in its attempt to forge a new close relationship with GOP officials in the executive branch. It was a strategy that infuriated Israel's strongest friends on the Hill—especially partisan Democrats—who felt taken for granted. But the administration quickly and clumsily proceeded to undermine this strategy and to reunite AIPAC with its bedrock Hill supporters.

With President Reagan still recovering from an assassination attempt, the NSC decided the first week in April to sell the full complement of F-15 enhancements to Saudi Arabia. The NSC also decided to include the sale of five AWACS aircraft as part of the package. The President ratified the decision from his bed at George Washington University Hospital.

Protest was swift and effective. On April 5, Prime Minister Begin (who faced his own reelection challenge in less than sixty days) expressed his opposition to the proposed AWACS transfer in the strongest terms. Begin warned Alexander Haig during the secretary's visit to Jerusalem that AWACS would provide the Saudis with a devastating battle management capability. On April 6, AIPAC came off the fence and sent out an "action alert" calling for all-out grassroots opposition to the AWACS package. On April 7, Congressmen Jack Kemp of New York and Jim Blanchard of Michigan led dozens of House colleagues in an antisale colloquy on the House floor. On April 9, then-Minority Leader Byrd indicated strong reservations in a public letter to the Secretary of State Haig that counseled delay.

The administration had already abandoned the fight in the House. Reagan aides proceeded later in the month to press their case in the Senate to prevent rejection of the sale. However, another problem arose from this strategy. The President was already employing his full political resources to push through a mammoth program of budget reforms, tax cuts, and defense spending increases. The fate of other critical items on the Reagan domestic agenda hung in the balance. Belatedly, the White House congressional relations staffers recognized the difficulty of waging a two-front war on the Hill by adding an extraordinarily controversial foreign policy item to the agenda. So the administration reversed itself. On April 26 the White

House abruptly shelved the Saudi arms proposal, indicating that the request would be renewed in a matter of weeks. Their strategy was simply to cool passions, to avoid discussing the proposal in any detail, and to urge troubled senators to reserve final judgment.

The effect of the administration's false start was to give the opposition a clear target and a virtually uncontested field. The gauntlet had been thrown down. A steady, unanswered drumbeat of criticism developed. Declared opposition to the sale became a test of faith among friends of Israel on the Hill. Senators due to face the polls took note. As Senators Packwood and Cranston continued to work the cloakrooms, AIPAC worked the phones. These closely coordinated forces relied upon both frontal assaults and "bank shots"– the strategy of inducing key opinion leaders to lobby swing Senate votes. By June 24, Packwood was able to tell a crowded Washington press conference that fifty-four senators—a comfortable majority of the Senate—had signed a letter to the President urging that the proposed sale be withdrawn. The letter attracted signatures of thirty-four Senate Democrats and twenty members of the President's own party.

The White House kept its cool and pressed for the completion of its domestic economic package, which gained final passage on August 5. On August 24, in the midst of a congressional recess, the Reagan administration sent informal notification to the Hill that the Saudi arms request would proceed. Packwood and Cranston again responded with an effort to kill the deal without a vote. A total of fifty-one senators signed on to their resolution of disapproval. With a bipartisan majority of representatives sponsoring a similar resolution in the House, it appeared to many observers that the proposal was dead in the water. But the serious lobbying was just beginning.

The fall campaign on the Saudi package featured escalation on both sides. AIPAC ultimately made opposition to the sale a crucial test for senators, who were challenged to demonstrate their sensitivity to Israeli security concerns. Several million dollars in PAC funds from scores of pro-Israel fund-raising organizations—many of which are responsive to the AIPAC executive board—hung in the balance.[27] Conversely, the Reagan administration made the issue virtually a test of patriotism, warning that the very capacity of the President to govern was at stake. The Saudis heightened the pressure by making it clear that, despite extensive past U.S. support, they viewed the vote as an essential "litmus test" of U.S. friendship. This assertion that the sale constituted yet another test of American goodwill especially irked Senate critics. As Democratic Senator Christopher Dodd of Connecticut argued:

> If the real issue is symbolic, then I would suggest there will always be new symbolic requests for the most sophisticated U.S. military equipment in the years to come. If we cannot make the distinction between realistic military requirements with U.S. controls and symbolism, then we should not be starting down this path.[28]

The immediate consequence of the escalation of rhetoric was that President Reagan was forced to commit political resources and personal time far in excess of the intrinsic value of the sale to U.S. security. Questions had been raised initially about the depth of Reagan's commitment to the controversial sale. But the threats of the White House staff and their dire predictions of the consequences of defeat in turn threatened to become a self-fulfilling prophecy; the President necessarily became deeply engaged in lobbying for individual votes. *Time* magazine breathlessly warned that if this weapons proposal for the distant desert kingdom were blocked by the Hill, "Ronald Reagan's ability to conduct any effective foreign policy at all would be called into serious question."[29]

In order to win, the administration had to hold all its votes and it had to pry several opponents of the sale off the Senate resolution of disapproval. Especially important in this effort were freshmen Republicans. As a group, these senators were highly vulnerable to White House pressure. Many had won narrow election victories in 1980 solely on the strength of Reagan's coattails. Other GOP colleagues faced difficult reelection battles in 1982 and 1984 and needed personal appearances from the President to rally troops and raise dollars. They also had vested interests in not weakening their party leader at the outset of his administration. Finally, junior Republican senators appreciated far better than White House lobbyists the need for a tangible concession to the legitimate concerns of sale opponents. These senators needed changes in the sale terms for which they could take credit, shielding them from the disapproval and disappointment of sale opponents in their home states. The senators would then be in the position of giving the President their vote while trumpeting the restrictions and improvements they had introduced as the price of their reluctant support.

There emerged two key groups from these endgame negotiations. The first consisted of half a dozen GOP freshmen: Dan Quayle of

Indiana, Slade Gorton of Washington, Mark Andrews of North Dakota, Robert Kasten of Wisconsin, Mack Mattingly of Georgia, and Frank Murkowski of Alaska. They worked with Vice President George Bush and other White House officials on a series of conditions to govern approval of the sale. A second group centered on senior, more conservative senators from foreign relations and armed services—men like Sam Nunn, John Warner, and John Glenn—who could provide their own votes, and several more, if some criteria were established to govern AWACS transfer and technology security.

Senator Glenn negotiated directly with Saudi Prince Bandar in an extraordinary Capitol Hill meeting arranged by the White House. Nunn and Warner worked privately with key White House officials like Jim Baker and Ed Meese. The Nunn-Warner proposal was to establish generic rules governing the transfer of AWACS to *any* country; it had the virtue of not singling out the Saudis for restrictions. This proposal was soon merged with the conditions put together by the Quayle-Gorton group. These conditions addressed six key issues: security of the AWACS technology, command and control of AWACS, screening of Saudi air force personnel, AWACS flight operations, Saudi command structure, and Saudi support for peace initiatives. Specifically, delivery of AWACS and future arms requests was to be conditioned on evidence that the Saudis were providing "substantial assistance" to making "significant progress" in the regional peace process.[30] (Glenn's insistence on joint crewing arrangements was rejected; he ultimately voted against the sale.)

While the Reagan administration was working to build support for a compromise—a conditional resolution of approval—it was also waging an all-out pressure campaign against opponents. In a stunning game of very public political hardball, the White House intensified the pressure on vulnerable GOP freshmen Senators Charles Grassley and Roger Jepsen of Iowa. Jepsen was one of the original "gang of four" senators who had first circulated a "Dear Colleague" letter opposing the sale. By virtue of that letter, Jepsen was publicly identified as a leader of the opposition. But the President's men pressured Jepsen relentlessly to reverse himself. After weeks of White House-generated lobbying from back home, Jepsen was strong-armed in a meeting with the President's political advisers. "We just beat his brains out," one Reagan aide later bragged to the *Des Moines Register*, "We showed him his political grave [if he refused to reverse himself]."[31] Jepsen and Grassley abandoned the opposition and joined the President, inaugurating a campaign catchphrase of the 1980s: the "flip-flop."

White House efforts to influence other votes met with mixed success. Senator DeConcini of Arizona bitterly rejected a trial balloon from an administration official, who pledged that Reagan would not campaign against DeConcini if the Democrat backed the Saudi sale. Robert Byrd scoffed at administration attempts to win his vote by offering to restore Amtrak routes through West Virginia. Grassley argued that clumsy efforts to link his support for the sale to appointment of one of his supporters to a federal judgeship might make it more difficult for him to back the President. Yet, as in the Panama dispute, Hayakawa of California publicly tied his vote on the pending controversy to another pet project, this time the sale of advanced U.S. fighter aircraft to Taiwan.[32] At least two senators who ultimately supported the sale—Gorton and Democrat John Melcher of Montana—won special favors for home-state projects, including federal funds for hospital renovation and renovation of a coal-burning plant.[33]

By late September, the Reagan administration began to develop momentum. Soundings still indicated that the Saudi sale was deeply unpopular at the grass-roots, with 59 percent opposed in a late summer Harris poll. But the White House was making demonstrable progress on the Hill, where senators were being bombarded with the argument that a vote against the sale would weaken the President's ability to pursue vital U.S. international interests. A letter from former President Carter was produced, arguing that a Senate vote to block the sale would undermine other U.S. international commitments. Carter argued:

> In the eyes of most nations, a commitment by the President of the United States is considered to be a promise by our country. A rejection of his commitment, rightly or wrongly, will be considered by our allies and potential adversaries as the breaking of a solemn agreement by the United States.[34]

Then the Armed Services Committee, which had no formal jurisdiction over the proposed sale, stole a march on the foreign relations panel by issuing a report on October 15 favoring the sale by a 10–5 margin. The White House draft of a letter providing assurances to the Quayle and Nunn groups was held back until the final floor vote. Together with the Jepsen-Grassley flip-flop, this proved to be the key to victory. The President's letter was drafted as a "living document." The text was altered daily, as necessary, to meet the concerns of swing senators; changes were rapidly edited into this catch-all draft. But the final document itself was not signed by President Reagan and delivered to senators until hours before the final Senate vote.

The last days of the Saudi sale fight were bitter ones. The rhetoric escalated to new heights of excess. Backers of the proposed sale savaged the alleged dual loyalties of sale critics. White House confidant William F. Buckley excoriated sale critics for "trying to outdo each other in servility to [Israeli Prime Minister Menachem] Begin."[35] Saudi lobbyist Dutton told the *Washington Post*, "If I had my way, I'd have bumper stickers plastered all over town that say 'Reagan or Begin.' . . . That kind of stuff really plays in Peoria."[36] An obviously irritated President Reagan himself warned the pro-Israel lobby in an October press conference that "it is not the business of other nations to make American foreign policy."[37] A distressed former President Nixon was encouraged to drive the point home, telling the press that "we know, the Saudis know, and everyone in the Middle East knows that if it were not for the intense opposition by Begin and parts of the American Jewish community, the AWACS sale would go through. This is the cold fact."[38]

Tensions ran high within the pro-sale camp as well. When national security adviser Richard Allen encouraged the Glenn proposal for joint crewing, Secretary Haig exploded that he did not want "any [obscenity] Senators running foreign policy," to which his ally Howard Baker retorted that he did not want "any [obscenity] Secretary of State running the Senate."[39] Sale opponents chimed in to criticize the hypocrisy of the administration blasting the Israelis for lobbying *against* the sale while a Saudi prince was given a Senate office from which to lobby *for* it. Sale critics were also dismayed by the implication that if the sale were defeated, Israel would be blamed for any strains in U.S.-Saudi ties. The director of the American Jewish Committee Washington office, Hyman Bookbinder, lamented this fact in an impassioned open letter to the White House liaison with the Jewish community: "Once again, I fear Jews and Israel are being prepared for our centuries-old curse, being scapegoated for problems not of our doing."[40] (A similar argument was ultimately advanced by Republican Senator William Cohen of Maine, who reversed himself and voted *for* a sale he concluded was not in the American interest because Israel was in a "no-win situation.")[41]

The President made his final appeal a defense of his office and his ability to govern. But Reagan's bipartisan pitch alienated Democratic leaders like Byrd—who recalled similar appeals ignored by Reagan when as a candidate for president he had assaulted the Panama Canal and SALT II treaties. And when President Reagan privately urged GOP senators to back him as a matter of party interest, it was a clumsy appeal as well. Here was a partisan appeal, scorned by Democrats, to a group of Republicans who had chosen as the head of their Senate campaign committee, Bob Packwood, the leading opponent of the Saudi sale.

The acrimonious Senate debate ended on October 29. The oft-revised draft of President Reagan's letter of assurances was finally signed and delivered to the Senate chamber just hours before the 5:00 p.m. roll call. By a vote of 52–48, the sale was approved. The President hailed the vote to authorize the Saudi sale with the same hyperbole that had marked both sides of the entire debate, proclaiming that with clearance of the $8 billion weapons package, "peace [was] again on the march in the Middle East."[42]

SELLING ARMS IN THE 1980s

It took nine months and an extraordinary amount of Reagan administration political capital to prevail in the 1981 Saudi arms fight. The scars incurred in the process endured throughout the 1980s. Even the radical change in the Arms Export Control Act brought by the 1983 Supreme Court decision on the legislative veto offered little solace for the Reagan administration. Indeed, it was after this 1983 decision—which meant that a two-thirds vote, not just a simple majority, would be required for *joint* resolutions of disapproval blocking arms sales—that the administration faced overwhelming opposition to new Arab arms requests.

The first casualties of the 1981 sale included a number of its key Senate backers. Ten of the sale's supporters were defeated in their next reelection bid; another half-dozen retired, for a variety of reasons. In some of these ten contests, the AWACS vote was a peripheral issue that did not have a major impact on fund-raising or voter support. But in several key tests, AWACS seemed occasionally to be the *only* issue. Senator Jepsen's flip-flop was exploited unmercifully by maverick Democratic challenger Congressman Tom Harkin, who received strong financial support from Israel backers. And Senate Foreign Relations Committee Chairman Charles Percy was targeted by pro-Israel PACs angered by his defense of the Saudi sale. Challenger Paul Simon's campaign benefited from a flood of nearly $3 million in anti-Percy TV commercials aired in Illinois. In an effort to retaliate against the moderate Republican, one Israel-backer, a Southern California businessman named Michael Goland, spent more than $1.4 million of his own funds on anti-Percy spots. Percy lost by less than 2 percent of the final vote.

By the end of his first term, President Reagan had lost patience with the troublesome politics of Middle East policymaking. Efforts to move the peace process forward had been met with rejections both in Arab capitals and in the Israeli cabinet. The AWACS package did little to alter the status quo: King Fahd of Saudi Arabia continued to oppose Camp David and a follow-on 1982 Reagan plan. Fahd's own peace plan offered the distant prospect of direct negotiations if Israel first ceded Jerusalem, its capital city, and all territory seized in 1967 after a generation of Arab assaults. The Israelis, too, frustrated the White House. Their military actions in Lebanon appeared to violate U.S. laws limiting the use of American arms to defensive missions. The failure of Secretary of State George Shultz's Lebanon disengagement plan, and then the calamity at the Beirut Marine barracks, left few in the administration with any desire for involvement in Middle East diplomacy. By early 1984, White House insiders were warning that First Lady Nancy Reagan wanted her husband to avoid the turbulent politics of the region.

In light of these White House frustrations, President Reagan's disastrous second-term run-ins with Congress over arms export laws were all the more surprising. The administration was not eager for continued confrontation over Middle East policy. White House officials knew the political and diplomatic costs such a course would entail. But while President Reagan had a strong record of support for Israel on issues like trade and strategic cooperation, administration officials continued to view the Middle East primarily in terms of a U.S.-Soviet struggle for influence and friendship. The obligations of leadership—and a desire to move beyond an always unsatisfactory status quo in the region—led President Reagan to take substantial risks in pursuit of his vision of U.S. national interests. With the peace process moribund, U.S. arms sales became a substitute for diplomatic initiative.

Five times between 1985 and 1988, the Reagan administration sought to undertake significant arms transfers to Middle East nations beyond the consensus "Camp David" recipients, Israel and Egypt.

One effort ended in failure and was abandoned. A second proposal resulted in rejection by strong congressional majorities—and survived in skeletal form only through a veto override sustained by a Senate margin of one vote. A third arms export scheme ended in the indictment of several top presidential advisers. Of the five attempts at arms transfer, only the last two, which were pressed at the height of U.S. deployments in the Persian Gulf, passed muster unscathed on Capitol Hill.

The initial arms sales battle in President Reagan's second term loomed once again on a request for Saudi Arabia. The administration had been quiet on all post-AWACS Saudi requests until after the November 1984 elections. But in January 1985, a Saudi shopping list resurfaced, bringing near instantaneous reaction on Capitol Hill. Twenty-four hours after the press reported that President Reagan was favorably disposed toward the new Saudi arms request, sixty-four senators signed a Cranston-Packwood letter to the President expressing "serious reservations" about more arms for the Saudis in light of their failure to support U.S. peace efforts.

The swiftness of the reaction was astonishing. For some senators, it was simply the politic thing to do. They were frustrated that the Saudis were not willing to take more risks to make peace with Israel and took note of the 1981 Reagan pledge in his letter to senators that there would be no more U.S. arms for the Saudis until they made greater strides toward peace. Domestic political pressures also militated against showing any sympathy for the Saudi kingdom. For in the wake of the 1984 elections, AIPAC was as powerful as ever. It also helped senators to know that opposition to another Saudi sale looked to be a "free vote"; since the 1983 Court decision on the legislative veto, it would take two-thirds in both houses to block a sale. If the sale proved to be of such importance to U.S. interests, many senators reasoned, let thirty-four White House loyalists stand to defend it.

In the face of the formidable Senate protest, the President promptly reversed his plan to send a Saudi sale notification to Congress in February 1985. The administration instead deferred all such requests, announcing that a comprehensive, regionwide study would be conducted on Middle East arms requirements. This delaying tactic permitted time to regroup and to establish lobbying priorities. What emerged was a risky effort to provide arms first to Jordan, a nation far more important than Saudi Arabia to efforts to move the stalled Arab-Israeli peace effort beyond square one.

With the Jordan arms proposal, yet another debate ensued over arms sales being made the centerpiece of U.S. diplomacy in the volatile Middle East region. King Hussein sought the whole gamut of top-of-the-line U.S. arms, including F-15 fighter aircraft, Sidewinder air-to-air missiles, and mobile Hawk surface-to-air missiles. He also sought Stingers, the suddenly popular, shoulder-fired antiaircraft weapons. Jordan had a legitimate fear of Syrian forces—which could threaten the tiny kingdom if it made peace with Israel. Hussein had repeatedly pursued secret negotiations with Israel, placing himself in great personal danger. And the King was once again entertaining Soviet offers of military hardware, if only to appease his nervous generals and to prod the United States into sweetening its own offers. The 1985 Jordan request caused consternation on the Hill. Hussein *was* a moderate, as well as the key to building upon the peace process that had been stalled since Camp David. Clearly, an arms-purchasing relationship with the United States would be an inducement for Hussein to be more helpful in the peace process. Yet U.S. legislators balked at the principle of arms before peace—even though it had succeeded with Sadat prior to Camp David. There was great concern that consummation of the arms sale would reduce Hussein's incentive to conclude a separate peace with Israel—while increasing an immediate and direct threat on the border of the Jewish state. At a minimum, the sale would increase arms-purchasing requirements for an Israeli government already devastated by runaway inflation. Thus, senators who wanted to gamble on Hussein's courage were torn.

Into this breach stepped AIPAC. The formidable organization's lobbying promptly narrowed the policy alternatives. Members of Congress became aware that their absence from antisale resolutions would be scored against them in the next election cycle. The better part of wisdom seemed to lie in joining the anti-Jordan effort while endorsing the proposition that Jordan should make peace with Israel before receiving American arms. In a matter of weeks, selling arms to Jordan simply became politically unacceptable. Democratic Senator Edward Kennedy of Massachusetts and Republican Senator John Heinz of Pennsylvania enlisted a veto-proof "supermajority" of seventy-three senators as cosponsors of an effort to block any Jordan sale before direct, sustained, face-to-face talks between Israel and Jordan were under way. Secretary Shultz did salvage a modest direct U.S. aid program for Hussein and a pledge from congressional leaders to respond promptly if the King stepped forward for peace talks. But on more immediate arms sales to Jordan, Congress had spoken. The

Jordan arms package was withdrawn without ever having been formally proposed.[43]

In the wake of the Jordan arms fiasco, the Reagan administration was anything but eager to revisit the Saudi request. But the President felt obliged to follow through, and the State Department and the Pentagon pressed the case. The Saudis were alarmed by escalation of the Iran-Iraq "tanker" war, during which more than one Iranian fighter strayed into Saudi airspace. Riyadh was determined to purchase additional arms—either from the United States or from others—as an added deterrent against Iran. The Pentagon, which had met with little success in drawing the Saudis into more direct military cooperation in the Gulf, backed the follow-on sale as a means of expanding U.S.-Saudi ties. The CIA—which was deeply involved in a number of joint, covert projects with Saudi leaders—urged President Reagan to proceed. Thus, administration officials, using the Gulf conflict as its immediate justification, trudged once more up to the Hill with a Saudi request in early 1986.

The original package sought by the Saudis in February included a host of weapons: another squadron of F-15 aircraft, M-1 tanks, bomb racks, Blackhawk helicopters, enhanced electronic packages for the F-15s, Sidewinder missiles, Stingers, and Harpoon (antiship) missiles. Critics in Congress immediately assailed the proposal. Most of the arguments were familiar, but Democratic Congressman Mel Levine of California added a new nationalistic twist: "President Reagan has won warm approval from Americans when he has talked tough to Third World dictators and monarchs. Yet in the Saudi case, we now see the Administration reflexively filling orders for our most sophisticated weapons from a nation that has scorned basic American foreign policy objectives." Levine noted the many U.S. interests in the region beyond access to oil, including broadening the peace process, combating terrorism, and aiding Egypt and Israel. But like many in Congress, Levine concluded that "the Saudi Kingdom has not only failed to support the administration in each of these crucial areas—it has actively opposed us."[44]

The administration faced unremitting hostility to the sale on the Hill, where it enjoyed virtually no Democratic support. From the outset of this new Saudi arms struggle, the administration adopted a strategy of defensive retreat worthy of the great Chinese generals. Once again, the House was written off. Then, in a novel post-*Chadha* strategy, the administration focused not on a Senate majority, but on a "veto-proof" hard core of thirty-four. This meant it could gain authority to consummate the sale simply by obtaining less than three dozen GOP votes in the Senate. Yet with few senators willing to defend the proposed sale, even this modest goal was extremely difficult to obtain. Senators were not eager to reward the Saudis for their failure to stop funding the Palestine Liberation Organization or for their feeble efforts in behalf of U.S. peace initiatives in the Middle East. And with AIPAC fighting the sale vigorously, the ghosts of former Senators Percy and Jepsen haunted would-be White House loyalists.

Support for the sale was left to a lonely band of five on the Foreign Relations Committee, including Senators Charles Mathias of Maryland and Daniel Evans of Washington. They noted that "for thirty years, our security assistance and arms sales programs have been a primary instrument for achieving [U.S. interests]" and concluded that rejection of the sale would "have enormous symbolic significance and lasting adverse effects on our interests."[45] Their unenviable task was made somewhat easier when the administration dropped the helicopters, tanks, and additional F-15 aircraft from the package. This not only diminished the military significance of the proposed exports, it also highlighted the alternative to American sales. The Saudis promptly contracted to buy British Tornado jets. While arms sales could not be justified solely on the basis of balance of trade, this costly forfeiture of a $10–15 billion sales package, combined with the loss of American control over spare parts and maintenance services, got the attention of some wavering senators.

Even the scaled-down, missiles-only sale lost in its initial Hill tests. Indeed, it was trounced. The May 6, 1986 Senate vote was 73–22; the House vote the next day was 356–62. The administration was shaken both by the wide margins and by the fact that Senate opponents had exceeded the magic number of sixty-seven necessary to override a veto. "The Administration dozed off until it was too late," Joel J. Johnson, an arms industry lobbyist, lamented. "Everyone thought there was a free vote, and this built up momentum against the sale."[46] The point was conceded by a senior administration official, who noted that even for GOP senators, "there were no consequences for voting against the sale"—and against the President.[47]

But the White House showed admirable persistence. Still more missiles, including the Stingers, were dropped out of the proposal. The package now totaled less than 8 percent of its original dollar value when proposed fourteen months earlier. New pledges were made to the Senate relating both to politics and policy. And a successful partisan appeal was made to secure Republican senators holding relatively safe seats. As an effort to override the President's veto of the resolution of disapproval loomed, White House stalwarts like Pete Domenici of New Mexico and William Roth of Delaware flip-flopped, as did more hard-line conservatives like Jesse Helms of North Carolina and Chic Hecht of Nevada. On June 5, the Senate failed by just one vote, 66–34, to override the veto. The sale thus went forward, despite the fact that nearly five-sixths of the members of Congress voted to bar it—a ringing testimony to the sorry state of affairs in arms export policymaking.

At the same time that the administration was seeking congressional approval for the Saudi sale, it was engaged in a covert effort to sell weapons to Iran. This risky endeavor, of course, became a full-blown scandal when it was subsequently revealed that U.S. government profits from these sales were diverted to fund the Nicaraguan Contras. The full sweep of this controversy is beyond the scope of this work. But it is important to note here the severity of this self-inflicted executive branch wound. Once again, the administration had been burned, and burned badly, with a Middle East arms sale. This controversy had devastating consequences, producing more than a year of revelations, recriminations, resignations, and indictments.

The administration's public justification for the sales to Teheran was that they could prove useful in reestablishing a dialogue with less extreme members of the Khomeini regime. Whatever the original impulse, the sales quickly degenerated into what President Reagan later conceded was "arms for hostages." The furor over these sales did not begin until days after the November 1986 congressional elections. Press leaks emanating from Iran prompted limited White House confirmations. Initially, the outcry in Congress focused narrowly on issues of process and policy: Why wasn't Congress consulted? What was the administration doing arming a terrorist government at the very same time that the United States was maintaining an arms embargo on Iran? In the early phases of the unfolding scandal, much attention was paid to the Arms Export Control Act and various intelligence activity reporting requirements. The provisions of law barring such sales and requiring congressional notification of covert operations had clearly been violated, as had the declared Reagan administration policy—pursued internationally with great fanfare—of barring all arms sales to terrorist nations.

But these questions of process and law were soon overwhelmed by the revelation that the Iranian arms sale was but one aspect of a whole series of covert operations run out of the White House basement by renegade National Security Council staff members. Congressional inquiries about process and policy gradually grew into a criminal investigation of how U.S. government funds were used, how U.S. government documents were shredded, how Congress was deceived. Violations of the Arms Export Control Act became the least of the executive branch's concerns. The President's credibility was at stake. Criminal culpability in the White House became an issue for daily public debate. The scandal-induced weakening of the Reagan administration continued through months of nationally televised congressional hearings and grand jury proceedings.

At the outset, some executive branch officials sought to shift at least some of the blame for the disastrous scheme to Congress. The argument made by administration champions was quite direct: Congress, after all, had cut the funds for the Contras. Congress had enacted a host of laws requiring CIA reporting of covert operations. If something as risky as the Iran sales had been reported to the Hill, surely, administration hard-liners alleged, it would have been leaked, scotching the effort to free Americans held hostage by Iran-backed terrorists. With Americans being held under deplorable conditions in Beirut—an American intelligence officer had already been tortured to death—the White House was justified in pursuing extralegal means, its defenders maintained. And the on-again, off-again, on-again congressional funding for Nicaraguan freedom fighters justified, in the minds of some, extralegal attempts to secure Contra funding by skimming profits from covert arms sales. Lives were at stake and leadership was required, they argued, even if laws were broken in the process.

The most articulate employer of this line of defense was Lieutenant Colonel Oliver North, a key NSC aide who faced criminal prosecution. While his congressional testimony won substantial public sympathy, his underlying logic did not. The public was ready for a certain amount of criticism of congressional foreign policy meddling. It was easy to caricature the inconsistent foreign policy pronouncements of the divided legislature. But the proposition that the

White House could violate laws if it did not agree with them appealed only to the most zealous of administration defenders. If Congress enacts unwise prohibitions, the American system requires that they be fought in the policy arena—or the courts—but not through the misappropriation of government funds. And covert reporting requirements are there for a good reason: to ensure that schemes as risky (many would say, as stupid) as the Iran-Contra plan will be scrutinized by thorough internal debate. As one leading weekly editorialized: "Implicit in the law is a decision that the benefit of democratic review is worth the risk of leaks."[48] Indeed, to say that the Iran-Contra scheme would not have gone forward if congressional leaders had been briefed is an argument *for* such reporting requirements, not against them.

The overlapping investigations of North and his colleagues came to focus heavily on personality and legal principles. Vigorous public debate was revived over the proper division of foreign policymaking authority, while political intrigue developed over questions about the scandal's impact on the governing authority of President Reagan and damage to the presidential bid of George Bush. Once again overshadowed in the ensuing debate were fundamental questions about policy and process. How could laws like the Arms Export Control Act be upheld when they were so clearly violated? What could be done about violations of intelligence statutes requiring formal findings and timely Hill notification before proceeding with such risky operations?

The report of the special Iran-Contra Committees did little to answer these broader questions, though it was conclusive on what happened: "The Committees find that the Administration's approval of [the arms sales] violated the Arms Export Control Act. . . . The President's authorization of [the sales was] made without even a pretense of compliance with the AECA."[49] Even the President's staunchest defenders conceded that point. As Secretary of Defense Caspar Weinberger testified, "My own view is that our Arms Export Control Act would make that kind of transaction illegal."[50] But little attention was paid to the broader warnings of committee member David Boren of Oklahoma: "What we've been looking at are symptoms of an underlying disease—the breakdown of bipartisanship in foreign policy. We'll make a big mistake if we only treat the symptoms—[White House officials] trying to get around the law."[51]

In the end, the Iran-Contra affair dealt a harsh blow to executive branch credibility—both on the Hill and overseas. It weakened the presidency while inviting reassertion by Congress of powers that had been on the wane during the first Reagan term. Ironically, it made inevitable still more of the legislative "meddling" in diplomacy that the creators of the Iran-Contra scheme so deplored.

There was a peculiar footnote to the scandal created by the secret Iran arms sales. In the wake of the arms-to-the-Ayatollah scandal—indeed, when congressional outrage over the criminal activity was at its height—the Reagan administration succeeded for the first time in gaining swift congressional approval for a controversial Arab arms request. Stranger still, this was a request for Saudi Arabia. This 1987 Saudi arms deal went through relatively smoothly, and even stalwart Saudi critics like Levine and Cranston publicly accepted the premise behind the proposal. There were two rather simple reasons for this remarkable policy reversal. The first was a change in Saudi policy on cooperation with U.S. military forces in the Persian Gulf. After years of criticism for not assisting American forces in the region more generously, the Saudis developed a more cooperative spirit. This assistance was a direct result of the escalating Iranian and Iraqi attacks on Gulf shipping. The Saudis were nervous and had finally become willing to work more closely with the extensive U.S. military contingent in the region. At the same time, the Saudis were turning to Britain as an alternative supplier of enormous amounts of military hardware, demonstrating that Washington's leverage in Riyadh would further decline if Congress balked at a new arms sale proposal.

The second reason was an unusual cooperative spirit that developed between congressional leaders, the new national security adviser Frank Carlucci, and White House chief of staff Howard Baker. It was a spirit born of shared burnout over the seemingly unending Iran-Contra scandal. But it also reflected a recognition by pro-Israeli legislators and AIPAC strategists that it was not a good time to pile on a staggering Reagan administration. As a senior aide to Senator Byrd observed: "The history of Congress rejecting sales to Arab nations is becoming a little unhealthy. . . . It's important to break the cycle of rejection. There is some feeling that a modest package is in the national interest."[52]

Carlucci sought out key Saudi critics on the Hill and actively worked for a compromise resolution of the sale well before battle lines were drawn. The new NSC team effectively used classified information regarding U.S.-Saudi military and intelligence cooperation to demonstrate that Saudi Arabia was finally being more forthcoming in aiding the U.S. military posture in the Persian Gulf. Carlucci used his personal entree as the new national security adviser, untainted by the spreading scandal, to appeal for an interbranch truce. Hill peace terms were modest. The number of missiles sought by the Saudis was reduced by a token amount, whereupon the sale went forward without a hitch—a rarity in U.S.-Saudi annals. Similar success was had with a 1988 request to sell planes and missiles to Kuwait; a package proposal went forward to that Gulf state after token reductions and restrictions were negotiated between the White House and congressional leaders.[53]

ARMS SALES AND THE REAGAN LEGACY

Proposals to export American arms caused the Reagan administration more grief on Capitol Hill than any other foreign policy endeavor. As we shall discuss in our review of the Contra funding issue in Chapter 8, it was not just in the Middle East but in Central America as well that the White House met with bruising congressional resistance to arms transfer schemes. The President enjoyed the post-*Chadha* advantage of an ability to veto joint resolutions that disapproved arms sales. Yet he met with effective resistance.

These repeated confrontations brought into sharp relief the divergent perspectives of typical executive and legislative branch policymakers. Reagan administration officials viewed Congress with undisguised disdain on most military security issues. Congress, they insisted, was meddlesome. Congress was parochial. Congress was unwilling to pursue necessary—though often unpopular—policies to assist friends abroad. Congress ignored the reality that potential customers like the Saudis would turn away from the United States to alternative suppliers, leaving fewer restraints and diminished U.S. influence. Such administration claims led to an executive branch consensus that Congress should be kept in the dark about the broader outlines of arms sales policy. Sales were rarely discussed in advance with Hill leaders. Indeed, by 1986, State Department officials had concluded with some disgust that, inasmuch as Israel supporters rushed to introduce resolutions of disapproval even *before* Congress had been formally notified of a sale, there really was no reason to uphold the practice of providing even a token 20-day prenotification of a major sale. Administration officials felt that the Pavlovian response the Hill offered against any sale justified their decision to keep sales secret as long as possible. Springing major sales on the eve of congressional recesses, they concluded, was wisdom, not foolishness.

Congressional leaders were angered by the pattern of brinksmanship employed by Reagan officials for most arms sales. The administration would present Congress with a fait accompli. The President—and the nation—had made a commitment, Congress was told. Congress balked at a rubber-stamp role. Resentment over procedural abuse exacerbated concerns about the substance of an arms sales policy. And in opposing controversial sales, Congress was pressing some legitimate, commonsense concerns. There was much to question in the wisdom of arming adversaries of American allies, of tolerating a "least common denominator" approach to weapons proliferation, which encouraged the United States to sell whatever its least responsible competitor would make commercially available. The politics of arms sales also made it easier for legislators to "just say no." The post-*Chadha* system, which allowed a sale to go forward if only thirty-four senators or 134 congressmen voted for it, proved a mixed blessing to the President because it made the temptation to object virtually irresistible. The executive branch was constantly on the defensive, operating in a damage limitation mode. Congress was sharply polarized as lobbyists descended with campaign fund-raising promises and political threats. The process of achieving compromise with moderate, experienced legislators was made extremely difficult. Indeed, it was the very familiarity of this high-stakes legislative game of chicken that ultimately allowed interbranch controversies to be resolved without too much damage to U.S. national interests.

Few participants in this policymaking process have been pleased by this state of affairs. Yet efforts to reform this mutually distressing arms export review system have faltered. In January 1987, a major initiative was undertaken on the Hill to rewrite the oft-amended arms export laws. Had it been advertised from the outset as a "good government" measure—especially in the wake of the scandal caused by secret arms sales to the Ayatollah—the legislative proposal might have borne some fruit. Clearly, there was a need to introduce greater certainty into the process, to clarify the rules for reviewing exports, and to reduce the number of sales subject to legislative challenge. In the wake of the *Chadha* decision, Congress was forever tinkering with the general terms of AECA, even in the midst of a specific export challenge. Dollar thresholds were changed. Long-range sales projections were required from the executive branch. To protect against Senate filibusters, expedited procedures were secured for joint disapproval resolutions. Loopholes in reporting requirements for covert arms sales were closed. But there remained a clear need for a more comprehensive reform approach.

In early 1987, Senator Biden and Congressman Levine sought to provide such a remedy, introducing the Arms Export Reform Act. Their logic reflected arguments made in the 1974 debate on the original Nelson-Bingham version of AECA. As Biden stated the post-*Chadha* case:

> We have on occasion seen an unholy alliance between U.S. arms manufacturers anxious to increase sales and an administration anxious to appease regional client states. This legislation would restore the checks and balances needed to prevent the casual distribution abroad of frontline U.S. weapons.[54]

But the Biden-Levine effort at sweeping reform was virtually stillborn. The reasons were quite simple. First, the 1987 bill sought to resolve the executive-legislative struggle by giving Congress the whip hand. Under the Biden-Levine proposal, *all* arms sales above certain thresholds would be subject to congressional approval (though sales to treaty partners in NATO, ANZUS, and the parties to the Camp David agreements were exempted). While Biden lamented the fact that wildly unpopular proposals like the 1986 Saudi package could go forward with only a handful of senators in support, his remedy proposed to grant legislators a "one-house" veto over the most sensitive arms export proposals.

Second, the effort to "reform" a process that had repeatedly brought grief for policymakers at both ends of Pennsylvania Avenue opened the door to still more controversy. A requirement that Congress act before many sales would be authorized meant that an already overloaded congressional schedule would be flooded with scores of additional floor votes. Hill leaders like Byrd and Fascell were distinctly unenthusiastic about this feature.

Finally, while reform could well be justified as a means of restoring the congressional prerogatives undermined by *Chadha* and lending greater regularity to a contentious process, the motives of the spon-

sors of the 1987 bill were widely suspect. Critics acknowledged that
Biden and Levine were regarded as serious legislators. But to many,
the measure was a transparently anti-Arab measure. Biden was running for president, enjoying enthusiastic support and funding from
the pro-Israel community. And Levine, who represented the wealthy
West Side communities of Los Angeles, had been a leader in virtually
every move to block Arab arms purchases from the United States.
They never succeeded in overcoming the impression that their bill
was an "Arab-bashing" measure. As Chairman Fascell observed,
"What is really at issue is, to whom do you want to stop selling arms?
It's a political fight."[55]

The administration got out ahead of the curve in responding to the
reform proposal. Executive branch officials recognized the challenge
posed to their prerogatives by the Biden-Levine measure and lobbied
hard to deter legislators from cosponsoring it. AIPAC made a tactical
decision to keep a low profile—in an effort to avoid the Arab-bashing
charge. Into this vacuum stepped a previously moribund industry
lobby—the American League for Exports and Security Assistance,
which was revitalized and sent to work to gain public White House
opposition. At the very first hearing on the bill, the senior Republican on the House Foreign Affairs Committee, William Broomfield of
Michigan, took the unusual step of announcing that a presidential
veto was assured if the measure passed. Effective pressure from arms
manufacturers then kept many members from pushing the bill, while
the low-key AIPAC role meant there was little counterpressure from
off the Hill. A "good government" argument and more moderate
sponsorship might possibly have moved the reform debate forward
in the 100th Congress. But formidable industry efforts stalled all
efforts to revise congressional arms review procedures in 1988. There
was consensus throughout Washington that the process was "broke."
But conflict proved insurmountable when efforts were made to fix
it. The challenge of revising an arms export review system that
pleased few policymakers remained unfinished business.

NOTES

1. Harold Saunders, "The Middle East 1973–84: Hidden Agendas," in Muskie,
   The President, the Congress, and Foreign Policy, p. 195.
2. Richard Nixon, as quoted in House Foreign Affairs Committee (HFAC),
   "Changing Perspectives on U.S. Arms Transfer Policy" (staff report),

September 25, 1981, p. 4. The neo-isolationist strain was overshadowed by the more overt message of the 1972 presidential candidacy of Democratic Senator George McGovern of South Dakota: "Come Home, America."

3. Presaging the war powers debate, Congress had voted as early as 1967 to make it clear that foreign aid was not to be construed as creating a new commitment to use Armed Forces of the U.S. for the defense of any foreign country. Yet Congress still approved the annual DOD spending requests that were needed to fund the war effort.

4. As quoted in HFAC, "Changing Perspectives," p. 4.

5. At this time, the use of concessionary loans or credits for arms purchases was growing through the Foreign Military Sales (FMS) Program, while the use of grant aid through the Military Assistance Program (MAP) was being phased out. Direct, bilateral aid could also be offered through the Economic Support Fund (ESF) Program—which typically was for balance-of-payments assistance—or through international military education and training (IMET).

6. This distinction was elevated to policy prominence later in the decade by Jeanne Kirkpatrick in her widely noted *Commentary* article, "Dictatorships and Double Standards" (November 1979, pp. 34–45).

7. The United States provided Israel with inconsequential amounts of government-to-government assistance from 1948 until the early 1960s. While private contributions were essential to Israel's security, the U.S. government provided no arms and even rejected an Israeli plea for weapons after Egypt turned to the Soviet bloc for arms in 1956. In the years preceding the Yom Kippur War, U.S. *loans* to Israel totaled less than $300 million a year for both military and economic assistance. By 1988, the direct *grant* assistance had grown to more than $3 billion per year.

8. The President personally lobbied more than 100 House members, and most of the congressional leadership voted against the embargo. But skepticism of administration willingness to press the Turks overcame this effort. As one key study concluded: "The intensity of the opposition was attributable in part to the Greek-American lobby, but . . . a far more important factor was Congress' sense that Kissinger was being unreasonably secretive, duplicitous, and uncompromising" (Heginbotham, "Dateline Washington," p. 165). See also Sundquist, *Decline and Resurgence*, pp. 283–86.

9. See Bernard Schwartz, "The Congressional Veto in Foreign Policy," in Franck, *Tethered Presidency*, p. 93.

10. *Congressional Record*, December 4, 1974, p. S38074.

11. *Congressional Record*, December 10, 1974, p. H38771.

12. Subsequent to the 1976 act, changes in AECA terms were made in 1977 (veto over third-country transfers added), 1978–1979 (requiring detailed "Javits" reports on prospective arms sales), 1980 (commercial sales cov-

ered), 1981 (dollar thresholds raised), and then again—post-*Chadha*—in 1985 (to ensure expedited procedures for *joint* resolutions of disapproval). Today, sales of more than $14 million in services, $50 million in arms, or $200 million in design and construction of military projects are subject to review by Congress.

13. The same argument was made in advancing contemporaneous legislation to bar cooperation by U.S. firms with the Arab boycott of Israel. Since this boycott hurt the economy of Israel, which was increasingly dependent on U.S. aid, it was in the U.S. interest to take steps to counter the boycott's effectiveness. Antiboycott legislation sponsored by Congressman Bingham and Democratic Senator Adlai Stevenson of Illinois was passed in 1977 as an amendment to the Export Administration Act (see Saunders, "The Middle East 1973–84," pp. 181–87).

14. *Congressional Record*, July 18, 1975, p. H23622. Senator Nelson noted that while the Joint Chiefs of Staff concluded that Jordan needed only three or four Hawk systems, the King sought fourteen.

15. The outlines of the compromise were written by a Senate Foreign Relations Committee staff member after visiting Hawk missile training facilities in Florida during the August recess (see Franck and Weisband, *Foreign Policy by Congress*, p. 102).

16. Israel's supporters had rallied earlier against a Ford administration "reevaluation" of its Middle East policy, announced by Secretary Kissinger after his shuttle diplomacy efforts faltered. Senior administration officials were irked at alleged Israeli foot-dragging on the peace process and openly mulled greater "even-handedness" in U.S. policy on the Arab-Israeli dispute. AIPAC countered with a letter signed by seventy-six senators rejecting the Ford move and reaffirming the primary of Israeli security as an American policy objective in the Middle East.

17. Jordan's King Hussein was so angry, he initially refused to consummate the deal. But the U.S. weapons technology was so clearly superior, he later relented. Efforts in subsequent years to allow Hawk batteries greater mobility were frustrated—and to date Hussein has still refused direct, bilateral peace negotiations with Israel.

18. Sidewinders are air-to-air missiles; Mavericks are TV-guided, air-to-ground missiles.

19. See HFAC, "Executive-Legislative Consultation on U.S. Arms Sales" (staff report) December 1982, pp. 11–13.

20. Saunders, "The Middle East 1973–84," p. 193.

21. Jimmy Carter, as quoted in ibid., p. 194.

22. Senator John Glenn, as quoted in ibid.

23. Details of Saudi assistance to projects as diverse as aid to the Afghan freedom fighters and assistance to the Contras first emerged years later. See, for example, Woodward, *Veil.*

24. For details on the Saudi lobby in the United States, see Emerson, *American House of Saud.*

25. Morrie Amitay, as quoted in Isaacs, *Jews and American Politics*, pp. 264–65.

26. *Wall Street Journal*, February 20, 1981, p. 3.

27. AIPAC is technically not a political action committee, but rather a lobbying organization. However, many of its board members serve on legally separate fund-raising committees that support legislators who vote with AIPAC (see Robert Kuttner, "Un-Holy Alliance," *New Republic*, May 26, 1986, pp. 19–25).

28. Senate Foreign Relations Committee Rept. 97–949, October 22, 1981, p. 12.

29. *Time*, November 9, 1981, p. 12.

30. See HFAC, "Executive-Legislative Consultation," p. 30. Pledges regarding Saudi support for the peace process were elevated to a statutory certification requirement in 1985.

31. *Des Moines Register*, October 29, 1981, p. 1.

32. *Wall Street Journal*, October 14, 1981, p. 1.

33. *U.S. News and World Report*, November 3, 1981, p. 20.

34. Jimmy Carter, letter to Robert C. Byrd, October 11, 1981, reprinted in *Congressional Record*, October 21, 1981, p. S11763.

35. William F. Buckley, Jr., as quoted in *New Republic*, October 3, 1981, p. 5.

36. *Washington Post*, September 28, 1981, p. 4.

37. *New York Times*, October 6, 1981, p. 1.

38. Richard Nixon, as quoted in ibid.

39. *Wall Street Journal*, October 2, 1981, p. 1.

40. *New York Times*, October 6, 1981, p. 1.

41. *Washington Post*, October 29, 1981, p. 1.

42. *Time*, November 4, 1981, p. 12.

43. See "The Jordan Package: Revival of an Old Debate," *Congressional Quarterly* 43 (October 26, 1985): 2136–39.

44. Mel Levine and Alan Cranston, *Washington Post*, March 22, 1986, p. 17.

45. Senate Foreign Relations Committee Report #97–249, October 22, 1981, p. 12.

46. Joel J. Johnson, as quoted in *National Journal*, March 21, 1987, pp. 667–71.

47. Ibid.

48. *New Republic*, March 23, 1987, p. 7.

49. Iran-Contra Committee, final report, S. Rept. 100–216, p. 418.

50. Ibid.

51. Senator David Boren, as quoted in *National Journal*, August 8, 1987, p. 2019.

52.   Senator Robert Byrd, as quoted in *National Journal*, October 17, 1987, p. 2606.

53.   See *Defense News*, August 8, 1988, p. 7.

54.   Senator Joseph Biden, as quoted in *National Journal*, March 21, 1987, p. 669.

55.   Ibid. See also *New York Times*, January 28, 1987, p. B8.

8 FOREIGN AID AND BILATERAL RELATIONS
Congress Sets the Agenda

> The executive branch propounded the strange idea that it was some-
> how an unwarranted intrusion into the President's foreign policy
> domain for Congress to specify the purposes of the aid we autho-
> rized and appropriated.
>
> —Congressman Michael D. Barnes, 1986 [1]

Foreign policy confrontations in Washington are most likely to be
page-one news when they involve stark issues of war and peace. The
battle lines are sharply drawn in a Senate treaty fight or a showdown
over war powers. And passions are easily aroused at the White House
and on Capitol Hill by proposals to sell arms to Middle East belligerents. But the area in which day-to-day executive branch management
of diplomacy is most frequently subjected to challenge and change
by Congress lies in the far less glamorous realm of foreign aid.

Foreign aid issues rarely make headlines. Disputes among Washington policymakers about programs like ESF, FMS, and IBRD read like
inside-the-Beltway quarrels over alphabet soup. [2] Sending U.S. taxpayer dollars overseas has never been especially popular with the general voting public—even though three-quarters of the $14 billion
annual foreign aid budget is spent each year in the United States for
the purchase of American arms and grain. [3] It is an issue ripe for
cheap shots at election time. More than one member of Congress has
been singed by the charge that he voted to "give away" taxpayer dol-

lars to foreign dictators and Communists, or to nations that consistently oppose U.S. foreign policy objectives.[4] Thus, legislators have moved relentlessly to place limits upon international assistance programs. It is here in the debate over what strings the United States should attach to its foreign aid that the determination of Congress to influence international relations is most often felt today by the president and his staff. It is here where Congress insists upon a quid pro quo for U.S. aid that legislators' foreign policymaking powers remain the strongest—even in the wake of the Reagan counterreformation. It is here, in using its powers to control the public purse, that Congress retains its greatest influence in setting the agenda for American diplomacy.

The key to understanding how Congress exercises these important powers is to appreciate the new watchword for U.S. foreign aid funding struggles: conditionality. By attaching restrictions, provisos, and presidential certification requirements to dozens of foreign assistance accounts, Congress has placed its imprimatur on virtually the entire sweep of U.S. foreign aid programs. Congress has thereby elevated to the forefront of the international dialogue U.S. concerns about issues as diverse as human rights, nuclear nonproliferation, and drug interdiction. Legislators have forced U.S. diplomatic personnel to press these issues and to make satisfaction of U.S. standards on these matters a condition for continued aid. Ultimately, the executive branch is able to extract funding from Congress for most international programs. The argument that foreign aid is a cheap way to fight communism while funding U.S. jobs has proven persuasive. But Congress has shown tremendous ingenuity and determination in forcing strict conditions onto the most controversial foreign aid efforts. Successive chief executives have complained about these initiatives, alleging, in the words of Gerald Ford, that they impose "impermissible shackles on the President's ability to carry out the laws and conduct the foreign relations of the United States."[5]

At best, these legislative efforts have injected an essential dose of common sense into U.S. aid programs. By pressing popular concerns, Congress has fueled diplomatic campaigns to advance American priorities, offering a powerful incentive for aid recipients to promote Washington's agenda. At worst, these congressional initiatives have been insulting and counterproductive. They have exasperated professional diplomats while crippling executive branch flexibility and alienating would-be allies. By introducing single-issue politics into the complex web of foreign relations, these initiatives have made efforts to implement sophisticated diplomatic strategies more difficult.[6] Regardless of their virtue, these initiatives have become a fact of life worthy of more detailed examination—a key element in the complex relationship between the modern foreign policymakers at each end of Pennsylvania Avenue.

FUNDING FOREIGN AID:
THE COLLISION COURSE

The best illustration of legislators' powers to reshape international priorities lies in the annual foreign aid bill. The process of writing one of these omnibus funding measures is anything but elegant. In recent years, building a consensus among State, Defense, the Office of Management and Budget (OMB), and the numerous Hill committees has proved to be a Herculean task. Indeed, only two annual authorization bills survived this gauntlet in the eight years of the Reagan presidency. The other six stalled and were never passed—or were wrapped into the gargantuan, catch-all continuing resolution on appropriations that Congress often forces through an adjournment eve.

The reasons for these failures were diverse. In some cases, the White House opposed enactment of omnibus measures because of objections to a single proviso—such as the curb on aid to Turkey proposed by pro-Greece legislators in 1987. In other instances, there were not sufficient House votes to pass *any* foreign "giveaway" bill, or there were so many mischievous amendments pending that floor debate appeared to be an unpromising prospect for the Senate leadership.

A good example of this troubled legacy is the tortured (and ultimately fruitless) course of the $12 billion foreign aid authorization bill of 1984. This voluminous executive branch proposal was vetted through the State Department, the Pentagon, OMB, and the NSC before being sent to the Hill. After rigorous in-house negotiations, the executive branch saw the proposal pummeled before congressional committees through twenty-four days of hearings. One hundred and thirty-three different witnesses addressed its virtues and demerits in public testimony. Then it weathered more than four days of line-by-line consideration in a House Foreign Affairs Committee markup, twenty-seven hours of floor debate, and the addition of a total of forty amendments, before being adopted by the full House of Representatives. And then it died. It was not vetoed. It did not even make it to a House-Senate conference. It was so overburdened with controversial proposals that it was never brought to a vote in the full Senate.[7]

A postmortem on the measure reveals a simple explanation as to the cause of death: an excess of baggage. Legislators' eagerness to condition various aid provisions on greater foreign sensitivity to American concerns had produced a measure so burdened with restrictive provisos that it sank of its own weight. It should be noted that such "piling on" is by no means unique to foreign aid legislation. In a domestic funding bill, this process is disparagingly called "decorating the Christmas tree." A bill containing tax breaks or appropriations for popular programs provides incentives for its advancement: special interest "ornaments" can be safely hung on a must-pass bill. But in a foreign aid measure, the burden of restrictive, single-issue amendments is not offset by essential provisions and can prove fatal. Thus, in 1984, the adoption of so many provisos making aid for would-be allies contingent upon performance on issues like human rights and drug interdiction made adoption of the measure not worth the trouble for the Reagan administration. The White House chose to bypass the authorization process entirely and to cut their own deal with the appropriations panels. The executive branch did not get as much money as it sought. And the funding approved by the appropriations panels still had a number of strings attached. But the administration chose to have no authorization bill at all and to seek continued funding through a catch-all appropriations bill rather than accept so much conditional authorization language, which could tie its hands.

The foreign aid authorization bill has become a bone of contention between executive branch and congressional officials simply because it is such an inviting target. Since there is no guarantee that a major arms sale, a treaty question, or a war powers dispute will arise in a given year, the foreign aid measure is the one vehicle upon which legislators know they can make manifest their international policy concerns; it is the one regularly scheduled opportunity for foreign policy debates. And lacking a broad constituency beyond selected ethnic lobbies and American exporters—a political engine to drive it forward—this measure is especially vulnerable to burdensome legislative riders. The foreign aid bill is where even the most junior legislator can easily reshape U.S. international relations through irresponsible but irresistible floor amendments. Here is where a host of foreign spending projects on a State Department or Pentagon wish list can be pared. Here is where legislators can attempt to steer foreign procurement contracts toward local firms. Here is where the specter of "535 secretaries of state" is inevitably raised by critics of an aggressive congressional role.

This executive-legislative struggle over foreign aid legislation proceeds today in a crisis atmosphere. The U.S. foreign assistance program has been hamstrung by a series of related setbacks. This is not simply a result of the fact that international assistance, however self-interested, has never been very popular with the American voters. It stems from the reality that the U.S. aid effort has been caught in the vortex of forces over which neither the Congress nor the executive branch has firm control. Changes are being forced upon the program that will almost inevitably put a new face on American aid efforts in the months and years ahead and will change the way Congress and the White House deal with each other on the aid issue.

Three factors have combined to lay siege to foreign aid priorities. The first is the federal budget crunch. Even an outspoken critic of federal spending like Ronald Reagan saw the desirability of using foreign aid as a diplomatic lever once he assumed the presidency. For the first four years of his administration, the White House sought substantial increases in foreign military assistance. But then the Reagan administration was confronted by the Gramm-Rudman-Hollings balanced budget measure. This legislation forced reductions in foreign aid through its program of mandated annual cuts in the U.S. budget deficit.[8] The foreign aid account, though only 1.2 percent of the total federal budget, has become a most inviting target for these required cuts. With the federal budget being cut, members of Congress have invariably sought to reduce foreign aid and transfer funds to domestic programs. Each year of Reagan's second term, legislators slashed $2–3 billion (nearly 20 percent) from executive branch foreign aid requests. As the chairman of the House Appropriations Subcommittee, Democrat David Obey of Wisconsin, has stated: "The country will not tolerate increasing foreign aid by paying for it by gutting cancer research, gutting educational opportunities, squeezing highways, and squeezing the investment portion of the budget here at home."[9] This perspective was one shared by even the most stalwart White House loyalists. As Republican Senate Budget Committee Chairman Pete Domenici snapped in 1986, "You can't cut every-thing, raise [foreign aid] and still have no revenues added to the pot."[10]

A second factor is directly related to the first. As the total amount of money allocated each year to international programs has been frozen, then reduced, Congress and the executive branch have com-peted to assert differing perspectives on which recipients should get priority treatment. Legislators influenced by both strategic consider-ations and ethnic politics insist on maintaining high levels of funding for favored nations like Israel, Egypt, Greece, and the Philippines.[11] Indeed, support of pro-Israel legislators has proven essential to the Reagan administration's success in obtaining votes for passage of foreign aid funding. Grain state lawmakers have joined to defend the Food for Peace Program, which exports agricultural products from the American Midwest. In response, the executive branch has scram-bled to protect important but less popular accounts, such as Turkey, Pakistan, and Honduras, with whom the United States enjoys valu-able military ties. Thus, before State Department allocations even begin for the dozens of countries and international development pro-grams to which the United States makes contributions, the vast majority of American aid dollars in the budget have already been ear-marked. The result has been that, to a severe extent, less visible pro-grams have been crowded out. Budgets for everything from African famine relief to construction of more secure U.S. embassy facilities abroad have been cut deeply, while earmarked accounts and funds dedicated to countries where the United States has cooperative mili-tary projects consume nearly four-fifths of the total bilateral aid funds available worldwide.[12] For example, in the case of global allo-cations of the 1988 ESF (cash transfer) accounts, only $99 million in discretionary spending was left of the $3.2 billion total after congres-sional priorities and aid to base rights countries were earmarked.[13]

A third divisive and debilitating factor has been the change in priorities reflected in executive branch foreign aid requests. In recent years, these requests have come to strongly favor military aid pro-grams and large grants of cash over economic development projects. The function of foreign aid has undergone a profound shift from the financing of programs to meet basic human needs to cash transfers necessary for weapons purchases and debt servicing. In 1977, secu-rity assistance was just over 25 percent of the total budget; in 1980, it was only 22 percent. But by 1984, it had soared to more than 42 percent of the overall foreign aid program.[14] Of course, foreign aid has *always* had a heavy security component, and a heavy degree of American self-interest. Much assistance has been advanced in the form of military sales credits, which are used to buy American weapons and finance American jobs. The enhancement of the military capacities of foreign aid recipients and the securing of base rights have always been a part of the picture. But the dramatic increase in cash transfers and military aid has cost foreign aid support among legislators, especially among liberals who support development assistance. To the extent that foreign aid has had any support from the electorate beyond the grain-growing states and selected ethnic constituencies, it has been heavily reliant on the perception that U.S. aid has promoted economic development abroad. In the popular imagination, foreign aid meant aiding the poorest of the poor, fighting hunger and disease around the world. In its youth, the U.S. foreign aid program was rooted in the effort to rebuild a shattered Europe after World War II; the romantic image was of U.S. planes airlifting food supplies to the children of Berlin. The image flowered in the 1950s and the early 1960s as an effort to combat Communist influence by promoting economic growth in the Third World through the Agency for International Development, the World Bank, and the Peace Corps.

More recently, the U.S. aid effort has become more of a funding program to equip Third World military forces and service their debts to international banks. To more cynical voters and policymakers alike, foreign aid has become just another bill to be paid at the end of the year. Its harshest critics portray the aid package as just another $1 billion for the quarreling Greeks and Turks, NATO members who often seem united only in their disdain for Americans; another $600 million each year to arm Pakistan, which continues its not-so-secret quest for nuclear weapons; another $3 billion for Egypt, to keep this undemocratic but most moderate of Arab nations from rejecting its Camp David pledges; another $3 billion for Israel, which is surrounded by heavily armed U.S. friends in the Arab world but channels much of its military might into the frustrating occupation of Palestinian communities on the West Bank; and another several hundred million dollars to keep the tottering Philippines afloat, while ensuring that the United States is not tossed out of Clark Airfield and Subic Bay. (The United States pays not only rent for bases used to help protect allies overseas but "protection" money to discourage recipients from cooperating with U.S. adversaries.) When U.S. legislators add up this tab—which does not even include the enormous sums spent each year to support U.S. troops in Europe and East Asia—they often feel like they have been shaken down. The shift in emphasis that occurred in the Reagan years favoring military programs over development aid has exacerbated such cynicism. Add to it the backlash caused by the foreign imports displacing American workers and you have a prescription for a rise in neo-isolationist sentiments. Consequently, the already limited appeal of foreign aid at the grass roots has diminished even further. And votes in Congress for key aid programs are not easy to come by. Indeed, it is only through sustained anticommunist rhetoric and a concerted campaign by supporters of Israel that foreign aid monies are advanced each year in Congress.

These three challenges confront foreign aid programs at a time when the U.S. Congress is as powerful as ever in placing its mark on foreign assistance legislation. Unlike other areas of policymaking, such as war powers or treaty prerogatives, there has been no diminution here in the ability of Congress to assert itself. There has been no rollback from the advances Congress made in the 1970s, when it forced its way into the details of foreign aid. The consequences for executive branch officials intent upon an aggressive American presence in the world have been serious. "Congressional cuts in the foreign affairs budget threaten the stability of our allies," Secretary Shultz charged in a 1987 broadside against the Hill. "They threaten our war on drug traffickers and terrorists. They threaten our efforts to promote democratic values and reforms. "They threaten our ability to understand and to influence [world] developments." [15]

Most legislators reject these executive branch views, however. In recent years, Congress has proved even more imaginative and effective than before in placing conditions on American efforts to cooperate with friends and allies abroad. The result has meant still more headaches for an executive branch already finding it hard enough to work with other nations without Congress writing the blueprints. In examining the broad scope of foreign aid programs, we shall therefore consider how this legislative hunger for conditionality has succeeded in setting the bilateral agenda in a number of crucial areas, including human rights, drug interdiction, nuclear nonproliferation, and military assistance policy.

HUMAN RIGHTS, DRUG INTERDICTION, AND THE CERTIFICATION CRAZE

The weapon of choice in legislators' efforts to reshape administration foreign assistance programs is the so-called certification requirement. Typically, such a provision conditions the funding of a given U.S. aid program on certification by the president that the recipient nation is in conformity with a set of defined standards on issues of concern to the United States. For example: no aid to the Philippines unless the president certifies that progress is being made toward restoring democracy. Or, no military assistance to Pakistan unless the president certifies that it has halted its nuclear bomb program. Such certification requirements are blunt efforts to exact a quid pro quo for U.S. foreign aid, to take a carrot-and-stick approach. The bottom line of such legislative gambits is usually quite simple. Congress seeks to ensure that aid is extended only to nations that are responsive to U.S. interests. In a given bilateral relationship, these interests might be respect for human rights and democratic elections, cooperation on blocking narcotics production, or curbing the spread of nuclear weapons–usable materials.

Since the decline of the Nixon presidency, Congress has had tremendous success in attaching such conditions to scores of bills. The executive branch has, not surprisingly, balked at this practice. Successive administrations have bemoaned the attachment of such conditions limiting executive branch flexibility in diplomacy. Here is an area where President Reagan's rhetoric sounded virtually identical to that of Presidents Ford and Carter.[16] But on Capitol Hill, liberals and conservatives alike have pressed the commonsense notion that U.S. aid should be conditioned upon some minimum degree of sensitivity to U.S. concerns. The White House is regularly derided in congressional debate for failing to press American concerns—for allowing assistance from Uncle Sam to become payoffs from "Uncle Sucker."

Ironically, the preferred means of pressing such concerns—attaching a certification requirement—has proven a double-edged weapon. The best example of this dilemma is one of the most recent. During the height of the 1986 campaign season, a wave of popular concern about the drug problem swept the nation. A voter-sensitive Congress reacted with lightning speed, pressing an omnibus antidrug measure, the Anti-Drug Abuse Act of 1986, swiftly through both houses on near unanimous votes.[17] Lawmakers expressed their frustration at a State Department that had been too insensitive for too long about narcotics production in nations receiving U.S. aid. This measure included a requirement that any nation found to have failed to cooperate with the United States to interdict the supply of drugs would be subject to an automatic 50 percent cutback in existing bilateral aid, a prohibition on any direct U.S. aid in subsequent years, and U.S. opposition to multilateral development bank loans. The proposition seemed irrefutable: why should U.S. taxpayers give money to nations that refused to help combat America's new Public Enemy Number One? In the rush to judgment, few in Congress spoke against the procedural means devised to apply this test. No politician was eager to stand against the tide in an election year and risk being accused of weakening an antidrug bill.

So it was established that the president must certify in writing every March 1 that each aid recipient on a "watch list" of nations with poor drug enforcement records is cooperating fully in efforts to combat narcotics production and distribution. Yet this certification process presented a number of problems. What should the president do in the case of a nation that is cooperating modestly but whose drug interdiction efforts are sorely in need of improvement? What about a case where the national government is trying to work with Washington but is unable to control provincial authorities aligned with drug cartels? In such cases, the president is given two principal choices. The first is to certify a lie: to secure continued provision of foreign aid by asserting that a country is being very helpful to drug interdiction efforts when in reality it is not. The second is to deny certification—thereby precipitating a cutoff in U.S. aid and a crisis in the bilateral relationship. A third option—withholding certification, but then waiving the requirements on national security grounds—has proven nearly as confrontational as the second. Thus, by elevating drug interdiction to the top of the U.S. bilateral agenda with a host of countries, Congress advanced American concerns but created a serious dilemma.

In just the first two years of experience under this law, lawmakers have had great difficulty reconciling procedural requirements with policymaking priorities. The first test arose in February 1987, when President Reagan certified that the government of Panama was cooperating satisfactorily in drug interdiction efforts. In fact, Panama was under the control of a drug-running gang in the Panamanian Defense Forces. Led by Manuel Noriega, these Panamanian authorities allowed the isthmus to become a center for narcotics traffic and money laundering throughout the hemisphere—a fact of which most U.S. policymakers were fully aware. Yet the President was reluctant to let fly the guillotine on aid to Panama—in part because of concern about the security of the Panama Canal, and in part because of fears that Noriega would embarrass the United States with revelations about his former long-standing relationship with the CIA and the Contras.

Under the automatic provisions of the Anti–Drug Abuse Act, the President was forced to decide. When the President chose to certify a lie, it had the double negative effect of infuriating Congress while giving the odious Noriega a good "report card" and a propaganda coup back home. To second-guess the certification, senators took advantage of provisions in the act that ensured a prompt roll call: antifilibuster procedures that guaranteed a clear shot for critics of both Reagan and Noriega. But the Senate debate on a resolution to overturn the Reagan certification was exploited effectively by Noriega to accuse Uncle Sam of intervention in Panama's domestic affairs.[18] The certification process was a bitter disappointment. National interests forced the White House to issue a bogus finding, while Noriega was able to make a strong pitch for nationalist sympathy.

A similar dilemma confronted Congress in 1988 when presidential drug certifications for Colombia, Mexico, and the Bahamas were at issue. Ironically, the country from which cocaine flooded the United States—Colombia—was the easiest to certify. In that nation, a drug war was under way between the Bogota government and regional drug lords that had cost the lives of police officials, supreme court justices, and the Colombian attorney general. However ineffective the Colombian efforts, Congress could only conclude from Bogota's casualty list that the Colombian authorities were demonstrably sincere.

The Bahamas proved a trickier case. The only nation that permitted U.S. "hot pursuit" of suspected smugglers inside its territorial waters, the Bahamas was led by a man suspected of ties to drug sales. Yet the Bahamas escaped the senators' wrath. Certification of Bahamian cooperation passed the Senate 53–40 on April 14, 1988.[19]

Later that same evening, the Senate debated a resolution to disapprove the certification of Mexican cooperation on drug interdiction. The dynamics of the chamber were such that many legislators who had voted with their heads—and with the executive branch— on the first vote were tempted to vote their hearts (and their frustrations) on the Mexico question. Senators were concerned by reports that a host of Mexican state governors were on the take from marijuana smugglers. And Washington was still angered by the assassination of a U.S. Drug Enforcement Agency (DEA) agent in Mexico, as well as the continued refusal of Mexico City to allow hot pursuit by DEA agents working the U.S. border. The temptation to beat up on Mexico—and to gain the political cover of at least one "tough on drugs" vote against a certification—became irresistible. Led by an extraordinary alliance between Senators Helms and Kerry—the Senate's right-wing champion and one of its most liberal members—an angry chamber voted 63-27 to bar future U.S. aid to Mexico.[20] The action came in spite of the fact that virtually all direct U.S. aid to Mexico was used for drug interdiction programs. Unavoidably, the Senate action provoked a bitter round of recriminations and renewed nationalist resistance in Mexico City to any cooperation with the U.S. antidrug effort.

The awkward drug certifications are illustrative of the difficulties inherent in congressional efforts to commit foreign nations to shifting American priorities. Congress performed an important service in raising the drug issue with the State Department and foreign governments. For too many years, diplomats had ignored the fact that many U.S. aid recipients were doing little to impede the flow of narcotics into American cities. Yet the mechanism established by Congress to press this concern left much to be desired. These procedures contrast unfavorably with congressional efforts to elevate human rights on the international agenda. Here Congress has enjoyed important and sustained successes. Perhaps the greatest victory has been to enshrine the notion that advancement of human rights is a central purpose of American foreign policy. Promoting democracy had always been a goal of American foreign policy. But broad acceptance of the notion that a democratic ally was a more stable and desirable ally was new. The readiness of Presidents Carter and Reagan to advance this view has added immeasurably to the success of legislative efforts. In the early years of this campaign, 1973 and 1974, the human rights focus of junior members of Congress like Democratic Congressmen Tom Harkin of Iowa and Don Fraser of Minnesota irritated the Hill leadership and sparked interbranch confrontation. But it also produced laws institutionalizing an emphasis on expanding liberties. Explicit annual human rights reports by the State Department were mandated and efforts by Secretary Kissinger to evade the requirements were blocked. A special human rights secretariat was established in the State Department. A commission to monitor compliance with the human rights components of the Helsinki accords was set up. And many laws were written linking U.S. military and economic assistance to respect for human rights and free elections.[21]

These efforts were not simply a moral crusade to make it clear where the United States stood. They represented a hard-headed assessment of national security objectives as well. In time, even the most conservative opponents of such measures came to see the wisdom of linking aid to progress toward democracy. One notable convert in 1985 was then-chairman of the Senate Foreign Relations Committee, Richard Lugar. Lugar joined traditional critics of oppressive governments in South Africa and the Philippines to endorse modest U.S. actions to distance Washington from these regimes. As the Republican senator from Indiana stated the case in a 1986 speech: "Democracy is the strongest suit of American foreign policy. Promoting and protecting democracy is in the best interests of the United States. Democratic countries celebrate human rights. They enhance our security interests, and they are good trading partners."[22]

The combined pressures of Congress and executive branch diplomats made substantial contributions toward democratic developments in nations as diverse as South Korea, Argentina, and the Philippines. At the same time, the United States pressed for change in repugnant regimes that headed nations like Chile and South Africa. These moves helped improve the chance that Washington might achieve better relations with the successor regimes in these nations, saving many thousands of lives in the process. The challenge was to promote democratic change and to develop ties to nonextremist opposition forces. The American experience of backing the Shah and Somoza for too long and ending up loathed by the extremist regimes of Khomeini and Ortega haunted American policymakers. The lesson taken from these experiences divided most liberals and conservatives in Congress. Liberals maintained that the United States should curb ties with right-wing dictators more promptly in order to ensure that moderates, not extremists succeeded them. Conservatives made a distinction between authoritarian right-wing regimes that support Washington, and their left-wing opponents who are pro-Marxist and

anti-American, arguing that the United States should avoid undermining the former to the benefit of the latter. Liberals argued that
the United States should impose sanctions on repugnant right-wing
regimes. Conservatives generally maintained that through "constructive engagement" with such nations, U.S. diplomats could do more
to encourage reform. Liberals argued that the United States should
use its influence against those authoritarian allies with whom it has
leverage. Conservatives decried the selectivity of this approach, which
often seemed to single out anticommunist regimes for criticism while
ignoring the abuses of leftist totalitarian regimes in Beijing, Havana,
and elsewhere. Despite this divergence in view, Congress was more
unified than ever in the 1980s behind the proposition that human
rights promotion was essential to U.S. national security interests.[23]
Thus, Washington successfully employed conditionality to use American leverage where it existed.

The record of success in pressing the human rights issue is not
unblemished, however. The very same difficulties that have beset
recent drug interdiction efforts are familiar to the human rights campaign and have resulted in some awkward and embarrassing legislation. Even the most flexibly drafted human rights provisos can leave
the president with but two unhappy choices. Take the case of U.S.
foreign aid to the government of Philippine dictator Ferdinand
Marcos circa 1984. Marcos critics in Congress argued throughout this
period that U.S. military aid should be curbed, on human rights
grounds. But proponents argued that such a move could have imperiled the U.S. bases at Clark Airfield and Subic Bay and could have
ignited a nationalist wave of sympathy for the tottering regime.
When certification requirements were enacted, the White House felt
obliged to grant Marcos what amounted to the "*Good Housekeeping*
Seal of Approval"—a finding which Marcos trumpeted all over Manila
that the human rights situation was improving. Congress recognized
the necessity of distancing the United States from a corrupt regime,
making a moral statement of sympathy with the Philippine democratic opposition, and rejecting business as usual with Marcos. But
the unsatisfactory means to send the message risked advertising
American weakness and arguably strengthened the dictator's hand.

In fact, presidents of both parties have chosen most always to
certify the uncertifiable in order to send foreign aid. The White
House has continued to prefer the aid carrot to the legislative stick;
presidents have chosen to remained engaged rather than curb U.S.

ties with unsavory regimes. The executive branch can articulate a commitment to apply diplomatic pressures in private. (In the Carter years, such jawboning by Assistant Secretary of State for Human Rights Pat Derian often occurred in public.) But the State Department diplomats and Pentagon policymakers remain susceptible to "clientitis." Congress is invariably infuriated by this State Department habit of placing a greater priority on maintaining a smooth bilateral relationship than on pursuing broader principles and long-term goals. Congress tries to advance more general causes, arguing that what is American foreign aid about if not to advance human rights, nuclear nonproliferation, and the antidrug crusade? But the executive branch must manage the specifics of a day-to-day relationship with sovereign powers. The tensions between the two branches, here as elsewhere, are inherent. Where one stands on a given issue is often determined by where one sits.

The certification system *can* work. When it is used in moderation and then pursued by a consistent legislative-executive partnership, it can measurably advance the American agenda. The best example of limited success for the certification system is the case of aid to El Salvador during the Reagan presidency. By conditioning expanded U.S. military aid upon democratic reforms and the curtailment of vigilante death squads, Congress and the Reagan administration together prodded the Salvadoran government into making some significant improvements from 1980 through 1987. This progress not only broadened the base of popular support in El Salvador for a democratically elected, pro-American government, it also laid the foundation for a domestic consensus in the United States which supported the costly Salvadoran aid program for a number of years.

In 1981, bitter divisions over this issue were apparent. Rhetoric was supercharged. Democrats in Congress warned of another Indochina debacle, arguing against any U.S. involvement in foreign civil wars. The Republican administration invoked the domino theory, warning of Communist insurgents advancing north on Mexico, toppling governments one by one. State Department efforts to gain a fivefold increase in the aid rushed to El Salvador in January 1981 by the Carter administration were complicated by the fact that Reagan appointees had excoriated efforts to use aid to keep Nicaragua from drifting into the Communist orbit. Corrupt army officials in San Salvador were then showing no ability to curb right-wing death squads, and the Marxist guerrillas in the Salvadoran hills enjoyed some sympathy on Capitol Hill for their resistance to an unsavory military regime. As the first Reagan request for unpopular Salvadoran aid was considered, all the ghosts of Vietnam stalked the halls of Congress.

But after a flurry of speech-making, the substantive Hill response was notably constructive. In this case, conditionality provided a sound approach. Under the leadership of former Peace Corps volunteer Senator Chris Dodd and Democratic Congressman Michael Barnes of Maryland, Congress wrote a series of guidelines to govern U.S. aid. Conditions were established to determine whether human rights progress had been made before more aid would be sent. A strict cap was placed on direct U.S. involvement through military advisers. Land reform and free election timetables were established. And flexibility was provided for a presidential waiver in case standards had not been met but U.S. national interests required continued aid.

The framework was sound. A government that enjoyed broader popular support through a commitment to democracy would be a more stable and defensible ally. But it was execution of the conditional U.S. aid program that would determine success or failure. Congressional oversight of the program was at first used to press for reforms. Administration diplomats used the stick afforded by the aid legislation to press Salvadoran authorities directly in a classic "good cop, bad cop" routine. By tempering the debate and focusing on agreed means, activists at both ends of Pennsylvania Avenue had their way for several years. For the first time since the Vietnam War, the White House sold the Hill on a program of sustained U.S. involvement in a foreign civil war.[24] Skeptics in Congress succeeded in limiting U.S. involvement and emphasizing their own human rights agenda. Several years and several billion dollars later, some progress was apparent. Throughout most of the 1980s, a popularly elected, pro-American government ran El Salvador. Civilian authority was restored. And while terrorist activities by both Communists and rightists continued, their frequency and severity diminished between 1982 and 1987. With Jose Napoleon Duarte's passing from power, the future of Salvadoran democracy remained uncertain. There remained the possibility that renewed violence by extremists from both ends of the political spectrum could undermine centrists in San Salvador. Yet Washington policymakers were united in their opposition to both the death squads on the right and the Communist guerrillas on the left, who preyed upon civilian and commercial targets. Thus, an American military aid program that provoked bitter divisions in Congress in 1981 enjoyed consensus support at least through the end of the Reagan years.[25]

NUCLEAR NONPROLIFERATION: LIMITS OF A SINGLE-ISSUE AGENDA

The clash between general values and specific needs has been a common theme in the fight to shape foreign aid policy. This clash has produced repeated controversies on the drug certification issue. It led to the forging of an effective partnership between Congress and the White House on many human rights initiatives. The experience in the effort to curb the spread of nuclear weapons has been mixed. In nonproliferation debates, the proclivity of diplomats to look for day-to-day tranquility while elected representatives press for broader, long-term objectives has produced frequent confrontations. As these struggles have unfolded, sharply defined battle lines have been established and retained.

In its simplest form, the story of American nonproliferation initiatives since 1973 is one of congressional resurgence and decline. For a time, activists in the legislature pressed the issue to the forefront of the executive branch agenda. Legislators rewrote a host of laws, linking nonproliferation concerns with U.S. aid efforts and setting new standards for nuclear exports. Nevertheless, they failed to enshrine the notion that the nuclear nonproliferation issue was not merely some naive do-gooder's concern, but rather a hard-headed national security imperative. Thus, advances made in the Carter years, when interbranch cooperation on the issue was at its height, were offset by the bitter and fruitless policy divisions of the Reagan years. With the passing from the scene of a generation of nonproliferation experts—legislators like Bingham, Percy, Proxmire, and Ribicoff—and with the devastating effect of the *Chadha* decision overturning legislative veto procedures that were central to much of the nuclear export control legislation, Capitol Hill activists are still in retreat.

Nuclear export control initiatives were an important part of the assertive congressional role in foreign policymaking that occurred in the mid-1970s. Like arms sales disputes, here was another area where legislators suspected executive branch laxity. Congress railed against the failure of the State Department and the Atomic Energy Commission (AEC) to condition U.S. technology transfers on commitments to curb nuclear weapons proliferation. The legislative debate was precipitated by the August 1974 Indian explosion of a nuclear warhead. This weapon was manufactured in part through the use of U.S.-source material (heavy water) imported with a vague "peaceful use" assurance. The initial outcry on Capitol Hill focused on the appalling misappropriation of resources by this struggling Third World power—a U.S. aid recipient. But the failure of the White House to press nonproliferation concerns, and the danger of a countervailing Pakistani nuclear bomb effort, fueled a nonproliferation crusade in Congress.

The immediate Hill concern was to bar recipients of U.S. aid from pursuing a nuclear weapons capability. The United States was complicit, however modestly, in the unnerving Indian effort. Legislators like Democrats Stuart Symington of Missouri and John Glenn wrote provisos barring future U.S. aid to countries with nascent bomb programs.[26] The Ford White House preferred to address nonproliferation issues through private diplomacy and balked at restrictive export control standards drafted by House and Senate committees as a follow-up to the Glenn and Symington measures. But then a strange thing happened. The esoteric nuclear nonproliferation issue became embroiled in a presidential election campaign. The Democratic standard-bearer, Jimmy Carter, was a former nuclear engineer who articulated concerns expressed by Congress about the nuclear weapons spread. During the campaign, nuclear export critics on the Hill succeeded in scuttling an elaborate uranium enrichment export scheme that would have cost taxpayers billions through privatization and federal loan guarantees. Then President Ford took an extremely significant step, placing the United States firmly on the record as being against the widespread commercial use of plutonium, a weapons-usable product of fission generators. Under congressional prodding, the Ford administration also leaned heavily on France to abandon a scheme to sell South Korea and Pakistan sensitive nuclear fuel facilities.

Legislative activists had a limited ability to go beyond this defensive agenda and to initiate new, more restrictive nuclear export control policies. The barriers here were institutional. In the executive branch, nuclear export policy had been the exclusive province of the Atomic Energy Commission—which was still charged with promoting the atom even as it regulated its use. On the Hill, all nuclear-related legislation was under the purview of the formidable Joint Committee on Atomic Energy (JCAE). In 1974, Congress split off the regulatory responsibilities of the AEC, establishing the independent Nuclear Regulatory Commission (NRC) to license domestic reactors and commercial exports. But on the Hill, the JCAE was firmly controlled by nuclear industry friends and export proponents. Committee members succeeded in blocking all efforts to tighten export standards through the mid-1970s.

The solution proposed by industry critics like Common Cause—to abolish the JCAE—at first seemed unrealistic. But House liberal Jonathan Bingham succeeded in the improbable coup, steering oversight of nuclear export legislation to the subcommittee he chaired and opening the door to several years of sustained reform efforts. In blindsiding the JCAE, Bingham exploited his position on the panel of senior Democrats that made committee assignments for newly elected members. Bingham exacted pledges for his reform proposal, to which he was able to commit the House Democratic Caucus in a close 133–99 vote on December 8, 1976.[27] The majority caucus was then committed to ratifying the decision on a party-line vote in the full House when new rules were adopted the next January. Thus, the JCAE was abolished through a maneuver endorsed by less than one-third of the House membership.

Bingham then stole a march on the incoming Carter administration, quickly moving a comprehensive proposal to overhaul all U.S. nuclear export laws. The focus of this bill was to deny nuclear exports to any nation flirting with a nuclear weapons option. The American nuclear industry was steadfastly opposed to the legislation, which barred commercial plutonium use. Industry officials viewed it as a naive and futile effort to put the nuclear genie back in the bottle; they derided this policy of "technological denial." The bill threatened to cost the slumping U.S. nuclear industry both jobs and the ability to wield influence in the international nuclear marketplace. But nonproliferation proved a "motherhood" issue. Bingham was able to forge a coalition between liberal opponents of nuclear energy and conservative critics of the burgeoning nuclear capabilities of Third World powers hostile to American interests.

The comprehensive legislation that emerged sought to give the United States clear nuclear export standards for the first time since the advent of the permissive 1954 Atoms For Peace Program. The

1977 legislation advanced a basic concept: the United States would expedite the shipment of nuclear energy production technology to nations willing to forgo fuels readily convertible to military use and willing to allow international inspection of all their nuclear facilities. The bill's export standards were strict. But it granted the president the authority to waive these restrictions and to overrule any NRC license denial in the case of compelling national interest. Congress retained the right of final approval: a legislative veto, included in the final version of the 1978 Nuclear Nonproliferation Act, could be used if the United States forged any new nuclear agreements for cooperation or granted any export licenses that were at variance with the act's standards.[28]

Typical legislative and executive branch roles in foreign policy-making were now reversed on the proliferation issue. The White House scrambled to respond to the Hill's international agenda. President Carter seized the issue presented by congressional activists and promptly undertook a diplomatic initiative of his own. Envoys were dispatched in 1977 to potential nuclear weapons states like Brazil, Argentina, Pakistan, India, South Korea, and Taiwan; U.S. officials warned of American wrath if further steps toward a military nuclear capability were taken. Other nuclear supplier nations were enlisted into an effort to "reevaluate" the nuclear fuel cycle—a transparent Carter move to stall the international nuclear industry's rush toward commercial use of bomb-grade plutonium.

The bluntness of the Carter efforts unnerved professional diplomats. State Department officials regarded them as a serious threat to the maintenance of smooth bilateral relationships. Yet Carter enjoyed some modest successes. The nonproliferation issue was pressed to the forefront of the international agenda. The diplomatic costs of irresponsible sales and practices were magnified. Standards for international nuclear commerce were elevated. It no longer appeared so likely that a host of regional nuclear arms races would emerge in the next decade. Where President Kennedy had once warned of twenty-five nuclear powers shadowing the planet by 1980, Carter-era aides like nonproliferation specialist Joseph Nye were able to focus on only a "nasty nine"—the five UN Security Council powers (the United States, the Soviet Union, China, France, and the United Kingdom) together with Israel, India, Pakistan, and South Africa.

Carter's moves also helped to slow a drive on Capitol Hill towards even more antinuclear legislation. The President had won credibility on the issue with all but the most zealous nuclear critics in Congress. And when House strategists chose to pass a weaker, slightly muddled, compromise Senate version—thereby ducking a conference committee likely to be dominated by the administration—it was a tacit concession that, by the second year of the Carter presidency, the executive branch had regained the lead in setting nuclear nonproliferation policy.

This executive-legislative partnership on nuclear export policies was effective for a time. A condominium was achieved among senior policymakers in both branches who were able to employ the "good cop, bad cop" routine in dealing with foreign nations. Legislators gave voice to nonproliferation security concerns in the starkest terms, threatening to disrupt business as usual in international nuclear commerce. Savvy diplomats like Assistant Secretary of State Nye and special nonproliferation ambassador Gerard Smith parlayed these Hill threats to obtain modest concessions in international negotiations. Senior members of Congress were able in turn to rein in their own hard-liners. Working together with Senator Glenn, Congressman Bingham was particularly effective in guarding against the danger that efforts to prevent nuclear weapons spread would be spearheaded by those opposed to *all* use of nuclear power for U.S. energy production. In one key 1978 test, Bingham pulled his own punches, narrowly losing a vote to interpret the new nonproliferation act more strictly and thereby block a pending nuclear shipment to India. The New York Democrat wanted a close vote in order to send a shot across the Indians' bow. Yet he was not eager to win and thereby precipitously deny the executive branch the bargaining chip for continued dialogue with the Indian government of Morarji Desai.[29]

Such a fine line could be walked only for so long, however. And while interbranch consensus was attainable on broad issues like comprehensive export standards, it began to break down when specific export licenses were at issue. Once again, the subject of divergent policy recommendations in Washington was South Asia. Pakistani Prime Minister Zulfikar Bhutto had made a secret national commitment to counter India's nuclear option with a bomb for his military. Under the terms of the Glenn and Symington amendments, U.S. ally Pakistan was no longer eligible for military aid. The Carter administration first sought to get around the prohibition. Then, when Pakistan's nuclear intentions became transparent, the White House invoked an aid cutoff. But the Soviet invasion of Afghanistan in December 1979 changed the entire equation. A Carter administration vulnerable to election-year charges of being soft on communism scrambled to revive the Pakistan aid program.

The Pakistan case proved over the course of the next decade to be a running sore in executive-legislative relations on nonproliferation issues. The issue presented fundamental questions. Should Washington subsidize a clandestine nuclear bomb program by funding Pakistan's military? Would a U.S. cutoff of military assistance fuel Pakistan's hunger for its own nuclear deterrent? What meaning did U.S. nonproliferation laws have if the United States armed the Pakistanis while Islamabad continued its secret bomb production effort? Legislative literalists insisted on using the nonproliferation laws in an effort to leverage Pakistan into halting its drive for a nuclear weapons production capability. Practitioners of realpolitik in the executive branch and Congress sought to waive the aid cutoff; White House officials subordinated nonproliferation purity to the need for Pakistani cooperation in resisting Soviet aggression and funneling arms to the Afghan resistance.

Nonproliferation champions on the Hill fought a long and painful retreat. Each year that a new aid request for Pakistan came to the Hill with a waiver of sanctions, legislators drew a line in the sand a little farther back. First, the president was called upon to certify that the Pakistanis were not enriching weapons-grade uranium. Then, when intelligence leaked that Pakistan had undeniably breached that crucial threshold, legislators adopted the Mathias amendment, which required that the president certify only that Pakistan did not actually have an assembled nuclear bomb on hand. In the end, nonproliferation laws were left in a weakened state. From 1981 to 1989, the United States provided Pakistan with the largest foreign aid program in the world outside of its NATO and Camp David commitments—more than $600 million each year. The aid kept up despite clear evidence that Pakistan was pursuing a nuclear weapons option in violation of pledges given to President Reagan by Pakistani ruler General Mohammad Zia. The Soviet presence in Afghanistan tipped the equation against pressing the nonproliferation concern; it seemed that all the executive branch lobbyists had to do in a Hill showdown was to invoke the word "Afghanistan" and the result was a foregone conclusion. Arguably, rearguard action on the Hill increased the disincentives for Zia to unveil his nuclear weapons—which would have spurred a perilous move to nuclear deployments on the Asian subcontinent. But the Pakistan dilemma forced legislative activists to confront the limits of their own power.

Few foreign policy issues saw such a reversal of legislative-executive strength from the 1970s to the 1980s as that which occurred on the nonproliferation debate. Congress was in the driver's seat during the heady days of reform in the mid-1970s. But the incoming Reagan administration scorned much of this work; it effectively buried the issue low on the list of national priorities. This sharp transition had been telegraphed during the 1980 campaign when candidate Reagan had suggested that it was "none of our business" if Pakistan decided to go nuclear. The new Reagan team convincingly portrayed the Carter efforts as naive and counterproductive. Reagan officials sought instead to advance nonproliferation by beefing up the conventional military security of potential nuclear states like Pakistan. They dismissed Hill efforts as having needlessly alienated allies. And they pledged to replace the congressional legislation with a pledge that the United States would again be a "reliable supplier" of nuclear materials to foreign customers. Succeeding Carter-era aides at the State Department was a team of Reagan policymakers determined to revive flagging U.S. influence in the international nuclear marketplace. Indeed, each of the early Reagan nonproliferation officials had worked on behalf of nuclear exporters and foreign clients of the atomic industry. The list included National Security Adviser Richard Allen, Assistant Secretary of State James Malone, and special nonproliferation ambassador Richard Kennedy. The stark changes in approach these aides recommended invited bitter confrontation on Capitol Hill. Senate challenges were raised to both the Kennedy and Malone appointments. Waivers necessary for the Pakistan aid were fought every step of the way. Lawsuits were filed by members of Congress against controversial new agreements with Sweden and Norway.

But Congress proved to be no match for executive branch nonproliferation policymakers during the Reagan years. Legislators protected the comprehensive Nuclear Nonproliferation Act of 1978 against Reagan administration designs for repeal. But the Hill was unable to prevent the administration from reversing direction on the day-to-day implementation of nonproliferation policy because Congress itself was divided on key questions. Legislative activists lost on specific issues like Pakistan because of the Afghanistan situation and anticommunist imperatives. They lost on more general ideological debates because the righteous nonproliferation initiatives of the Carter years were successfully caricatured by the Reagan team and fell into disrepute among many key swing voters on the Hill. Persistent nuclear export critics like Glenn and Cranston in the Senate and Levine and Michigan Democrat Howard Wolpe in the House pressed their case. But obtaining a majority proved increasingly difficult. Then came the *Chadha* decision. The Supreme Court's 1983 rejection of the legislative veto that was so central to congressional nonproliferation review powers marked the nadir for Hill activists on nuclear export issues.

The postscript to this struggle proved to be interesting, however. In full retreat by the end of Reagan's first term, nonproliferation activists in Congress rallied to challenge several key nuclear export proposals later in the 1980s. The Hill's principal weapon in this effort was better access to intelligence information. The complacent executive branch approach to nonproliferation required sustained efforts to hide intelligence on unpleasant developments from the Hill. But in a familiar Washington twist, dissenters to the Reagan administration policy working within the executive branch leaked to key Hill aides troubling details on proliferation-related developments. Legislators then used these revelations to exact modifications in permissive Reagan nuclear export policies. Congress retained few procedural levers with which to block new nuclear trade initiatives like the 1986 accord with the People's Republic of China; the *Chadha* decision required Congress to get a two-thirds majority in both houses to override a presidential veto of any resolution of disapproval. A frontal assault was thus unpromising—unless liberal nonproliferators could forge an alliance with more conservative, fervently anticommunist legislators. Information about irresponsible Chinese nuclear export practices did the trick. News stories about new U.S. intelligence linking China to Pakistan's bomb design and nuclear fuel production efforts were embellished and circulated by Hill critics of the nuclear pact with China. The old congressional left-right coalition from the 1970s on nonproliferation issues was temporarily revived as the pact was placed on hold. Embarrassed administration negotiators were forced by the Hill critics to go back to Beijing to seek revisions and new Chinese pledges. A conditional

resolution of approval imposing modest curbs on the pact's implementation was negotiated by Congressman Stephen Solarz and Senator Cranston and forced upon a reluctant White House.[30]

Similar use was made of various intelligence leaks in 1987. Efforts
to stall military aid deliveries to Pakistan were pressed and a move to
rewrite a controversial new U.S.-Japan nuclear trade pact nearly succeeded. Revelations about continued Pakistani smuggling of nuclear
weapons production components from the United States forced the
administration to make new demarches in Islamabad.[31] And Congress nearly rejected outright the nuclear accord with Japan, which
granted 30-year blanket approvals for commercial use of U.S.-source
plutonium. The pact was assailed in a December 1987 Senate Foreign
Relations Committee vote of 15–3, temporarily sidetracking approval. Ambassador Kennedy was lambasted for failing to achieve more
effective safeguards.[32] But in the wake of *Chadha*, Congress had few
options for trying to make such a preliminary vote stick. Before the
full Senate vote, the administration called upon its ambassador to
Japan—one-time majority leader Mike Mansfield—to lobby his former
colleagues on behalf of the accord. And lobbying by the Kentucky
delegation—which feared a loss of jobs at their Paducah uranium
enrichment plant if U.S.-Japan nuclear trade were slowed—sapped
the strength of nonproliferation activists. Once again, division on
Capitol Hill brought victory for the White House. Even then, the
executive branch was forced to make important concessions in the
form of written pledges to the Hill revising terms for implementing
the U.S.-Japan pact before critics in Congress dropped their opposition.[33] Thus, Congress was still able in 1988 to impose modest conditions on military aid and nuclear trade accords. Nonproliferation
activists on the Hill were down, but apparently not out.

MILITARY AID IN AN ERA
OF SHIFTING ALLIANCES

The struggle to shape foreign policy has been inextricably tied to the
central dilemma of postwar American diplomacy: how to promote
democracy while avoiding a direct superpower confrontation. Since
the Vietnam experience, Congress has remained fervently anticommunist in its approach to the Third World. But an eagerness to
combat the spread of communism and to undermine totalitarian

dictatorships has not translated into an eagerness to apply direct U.S. force. Economic sanctions and trade limitations have become a favored means of advancing policy. But in case after case, these tools have shown clear limitations. For example, antiapartheid legislation adopted by Congress in 1986 failed to improve the situation in South Africa—the 1980 grain embargo and the boycott of the Moscow Olympics were equally ineffective. Strong economic sanctions against Panamanian dictator Manuel Noriega—insisted upon by Congress in 1987—also failed to accomplish the prompt restoration of democracy in that beleaguered nation.

In a different era, covert operations and secret military assistance might have provided a more attractive option for accomplishing diplomatic goals. But as early as 1975, Congress raised substantial barriers to secret efforts to aid democracy. In December of that year, Congress voted to halt a Ford administration move to provide up to $30 million in covert aid to Angola.[34] Legislators were reluctant, in the wake of the Saigon withdrawal, to see the United States bogged down in a faraway conflict that did not appear crucial to national interests. And many members of Congress doubted the efficacy of a clumsy U.S. effort to intervene after so many years of support for Portuguese colonial forces. Since the trauma of the 1975 Angola debates, the executive branch challenge has been to find a means of checking the spread of communism and promoting democracy with a minimum of direct U.S. involvement. The question in Washington has often come down to a simple one: whom should the United States favor with its military aid?

The containment policy remains very much alive; it is advanced today more through the provision of conditional military aid than through assertive deployment of U.S. troops in global hot spots. It was not the resurgence of Congress in the 1970s that brought this new formula of sending guns, not troops. And it was not exclusively the idea of congressional liberals to export principles like human rights and free elections instead of troops. After all, it was a conservative Republican in the White House who spelled out the Nixon Doctrine, which called upon Asians to take up their own defense (and explicitly reversed the pledge of President Kennedy to "pay any price, bear any burden" to check communism). With the exception of his election-year stand on the Persian Gulf, President Carter echoed the neo-isolationist tone of many Nixon administration statements. Congress would be asked to send military aid to nations like Iran, Israel, Egypt, and El Salvador, as well as to the Afghan resistance. But U.S. forces would not become directly involved in any fighting. To a great extent, this policy of substituting U.S. military aid for direct military commitments continued through the eight years of the Reagan presidency. With the exception of a few brief skirmishes with unstable regimes in Grenada, Libya, Lebanon, and Iran, U.S. forces have not been committed to sustained battle since Saigon fell.

Cynics might call this a superpower's strategy of fighting wars with a checkbook; the caricature justifiably highlights the enduring features of Washington struggles over U.S. aid. Contemporary military assistance fights among policymakers in Congress and the executive branch usually focus on who gets how much and with what restrictions. Conditionality has become central to the entire military aid debate. This practice was born of efforts to link the final increments of U.S. military aid to the Southeast Asian nations with deadlines for terminating U.S. involvement. It has since escalated, from the Turkish arms embargo to the debates on aid to Pakistan and El Salvador in the late 1970s and early 1980s, finally erupting into a full-scale donnybrook with the fight to aid the opponents of Sandinista rule in Nicaragua, the Contras.

The evolution of this struggle offers evidence of how flexible both branches of government can be. For example, while committed to anticommunism, lawmakers in Washington have embraced a policy of military cooperation with the Chinese on *both* sides of the Taiwan Straits. Legislators have also rejected stereotypes in generously funding former combatants Israel and Egypt with an annual total of nearly $7 billion, while acquiescing in the sale of sophisticated arms to Israel's sworn enemies, the Saudis, and tolerating grants of U.S. taxpayer dollars to Jordan. But in the eight-year fight for Contra funding, ideology more often limited opportunities for flexibility and accommodation between executive and legislative policymakers.

The Contra aid struggle dominated the post-Vietnam debate between Congress and the President throughout the 1980s. It brought into play all the key elements in the contemporary battle for policymaking primacy. White House aid requests provoked confrontations and yielded compromises. These requests invited the imposition of conditions by Congress, but once rejected, they opened the door to illegal activities by the NSC staff. It was a battle that saw bogeymen raised by both sides. Fears of direct U.S. troop involvement in Nicaragua were systematically exaggerated by congressional liberals. Conversely, anticommunist fears were stirred by the "Great Communicator" in the Oval Office who repeatedly raised the specter of a Communist march north toward Texas. Yet for many years, until it became hopelessly ensnared in partisan politics, this struggle offered enough successes to placate moderates, while infuriating zealots on both sides of the policy debate.

The Contra aid fight began in Washington as it has ended—a shadowy struggle in which the main agenda of proponents and opponents was rarely laid on the table. From the fall of 1979, when the Sandinistas toppled the Somoza dictatorship in a popular revolution, to the spring of 1981, the debate in Washington was often not about Nicaragua per se. It was about the limits of power. It was about how best to check communism. It was about avoiding the establishment of another pro-Soviet base in the Western Hemisphere, and about avoiding the bitter recriminations of another debate over "who lost Cuba?"

This prologue to the Contra aid debate was played out almost exclusively for the benefit of the American electorate. President Carter risked voters' wrath in 1979 when he sought to appease leftist insurgents in Managua with a modest offer of economic aid to rebuild their war-torn nation. The effort was designed to test the Sandinistas by affording them an alternative to reliance on Moscow. The United States was culpable in the prolonged rule of the brutal Somoza dictatorship. By offering aid to the successor regime, Carter officials hoped to join belatedly in backing the winning side in Nicaragua. But Carter was pilloried by conservatives on the Hill, who leaked sketchy evidence that the Sandinistas were intent upon exporting revolution to El Salvador. The House added unrealistic and insulting conditions on the provision of $75 million in aid to Nicaragua. The money went forward, though there was no significant response from the Sandinistas. And the roll call on the aid request was used effectively by critics in the 1980 congressional campaigns. By January 1981, lame-duck President Jimmy Carter had lost patience with the anti-American rhetoric out of Managua. He abandoned the Nicaraguan aid effort and sought token military assistance for anticommunist forces in El Salvador. Again, the backdrop of this Washington policy debate was domestic politics. A history-conscious president was striving to deflect a judgment that he was soft on communism in Latin America.

The debate continued to focus on how to avoid "another Cuba" in the early months of the Reagan term. Secretary of State Alexander Haig sounded the alarm in February 1981 against what he alleged was Nicaragua's well-orchestrated international communist campaign" to export revolution from Panama to the southern borders of the United States.[35] The Reagan administration sought congressional authorization for vastly expanded military aid to El Salvador; by 1988, the total sum would approach $3 billion in U.S. commitments to that tiny Central American nation. But if the fight in 1981 was really about Nicaragua—and Cuba—much more would be needed.

Enter the Contras. In the middle of 1981, this military force consisted of but a few dozen snipers in the field, bluntly labeled by Pentagon internal analysts as "terrorists." They had the emotional support of (if not any material commitments from) Miami-based National Guard officers of the deposed Somoza regime. The Reagan administration was determined to create a firebreak against any further spread of Communist regimes. Administration officials were convinced that Managua was already firmly under the control of pro-Soviet Marxists. So the White House seized the opportunity presented by the dispersed Somoza followers. In essence, the Reagan administration created the Contras. Administration officials nurtured the idea of a military resistance to the Sandinistas. Through the Central Intelligence Agency and the National Security Council staff, administration officials recruited Contra members, wrote battle plans, provided public and private funding, enlisted direct donations from recipients of U.S. aid abroad, and tried to sell the program to the American people through the State Department's new Office of Public Diplomacy. U.S. officials even wrote a constitution for the ragtag band of military resisters to Sandinista rule.[36] In time, the Contra cause was able to develop a modicum of support in Washington, if not in the Nicaraguan countryside.

This struggle was waged courageously by President Reagan for eight years despite the fact that it at no time enjoyed broad support with the American people. Here was an unpopular cause that the President joined and stood by, committing resources far in excess of the recommendations of many of his media advisers.[37] Yet the Contra struggle was fought in large part on false pretenses. Reagan administration officials knew from the outset that, while the president had been sold on the concept of "rolling back" communism in Central America, a few thousand Contras never stood a chance against hundreds of thousands of committed Sandinista soldiers. So year after year, the controversial Contra aid program was defended on Capitol Hill with a vague and shifting rationale.

In 1981, the congressional intelligence committees were given a national security decision directive that envisioned a Contra force of less than 2,000 troops. The mission of this cadre, the Hill was told in November 1981, was to interdict the flow of arms said to be moving from Nicaragua to guerrillas in El Salvador. Yet even in this first Contra request, the White House was eager for more than Congress was willing to grant. The administration was already seeking to evade funding limitations negotiated with Congress. This 1981 program involved kickback grants to the military leaders in Argentina, who used U.S. assistance to fund Contra training, at the behest of Reagan administration officials.

In 1982, with Sandinista military imports from the Soviet Union showing an alarming rise, the Reagan administration was deeply divided over what long-term course to pursue. Some at the State Department and the Pentagon wanted more direct military action against Nicaragua—and even against what Secretary of State Haig alleged was the "source" of the Central American troubles—Cuba. Others in the executive branch were skeptical. The Joint Chiefs of Staff were particularly wary of drawing the United States into a commitment that might lead to an unpopular deployment of U.S. ground troops in Central American cities and jungles. A compromise reached with congressional critics barred use of Contra aid funds "for the purpose of overthrowing the government of Nicaragua."[38]

But what then was the goal of the controversial Reagan program? The flow of arms from Managua to El Salvador had never been substantial. And only the President and a few of the most fervent true believers in the bureaucracy actually believed the Contras could challenge the Sandinistas' firm grip on power. By 1983, congressional skeptics argued more insistently, warning that if an accommodation was sought with Managua, the administration had better start negotiating. But when Assistant Secretary of State for Latin America Tom Enders sought to open a diplomatic track to parallel the military aid program, he was undermined by administration hard-liners. He resigned in May 1983. Enders' notion of pursuing negotiations while pressing the Sandinistas militarily was anathema to conservatives, who were rallying around the Reagan Doctrine, which endorsed funding for proxy wars against undemocratic Third World regimes.

The dilemma for the White House was that even if the executive branch reached a consensus among its own policymakers about the objectives of the Contra aid program, if they articulated this vision on the Hill—if they told the truth—Congress would terminate funding. Congress was unwilling in 1983 to commit U.S. funds to a jungle force whose principal mission was simply to harass the Sandinistas, to keep them occupied with defending borders so that they could not consolidate their leftist revolution. And a majority of Congress was not convinced that pressing the Contra fight would win democratic reforms from the entrenched Sandinista regime.

This was the heart of the Contra aid problem. The Soviets had their Brezhnev Doctrine. They adhered to a commitment to back socialist revolutions around the world and to defend leftist governments once they were established. But Congress was reluctant to embrace an American corollary—the idea that any anticommunist rebellion warranted U.S. aid, however unpromising its prospects for success might be. To executive branch practitioners of realpolitik, this reluctance meant the Soviets could in effect sit back confidently and say, "What is ours is ours, what is yours is negotiable." Republican Senator Orrin Hatch of Utah summed up the broader ideological stakes in a 1986 plea for aid:

> We must once and for all put Third World conflict-promoting states such as Nicaragua on notice that national liberation is a two-way street. We must put our adversaries on notice that it is in the U.S. national interest to oppose alien-sponsored and Marxist-supported insurgencies throughout the Western hemisphere.[39]

While the Reagan Doctrine did enjoy substantial support on the Hill, the key swing votes in Contress were skeptical from the outset about the efficacy of the Contra effort. The Sandinistas had virtually no friends in Congress. But few legislators believed that the Reagan administration effort to overthrow them would succeed. Thus, administration options were limited. The White House felt a need to contain the Sandinistas. Reagan officials dreamt of forcing major democratic concessions from the Sandinistas by applying military pressure. But to Hill critics, this dream was a fantasy—the Contras appeared to be sure losers from the start and never seemed capable of militarily challenging the Sandinistas for power.

The manner in which the Contras waged war also proved unpalatable. American politicians found the proxy war distasteful, the Contras' abuses of civilian buses and crops unsavory, the reliance upon terrorism un-American. Thus, on July 28, 1983, the House voted 228–195 to terminate aid. Moderate Lee Hamilton summed up the prevailing Hill sentiment: "[The aid effort] is not working, it risks wider war, is opposed by the American people, and it is against the American character."[40] The convening by the White House of a "national bipartisan commission" on Central America served to freeze the Washington policy dispute for several months. Administration officials enunciated a broader strategy of economic assistance to the region, and the President managed to rally support for a request of $24 million in Contra aid, which was passed by the Senate in November 1983.

The cause seemed lost the following year, however. Congress objected to expanded U.S. involvement in the Contra war. More frequent U.S. saber rattling—troop maneuvers in Honduras and the massing of naval forces off Nicaraguan shores—backfired. These administration moves only unnerved swing votes, while failing to increase congressional resolve to back military aid as an alternative to U.S. troops. Revelations in the spring of 1984 that the CIA had been directly involved in mining Nicaraguan harbors seemed the last straw. In a bold election-year move, Congress prohibited any further U.S. aid, direct or indirect, to the Contras.[41]

Here the Washington policy struggle might have ended but for the initiative and determination of the executive branch. The weakness that President Reagan was able to exploit on the Hill was that while critics in Congress knew what they were *against*, they were hard-pressed to articulate and realize a practical program to accomplish what they were *for* in Central America. Congress was united in its opposition to communist consolidation in Managua. Reprehensible actions by the Sandinista regime in Managua made it an inviting target for criticism. Congress also was united in its opposition to the export of leftist revolutions in Central America. Legislators remained extraordinarily sensitive to the charge that they might be accountable for the "loss" of another nation to communism. Yet Congress was also firmly opposed to any type of direct U.S. military involvement. So while members could vote *against* Contra aid, there was little that they could vote *for*. The Contadora peace process, initiated by Nicaragua's neighbors during a conference on Panama's Contadora Island, offered an alluring vision. But Congress was powerless to conduct day-to-day diplomacy. Congress was unable to do much of anything to bring the Contadora vision of a regionwide settlement closer to reality, save pass motherhood resolutions extolling its virtues. So long as this peace process bore no fruit, the incantation of "Contadora" offered but a weak alternative to token funding of Contra aid.

By contrast, White House staffers had both the initiative and commitment—as well as the certitude born of ideological fervor—to follow through with their Contra aid program. And follow through they did. In the wake of the 1984 setback, a two-track policy emerged. One effort was overt: a full-court press against the Hill was led by President Reagan himself. An administration public relations team revamped the image of the Contra jungle fighters, dispatching dozens of speakers to swing districts around the United States and unleashing a barrage of favorable publicity from the Office of Public Diplomacy. A second, parallel effort was conducted covertly by members of the CIA and NSC staff. This shadowy group worked to provide sustenance for the Contra forces while the debate in Congress continued. They turned to third countries like Saudi Arabia and Taiwan—even to the Sultan of Brunei. They turned to private donors in the American conservative community and, ultimately, to illegal diversion of U.S. government assets to tide the Contras over. The Sandinistas played into the hands of Contra supporters throughout this period with Daniel Ortega's clumsy efforts to cozy up to Moscow. The Nicaraguan leader's April 1985 trip to the Soviet capital just four days after another Contra aid setback in the House embarrassed even the most virulent congressional critics of the aid program. The question was now moot whether Contra aid had driven the Sandinistas into Moscow's orbit, or whether Ortega had been a committed Marxist all along. The question for U.S. policymakers had simply become how best to respond to the Sandinista challenge. The surprising answer was found in the renewal of U.S. aid to the Contras.

Regardless of Ortega's stupidity or the inability of legislators to advance a diplomatic alternative to Contra aid, much of the credit for revival of the military effort was due to Ronald Reagan. The President made an extraordinary commitment of personal prestige to the aid effort. While some members of his NSC staff were systematically violating congressional strictures, the President pressed the public case for $27 million in "nonlethal aid" for 1985. Lobbying in Washington and at the grass roots was focused almost exclusively on two dozen "boll weevil" Democrats in the House. These conservative southern representatives were most sensitive to the concerns raised by the White House that abandonment of the Contras would lead to the spread of communism north to Mexico and hasten the flow of immigrants into the United States.[42] In a striking phenomenon, executive branch officials flew Contra leaders in from Honduras and Miami to lobby the Hill. One Contra fighter described how this unusual policymaking struggle was played out: "CIA officials told us we could change the votes of many members of Congress if we knew how to 'sell' our case and place [opponents] in a position of 'looking soft on communism.' . . . They told us exactly what to say and which members of Congress to say it to."[43]

But in the end, it was Reagan himself who simply wore down these swing votes in the House. As a leading Contra aid opponent, Congressman Barnes, put it: "The guys in the middle just got tired of being beaten up on both sides. They knew Reagan was going to come back and back and back on this. He was obsessed by it. . . . He just wore everybody out."[44] In June 1985, the Contras unveiled a new prodemocracy platform for their cause at virtually the same time the House was voting to restore "humanitarian" aid in the largely symbolic sum of $27 million.

Members of Congress had already cast more than a dozen separate votes on the Contra funding issue. Yet over the course of the next eighteen months, this seemingly endless policy struggle in Washington escalated markedly. By now, most of the debate proceeded amid an air of unreality. A foreign visitor or a political science novice would have been bewildered. On the one hand were Contra aid opponents in Congress. They spoke eloquently of the dangers of U.S. troops becoming involved. Yet they had no effective program of their own for confronting Nicaragua's Sandinistas, despite the fact that denying Contra aid arguably could hasten the day when U.S. troops would be called to defend neighboring countries. Contra critics held up the Contadora peace process as a panacea. But their "plague on both houses" platform had an isolationist ring. On the other hand was the White House: having identified the greatest threat to the Western Hemisphere since the enunciation of the Monroe Doctrine, Reagan officials then asked for but a pittance to address it. The Reagan administration sent mixed signals: having virtually declared war on the Sandinistas, it maintained diplomatic relations and kept a fully staffed embassy in Managua. Faraway Middle Eastern nations were granted nearly $60 billion in U.S. foreign aid during the Reagan years. But the key 1985 life-and-death struggle for Contra funding was over $27 *million* in fatigues and band-aids!

Adding to the sense of the surreal was the seriousness with which key NSC aides spent their days on the Hill crafting compromise legislative provisions, then returning down Pennsylvania Avenue at night to violate a number of previously adopted laws. Otherwise respected and honorable Reagan officials systematically misled elected representatives in Congress and lied to the American people; the list included two national security advisers, Robert McFarlane and John Poindexter, as well as Assistant Secretary of State for Latin America Elliott Abrams.[45] During these months, Washington was full of talk about the urgency of negotiating directly with Managua. But while some administration officials professed a commitment to this goal, senior State Department officials were privately threatening nations that sought a direct dialogue with Managua. In fact, senior White House officials worked systematically to sabotage the Contadora process so favored by Hill moderates.[46] The White House wanted to obliterate the Sandinistas; but it was politically unwilling and constitutionally unable to use the full force of a superpower to make them cry "uncle." Contra aid critics loved to twit the administration on this point; Senator Cranston noted that

> if the Administration truly believes that the Sandinistas are a threat to our national security, why doesn't the Administration just come out and say that its objective is the military overthrow of the Sandinista regime? The reason, I suspect, is that the "contra" effort is woefully inadequate to the task—and because the American people quite rightly reject the idea that U.S. military force should be employed indiscriminately to remake foreign governments in our own image.[47]

Contra supporters were also bitter about the fact that "compromise" with Capitol Hill ensured that the Contras would never get enough funding to pursue their goals. Halfway measures were clearly self-defeating, as conservative analyst Jeffrey Bergner noted: "U.S.

policy should either provide real, effective help to the contras or make peace with the Sandinista regime. Splitting the difference makes no sense. Yet this has been the result of an incredible and delicate balance between those who favor effective aid and those who do not."[48]

The Contra policy struggle between Congress and the President eventually disintegrated into a fight over abstractions. It became a battle waged through the creation of straw men and through scapegoating, subterfuge, and public relations offensives. The goals professed, and the means advanced to achieve them, bore little relationship to reality. President Reagan was able to maintain the initiative in this war of ideas, even though he was playing by the Hill's post-Vietnam rules. Championing his "freedom fighters," Reagan successfully claimed the moral high ground of anticommunism. And he held it for years, despite repeated revelations of Contra atrocities against Nicaraguan civilians. Indeed, most of the Contra war was waged against unarmed peasants, against soft targets like buses and bridges. Only rarely, and then in retreat, did Contras ever engage uniformed Sandinista soldiers.

Amid some of the ugliest fighting in 1986, the President came to the Hill with a bold request for $100 million in virtually unrestricted Contra aid. The wraps were off. The White House orchestrated a campaign of carefully timed media revelations of alleged new Sandinista excesses. And the President made yet another nationally televised, prime-time appeal for congressional support. This strong personal pitch from the Oval Office won sympathy from the beleaguered swing votes in the House. In the Senate, a rearguard threat of a liberal filibuster appeared. But ironically, this strategy was defeated through resort to a familiar series of parliamentary maneuvers. In 1984, liberals had cut off all Contra aid by tying the Boland amendment to a continuing resolution funding the entire federal government. In 1986, conservative Contra backers, led by Senate Majority Leader Robert Dole, linked the issue of Contra funding with a pending South Africa sanctions measure. This classic Senate parliamentary knot forced liberals to choose. Just as Reagan had decided not to veto the 1984 continuing resolution (and thereby halt federal government operations until the impasse was broken), legislative linkage also forced Senate liberals in August 1986 to back down. Liberals could obtain clear up-or-down votes on both South Africa and Contra aid, or on neither issue. After an election-year deal was cut freeing the antiapartheid measure, the Senate passed the Reagan Contra aid request by a 53–47 vote.[49]

Within six months of this historic victory, the Reagan Contra policy was doomed. The first blow came in the jungles of Central America. The Contras got their guns. But they failed to seize and hold any Nicaraguan territory. The Contras appeared increasingly to be only a force for vengeance, for futilely dragging on the fighting. After seven years of U.S. aid, they were capable of terrorizing rural civilians and pressing the Sandinistas for more generous peace terms. But they also gave Managua an excuse for domestic repression against external threat and were ineffective in rallying public opposition to the Sandinistas within Nicaraguan borders. The harder the Contras fought, the more the Sandinistas were able to justify internal repression and reliance on Soviet bloc allies.

A second blow came on election day 1986, when the Republicans lost control of the Senate. Several Contra aid supporters were replaced by staunch aid opponents. Parliamentary options for gaining new aid were severely limited by the ascension of Democratic committee chairmen and leadership.

The third blow to the Contras also came in November 1986, when reports of the secret U.S. arms sales to Iran began to leak out. There soon followed a hemorrhaging of details about the diversion of U.S. assets to the Contras during the months of the Boland ban, about kickbacks by U.S. allies to circumvent the congressional prohibition, and about White House deceit in establishing a covert network to privatize the implementation of foreign policy. The most sensational allegations of Contra aid critics on the Hill were now confirmed. Staffers in the White House basement had become so frustrated with congressional vacillation that they had created a government-within-a-government to circumvent legislative restrictions. As a mammoth congressional investigation of the Iran-Contra scandal unfolded, an echo of the Watergate-era morality tale was heard. Key executive branch officials asserted that the end—keeping the freedom fighters in the field—justified the means. Critics on the Hill maintained that the cause of democracy could not be advanced while subverting democratic principles. When Lieutenant Colonel Oliver North proved an articulate critic of the on-again, off-again inconsistency of congressional policy toward the Contra effort, the White House sought to mount a belated counterattack by blaming much of the fiasco on Congress. But this effort won few converts; by the summer of 1987 the scandal was sapping the ability of the Reagan administration to govern.

It is a remarkable commentary on the staying power of the central ideas at issue that even after these fiascos, the Contra aid debate remained a live one. Into late 1987, stopgap funding dribbled forward. It was only a gamble by the Contras themselves in early 1988 that essentially ended the prospect of new military aid. Through an elaborate series of maneuverings among the Sandinistas, the Contras, and House Speaker Jim Wright, the parties to the conflict were convinced to cut a deal separate from the White House. Peace—but not democracy—broke out in Nicaragua. Contra leaders apparently reached the conclusion that Democrats and Republicans in Washington were far more interested in using the Nicaragua issue to score political points than in advancing the interests of the Contras themselves. The U.S.-funded military aid campaign ground to a halt. The Contras risked making their own deal with Ortega under the framework of the Arias Plan, the successor to the regionwide Contadora peace process.

Even then it took the policymakers in Washington many months to grasp the fact that the military struggle was over, that the Contras had no future as a fighting force. Through the last months of the Reagan administration, the Washington maneuvering was almost exclusively driven by political concerns about who would ultimately be blamed for the Contras' failure. Democrats scurried for some political cover in case the negotiations in Managua turned sour. A package of $48 million in refugee relief and assistance for a cease-fire monitoring team was rushed through Congress with lightning speed in March 1988. House Speaker Jim Wright advanced an extensive plan for regionwide aid. GOP defenders of the Contra cause sought parliamentary guarantees that military aid could be put to a quick vote if peace talks broke down. The White House continued to assail congressional Democrats for opposing military aid, while the State Department remained suspicious of any peace worked out directly among the Central Americans. Within ninety days of the beginning of the Managua peace talks, Secretary of State Shultz was futilely calling upon Congress for renewal of military aid to the hapless Contras. Even when the Sandinistas and Contras failed to implement the Arias accords, the best the Reagan administration could achieve on Capitol Hill was an August 1988 vote for refugee relief for Contras encamped in Honduras. Through his very last days in office, President Reagan assailed Hill opponents of new military aid to the Contras, blaming U.S. critics for the Contras' failures in the field.

The prolonged struggle to shape Contra assistance policy illustrated a host of truths about the nature of the military aid debate in the post-Vietnam era:

• Because extended commitment of U.S. combat troops remains unpopular, policymakers in both branches of government will go to extraordinary lengths to achieve face-saving compromises: the Contra mission was always vague and unpromising. Yet it won Hill and White House support for years because more extreme alternatives had less appeal.

• Covert military aid remains in disrepute: while some CIA actions require diplomatic deniability, executive as well as legislative policymakers preferred to debate Contra aid in the open, with advancement of human rights the common goal.

• Conditionality provides the ground for ultimate consensus in contemporary executive-legislative negotiations on aid policy, even if the result is to build a bridge halfway across a river. Washington negotiations ensured that the Contras were given just enough aid to keep them alive—and to provide Ortega with a foreign foe—but never so much that they might have really threatened Sandinista rule.

• End-run efforts usually lead to disaster; their eventual exposure provides opponents of presidential initiatives with a procedural club that can be used to press what in reality are objections to the substance of policy. The decisions by senior executive branch officials to privatize foreign policy and to ignore congressional prohibitions ultimately weakened the Contra cause.

• Presidential tenacity pays dividends; but Congress will support success and abandon a failure: Skepticism about the efficacy of the Contra effort repeatedly hamstrung the President's aid requests. (Contrast with the U.S. policy of granting hundreds of millions of dollars in aid to the Afghan resistance—a program that won unanimous Hill support in good measure because it was viewed as a success.) Anticommunism remains a potent rallying cry. But an effective program is still a sine qua non for maintaining a long-term national commitment of troops or money.

• Finally, it should be underscored that despite the enormous stakes of the Contra aid dispute, it was procedural gimmickry that often determined the outcome of legislative showdowns. Sage use of parliamentary devices carried the day for both the Boland aid cutoff in 1984 and the Reagan $100 million Contra assistance request in 1986. Today in military assistance programs, no less than in so many other diplomatic endeavors, procedure can make or break policy. This is as true in the struggle to shape foreign aid programs as anywhere else in the enduring policymaking struggle between the president and Congress.

NOTES

1. Michael D. Barnes, "The Constitution and Foreign Policy: The Role of Congress," in Pollock, *Renewing the Dream*, p. 68.

2. There are four principal accounts in the foreign aid bill. ESF (Economic Support Fund) grants are cash transfers used for anything from balance of payments to purchasing foodstuffs. FMS (foreign military sales) credits are used to purchase U.S. arms. MDBs (multilateral development banks) are institutions like the International Bank for Reconstruction and Development (IBRD) to which the United States makes annual contributions for international loans. Development assistance (DA) includes projects funded through Agency for International Development (AID) programs, as well as P.L. 480 (Food for Peace) gifts of grain.

3. For example, the fiscal year 1988 appropriation of $14.013 billion broke down as follows—MDBs: $1.3 billion; FMS: $5.4 billion; ESF: $3.2 billion; food aid: $1.1 billion; other bilateral and economic aid (principally AID): $3.0 billion. The State Department must also seek funding for running its own bureaucracy and securing its embassy facilities overseas. The "international affairs function 150" of the Congressional Budget Resolution also includes spending for the Export-Import Bank and international information programs.

4. One egregious example occurred in August 1983 when Democrats heeded a Reagan White House plea to resist a bar on International Monetary Fund (IMF) loans to "communist dictatorships"—a line-item veto that no donor nation is allowed to make. After the Democrats helped the President, the Republican Congressional Committee mailed news releases to their districts assailing their votes (see Destler, et al., *Our Own Worst Enemy*, p. 148). See also "Rethinking Foreign Aid" (Heritage Foundation backgrounder), June 1, 1988, which criticizes U.S. aid totaling $1 billion to nations that opposed the United States in a majority of UN votes.

5. Gerald Ford, veto message on Foreign Assistance Bill, May 7, 1976, *Public Papers of the Presidents: Gerald Ford*, 1975–1976, p. 1481.

6. See Flora Lewis, *New York Times*, June 20, 1988, p. A15.

7. See Senate Foreign Relations Committee Rept. 98–400 on S. 2582.

8. Gramm-Rudman-Hollings requires that an increasing percentage of the federal budget deficit—which ran at $146 billion in fiscal year 1989—will be cut each year. Automatic cuts fall most heavily on spending programs like foreign aid, which are not entitlements but do pay out 100 percent cash in the pending fiscal year.

9. Congressman David Obey, as quoted in *National Journal*, September 20, 1986, p. 2238.

10. Senator Pete Domenici, as quoted in "Defense Torpedoes Foreign Aid Request," *Washington Post*, May 14, 1986, p. 21.

11. Aid for favored nations is often "bid up." The State Department submits to the Hill a figure that supporters increase in committee. With total spending for the Israel account often moving up, this requires balancing increases for Egypt. When Turkey receives increases, supporters of Greece insist upon parallel moves to maintain the traditional 7:10 ratio in U.S. aid to the two southern Mediterranean antagonists.

12. Base rights countries have received aid increases of some 60 percent between 1981 and 1987 (see David Obey and Carol Lancaster, "Funding Foreign Aid," *Foreign Policy* 71 [Summer 1988] : 152).

13. Consequently, as AID administrator Alan Woods lamented, "there [wasn't] room in the non-earmarked part of the budget to satisfy all our priorities and obligations. In some cases, we'll be able to make only token gestures. And in others, we won't be able to do anything at all" (see "Hill's Aid Allocations Faulted," *Washington Post*, January 13, 1988, p. 8).

14. See "Foreign Aid: The Evolution of U.S. Programs," *Congressional Research Service*, April 16, 1986, p. 17.

15. George P. Shultz, "Why We Need to Keep Foreign Aid Flowing" (a reprint of Shultz's congressional testimony), *Newsday*, March 2, 1987, p. 53.

16. See, for example, Ford's comments in *New York Times*, September 2, 1976, p. 1.

17. P.L. 99–570. Congress passed another omnibus antidrug bill days before the 1988 general election.

18. On April 3, 1987, the Senate passed S.J. Res. 91 disapproving the Panama certification. But the measure died when the House failed to pass it within the required thirty legislative days.

19. See S. Res. 292, *Congressional Record*, 14 April 1988.

20. S. Res. 268, April 14, 1988. If sustained, the vote would also have required the United States to oppose World Bank loans to Mexico—loans that are used primarily to service debts to American banks.

21. For example, the 1975 Harkin amendment, threatening aid cutoffs for consistent violators of human rights, was adopted on the House floor over the objections of Democratic Foreign Affairs Committee Chairman Thomas ("Doc") Morgan of Pennsylvania. It survived in the Senate despite similar leadership objections. After being watered down in the Foreign Relations Committee by Senator Hubert Humphrey, it was revived and adopted in

its original form under the sponsorship of Senators Cranston and Abourezk (see Franck, *Tethered Presidency*, p. 85).

22.   Richard G. Lugar, "Democracy and American Foreign Policy: A Corollary
to the Reagan Doctrine," speech to Young Republicans, Washington, D.C.,
March 15, 1986. Reprinted in *Congressional Record*, March 18, 1986,
S2963.

23.   The Marshall Plan and U.S. aid to South Vietnam were other efforts advanced for human rights, broadly defined. But where John Kennedy succeeded in linking such themes to the anticommunist cause, LBJ and Nixon
failed. Even a flood of Indochinese boat people and the scourge of Cambodian genocide did not produce a consensus in Washington that the Indochina conflict was a human rights cause.

24.   Efforts to trigger the War Powers Act over El Salvador consistently failed.
But efforts by legislators to invoke the act did provide Congress with some
useful leverage in negotiations with the White House.

25.   For an alternative view, see "Bankrolling Failure: U.S. Policy in El Salvador and the Urgent Need For Reform," staff report of U.S. Congress Arms
Control and Foreign Policy Caucus, November 1987.

26.   U.S. nonproliferation statutes provided an implicit waiver for Israel's
clandestine nuclear program. Israel remained eligible for vital U.S. economic and military assistance because its nuclear program had been started
before the restrictive legislation of the 1970s was passed.

27.   See Franck, *Tethered Presidency*, p. 112. The unilateral House action of
refusing to send legislation to the JCAE neutralized it; the House and Senate later acted together to disband it.

28.   P.L. 95-242. The original House bill was H.R. 4409; the weaker Senate
bill, heavily amended on the Senate floor, was S. 897.

29.   A view of this debate from the perspective of an antinuclear activist is
chronicled in Congressman Ed Markey's *Nuclear Peril: The Politics of Proliferation.* See especially Chapter 7, "The Just Barely Nuclear Congress."

30.   S.J. Res. 238, adopted December 11, 1985. Criticism of this bargain is
articulated in Paul Leventhal and Daniel Horner, "The U.S.-China Nuclear
Agreement; A Failure of Executive Policymaking and Congressional Oversight," *Fletcher Forum* 11, no. 1 (Winter 1987): 105-22.

31.   Pakistan escaped the Hill's wrath when its embassy lobbyists succeeded in
linking anti-Pakistan sanctions with new, severe anti-India measures. These
subsequently were stripped off a key bill together (see "Bill on Atom
Arms Would Punish India," *New York Times*, December 5, 1987, p. 3).

32.   See S. Con Res. 96. See also "Senate Panel Rejects U.S.-Japan Pact on
Shipping Plutonium," *Washington Post*, December 18, 1987, p. 7.

33.   See "Restrictions Added to Plutonium Pact with Japan," *Washington Post*,
June 6, 1987, p. 16.

34.   See Sundquist, *Decline and Resurgence*, pp. 286-89.

35. Alexander Haig, as quoted in Joanne Omang, "Rebel Fund Diversion Rooted in Early Policy" (two-part series), *Washington Post*, January 1, 1986, p. 1.

36. See Edgar Chammorro and Jefferson Morley, "Confessions of a Contra: How the CIA Masterminds the Nicaraguan Insurgency," *New Republic*, August 15, 1985, p. 18.

37. "[White House public relations specialist Michael] Deaver hated this issue," Reagan supporter Peter Flaherty noted in 1986. "He didn't want Reagan messing with it and ruining his popularity" (as quoted in Omang, "Rebel Fund Diversion, p. 1).

38. This compromise became known as "Boland I," after the chairman of the House Intelligence Committee, Edward Boland of Massachusetts, who at that time supported Contra aid. P.L. 97–377 was signed December 21, 1982.

39. Senator Orrin Hatch, *Congressional Record*, March 27, 1986, p. S3667.

40. Congressman Lee Hamilton, *Congressional Record*, August 2, 1984, p. H8282. See also Omang, "Rebel Fund Diversion."

41. "Boland II" (P.L. 98–473) was attached to the fiscal year 1985 continuing resolution and proved veto-proof. It was signed into law October 21, 1984.

42. "Boll weevils" were first targeted by OMB Director David Stockman for votes among the Democratic ranks in support of Reagan tax and spending cuts. These House votes were key on the Contra issue because the GOP-controlled Senate offered steady, but slim, margins in favor of aid through 1986.

43. Edgar Chamorro, testimony before the World Court, November 1984, as quoted in Omang, "Rebel Fund Diversion," p. 1.

44. Congressman Michael Barnes, as quoted in Omang, "Rebel Fund Diversion," p. 1.

45. See Iran-Contra Committee, "Executive Summary" of the final report. Subsequently, McFarlane pleaded guilty to criminal charges, Abrams was barred from testifying before key Hill committees until he apologized for lying, and Poindexter was indicted by the special prosecutor.

46. Ibid.

47. Senator Alan Cranston, Senate Foreign Relations Committee, hearings, February 26, 1986.

48. Jeffrey Bergner, "Organizing the Congress for National Security," *Comparative Strategy* 6, no. 3 (1983): 298.

49. Senate Republicans split 42–11 in favor of continued aid. It was kept alive through the support of eleven of the Senate's forty-seven Democrats, including eight southerners, Dixon of Illinois, Bradley of New Jersey, and Boren of Oklahoma.

9 CONGRESS AND THE PENTAGON Shaping National Security Policy

> Today there is no rational system whereby the Executive Branch and Congress reach coherent and enduring agreement on national military strategy, the forces to carry it out, and the funding that should be provided.
>
> —Packard Commission, 1986[1]

The single greatest failure in the tortured international affairs policy-making struggle between the modern Congress and the president has been the inability to construct a reliable system for resolving defense spending and arms control disputes. This is a problem that grew in severity during the late 1930s and early 1940s, years when America took halting steps to assume global responsibilities. The challenge was met for a time thereafter: the Atlanticist consensus aided President Truman, while anticommunism and containment gave the nation a unified strategy. President Eisenhower was articulate in expressing frustration over the "undue influence" of the new "military-industrial complex."[2] But the general in the White House enjoyed unique support from both the military services and Capitol Hill appropriators. Through the early years of the Nixon presidency, setting military strategy and obtaining funding was not usually the subject of prolonged interbranch warfare. But over the course of the last fifteen years, a burgeoning Pentagon bureaucracy determined to recover from the harrowing Vietnam experience has collided with a resurgent Congress. Successive presidents have been bedeviled by effective Hill resistance to their nuclear arms production and arms control negotiating priorities. Budget disputes and procurement scandals have crippled efforts to build a sustainable consensus on defense spending levels. And the roller-coaster ride of steep defense increases followed by sharp cutbacks has careened onward through scandal after scandal. Here is a portrait of a policymaking system out of control.

Voters are not innocent witnesses to this disaster; they must bear a measure of the responsibility for Washington's failure to right the system. Wild vacillations in the public mood have exacerbated the challenge of establishing an enduring Pennsylvania Avenue consensus on international security priorities. With voters demanding first less funding for the Pentagon (1973–1979), then much more (1980–1985), and then recently less again, serious debate on military strategy has often been reduced to an absurd bidding ritual. Discussion of defense priorities at times bears little relationship to any objective reality. The guns versus butter debate has preyed upon politicians' traditional fears of being labeled "soft on defense" or callous on domestic "fairness" issues, yielding timidity instead of leadership. Symbolism has come to overshadow military strategy; the input of dollars has obscured the output of results. In this climate, an otherwise rational policymaker can publicly maintain (as Secretary of Defense Caspar Weinberger did in 1983) that a penny less than a 10 percent rise in the subsequent fiscal year's DOD budget would bring the Russians up the Potomac.[3] Conversely, a champion of domestic spending programs like Reverend Jesse Jackson, who has no professional experience in formulating military strategy or procurement priorities, can maintain with a straight face that as much as $60 billion can be cut from the military budget without any harmful impact upon national security.[4]

The prodigious sums dedicated to international security efforts have transformed the Pentagon budget into the nation's largest federal jobs program, ensuring that it will be larded with fat. Those in Congress who earmark appropriations insist on funding home-state bases that the military does not need and locally produced weapons that the Pentagon does not want. There are thus clear limitations on the ability of Congress to legislate the military out of its current mess. Hawkish Republican Congressman Jim Courter of New Jersey has even suggested that "bills are needed to regulate Congress as well as the Pentagon. We're always saying 'Shame on your house.' But we have our own shame here. We can't reform the Pentagon until we've reformed ourselves."[5] Courter's scorn ignores the fundamental issue; Congress approved the vast majority of Pentagon programs—$2.2 trillion of the $2.3 trillion in defense spending sought by the eight-year Reagan presidency. Where Congress falls short is in failing to exercise more effective oversight of spending requests and in insisting on funding its own pet projects. Managing the Pentagon is such a tough challenge that the president, the Joint Chiefs of Staff, and the civilian secretary of defense need all the help they can get on Capitol Hill.

THE MODERN CONGRESS AND CIVILIAN CONTROL

The challenge of forging an executive-legislative consensus on international security priorities has always had a singular subtext: in the United States, civilian control of the military is a fundamental constitutional principle. But the American experience since King George III has been to identify the executive with the armed forces, to be suspicious of White House military proposals, and to be jealous of the commander-in-chief's prerogatives. Since 1792, when the nation's most revered general assumed the presidency, the uniformed military has been at the beck and call of legislative investigators. A finger-pointing postmortem conducted in the first year of Washington's administration by a special House committee on the military disaster at the hands of the Creek Indians set crucial precedents for legislative predominance.[6] Congress would not only pay the military's bills; it would also attempt to use the purse strings to set defense policy and oversee its execution. This, of course, was a basic design of the Constitutional Convention. Not only was Congress granted the sole power to declare war, it was granted the express authority to "raise and support armies," to make "rules for the Government and Regulation of the land and naval forces," and to provide for "calling forth, organizing, arming and disciplining the militia." And congressional control over the defense budget was so clearly established that a uniquely detailed prohibition on military appropriations exceeding two years was actually written into the

Constitution as a protection against a neo-royalist president prosecuting a war without the continued popular support of the legislature.

The modern Congress has lived up to this vision in many respects. As American obligations around the globe have multiplied in the nuclear age, Congress has developed new means of influencing military policy. Congress has altered military funding priorities; legislators have curbed key nuclear weapons delivery systems, while initiating development of others; Congress has changed the strategic arms negotiating priorities of four successive presidents; and Congress has shuffled the military's own command structure through reorganization of the Department of Defense and the Joint Chiefs of Staff.

Yet when compared with the struggle over foreign aid and other diplomatic endeavors—where Congress was resurgent in the 1970s and subject to counterreformation in the 1980s—the national security policymaking picture is markedly different. Congress has played a far weightier role in asserting its views on diplomatic policy, on which its influence has been far more substantial and sustained than on military policy. In the defense field, the impact of Congress is still on the rise. But the effectiveness of Capitol Hill defense experts in challenging the executive branch and helping to clarify national priorities still lags behind that of their foreign relations counterparts.

There are many possible explanations for the inability of Congress to master defense issues and to exercise more effective guidance in establishing defense spending priorities. The technical details often seem impenetrable to many an overworked legislator; time demands are such that only a handful of members are truly expert in national security strategy. Yet defense procurement debates remain ripe for simplistic sloganeering. Fickle public support for the Pentagon undermines efforts to achieve a Hill consensus behind a sustainable rate of funding. And the national security mystique of nuclear weapons doctrine and covert intelligence requirements sometimes makes legislative passivity appear the better part of patriotism. The intimidating impact of uniformed military officials providing expert advice cannot be minimized either. But with public concern about costly defense programs at an all-time high and the contemporary headlines full of stories about Pentagon waste, fraud, and abuse, one thing is clear: more vigorous congressional oversight is needed to help the president and the secretary of defense sort out the competing demands for military spending.

To an extraordinary degree, blame for this particular policy integration failure must lie at the feet of the executive branch. It is the president, after all, who is charged with administering the federal agencies in their day-to-day operations. The Pentagon makes thousands of procurement decisions every twenty-four hours; many are wise, many are sound. But it is the president who is the company CEO when someone buys a $7,000 coffeepot.[7] The president controls the NSC. He handpicks the heads of the JCS, OMB, and DOD. But frustration in establishing responsible and sustainable Pentagon spending practices is a problem as old as the mammoth Arlington, Virginia building itself. Dating back to Harry Truman (who had his own Hill experience as an investigator of defense fraud and production bottlenecks during World War II), the White House has been bedeviled by the unmanageability of the defense establishment. A long and tired path has been beaten by successors to the Truman Committee—the Grace Commission, the blue ribbon Packard Commission, and others. The main difficulty has always been keen interservice rivalry; turf battles between the Army, the Navy, the Air Force, and the Marine Corps ensure duplication and redundancy. For example, the Air Force and the Navy are developing nine different systems for detecting hostile radars—programs with a total price tag of $7 billion—even though they will all function on common principles. Similarly, there are four distinct and separate Pentagon programs funded to develop a remotely piloted aircraft. Efforts to halt such duplication are sidetracked by interservice jealousies. One official who recently tried, Pentagon Undersecretary for Acquisition Richard Godwin, resigned in disgust after less than twelve months; Godwin testified before Congress that "anyone who tries to make changes [in Pentagon procurement practices] will meet the status quo head on."[8] The converse of such interservice rivalry is a form of bureaucratic unification: a tacit conspiracy of silence warns top brass away from others' pet projects in the hopes that their own will escape criticism. Even a Pentagon-defender like Senator Barry Goldwater has publicly chastised the military in this regard, observing that "the services are unable to put national interest above parochial interest."[9]

Throughout the Reagan years, the challenge of building a coherent program that enjoyed consensus Hill support was made more difficult by the confrontational style of Secretary Weinberger. Determined and unyielding, Weinberger at first enjoyed tremendous success—measured solely in dollar terms. Defense won consecutive 25 percent increases in appropriations in 1981 and 1982 and impressively rolled over its critics. But such success was calculated only in terms of financial input, not results. Secretary Weinberger accelerated Carter-era plans to improve each leg of the nuclear triad, while expanding the Navy and deploying INF weapons in Europe. Weinberger's "more of everything" restored military morale. Yet it ultimately cost the Pentagon support from even GOP stalwarts. Weinberger alienated key Hill moderates—and even some conservative Republicans—with his constant brinksmanship and reliance on budget flimflammery. DOD would submit unrealistically high requests for budget increases. Then when the Hill increased the budget by a lesser amount, the secretary of defense would publicly assail these alleged "cuts" of defense "muscle and bone." Under Weinberger, the Pentagon systematically overestimated the inflationary costs of purchasing weapons each year. The Pentagon would then use monies stockpiled in this in-house slush fund to pay for programs cut by Congress. It was an impressive game while it lasted. But it alienated key Hill allies and diminished DOD's credibility at the very time that the Pentagon had the opportunity to establish a sustainable domestic consensus behind a long-term defense strategy.[10]

The responsibility for authorizing and appropriating monies for the Defense Department, however, lies with Congress. And it is Congress that has failed to make systematic improvements in the defense management process. The principal weakness in Congress's approach to military security issues is that while legislators are often intimidated by military officials on broad policy issues, they are all too ready to substitute pork-barreling for policy making. Military strategy debates quickly degenerate into aggressive attempts at constituent servicing. The defense bill—fully one-third of the federal budget—has become one mammoth employment program.[11] The membership of the House and Senate armed services panels has long been weighted by senior members adept at steering extraordinary sums in Pentagon contracts and military base commitments to their home states. The practice is by no means a new one. As early as 1960, the frustration of Pentagon officials who sought to curb retention of antiquated military bases, only to be overruled by local legislators, led wags to call the House Armed Services Committee the "House Military Real Estate Committee."[12] Today, a far more critical brand of leadership controls these two key committees, maverick Les Aspin in the House and widely respected conservative Sam Nunn in the Senate. But the "iron triangle" legacy continues to beset the two panels, whose members today are so richly endowed by defense contractors' PACs.[13]

With the U.S. assumption of more global obligations in the nuclear age, the sums involved have grown exponentially. Defense spending grew from $130 billion in 1979 to nearly $300 billion in 1988: a 60 percent increase after inflation, and a 20 percent increase over 1968, the costliest year of the Vietnam War.

Congress still usually fails—except in the rather unique area of strategic nuclear arms policy—to look at the big picture in defense debates. Congress approves virtually every major weapons system and some 95 percent of executive branch defense spending proposals. Yet thousands of relatively minor details are subject to intense scrutiny. Money is added for bases and weapons the military does not want and cannot use, and an average of $2.2 billion in research and development programs were tacked onto the Pentagon request by Hill appropriators each year of the Reagan administration. Yet crucial issues of national strategy and priorities are overlooked. The annual encampment of the defense authorization bill on the House and Senate floors has too often become a public spectacle, a free-for-all circus where there is always something for everyone. As a consequence, Congress has hampered its ability to be a major player in the crucial effort to marry force with diplomacy in U.S. national security policymaking.

PROCRASTINATION AND PORK: THE PENTAGON BUDGET MESS

How bad has Pentagon procurement and congressional oversight of the defense budget become? Consider the 1986 DOD authorization bill as one example. Certainly this Reagan administration request for $286 billion in new spending authority did not suffer from indifference on the Hill. Coming on the heels of an unprecedented seven-year rise in real defense spending outlays, the 1986 measure was received with intense interest both by legislators who wanted more and by those who saw the need to cut back. This was the year that Gramm-Rudman-Hollings was born, mandating significant reductions in the soaring federal deficit. Defense was a prime target for budget-cutters, so the Pentagon's enormous request presented fundamental issues to members of Congress. The four authorizing and appropriating committees held 142 separate hearings, publishing 21,738 pages of testimony.[14]

The committee hearings focused on broad questions of strategy as well as the specifics of which weapons to buy. Yet when it came time for floor debate and votes, no issue was too small for legislative review. For instance, provisions debated and then attached to the 1986 Defense Authorization Act reduced fees at DOD veterinary clinics from $10 to $2 per visit, required a demonstration project to establish the feasibility of selling U.S. meat at overseas commissaries, and authorized the commercial sale of tapes from a 1985 Air Force Band concert.[15] After the two chambers wobbled through four weeks of debate on a total of 199 separate floor amendments, a lengthy House-Senate conference had still to be weathered. The awkward spectacle was later summarized by an exasperated Senator Nunn:

> We are focusing on the grains of sand on the beach while we should be looking over the broad ocean and beyond the horizon. We are not fulfilling our responsibilities to serve as the board of directors for the Department of Defense. Instead, Congress has become 535 individual program managers that are micromanaging the Department at an alarming rate. . . . I cannot remember when we have had a debate on our national military strategy and how well we are doing in carrying out that strategy.[16]

Nunn is not alone in bemoaning alleged congressional micromanaging. The complaint is a familiar one—and was a central criticism of the industry-dominated Packard Commission study. Yet there is a contradiction here. The micromanagement charge fails to explain how so much waste, fraud, and abuse has persisted in Pentagon spending practices. One would think that all the thousands of hours of scrutiny on the Hill would have tightened up buying practices and made a coherent whole out of the many contracting enterprises. But even with the adoption of dozens of proposals advertised as "procurement reform," Congress has barely made a dent in DOD's profligate spending practices.

Part of the problem is the limited legislative attention span. Having debated and adopted a series of modest procurement reforms in 1985 and 1986, many legislators sensed that time was needed to "let the dust settle," to provide a breathing space to see if the reforms had the desired effect. There was insufficient follow-up to toughen the incremental measures enacted. Even through the summer of 1988, when the most pervasive "Pentagate" procurement scandals erupted, Congress repeatedly rejected or watered down legislation advanced by reformers intent upon tightening up Pentagon buying practices. The story was a familiar one. At the height of earlier procurement scandals, Senators Pryor and Grassley moved to require more competitive bidding and to curb revolving-door practices that had the industry luring away Pentagon officials to bid on contracts they had been in charge of drawing up. In its key test, this 1985 initiative was rejected by an overwhelming Senate vote of 67–22.[17] The White House and the Pentagon clearly had not cleaned up their act. But neither had Congress. So cowed were legislators by their fear of the "soft on defense" label that they ignored the clear message: sustainable military growth requires both ethical management and vigilant oversight. Ultimately, some revolving-door legislation was passed. But Pentagon efforts at self-policing failed in the interim. And Congress flinched when the issue most needed timely attention.

To the credit of Congress, it should be noted that procurement reform and revolving-door protections are essentially administrative issues on which legislators have seized the initiative. These were issues that had gained virtually no attention in Washington through the 1970s. While reformers were pressing the president's foreign policy prerogatives at every turn and the intelligence community was being turned upside down by a congressional inquisition, the Pentagon was virtually exempt from procedural challenges. The problem was that the authorizing and appropriating committees were firmly in the hands of those who benefited tremendously from the status quo. Even while defense spending was reduced, their home-state bases got funded, and their local plants got the contracts.

Horror stories still abound regarding the excessive zeal of lawmakers intent upon funding home-state military projects. Among the most notorious was a 1986 competition between Kansas and New York for an Air Force trainer aircraft contract: Majority Leader Dole, Republican Senator Alfonse D'Amato, and House Armed Services Committee conferees nearly managed to bring all federal government spending to a temporary standstill over the question of whether the United States would buy a (Kansas-built) Cessna T-37 or a (New York-produced) Fairchild T-46.

Even the most consistent critics of increased military spending get in on the pork-barrel action. Ted Kennedy plumps for the Massachusetts-built F-18 fighter; nuclear freeze advocate Alan Cranston champions the California-built B-1; and Levin of Michigan fights for Detroit's M-1 tank. Occasionally, the liberals' frustration at their sense of misplaced priorities yields extraordinary frankness. Congressman Thomas Downey of New York, an ardent arms control advocate who figured prominently in the T-37 versus T-46 dispute, summed up the dilemma he faced pursuing contracts for his Long Island district:

> This is not what I envisioned my career being, hustling people for weapons. [But] the Texas guys will make sure they rally around LTV, the St. Louis guys around General Dynamics and the Seattle guys around Boeing. The issue is straight jobs. Everything is couched in a national security hue. But that level of analysis stops with the first person who makes the screws for the windshield wiper on the plane.[18]

Rare is the legislator who has not felt similar pressures. Thus, it is lawmakers from states with few DOD contracts—places like Arkansas (Pryor) and Oregon (Hatfield) and Wisconsin (Proxmire)—who feel the fewest political restraints in assailing Pentagon foul-ups.[19]

Ironically, it was the aggressive defense spending of the Reagan years that jarred the Hill committees into a more critical approach. And it was this same spending buildup—with an accompanying surge, then waning, of public support for more Pentagon funding—that sparked an enduring debate about military priorities. The struggle of Congress to meet this challenge proved to be a "forest and trees" problem. Congress focuses on individual saplings—the minutiae of home-state contract awards. Or Congress argues about the overall size of the forest—the annual testy floor debate over what modest percentage change should be made in the defense budget request of the White House. But the abstraction of X billion dollars more for defense is primarily a question of political symbolism. A token percentage change usually has negligible impact upon American security—particularly with the enormous stockpile of DOD funds set aside for previously authorized contracts and excessive inflation allowances. And petty disputes over legislators' home-state interests do little to improve American security; they are irrelevant at best. Legislators have failed to help the Pentagon integrate this clumsy micro/macro mix into a coherent military strategy that can advance security interests. Of course, the same problems beset the executive branch bureaucracy; but here the awkward process is usually hidden from public view and more insulated from political accountability.

The effort to devise a responsible legislative role in defense policymaking has also been severely hampered by legislators' ready demagoguery on the Pentagon budget. Whenever public fears of the Soviets run high (as after the invasion of Afghanistan in 1979), politicians outdo themselves in their eagerness to pour money into defense. Career military officials struggled valiantly in the wake of the post-Vietnam cutbacks to make the case for essential spending on operations, maintenance, and personnel. It was an uphill struggle; they confronted righteous Hill critics and an isolationist public for nearly a decade. Then when public support for a Pentagon buildup finally came, it came with a fury that did not allow time to build a solid foundation. So great was Jimmy Carter's political danger in 1980 of being viewed as "soft on the Russians" that the relatively frugal Democratic president announced an unrealistic five-year budget projection that would have committed more money to defense than even Cap Weinberger proved capable of spending. Carter's last defense budget had little credibility; it was an election-year political document, and the projected figures for the "out years" were just too high. Yet the Trident II submarines, the D-5 missile, cruise missiles, the MX missile, and the Pershing II were all Carter-era weapons that Reagan simply continued to fund as overall defense numbers were bid up in the early 1980s.

Conversely, whenever the budget squeeze is on, there is a widely held opinion on Capitol Hill that the defense budget is a virtual reserve fund for every social spending program that might be imperiled. Attempts are repeatedly made during floor debates to transfer X billion dollars from the Pentagon to aid farmers or the homeless. It is a dialogue ripe for misplaced moralism. With such a simplistic guns versus butter debate, consideration of real defense needs is reduced to empty sloganeering. What is the mission of a 600-ship Navy? What forces should be funded to counter terrorist threats? Should the Air Force still be flying ground-support combat missions? Clearly, many of these questions are beyond the capacity of a congressman from Topeka to resolve; it is the uniformed military and career Defense officials who must provide initial guidance. But there is also a crucial review and oversight role for the popularly elected Congress, which must vote the appropriations. In addition, many vital questions attract only the most desultory of debates in an atmosphere beclouded by political rhetoric. Analyst Larry Smith describes this debilitating polarization:

> For years we have been crippled in trying to reach a sensible basis for defense policy through a ritual with predictable moves. One set of people has instinc-

tively, reflexively opposed virtually any weapons system. The other set, with equal failure to discriminate, has asserted that all weapons systems are equally virtuous, equally deserving of support. We have developed a ritual of indiscrimination, with a heavy moralistic overtone on either side.[20]

Debate over the defense budget—at OMB and the White House no less than on the Hill—has thus become a debate over symbols rather than strategy. Individual weapons systems like the MX missile and the B-1 bomber are singled out for annual debates not so much on their merits but as bellwethers of popular sentiment. They are more like icons to be worshiped or devils to be purged; their strategic rationale is rarely the focus of debate. "One military program after another," journalist James Fallows has observed, "becomes a mere proxy for a general world view that the United States is too weak or too strong."[21] Often these debates are strung out over the course of six or seven years before a binding decision is reached. For example, each year from 1976 through 1982, the Congress had knock-down-drag-out fights over the question of replacing Korean War–era B-52 bombers with the B-1. Similar debates over how to deploy the MX missile have unfolded without resolution each year since 1978. And funding for chemical weapons production start-up has sparked bitter controversy while being discussed ad nauseam for more than a decade. Such debates rarely yield any clear policy direction. The necessity for political compromise often results in a split-the-difference approach: the United States builds half as many of a given system instead of achieving a consensus that full funding is justified or that it should be scrapped altogether. Another budget compromise gimmick, the production stretch-out, inflates the overall cost of weapons in future years in order to meet immediate political needs to reduce spending. Defense contractors welcome it. Vote-hungry legislators find comfort in it. But the public interest and the federal deficit suffer.

Three other factors have added to the difficulty of effectively devising sound executive branch management and sound congressional oversight of defense spending. One is the increased Pentagon reliance on funding programs through the "black budget." Crucial R&D efforts like the Stealth bomber are classified at levels above top secret. At "codeword" level and above, information on these costly programs is accessible to a very limited number of staffers and members of Congress. The budget requests are buried in the overall DOD budget—insulated from routine internal and legislative review and subject to no public debate. A 1988 GAO report on such "special access programs" warned of the DOD practice of "placing growing numbers of programs and amounts of dollars in the special access budget with either the intent, or at least the result, of hiding programmatic or budgetary problems."[22] And Senator Lowell Weicker berated Secretary of Defense Carlucci, noting that "no one seems to know how many special access programs exist and [the secretary's office] does not maintain a listing."[23] Here, where top secrets are at risk, the ability of the Pentagon to intimidate Hill inquisitors seems unimpaired by assertive congressional moves in other areas of international security policymaking.

A second bar to more effective oversight of the defense budget has been the creation of a bow wave effect in the weapons procurement efforts of the Reagan administration. The Reagan team took office only one year after defense spending had begun to rise. As a candidate, Reagan had pledged to greatly expand monies committed to all major defense accounts. His top aides pursued a deliberate strategy of locking the United States into long-term weapons-buying contracts in order to guard against any subsequent diminution of popular support for the defense buildup. As the procurement portion of the budget doubled in less than four years, actual outlays lagged behind—because the first few years of such contracts entailed fewer expenditures.[24] But three to five years after start-up, there was an enormous bulge of spending (like a bow wave on a graph) as assembly lines reached full production under previously signed contracts. Thus, with relatively modest impact on the immediate budget, shrewd administration officials like Navy Secretary John Lehman had won enormous commitments of national resources for the out years of the military budget. When Gramm-Rudman-Hollings forced cuts and Weinberger's successors were required to reduce defense spending, controlling these prior spending commitments was difficult. By mid-1987, the Defense Department had accumulated some $300 billion in unfunded defense contracts for the coming half-decade. Weinberger had resigned, and Lehman had left to open his own defense consulting operation. But Congress was left with few responsible options for controlling the bow wave. Scrapping production plans would mean wasting the substantial sums already spent—and literally getting nothing for the money. Such contract terminations often require large severance payments. Stretching out the length of the production schedule would only increase unit costs and ensure that final payments would be made in future, inevitably inflated, dollars. Finally, even if the costly weapons projects were completed, funds to operate and maintain them would be hard to come by on the Hill. "Budgets are shrinking," a key Center for Defense Information study noted in 1987, "just as the new weapons are coming off the production lines, and funding readiness and sustainability is becoming fodder for the fiscal retreat."[25]

A third weakness besetting efforts to establish defense priorities has been the failure of both the Pentagon and Congress to get on top of the "consultant problem." This issue lay at the heart of the Pentagate scandals of 1988. It was equally infuriating to Pentagon military officers and Hill legislators. The source of the dilemma lies in the way the United States buys weapons. Each military service has its own wish list related to strategy and mission—and subject to intense interservice rivalry and resultant duplication. Legislators have their individual pet projects and home-state priorities. But the key determinant is often a layer of civilian weapons-buyers sandwiched in the middle. These are men and women from the private defense industry who come to Pentagon weapons-buying jobs and then usually return to industry after their stints in the public sector. They are the contracting and production specialists who know what it takes to produce military hardware and make a profit in the business world. They are uniquely skilled in this area. But the revolving door on their government offices is vulnerable to extraordinary abuse, particularly since Pentagon salaries pale in comparison to those offered by the booming defense industry. At the heart of the 1988 Pentagate scandals was the reality that few military officers or Hill legislators really have a handle on weapons buying. It is the weapons-buying consultants and contract writers—an industry that does some $10 billion in business each year, according to GAO estimates—who dominate this key policy realm.[26] "There's just a different ethic between the troops and the political appointees," lamented one Navy officer at the height of the 1988 procurement scandals. "The guy who's going to pay is the sailor sweating down in the boiler room in some ship out there in the Persian Gulf."[27]

Even before the stories about $640 toilet seats and procurement scams broke, Congress was taking halting steps to address its shortcomings in performing defense policy oversight. Ironically, many of these moves are associated with the discredited political ambitions of Coloradan Gary Hart, who fought tenaciously for reform in defense policymaking during his Senate tenure.[28] An organizational beginning was made in 1985, when a coalition of budget-conscious moderates led by Senators Nancy Kassebaum and David Pryor, together with Congressmen Mel Levine of California and Denny Smith of Oregon, established the Military Reform Caucus to focus on procurement issues. Despite a series of initial legislative setbacks, this coalition of members—few of whom served on the military authorizing committees—demonstrated a willingness to question key Pentagon practices without fear of the "soft on defense" label. There were even a few notable successes: for example, in 1985, caucus cochairman Smith, a conservative Republican, pressed successfully, and almost single-handedly, for cancellation of the Army's flawed $1.8 billion Divad gun program. Congress also established an independent inspector general's office at the Pentagon, as well as an operational testing and evaluations office, and a new procurement czar.

It was a measure of this new reformist zeal that House reformers in 1985 took the extraordinary step of unseating the chairman of the House Armed Services Committee, Democrat Mel Price of Illinois. A coup was effected by Les Aspin, who vaulted over four more senior members to seize this key post in a House democratic Caucus struggle. Aspin moved the committee toward more thorough and effective oversight; yet he had his own political troubles with House liberals, which limited his room for maneuver.[29] In less dramatic fashion, the replacement of Barry Goldwater by Sam Nunn—who became chairman of the Senate Armed Services Committee with the new Democratic Senate majority seated in January 1987—brought a fundamentally new approach to congressional review of DOD budgets. Nunn promptly convened three months of mission-oriented budget hearings in which Pentagon requests were weighed primarily as component parts of an overall national security strategy. It was a measure of how far-gone the process was that this commonsense approach was considered a landmark departure at the time.

These congressional initiatives went forward in the wake of an extraordinary defense buildup, the first time in U.S. history that Pentagon budgets had risen for seven consecutive years. These increases enjoyed consensus support on the Hill, even though they helped produce a doubling of the national deficit, and despite the fact that they were unaccompanied by any substantial redistribution of the defense burden among American partners in NATO, Japan, and South Korea. Especially puzzling was the absence of any "great debate" on the burden-sharing issue. These were years of impassioned debate about budget shortfalls and the balance-of-trade deficit. And allied trade practices combined with slumping economic competitiveness at home were battering the dollar exchange rate. But there was little sustained and focused discussion about the failure of Europe and Japan to commit more of their own resources to Western security. Part of the explanation was the eagerness of the Pentagon to maintain voters' backing for costly European programs like the INF deployments.

The need to guard against any erosion of support for the Atlantic alliance led to all kinds of numbers juggling, as former Assistant Secretary of Defense for International Security Policy Richard Perle testified in 1988: "The exercise of preparing the annual report on burden sharing is largely an exercise of thinking of ways to put the best gloss on some pretty dismal figures. . . . We look for statistics that make the allies look good."[30] But the numbers are inescapable. The United States spends more than $50 billion each year to deploy half a million troops in Europe and the Far East, and the nation's strategic nuclear forces serve allied interests as well. Americans spent $1,115 per capita for defense in 1987, versus $488 in Britain and $453 in West Germany. Americans spent nearly 7 percent of their gross national product on defense, the Japanese just one percent.[31] Even the most pro-NATO Europeans wondered how the Americans tolerated the disparity. As the venerable *Economist* editorialized:

> Future historians will scratch their heads when asked to contemplate the fact that the United States, with fewer people and less government spending than Western Europe, nevertheless provides most of Europe's nuclear protection, a large chunk of its non-nuclear defense, and almost all of the men, ships, and aircraft which guard the Gulf oil that European industry depends on while Europe provides no reciprocal service for the United States.[32]

But while Europeans could marvel, Americans approached the subject only for fringe demagoguery, not serious debate. The legacy of the Atlanticist consensus, and the cold calculation that Americans would have to act responsibly even if Europeans were unwilling to, led to a virtual silencing of any legislative proposals to address the growing disparities of burden sharing. Mainstream legislators of both parties were keenly aware of the horrid legacy of congressional isolationism between the two world wars. And history had not treated kindly the calls for retreat, from William Borah on the right to George McGovern on the left. Fear of the isolationist label postponed indefinitely any serious questioning about the basic fairness of how the Western defense spending burden was shared.

Through the years of the Reagan buildup, Congress did initiate one enduring debate about defense spending priorities. The question of nuclear versus conventional spending presented clear choices about military strategy. Should the United States buy more new nuclear systems to modernize and refine its deterrent? Or should the United States commit more resources to improving conventional military capabilities—more ammunition and antitank weapons and fuel—thereby raising the nuclear threshold? The issues were fundamental. But the otherwise thoughtful debate was hampered by the thinly disguised political motives of key disputants. Advocates of the Pentagon's nuclear buildup were pitted against champions of more aggressive nuclear arms reductions efforts. Indeed, the nuclear versus conventional debate was framed by Hill Democrats as a way to curb the Reagan defense spending boom without being vulnerable to the antidefense charge. The strategy adopted under the leadership of Democratic Senator Carl Levin was to call for substantial slashes in key nuclear weapons programs—but to offer to transfer the budget savings to underfunded operations and maintenance accounts. Levin charged the Reagan administration with spending "too much for fancy aircraft, vulnerable surface ships and redundant strategic nuclear weapons, while spending too little on the nuts and bolts and staying power of conventional-forces readiness."[33] His transfer amendments provided critics with a chance to be *for* something on defense—for the unglamorous operations and maintenance accounts, for pay raises for service personnel—while opposing key parts of the Reagan nuclear modernization effort. Here, finally, was a serious Hill debate about military spending priorities. The "guns versus guns" argument was used effectively to introduce some restraint into nuclear modernization. And it ensured that all the new weapons coming down the line would have the support necessary to maintain them. Indeed, it was in such challenges to the strategic nuclear weapons plans of both the Carter and Reagan administrations that the modern Congress has proved most successful in altering international security priorities.

CONGRESS AND NUCLEAR WEAPONS:
CHALLENGING EXECUTIVE AUTHORITY

The success of Congress in checking presidential moves on nuclear weapons policy has been a direct result of the closeness of the legislative branch to the voters. Time and time again in the nuclear age, Congress has manifested popular will in crossing the executive on nuclear policy initiatives. Sometimes more hawkish than the White House, often more skeptical of spending for new nuclear weapons systems, Congress has not been shy about placing its imprimatur on proposals from the Baruch Plan to the B-1 bomber. In so doing, Congress has demonstrated both the ignorance of a general populace awed by devastating nuclear technology and the common sense of a people not about to be hoodwinked by the mumbo jumbo of the more doctrinaire Pentagon strategic thinkers.

For the first thirty years of the atomic age, Congress moved only in *reaction* to the executive on nuclear matters. The legislature was an inherently conservative force, reacting to revelations about the Manhattan Project with a firm insistence that every kind of nuclear research be kept secret.[34] The Congress reacted to news in 1949 of the Soviet atomic bomb with a pell-mell rush into foreign military aid and support for developing a U.S. hydrogen bomb. The 1957 launching of Sputnik by the Soviets spurred allegations in Congress of a "missile gap" and gave rise to programs to challenge the Soviets for mastery in developing space rockets for both scientific exploration and nuclear weapons delivery systems. These were issues that legislators like John Kennedy and Lyndon Johnson exploited effectively in their presidential campaigns.[35] Similarly, during the 1962 crisis over the Soviet deployment of nuclear missiles in Cuba, Capitol Hill was the source of the most bellicose proposals. Sentiment on the Hill leaned towards an immediate bombing of the Cuban missile sites, if not a full-scale U.S. invasion.

But as skepticism of presidential authority grew during the Vietnam War years, so too did the ability of liberals in Congress to reshape White House initiatives on nuclear weapons policy. The bellwether debate came in 1969, when the Senate nearly scrapped funding for antiballistic missile systems; the skepticism in Congress forced President Nixon to seek a prompt agreement with the Soviets for mutual curbs on ABM deployments. By the time Ronald Reagan assumed the presidency a decade later, there occurred the striking phenomenon of Congress not simply moving to check the executive—the legislature actually tried to initiate international negotiations on key arms control questions, like nuclear testing bans, by freezing funding of certain military programs. Liberals in Congress seized the diplomatic reins to curb funding for certain U.S. military programs (so long as the Soviets showed parallel restraint). Early in the 1980s, grass-roots pressure from the movement for a bilateral nuclear deployment freeze, as manifested in Congress, hastened President Reagan's return to the negotiating table with the Soviets. For a time, pro-freeze sentiment helped the Hill to set the parameters for the Reagan arms control negotiating agenda and kept White House proposals for new nuclear deployments like the MX missile on a short leash. But U.S. deployments of INF systems in 1984, the Soviet walkout from Geneva, and Reagan's landslide reelection blunted support in Congress for the bilateral freeze proposal.

There is a striking paradox in the assertive nuclear weapons policymaking by Congress that has occurred since the beginning of the Nixon administration. It was *liberals* who first mastered the legislative tools and mustered the political will to reshape executive branch nuclear policy initiatives. Liberals doomed ABM in 1969. Liberals first stalled MX production in the 1970s. Liberals limited funding for the Strategic Defense Initiative in the 1980s. But it was *conservatives* in Congress who won perhaps the most significant arms control battle, blocking SALT II ratification and setting back efforts to ratify a strategic arms reduction treaty for more than ten years. Led by Democratic Senator Henry Jackson, Hill conservatives used their muscle as early as 1972 to set parameters for SALT II. They made "detente" such a dirty word under the Ford presidency that the whole policy—and any prospect of transforming the accords reached by U.S. and Soviet negotiators at Vladivostok into an arms reduction pact—was shelved for the 1976 campaign. And conservatives kept the B-1 bomber alive throughout the Carter administration. Finally, congressional conservatives were so successful in asserting the existence of a "window of vulnerability" through which land-based U.S. intercontinental ballistic missiles (ICBMs) could be destroyed that they ensured that the key strategic debates of the early 1980s would proceed on their terms.

The legacy of these enduring debates is one of severe polarization. Differences among policymakers have grown so sharp that it is important to sort out areas of change from those of continuity in recent nuclear policymaking struggles between the White House and Capitol Hill.

FUNDING STRATEGIC MODERNIZATION

It is an extraordinary challenge for a democracy to pursue rational policymaking in a field as ripe for demagoguery as nuclear deterrence. Isn't it immoral to buy more weapons of mass destruction when human needs at home go unfunded? What about the callousness of forgoing possible protections against Soviet nuclear attack—how can politicians leave their people defenseless? Such rhetorical questions highlight the emotionally charged nature of nuclear policy questions and the degree to which this Washington policy debate hinges on theoretical psychology. "If the Soviets attack our missiles in Europe, will they believe that we'll launch nuclear missiles from the United States when we know that will provoke an attack on our homeland?" This lends itself to all sorts of convoluted readings of nuclear doctrine.

Such an abstract debate was at the heart of the first key nuclear funding challenge by Capitol Hill, the August 1969 ABM dispute. The Senate came within one vote of halting new funding because legislators did not believe that defense against massive nuclear missile attacks was possible; legislators worried that an ABM deployment race would lead to a costly, destabilizing, and ultimately futile search for nuclear "superiority." This congressional challenge had extraordinarily far-reaching consequences. It laid the groundwork for legislative-executive consensus on basic strategic weapons issues. It set the ball in motion for the ABM and SALT I agreements. And it enshrined U.S. reliance on a stable deterrent—composed of the triad of land-, sea-, and air-based nuclear weapons delivery systems—for security in a new age of nuclear parity between the superpowers.

This interbranch consensus frayed when Presidents Ford and Carter moved toward conclusion of a SALT II treaty based upon a framework agreed to at Vladivostok in 1975. It began to unravel because linkage advocates were suspicious of moves that might lull Americans into a false sense of security in relations with an aggressive Soviet leadership. But the first key post-ABM dispute over funding for strategic weapons modernization also tore at the fabric of this consensus between Congress and the White House. When President Carter moved early in his administration to cancel the B-1 bomber, congressional critics were outraged. The Hill was furious not simply because the President had "cashed in" a negotiating chip without any offsetting Soviet concession. The Carter move raised questions about the staying power of the triad deterrent as well. How credible was an air leg of the triad that rode upon the wings of a Korean war–era bomber? The Air Force was angry as well: how could men be sent on patrol for another decade in bombers older than the pilots? Carter promised a program of air-launched cruise missiles—and in political extremis, his aides leaked highly classified details of research on the new radar-eluding "Stealth" bomber, which promised to be more capable of penetrating Soviet air defenses.[36]

B-1 critics in Congress might have weathered the Air Force's criticism and concern for the viability of the nuclear triad. But the determination of defense contractors involved in the debate posed an even more formidable challenge. The principal builder of the B-1, Rockwell International of California, had worked assiduously for years spreading subcontracts to plants throughout the United States. This grass-roots job dispersal strategy created a remarkably diverse and effective lobby for full funding of the plane by Congress. Businesses in more than 400 of the nation's 435 congressional districts stood to gain from B-1 contracts, as did forty-eight of the fifty states.[37] It was only after a bitter and costly Hill fight that Carter succeeded in suspending immediate production of the plane—thereby escaping the fate of the Kennedy administration, which had been defeated in a similar 1961 fight when an irate House Armed Services Committee majority voted to "direct, order, mandate and require" the secretary of defense to purchase a congressionally favored B-70 bomber.[38] Though Carter halted full-scale production, the contractors' B-1 team was kept intact and ready for start-up in January 1981 when Reagan took office.

The sanctity of the nuclear triad was again at issue in the struggle over modernization of land-based ICBMs. Here Congress and the Carter White House reversed roles, with the Hill skeptical of the President's MX deployment proposals and the White House determined to proceed on prompt improvement of the land leg of the triad. The MX debate took on new urgency after the collapse of SALT II ratification and the Soviet invasion of Afghanistan. Conservative political winds were blowing on Capitol Hill, and widespread frustration at the holding of American hostages in Iran intensified the storm.

The Carter administration had already laid a hawkish foundation: the President had funded the Trident II and D-5 missile modernization program for strategic submarines; three separate cruise missile programs were moving forward; at Carter's instigation, the NATO alliance had committed to a two-track approach to INF missile modernization; and as a gambit to win Senator Nunn's support for SALT II ratification, the White House had tabled a projected five-year defense budget calling for extraordinarily large percentage increases each year. Nevertheless, critics of SALT II on Capitol Hill were unrelenting in their complaint that the United States trailed the Soviets in the subcategory of multiple-warhead ICBMs. The Soviet lead in heavy land-based missiles (less accurate but more powerful than U.S. systems) worried many on the Hill who were uncomfortable with asymmetries in U.S. and Soviet nuclear forces. These concerns were effectively exploited by private lobbying groups like the Committee on the Present Danger: using graphic displays, these lobbyists spread fears that the Soviet weapons were bigger, ignoring offsetting U.S. advantages in ICBM accuracy, as well as in sea- and air-based nuclear deterrents.

President Carter therefore felt it to be essential to press for agreement on how to deploy the ten-warhead MX missile. However, no consensus was reached regarding any deployment scheme that met the declared objective of enhancing the survivability of U.S. land-based missiles. When Carter officials maintained a commitment to a variant of the shell game known as the "racetrack scheme," conservative legislators from western states who were concerned about massive land and water requirements teamed with liberals who were skeptical about the need and cost to shelve the plan.

From this troubled beginning as a symbolic response to a political crisis, the MX debate developed a life of its own. Throughout the dispute, divisions within the executive branch hampered efforts to sell Congress on a production and deployment commitment. One study of the debacle by an MX supporter laid the blame for congressional reservations at the feet of the President's team:

> These reservations largely reflected internal disagreements within the executive branch. In the case of the MX, an entire history of executive branch confusion and inadvertence [strengthened Hill opposition], including such a

variety of basing schemes that it was inescapably clear that there was no consensus even within the executive branch as to how to proceed.[39]

Ronald Reagan campaigned in 1980 against an alleged "window of vulnerability"—charging that unless Washington moved swiftly to deploy mobile land-based ICBMs, the Soviets could wipe out the missiles in a first strike and the United States would be unable or unwilling to respond. A number of analysts questioned this premise, however; it ignored the redundancy of the triad's sea- and air-based legs, especially new, highly accurate U.S. sea-launched ballistic missiles (SLBMs). One modern American sub can wipe out the Soviets' 240 largest cities in a devastating SLBM attack. The vulnerability argument also ignored the devastation that would ensue from even a "surgical" Soviet first strike, an attack that the Kremlin would know invited massive retaliation. But the fact that ICBMs were in fixed sites, and thus targetable, and the fact that the Soviets might be reluctant to reduce their reliance on land-based heavy missiles loaded with so much destructive power if American diplomats had no system of its own to "cash in," were transformed into a broader theory of U.S. vulnerability.

This theory gained widespread acceptance with many of the nation's most respected nuclear strategists. On Capitol Hill, it soon became a catechism that the window of vulnerability had to be closed before the nation would be secure. Key Democrats and Republicans embraced this idea as gospel. Few in Congress rose to challenge the basic premise—that a whole new land-based system was needed to replace the modern Minuteman in concrete silos. And this doctrine of ICBM vulnerability drove the debate for nearly a decade, pushing the dispute over MX deployments into extraordinary contortions.

This debate was essentially about the cost of acquiring mobility, about getting U.S. land-based ICBMs out of easily targeted missile silos. When the new president assumed office, he peopled his national security bureaucracy with aides from the Committee on the Present Danger: Rostow, Nitze, Perle, Rowny, and (later) Adelman. Quite naturally, they took the MX off the shelf and pressed for its prompt deployment. But the Reagan team was deeply divided within itself over what role arms control would play in the coming defense build-up. These divisions hurt them on the Hill as they sought to sell first one, then another MX basing scheme. The Reagan military team, despite enjoying strong support on Capitol Hill through the President's first term, failed to come up with a basing scheme acceptable to a pliable Congress.

The MX became the missile without a home. Secretary Weinberger was determined to have a new land-based system with which to counter the Soviet heavy missiles and desperately cast about for a consensus alternative. One effort after another was ostentatiously delivered to the Armed Services committees: elaborate proposals with charts and graphs tagged with unfortunate acronyms like DUMB (deep underground missile basing) and CSB (closely spaced basing, or dense-pack). Fully thirty-seven different basing plans were reviewed, and nearly a dozen were sent to Capitol Hill for serious consideration. But in the meantime, even the Pentagon's biggest boosters on Capitol Hill were hard-pressed to defend MX funding. As Reagan's national security adviser Robert McFarlane later observed ruefully: "From 1981 to 1985, when we had the money and popular support for renewal of our strategic forces, the Pentagon's civilian leadership fumbled the opportunity through ineptitude and hubris."[40] Consequently, the MX program was cut repeatedly through the early 1980s. Finally, the Reagan administration fell back to a familiar strategy, calling for a truce with critics on the Hill while a bipartisan commission studied the issue anew. Under the leadership of General Brent Scowcroft, this panel prepared a blueprint for the future of American strategic forces. Scowcroft had great credibility with Congress, based upon his respected service as President Ford's national security adviser. But when the Scowcroft Commission's study could do no better than recommend that the MX missiles be put in those same, allegedly vulnerable ICBM silos, the MX program appeared doomed.

On the Hill, hawks and doves alike looked upon this interim "solution" with considerable scorn; the raison d'être for the MX had been mobility. (Few were willing to spend $30–40 billion on a missile as a bargaining chip to cash in at START.) The balance of power in the bitter congressional debate was held by a handful of powerful Democrats, including Aspin and Nunn. They sought to obtain leverage to energize the less-than-determined Reagan administration commitment to negotiated arms reductions by continuing conditional support for the President's MX schemes. But by 1985, the original program of 200 missiles met with overwhelming opposition in Congress. In a Reagan loss that marked a stunning departure from his otherwise free hand on defense, the program was capped at production of only fifty missiles until a survivable basing mode was agreed to. Never before had a major strategic weapons program been cut back so drastically by binding legislation.

Discussion of other mobile ICBM alternatives proceeded without decision year after year. In the 1988 debate on the Department of Defense authorization bill, a deal was cut that called for funding a railroad car–based MX and a single-warhead Midgetman missile with roughly equal dollar amounts. The two programs relied on virtually opposite strategic rationales—"to MIRV or not to MIRV" was the question they answered differently. But the stalemate on the Hill left it to Reagan's successors in the Bush Administration to set priorities and pass judgment on the latest MX proposal for a "rail garrison" deployment: launching MX missiles from railroad cars, which would be flushed out into the nation's commercial rail system in time of crisis.[41] The debate of the experts on nuclear doctrine was unending. But to Hill critics, it seemed that the worry was self-created. In the end, as former national security adviser McGeorge Bundy noted, "nothing ever came through the window of vulnerability that was so fearfully predicted in the 1970s, and it fell to a panel that Ronald Reagan appointed—the Scowcroft Commission—to make it clear in 1983 that this particular window had never been open in the first place."[42]

From the doctrinal struggles attendant to the MX, there arose two corollary debates that continue to dominate nuclear policymaking. The first was an initiative uniquely congressional: the Midgetman missile. Critics of the MX on Capitol Hill were eager to address the program's deficiencies on its own terms. And liberals were determined to have an alternative missile system that they were *for*, in order to escape the antidefense tag that had been nearly fatal with voters in the early 1980s. If the problem posed by putting a ten-warhead MX in a fixed silo was that it invited a first strike (because it would be such a high-value target), then the solution would be to disperse targets through deployment of a single-warhead ICBM in hundreds of silos. From such logic, the Midgetman was born; Pentagon critics even took to calling it the "Congressman." On Capitol Hill, it was considered a "Democratic" weapon, being championed by Senator Gore and Congressman Aspin. In spite of considerable Pentagon skepticism, these legislators pushed the program relentlessly, securing research and development funding and ensuring that monies would be available for the Midgetman to compete with the MX through the end of the decade.[43]

A second outgrowth of the MX debate was the wrangle over SDI. Here was an initiative taken by the President himself with virtually no consultation outside of a handful of White House political advisers. The program was born in March 1983, when the President faced mounting opposition in Congress to soaring defense budget requests. At the time, the nation was also being swept by a grass-roots campaign for a mutual U.S.-Soviet freeze on all nuclear weapons testing, production, and deployment.[44] And the MX was once again on the ropes, facing a series of key Hill votes. In a brilliant political stroke, the President countered by changing the entire nature of the defense debate. On March 23, 1983, the President stunned even the most hawkish of his Pentagon advisers by calling, in a nationally televised, prime-time speech, for research and construction of a defensive system to make nuclear weapons "impotent and obsolete." With characteristic optimism, the President dismissed nay-sayers and challenged scientists to produce a system that skeptics said would never work.

The Reagan SDI speech virtually ignored the $1.5 billion the United States was spending annually on ABM-related research, suggesting instead that the nation was standing still in the field. The President called for a new crash program to exploit technologies developed since the 1972 ABM pact was signed. His call for an astrodome-type defense of the United States, a "peace shield" (immediately dubbed "Star Wars" by the national press), sparked the imaginations of the uninitiated. Why not *defend*, instead of relying upon the blackmail of deterrence, which threatened only massive retaliation and mutual annihilation? The SDI proposal responded directly to the vulnerability concerns for which the MX was designed—even if few in the Pentagon believed it would ever work as advertised. And the SDI proposal had the virtue of distracting critics—who were left open to the charge that they were against defending American cities.

Liberals on the Hill were appalled by the President's move to undermine the ABM Treaty. Didn't he recognize that Star Wars might undermine START by inviting the addition of still more offensive Soviet missiles—cheaper than defense—to overwhelm any such system? Didn't the President understand that any SDI command and control systems would become the first targets at the outset of a nuclear conflict? And what about the fact that such a costly system would involve orbiting nuclear weapons, trillions of dollars, and decades of expanded nuclear testing—with no guarantee that it would ever work? For skeptics, the President's gambit to reverse the Pentagon's fortunes on the Hill threatened to undermine the central premises of arms control.

In the face of such criticism, the President pressed ahead with the faith of a true believer. Important victories were won: annual spending on ABM research steadily rose from less than $2 billion to more than $4 billion. The notion of constructing an impenetrable astrodome over North America fell rather swiftly into disrepute; even a 90 percent effective system would result in widespread devastation of the United States if 10 percent of the Soviets' more than 10,000 strategic nuclear warheads got through an SDI defense. But the idea of limited defense, once buried by the 1972 ABM pact, was resuscitated and slowly regained political legitimacy, however dubious the prospects for its realization. By the end of his presidency, Reagan had not only succeeded in challenging the fundamental premises of the ABM Treaty; he had unmistakably gotten the Soviets' attention as well. Indeed, many analysts credited Soviet concerns that SDI might work—or at least might spur yet another costly round of the arms race—with stimulating the new Kremlin readiness evident under Mikhail Gorbachev to deal on arms reduction pacts. By 1988, the Reagan initiative had even succeeded in producing new U.S. programs for research on antimissile systems offering "point" defense of military installations—programs that might prove especially promising to nations like Israel, which is surrounded by burgeoning arsenals of ballistic missiles and chemical weapons.[45] Expanded ABM research and development became a program institutionalized for the long term—even if transformed into an imperfect effort to defend ICBM silos and no longer promising "defense" of American cities.

President Reagan's SDI campaign confounded the experts and changed the terms of the whole nuclear debate. Politically, it was a no-lose proposition. SDI critics on the Hill were vulnerable to the charge that they would leave Americans defenseless against nuclear attack, that they supported the "immoral" doctrine of mutual assured destruction. And when the program failed to pan out as originally advertised, opponents were vulnerable to criticism for making allegedly "debilitating" and "irresponsible" cuts in the enormous Pentagon SDI funding requests.[46] In the end, despite widespread doubts about its efficacy that were shared by liberals and conservatives on Capitol Hill, SDI developed a life of its own. Its justification was ever shifting: at first, it was to be an astrodome to protect the populace; then it embodied the more familiar plan of reducing the severity of any attack on missile fields; at other times, it was the bargaining chip credited with bringing the Soviets back to the START negotiating table. But in the Reagan years, it was never "cashed in" by a president who believed perhaps more than any of his advisers that it was a panacea for the security of future generations.

Capitol Hill debates on SDI funding became almost theological; several days each year were consumed arguing over incremental changes. Should the President's request for a 30 percent funding increase be cut by $400 million or $500 million? Should the program grow at a rate of 7 percent or 9 percent? Ultimately, funding leveled off when the White House insisted that it was free to test components (none of which were yet ready to be tested), in violation of the traditional interpretation of the ABM Treaty. This attempt at ABM Treaty "reinterpretation" led to confrontations with both Capitol Hill critics and Soviet diplomats. In 1987, the White House lost the crucial support of Sam Nunn, who coauthored with Senator Levin legislation barring any SDI testing under the new White House ABM Treaty interpretation drafted by Abraham Sofaer at the State Department.[47] The President's determination not to reaffirm U.S. ABM Treaty commitments also slowed efforts to conclude a START treaty after nearly eight years of discussion. A half-decade after its inception, McGeorge Bundy concluded that SDI appeared "to have only one clear result. Its technical promise remains uncertain, its costs unpredictable, and even its purpose far from clear. But it has become a powerful barrier across the path of arms control."[48]

The debates on the B-1, the MX, and SDI offer evidence of a steady growth in the power of Congress on basic questions of nuclear strategy and international security. While Congress has been relatively ineffectual in altering the overall shape of defense policy, it has had an extraordinary impact on a select group or weapons decisions. Indeed, the annual defense budget debate is now marked by predictable disputes over one or two big-ticket items. Members have come to expect prolonged donnybrooks over funding for high-profile programs like the MX or B-1—indeed, members relish these confrontations for the leverage they afford those holding swing votes. Key nuclear weapons systems have developed a symbolism in the political life of the nation bigger even than the costly programs themselves. They represent essential tests for the end-of-session scorecards that both liberal and conservative lobbying groups maintain on legislative votes. Struggles over such icons have emboldened the Congress in related fields. Moratoriums have been initiated in areas like testing of antisatellite weapons (ASATS) and have been forced upon the President by Congress for as long as the Soviets adhere to a similar ban. And where Senate conservatives frustrated President Carter's drive to ratify SALT II and negotiate a comprehensive test ban, liberals in Congress repeatedly pressed a reluctant Reagan White House to take new initiatives in pursuit of negotiated U.S.-Soviet arms reductions. Through such means, arms control efforts have increasingly become a three-ring circus. The president negotiates with the Soviet leadership; the president negotiates with Congress; and Congress instructs the White House through the legislative process to make new proposals directly to Kremlin leaders. Thus, in nuclear weapons policymaking no less than in the broader realm of foreign affairs, with each passing day a new level of complexity is added to the challenge of charting America's course in a dangerous world. A model for more effective burden sharing by policymakers at both ends of Pennsylvania Avenue still escapes us.

NOTES

1. President's Blue Ribbon Commission on Defense Management (Packard Commission), *Interim Report to the President*, February 28, 1986, pp. 5-6.
2. Eisenhower noted in his January 17, 1961 farewell address that "the potential for the disastrous rise of misplaced power [in this "military-industrial complex"] exists and will persist." See *Public Papers of the Presidents: Dwight D. Eisenhower, 1960-1961*, p. 1038.
3. DOD's insistence that an arbitrary percentage was vital to national security cost the administration the support of the Republican majority on the Senate Budget Committee. In 1983, Chairman Pete Domenici rejected a personal plea from President Reagan and led a 17-4 vote to limit the fiscal year 1984 defense spending increase to only 5 percent (see Smith, *Power Game*, pp. 210-12).
4. During his 1984 presidential campaign, Jackson regularly called for across-the-board reductions in defense. In his 1988 bid, he pressed Governor Michael Dukakis to call for a freeze in defense spending levels and to make

cuts in the out years totaling $60 billion. See, for example, Jackson's May 24, 1988 address to the World Affairs Council of Southern California, reprinted in *World Affairs Journal* (Summer 1988): 28.

5. Congressman Jim Courter, as quoted in David C. Morrison, "Chaos on Capitol Hill," *National Journal*, September 27, 1986, p. 2302.

6. President Washington balked at providing all relevant documents to representatives investigating the disastrous battle, asserting executive privilege. But Congress pressed ahead with a thorough review of the military's performance (see Frederick M. Kaiser, "The Congress and the President: Allies and Adversaries in National Defense Policy," *CRS Review* [January 1988] : 8). A February 1986 report of the GAO estimated that an annual average of 1,306 Pentagon witnesses spend 1,420 hours testifying before 84 committees and subcommittees of Congress.

7. The early Reagan-era procurement scandals also featured shocking stories—ultimately confirmed—of contractors burying overhead costs by marking up prices on, for example, a $1,100 cap for a chair leg, a $9,600 wrench, and a $2,000 nut.

8. Richard Godwin, as quoted in "Pentagon Procurement Has Armor That Repels Reform," *New York Times*, September 27, 1987, p. 4.

9. Senator Barry Goldwater, *Congressional Record*, October 3, 1985, p. S12532.

10. Ironically, Weinberger earned high marks from military critics on the Hill for his reluctance to commit U.S. forces to battle. In Lebanon, the Persian Gulf, and Central America, Weinberger was notably less willing to use U.S. troops than his counterparts at the State Department. Career military officials welcomed Weinberger's caution, which kept them out of confrontations with irregular forces in the field and guarded against the danger that public support for U.S. defense spending increases would be squandered by involvement in an unpopular and protracted Third World conflict.

11. U.S. spending on national defense requirements exceeds $300 billion annually. Some argue that the total bill should include more than just the annual Pentagon budget for weapons procurement, personnel, operations, and maintenance. Also to be considered are the Department of Energy budget for nuclear weapons production, veterans' benefits, and money spent to secure foreign base rights for U.S. military facilities.

12. Sundquist, *Decline and Resurgence*, p. 119. In October 1988, Congress adopted legislation facilitating closure of antiquated military bases. The measure allows an independent panel to present DOD and Congress with a list of facilities to be closed that Congress can review only on an all-or-nothing basis.

13. The nation's top ten defense contracting firms gave an average of $13,000 in PAC contributions to members of military authorizing and appropriating committees for the 1986 elections. Some $236,000 was also given directly to these members in honoraria (see "Defense Firms Court Con-

gress," *USA Today*, June 24, 1988, p. 4). The chairman of the House Military Appropriations Subcommittee, Democrat William Chappel of Florida, received over $130,000 from these ten contractors in 1985–1986.

14. Morrison, "Chaos on Capitol Hill," p. 2303. For details on the following year's debate, see "A Military Bill Like None Other," *New York Times*, May 13, 1987, p. B12.

15. Center for Defense Information, "Trivial Pursuits: Congress's Way with Military Policy," *Baltimore Sun*, May 8, 1987, p. 9.

16. Senator Sam Nunn, as quoted in Morrison, "Chaos on Capitol Hill," p. 2302.

17. *Congressional Record*, May 20, 1985, p. S6559.

18. Congressman Thomas Downey, as quoted in *Washington Post*, July 3, 1988, p. A8.

19. See "New Breed of Military Reformer," *New York Times*, October 12, 1985, p. B8.

20. Larry Smith, as quoted in Fallows, *National Defense*, p. 177.

21. Ibid.

22. As cited in *Washington Times*, June 29, 1988, p. 3.

23. Senator Lowell Weicker, as quoted in ibid.

24. The procurement portion of the DOD budget grew by 25 percent for each of the first two years of the Reagan tenure, then by 17 percent in 1983. By 1988, weapons procurement consumed $81 billion of the $291 billion Pentagon appropriation, with another $44 billion going to R&D for weapons programs (see "The Pentagon Is Learning to Live with Less," *New York Times*, April 3, 1988, p. E5).

25. Stephen Daggett, "Up the Mountain and Along the Plateau: New Adventures of the Military Budget," a Center for Defense Information study, *Arms Control Today* (April 1986): 15. See also Flora Lewis, "A Lethal Defense Legacy," *New York Times*, December 1, 1987, p. 27.

26. In fiscal year 1987, the Pentagon reported spending only $155 million on consulting contracts, but the GAO subsequently found $2.8 billion in spending a more reliable, but still conservative, number. When the GAO included management reviews, special studies, and R&D support services, the price tag for fiscal year 1987 came to $18 billion (see speech of Senator David Pryor, "Consultants in the Pentagon," *Congressional Record*, June 21, 1988, p. S8293).

27. As quoted in "Scandal Pushes Apart Two Worlds Under One Roof," *New York Times*, June 29, 1988, p. 20.

28. See Hart's tract on military reform, *America Can Win* (coauthored with William S. Lind).

29. Aspin was himself almost the victim of a countercoup when liberals who were furious with his support for the MX joined with conservatives who were upset with his challenges to the Pentagon. This bid to unseat him fell short, however, and the chastised Aspin retained the gavel. One ironic

effect of Aspin's scare was that he became more reluctant than before to challenge dubious pork-barrel requests from his fellow legislators; as a consequence, the House Defense authorization bill became loaded down with questionable spending commitments.

30.   Richard Perle, testimony before House Armed Services Committee, February 2, 1988, as quoted in Congresswoman Patricia Schroeder, "The Burden-Sharing Numbers Racket," *New York Times*, April 16, 1988, p. 27.

31.   Figures from the Congressional Budget Office, as cited in Schroeder, "The Burden-Sharing Numbers Racket."

32.   *Economist*, May 18, 1984, as quoted in Senator William V. Roth, Jr., "Sharing the Burden of European Defense," *Christian Science Monitor*, December 3, 1984, p. 38.

33.   Senator Carl Levin, "Golden Arms, Leaden Readiness," *New York Times*, September 5, 1984, p. 23.

34.   Congress pressed restrictive legislation like the 1946 McMahon Act, which rested on the basic premise that all nuclear matters were top secret and, if withheld, could preserve the American monopoly. Even war-time allies like Britain, whose nationals participated in the Manhattan Project, were denied access to information on key technologies. And concern about Hill criticism prompted Truman and U.S. representative Bernard Baruch to take a hard line in UN discussions of internationalization of the atom.

35.   Kennedy compared the Eisenhower years to the isolationist 1930s, when England "slept" in the face of the growing Nazi menace. During his campaign, he proclaimed a desire to "turn back"—foreshadowing initiatives like the ill-fated Bay of Pigs invasion of Cuba. As an incumbent president in 1964, LBJ took the flip side of the national security debate, using crude television commercials to suggest that his opponent Senator Goldwater would be quick to use nuclear weapons (see Destler, et al., *Our Own Worst Enemy*, pp. 48–55).

36.   Carter aides also leaked a sensitive NSC document, PD–59, which put a tough face on administration military policy (ibid., p. 78).

37.   Smith, *Power Game*, p. 180.

38.   Robert C. McFarlane, *New York Times*, July 1, 1988, p. 38.

39.   Bergner, "Organizing the Congress," p. 283.

40.   Robert McFarlane, as quoted in Sundquist, *Decline and Resurgence*, p. 57. LBJ had a similar problem when Congress forced him to fund two nuclear frigates that Secretary of Defense Robert McNamara had rejected.

41.   The rail garrison proposal had its own major defects quite apart from the debate about cost. The plan required substantial advance warning of a Soviet attack to allow the missiles to be moved from easily targeted staging areas into the commercial rail system. But the whole point of having a mobile ICBM had been to reduce the perceived vulnerability of a surprise attack against a missile in a fixed site.

42. McGeorge Bundy, "The Evolution of U.S.-Soviet Relations to the 21st Century," address at Stanford University, December 4, 1987, p. 5 (unpublished).

43. Midgetman had major problems as well. When loaded on its hard mobile launcher, prototypes were extraordinarily heavy—and so costly that Air Force planners found its single warhead of dubious cost-effectiveness.

44. The fate of the bilateral freeze movement within Congress gets sympathetic treatment in Waller, *Congress and the Nuclear Freeze.*

45. Such SDI spin-offs were effectively used by program administrators to broaden the base of support for the controversial program. Headlines trumpeting European and Japanese "support" for SDI were produced by parceling out subcontracts to U.S. allies. And important inroads on the Hill were made by pressing the case for providing an antimissile system to Israel.

46. See, for example, "Politics of 'Star Wars' Misfire, and Plan Is Hit in Hail of Budget Cuts," *Wall Street Journal,* July 22, 1986, p. 1. Note that efforts by President Reagan to make the 1986 mid-term elections a referendum on Star Wars were unsuccessful.

47. The Levin-Nunn amendment produced an unprecedented four-month Republican filibuster of the 1988 DOD authorization bill. The amendment passed by a 58–38 vote on September 17, 1987.

48. Bundy, "Evolution of U.S.-Soviet Relations," p. 7.

10 CONCLUSION
A Blueprint for Peaceful Co-Existence on Pennsylvania Avenue

Over the course of the last generation, the stakes of foreign policy-making confrontations in Washington have grown higher, even as the achievement of domestic unity has proven a more elusive goal. A careful reading of history makes it clear that the struggle between Congress and the executive branch to shape the American course in the world has moved in cycles. But in the decade and a half since the end of the Nixon administration, this enduring battle has developed new characteristics. In no previous era of congressional ascendancy has the United States borne the burdens of world leadership. And in no previous era of presidential counterreformation has the White House confronted such a formidable array of procedural weapons at the legislature's disposal.

The sparks from repeated Pennsylvania Avenue clashes draw our attention. These conflicts have weakened successive presidencies while inviting criticism of excesses by both the Congress and the executive branch. But it is too easy to be distracted by the disappointments these repeated confrontations have produced. There is good news, we should recognize, as well.

There is an ideological convergence under way today in American foreign policymaking. Conservatives in both branches of government are now championing human rights. Liberals are advocating strong action against terrorism and the drug trade. Conservatives now recognize the imperative of embracing such causes as nuclear nonproliferation and mutual arms reductions, while liberals show new understand-

309

ing of the indispensable role force can play in promoting certain U.S. diplomatic objectives.

The wane of ideology as a decisive factor in Washington foreign policy struggles has yielded other important results. Bold presidential leadership has brought such achievements as the Panama Canal treaties and the Camp David accords, as well as the two-track decision to deploy INF missiles while negotiating reductions—a risky plan that weathered stormy political transitions in both Washington and Europe before finally bearing fruit in a U.S.-Soviet nuclear arms reduction treaty. In another sense, a results-oriented pragmatism has emboldened those in Congress who most vigorously apply the checks and balances provided by the current body of foreign policy laws. Veteran legislators have mastered the art of the "good cop, bad cop" routine in recent arms sales tests. Conditionality has provided valuable restraint in several risky aid programs. And interbranch consultation—even token White House efforts to communicate with congressional leaders—has yielded some modest, though useful, results. In many cases, deep disagreements remain over the best means for the United States to use in challenging antidemocratic regimes. But the containment of communism and the rejection of totalitarianism are still consensus objectives of policymakers in both branches of the federal government.

To put the lessons of the recent past to work, several strong measures should be undertaken. None of these reforms will be easy. Indeed, some are politically impractical, given the threat they pose to entrenched powers. But to build toward a more promising future, boldness is in order. Here, then, are seven specific suggestions that are derived from this work—proposals designed to enhance prospects for international success in U.S. foreign policymaking.

1. Centralize Congressional Powers. A central point of contact needs to be established on Capitol Hill for crisis communication and consultation on the most sensitive policy questions. An ad hoc national security consultative group should be established consisting of the chairmen and ranking members of the foreign affairs, intelligence, and armed services committees, the House and Senate minority leaders, the Senate majority leader, and the House Speaker. This group should convene informally each month with the cabinet-level members of the National Security Council; it should meet in formal session with the president to consult before any U.S. military forces are deployed in hostile situations. In addition, two congressional intelligence committees should be folded into a single, smaller, joint panel with representation on the consultative group. These steps can help reverse the debilitating diffusion of power—and diminution of trust—that overzealous reforms of the 1970s produced. They can also strengthen the hand of Congress in demanding greater executive accountability, while facilitating more productive communication from both ends of Pennsylvania Avenue.

2. Clarify Executive Branch Lines of Authority.   The national security adviser should be made subject to Senate confirmation and answerable to Capitol Hill, as well as to the White House, for his management of the NSC staff. His statutory mandate should stipulate, however, that the NSC head holds a *sub*cabinet rank, inferior to the secretaries of state and defense, as well as to the director of central intelligence. The NSC head and his staff should be barred by statute from involvement in operational aspects of intelligence and the implementation of diplomatic policies. But the national security adviser should be given clearer responsibilities to chair interagency groups on policy formulation. Such moves could greatly enhance accountability, while helping to contain the damage caused by inevitable executive branch "turf battles."

3. Rewrite the War Powers and Arms Export Control Acts.   Statutory provision should be made for swift and certain votes in Congress on whether to fund U.S. troop deployments in hostile situations. Definition of such situations should be the prerogative of a broadly constituted, bipartisan leadership body—ideally, the national security consultative group. As a complement to this leadership-dominated mechanism, a majority of members should be empowered to set, by petition, a prompt up-or-down vote on the question of funding military deployments under war-time conditions. On arms sales, similar efforts should be made to limit procedural wrangling, while facilitating timely congressional votes on key international controversies. Military exports to nations with whom the United States maintains current defense treaty ties should be exempted from routine AECA reviews. But above a $250 million threshold, new commercial transfers destined for nations with whom the United States does not have a defense treaty tie should require affirmative votes of both houses before being authorized for export. Of course, controversial sales to existing U.S. defense treaty partners would remain subject to challenge through the normal legislative process. But limiting the application of AECA procedures—while requiring congressional authorization only in those cases of greatest concern—would enhance accountability and limit abuse of the act's provisions. Such reforms could provide a substantive focus for differences of opinion, while reducing the prospects for debilitating procedural wrangling over crucial war and peace decisions.

4. Reform the Budget Process. A House and Senate leadership summit should be convened to bring internal legislative procedures into the twentieth century. To provide greater budget accountability and more effective management of international security policy, the respective bodies' committee responsibilities should be brought into conformity with those of their counterparts. Budget functions should be unified under the jurisdiction of a single committee in each chamber. Authorizing and appropriating responsibilities should be unified under the committees most expert in the substantive policy areas. Ideally, efforts should be made to abolish the appropriations panels altogether; their respective chairmen could take over a special budget panel composed of chairmen and ranking members of the standing legislative committees. As an antidote to the further empowerment of committee chairs that would result, the party caucuses on the Hill should adopt measures finally abolishing the seniority system for designating committee chairmen, opening up the selection process to more democratic, merit-based methods, and providing a remedy for any abuses of concentrated legislative powers. A more reliable legislative process would also be greatly aided by empowering the Senate Rules Committee to establish parameters for floor debate. This would reduce the irresponsibly frequent resort to delaying tactics—a recent development which has diminished the Senate's influence on key decisions and provided presidents with a ready excuse for refusing to work in partnership with the legislature on controversial international issues.

5. Curb the Influence of Campaign Contributions. A host of reforms are needed to stem the tide of money washing over the Washington policymaking process. For starters, public financing of all congressional general election campaigns should be established in order to blunt the dollar-giving powers of political action committees. The influence of "soft money" contributions funneled through the major political parties should be curbed by establishing—through a constitutional amendment, if necessary—a strict dollar limit on annual political contributions by an individual. Among the many results of such a prohibition would be a curb on the reprehensible practice of using important ambassadorial appointments as rewards for wealthy campaign contributors. All members of Congress should be barred from accepting honoraria or making personal use of excess campaign funds. Policymakers in each branch should be subject to far stricter sanctions against so-called revolving-door abuses—the practice of going directly from public service where one has access to classified information to working with foreign clients or domestic industries over which one previously had significant policymaking authorities.

6. *Educate the Nation.* A new federal commitment to literacy in international affairs would greatly advance U.S. interests in the century ahead. To succeed in an era of growing international interdependence—and economic competition—Americans require much better training in languages, economics, world history, and geography, as well as international politics and culture. Such training can help build the foundation for a broader policymaking consensus in Washington as well as at the grass roots, while facilitating greater success in international competition. This type of initiative would be an investment in the next generation, designed to aid U.S. diplomacy and trade opportunities while improving the prospects for achieving a more bipartisan consensus at home.

7. *Build Bridges Between the Executive and Legislative Branches.*
Washington policymakers need to devise a more effective "exchange program" of mid-career lateral entry into staff positions in Congress and the executive branch in order to help reduce institutional animosity. State Department officers should be rewarded for time spent on Capitol Hill. Legislative staffers should be encouraged to serve in the Foggy Bottom and Pentagon bureaucracies. Here, as elsewhere, the long-term goal should be to reduce routine confrontation and diminish lawmakers' insistence on applying binding legislative restraints to fluid international situations, while increasing executive branch respect for the rule of law and bureaucratic accountability. New means need to be devised to rally the respective branches into mutual support against foreign challenges without weakening the healthy checks and balances that thrive under the separation-of-powers system.

Few procedural reforms would be more valuable than modest efforts by the president and congressional leaders to establish greater mutual trust. Successful governance in a democracy requires inter-branch partnership. The democratic system is challenged in international affairs when it confronts totalitarian regimes that have an enforced unity of purpose in their bureaucracies. No doubt, America is strengthened by the prudent use of checks and balances; the many cases where excesses have been curbed by assertive legislators have been well chronicled. But ultimately, trust and credibility are essential to presidential leadership, just as reliability and discretion are needed for effective employment of congressional prerogatives. On the vast majority of occasions when the president has sought to end-run the legislature, the long-term political and diplomatic objectives of the White House have suffered. Conversely, excessive resort to procedural gimmickry and legislative literalism by Congress has diminished the influence of Capitol Hill. Congress will continue to favor legalistic remedies and binding conditions on authorizations. Presidents will continue to argue for greater executive branch flexibility. Efforts to strike a balance between these tendencies can provide greater maturity to American foreign policymaking in the decades ahead.

The congressional revolution of the 1970s produced an extraordinary fragmentation of power, just as the swelling of the executive bureaucracy resulted in a diffusion of authority. Both phenomena lengthened the policymaking process while frustrating unity of action. Opportunities for curtailing international initiatives multiplied, while the temptation grew for the president to act first, then deal with congressional complaints after the fact. Such efforts to set American policy unilaterally have usually backfired. There is still no substitute in American diplomacy for the strength afforded by a united executive and legislative branch team. Thus, recent American presidents have ultimately recognized that international initiatives cannot be sustained over the long term unless an executive-legislative partnership supports them. Wise leadership can use the new rules of the foreign policymaking game to strengthen the American hand, even as efforts are made to reform the process. The president and the members of Congress have an opportunity to build upon the lessons of the turbulent past to improve existing policymaking structures. Such bold initiatives are the key to charting a more promising course for the future of American diplomacy.

BIBLIOGRAPHY

Acheson, Dean. *Present at the Creation: My Years in the State Department.* New York: Norton, 1969.

Allison, Graham. *Essence of Decision.* Boston: Little, Brown, 1969.

Bailey, Thomas. *Diplomatic History of the American People.* New Jersey: Prentice-Hall, 1980.

Bernstein, Barton J., ed. *Towards a New Past: Dissenting Essays in American History.* New York: Random House, 1967.

Bolling, Richard. *House Out of Order.* New York: Dutton, 1965.

Bloomfield, Lincoln. *The Foreign Policy Process.* New Jersey: Prentice-Hall, 1982.

Brzezinski, Zbigniew. *Power and Principle: Memoirs of the National Security Adviser 1977–1981.* New York: Farrar, Straus, Giroux, 1983.

Corwin, Edward. *The President: Office and Powers 1787–1957.* New York: New York University Press, 1957.

Crabb, Cecil V., Jr., and Pat M. Holt. *Invitation to Struggle: Congress, the President and Foreign Policy.* Washington, D.C.: Congressional Quarterly Press, 1984.

DeConde, Alexander. *A History of American Foreign Policy*, Vol. I. New York: Scribners, 1978.

de Tocqueville, Alexis. *Democracy in America*, Richard D. Hefner, ed. New York: Mentor, 1956.

Destler, I.M., Leslie Gelb, and Anthony Lake. *Our Own Worst Enemy: The Unmaking of American Foreign Policy.* New York: Simon and Schuster, 1984.

Eagleton, Thomas. *War and Presidential Power.* New York: Liveright, 1974.

Emerson, Steven. *The American House of Saud.* New York: Watts, 1985.

Fallows, James. *National Defense.* New York: Random House, 1981.

Franck, Thomas M., ed. *The Tethered Presidency.* New York: New York University Press, 1981.

_____ , and Edward Weisband. *Foreign Policy by Congress.* New York: Oxford University Press, 1979.

Frye, Alton. *A Responsible Congress.* New York: McGraw-Hill, 1975.

George, Alexander L. *Presidential Decisionmaking in Foreign Policy: The Effective Use of Information and Advice.* Boulder, Colorado: Westview, 1980.

Hamilton, Alexander, James Madison, and John Jay. *The Federalist Papers,* Clinton Rossiter, ed. New York: Mentor, 1961.

Hart, Gary, and William S. Lind. *America Can Win.* Bethesda, Md.: Adler, 1986.

Hughes, Barry. *The Domestic Context of Foreign Policy.* San Francisco: Freeman, 1978.

Hunter, Robert E. *Presidential Control of Foreign Policy: Management or Mishap?* New York: Praeger, 1982.

Isaacs, Stephen D. *Jews and American Politics.* New York: Doubleday, 1974.

Isaacson, Walter, and Evan Thomas. *The Wise Men.* New York: Simon and Schuster, 1986.

Josephy, Alvin M., Jr. *The American Heritage History of the Congress of the United States.* New York: McGraw-Hill, 1975.

Kearns, Doris. *Lyndon Johnson and the American Dream.* New York: Harper and Row, 1976.

Kennedy, Robert F. *Thirteen Days: A Memoir of the Cuban Missile Crisis.* New York: Norton, 1969.

Kissinger, Henry. *White House Years.* Boston: Little, Brown, 1979.

Lieber, Robert J., et al. *Eagle Defiant: United States Foreign Policy in the 1980s.* Boston: Little, Brown, 1983.

Mann, Thomas, and Norman Ornstein, eds. *The New Congress.* Washington, D.C.: American Enterprise Institute, 1981.

Markey, Edward. *Nuclear Peril: The Politics of Proliferation.* Cambridge, Mass.: Ballinger, 1982.

Miller, Merle, ed. *Plain Speaking: An Oral Biography of Harry Truman.* New York: Putnam, 1974.

Muskie, Edmund, et al. *The President, the Congress, and Foreign Policy.* New York: New York University Press, 1986.

Neustadt, Richard. *Presidential Power: The Politics of Leadership.* New York: Harper and Row, 1960.

Nixon, Richard. *RN: The Memoirs of Richard Nixon.* New York: Warner, 1978.

O'Neill, William L. *American High: The Years of Confidence, 1945–1960.* New York: Macmillan, 1986.

Pollock, Ralph S., ed. *Renewing the Dream.* Takoma Park, Md.: Maryland University Press, 1986.

Roosevelt, Theodore. *The Words of Theodore Roosevelt*, George Huron Putnam, ed. Mt. Vernon, N.Y.: Pauper Press, 1970.

Rubin, Barry. *The Secrets of State.* New York: Oxford University Press, 1985.

Schlesinger, Arthur M., Jr. *The Cycles of American History.* Boston: Houghton Mifflin, 1986.

_____ . *The Imperial Presidency.* Boston: Houghton Mifflin, 1973.

Smith, Gerard C. *Doubletalk.* New York: Doubleday, 1980.

Smith, Hedrick. *The Power Game.* New York: Random House, 1988.

Smith, Page. *The Shaping of America*, Vol. 3. New York: McGraw-Hill, 1980.

Sorensen, Theodore. *Kennedy.* New York: Harper and Row, 1965.

Sundquist, James. *The Decline and Resurgence of Congress.* Washington, D.C.: The Brookings Institution, 1981.

Talbott, Strobe. *Endgame: The Inside Story of SALT II.* New York: Harper and Row, 1979.

Tugwell, Rex. *The Presidency Reappraised.* New York: Praeger, 1977.

Waller, Douglas. *Congress and the Nuclear Freeze: An Inside Look at the Politics of a Mass Movement.* Amherst: University of Massachusetts, 1987.

Woodward, Bob. *Veil: The Secret Wars of the CIA, 1981-1987.* New York: Simon and Schuster, 1987.

Yergin, Daniel. *Shattered Peace: The Origins of the Cold War and the National Security State.* Boston: Houghton Mifflin, 1978.

INDEX

319

Stevens, Ted, 154, 174
Strategic Arms Limitation Talks
  (SALT), 42, 52-53, 63, 67-69, 72,
  79-80, 83-84, 96, 102, 111,
  154-156, 160, 165-175, 212, 278,
  293-296, 303
Strategic Arms Reduction Talks
  (START), 81, 174, 278, 293, 297,
  302
Strategic Defense Initiative (SDI),
  82-84, 102, 162-163, 175, 293,
  300-302
Symington, Stuart, 52, 248, 251

Taft, Robert, 27, 34, 37
Taiwan (see China)
Talmadge, Herman, 158, 178
television, 37, 64-65, 85n8, 90, 107,
  266, 300
Thailand, 47
Thurmond, Strom, 176
Tower, John, 62
trade issues, 6-9, 17, 20, 52, 76, 93,
  96, 165, 168-169, 213, 255-256
Trible, Paul, 104, 148n22
Truman, Harry, 20-21, 29, 31-34,
  36-37, 41, 44, 46, 55n13, 62, 68,
  71-73, 166, 275, 279
Tunney, John, 180n4
Turkey, 51, 56n24, 63, 67, 102-103,
  185, 189, 191-192, 233, 236-237

United Nations, 22, 27, 30, 36, 75, 82,
  102, 270n4

Vance, Cyrus, 74, 79, 101, 121,
  150n49, 166, 177
Vandenberg, Arthur, 32-34, 55n10

Vanik, Charles, 52, 169
veto (presidential) (see also legislative
  veto), 10, 51, 93, 95, 123-125,
  138-139, 141-142, 192, 214-215,
  222, 225, 254, 266
Vietnam War, 34, 37, 39-41, 43-51,
  54n2, 55n23, 63, 68, 73, 99, 103,
  122-124, 129, 160, 164-165,
  187-190, 246, 256-257, 272n23,
  281, 292
Vladivostok accord, 70, 79, 169-170,
  293-294

Wallace, Henry, 71, 166
Wallop, Malcolm, 111, 174
Warner, John, 141, 209
Warnke, Paul, 96, 170
War Powers Act, 100, 108, 119-132,
  134-146, 272n24, 311
Washington, George, 8, 10, 13-17,
  23n13, 35, 156-158, 277, 304n6
Watergate scandal, 4, 43-45, 63, 73,
  89, 97, 123-124, 267
Webb, James, 137
Weicker, Lowell, 132, 138, 148n22,
  287
Weinberger, Caspar, 135, 220, 276,
  279-280, 285, 287, 297, 304n10
Whalen, Charles, 144
Wilson, Pete, 107
Wilson, Woodrow, 20-21, 55n20, 70,
  77, 102
Wolpe, Howard, 254
Wright, Jim, 162, 181n12, 268

Young, Milton, 49

Zablocki, Clement, 52, 123

ABOUT THE AUTHOR

Gerald Felix Warburg has played an integral role in most of the major Washington foreign policymaking disputes of the last decade and a half. As a legislative assistant to members of both the House and Senate leadership, as a consultant to presidential campaigns and agencies of the executive branch, and as an editorial commentator, he has been both a participant in and an analyst of the ongoing struggle to shape America's course in the world. A member of the Council on Foreign Relations, Mr. Warburg has lectured widely on American foreign policy at major universities and research institutions in the United States and abroad. He has participated actively in congressional delegations meeting with foreign leaders in the Soviet Union, the People's Republic of China, and elsewhere in Europe, the Middle East, Asia, and Latin America.

A graduate of Hampshire College, the author holds a master's degree in international relations from Stanford University, where he was a fellow in the arms control and U.S.-China relations programs. A native of Ross, California, just north of San Francisco, Mr. Warburg currently resides in Arlington, Virginia with his wife, Joy Jacobson and their daughter Jennifer Marian Warburg.